PERSPECTIVES
ON
ELECTION

PERSPECTIVES

ON
ELECTION

FIVE VIEWS

JACK W. COTTRELL
CLARK H. PINNOCK
ROBERT L. REYMOND
THOMAS B. TALBOTT
BRUCE A. WARE

EDITED BY
CHAD OWEN BRAND

ACADEMIC
NASHVILLE, TENNESSEE

ISBN 978-0-8054-2729-5

Published by Broadman & Holman Publishers
Nashville, Tennessee

Dewey Decimal Classification: 234.9
Subject Heading: PREDESTINATION \

DOCTRINAL THEOLOGY

Printed in the United States of America
2 3 4 5 6 7 8 9 10 11 12 • 15 14 13 12 11 10 09 08 07

Contents

This book is dedicated affectionately to

Regina, Mike, and Lance

Contributors

Chad Owen Brand
(Ph.D., Southwestern Baptist Theological Seminary)
Professor of Christian Theology
The Southern Baptist Theological Seminary
Associate Dean for Biblical and Theological Studies
Boyce College
Louisville, Kentucky

Jack W. Cottrell
(Ph.D., Princeton Theological Seminary)
Professor of Theology
Cincinnati Bible Seminary
Cincinnati, Ohio

Clark H. Pinnock
(Ph.D., University of Manchester)
Professor Emeritus of Theology
McMaster Divinity College
Hamilton, Ontario

Robert L. Reymond
(Ph.D., Bob Jones University)
Emeritus Professor of Systematic Theology
Knox Theological Seminary
Fort Lauderdale, Florida

Thomas B. Talbott
(Ph.D., University of California at Santa Barbara)
Professor of Philosophy
Willamette University
Salem, Oregon

Bruce A. Ware
(Ph.D., Fuller Theological Seminary)
Professor of Christian Theology
Senior Associate Dean, School of Theology
The Southern Baptist Theological Seminary
Louisville, Kentucky

Preface

Saunter into the cafeteria or coffee shop of any conservative Bible college or seminary in America today, and you will likely stumble on to two or three theological conversations, especially if it is mid-afternoon and classes are about over for the day. It is also likely that one of the topics will be the issue of the doctrine of election, or at least it will be about "Calvinism" or "Arminianism" in general. It is important of course to note at the outset of this volume that "Calvinism" (or Augustinianism, or Reformed theology in general) is not merely about the doctrine of election. That is only one component, albeit an important one, in such systems of theology. It is also important to note, as the discussion in this book will demonstrate, that even among the adherents to the Reformed tradition, as with the Arminian tradition, there is often disagreement as to just how the doctrine of election is to be understood. What that means, then, is that some of the red-faced people arguing with one another over their cappuccinos in the corner of the café may actually be largely on the same side on most issues but in disagreement over a fine nuance here or there. I guess at one level this is an important part of theological education, and as long as the antagonists can keep their teeth filed down and avoid grabbing sharp objects, such debates can be relatively harmless.

The purpose of this book is not to add fuel to the fire of such intramural contests. The goal of the book is to add clarity to the discussion and to further the discussion, insofar as it is possible, in an amiable manner. I am proud to say that the authors of the chapters in this book have behaved quite respectfully toward one another, even when it is clear that they are sharply divided on some key issues. And they are sometimes sharply divided! More of that in a bit.

My own thinking on this subject has been elevated by several excellent teachers. In college I sat under Alex Strauch, now a pastor in the Denver area, but once a college New Testament professor and an excellent one at that. Though I had done some personal reading on predestination, he was the first Bible teacher who really challenged me to work out the issues from the text of Scripture. Tom Nettles was one of my first seminary professors. Tom has published on this subject, and conversation with him has always been stimulating. I took a history course on John Calvin with William Estep, Baptist historian who has now gone to be with the Lord, and two historical theology classes with Jan Kiwiet on Reformation and post-Reformation studies. Those teachers gave me a lot to chew on, even in our disagreements. In doctoral work my main professor was James Leo Garrett Jr. Anyone who knows Dr. Garrett knows that he is a model of the gentleman scholar, with an encyclopedic grasp of bibliography and historical theology. It was a joy and a privilege to study under him and to work through some of these issues at another level of conversation. These men are all over the spectrum on this doctrine, but they all in one way or another helped me to clarify my understanding of the issues around the doctrine of election.

I want to take this opportunity to say a few words of appropriate gratitude. Anyone who has published a book knows that many hands go into the preparation. Pride of place in my case goes to my wife, Tina, who has learned to be patient with her overly busy husband. She has always been my support and has often done more than her share of family duties, especially with our children, and, as of April, 2005, with our twin granddaughters. I can never adequately state my love and appreciation for her. My three children, Tashia, Chad, and Cassandra, have all helpfully made room in their schedules for their dad to work on such projects, and the occasional break from the computer keyboard to play "Spades" with them always brings refreshment to my soul.

I am grateful to the faculty, administration, and trustees of The Southern Baptist Theological Seminary for wonderful support and encouragement as this project has moved (sometimes slowly) along. Dr. R. Albert Mohler Jr. sets a remarkable example as a scholar, administrator, pastor (to the seminary), cultural analyst, and friend. He has regularly encouraged me in the production of this volume, and that has helped enormously in the completion of the project. My two deans, Dr. James Scroggins and Dr. Russell Moore, have also prompted me with pep talks and with questions about the development of the book. I am also thankful to the seminary trustees, as it was during a sabbatical leave that this book was initiated. Two young men, Carl Lee Bean and Gabriel Martini, assisted in collecting materials for the research that went into my historical introduction in this book. If not for them, this book would still not be finished. I wish to express my gratitude to the two men who prepared the indices for this volume. Travis Kerns is a PhD student at The Southern Baptist Theological Seminary and adjunct professor of philosophy at Boyce College. Joe Harrod is an MDiv student in the School of Theology at SBTS. Leonard G. Goss at B & H Publishing Group has, as always, been a joy to work with. And I am also grateful to the rest of the team there including Steve Bond, John Landers, Ray Clendenen, and Tim Grubbs for all their encouragement along the way. I say "thank you" to all of these and to so many more who have helped in one way or another.

Without the five scholars who wrote the chapters of this book, there would be nothing to say. What I can tell you is that you are in for a treat. I could not have asked for a more dedicated group of scholars to pen these pages. You are about to find out that each one of them really wants to convince you, the reader, of the rightness of his position. This is great stuff! Let me say a word here about the order of the chapters. I have laid them out this way with a purpose. Most Protestants since the Reformation have held to views of one of the first two chapters presented—those of Drs. Ware and Cottrell. A significant minority in the Reformed churches have held the position espoused by Dr. Reymond. Because these three positions have had the larger constituency, it seemed good to me to place them first—as the positions most commonly held. Dr. Talbott's approach, a universalist viewpoint, has had many defenders in history, but they have always been very much in the minority at any given time, and that view has often been labeled as heretical. I think you will find it interesting that he attempts his defense from Scripture and not from philosophy. The perspective that Dr. Pinnock represents, that is, his understanding of election as vocational and corporate, has had quite a few defenders, though his addition of an "open" view of God gives it a bit of a twist. Since these two positions are representative of minority (though significant) traditions in the church, I thought it most helpful to treat them after the classical positions had been laid out. Of course, you can read them in any order you choose.

I have dedicated this volume to three people whom I love very much and who have known me all of their lives since I am their oldest brother. Though we are separated by twelve hundred miles of highway, I know I am never separated from them in spirit. I love and appreciate them very much and pray that the God and Father of our Lord Jesus Christ will bless them continually in all ways.

Now to the "blessed and only Sovereign, the King of kings, and the Lord of lords, the only One who has immortality, dwelling in unapproachable light, whom none of mankind has seen or can see, to whom be honor and eternal might. Amen" (1 Tim. 6:15–16 HCSB).

CHAPTER 1

Divine Election to Salvation:
Unconditional, Individual, and Infralapsarian

BRUCE A. WARE

Just a moment's reflection reveals how differently we commonly think within our evangelical churches from how Paul (and other biblical writers) thought about the doctrine of election. What is often to us a "controversial" and "potentially divisive" doctrine to be ignored, at best, and repulsed, at worst, was for Paul, most notably, one of the sources of his greatest joy and strength. Consider Ephesians 1. Paul begins this letter commending praise to God the Father for the many rich and wondrous blessings he has granted us in his Son (Eph. 1:3). And so as not to leave us wondering just what these blessings are that he has in mind, he proceeds to enumerate them in the verses that follow (Eph. 1:4–14). Where does he begin his recitation of God's wondrous blessings? What blessing tops the list?

Of all things, the very first blessing he extols, the one that, in the apostle's mind, constitutes the basis for the rest of the blessings that follow, is the truth that God "chose us in Him [Christ], before the foundation of the world [*ezelezato emas en auto pro kataboles kosmou*], to be holy and blameless in His sight" (Eph. 1:4 HCSB). And rather than leaving this notion quickly (as one would drop an unexpectedly hot pan picked up from the stove), instead he adds to this opening thought, marveling now that in love, God "predestined us to be adopted through Jesus Christ for Himself, according to His favor and will, to the praise of His glorious grace that He favored us with in the Beloved" (Eph. 1:5–6 HCSB). Let's not miss the significance here. When Paul thinks of why God is worthy of being praised, of what God has done for his people that should elicit from them deep, passionate, and wondrous worship, to the glory of his name, for the riches of his grace (Eph. 1:6), the very first thing that comes to his mind, and flows from his pen, is this truth: God chose us! God predestined us!

I cannot help but wonder if people in most of our churches were asked to list the reasons God is to be praised—that is, if they wrote down all of the blessings they could think of that God has provided for them—how many of our people would include election on the list? And, if it makes the list, for how many would election *top* the list? One thing seems clear: if we think one way about something, and Paul (and other biblical writers) think another way about the same thing, we are the ones in need of correction—not Paul or the Bible! Why does Paul value the truth that we often tend to shun? Why does Paul lead with a doctrine that many pastors wouldn't dream of preaching on lest they breed controversy and risk a possible church split? What did Paul have in mind with this teaching on divine election, and why is it so important?

This chapter proposes to explain and defend the position that Paul—and the Bible—understands and presents divine salvific election as unconditional, individual, and infralapsarian. Just a word of explanation of each of these elements of election may be helpful.

We are concerned with the Bible's teaching of "salvific election," that is, election to salvation. There is no question that election is used in other contexts and with other senses than election to salvation, per se. But the richest sense of the Bible's use of election is of sinners' election to salvation. As Paul writes, "But we must always thank God for you, brothers loved by the Lord, because from the beginning God has chosen you for salvation through sanctification by the Spirit and through belief in the truth" (2 Thess. 2:13 HCSB). It is this glorious election to salvation we wish here to explain and defend.

"Unconditional election" refers to the claim that God's selection of those whom he would save was not based upon (or, not "conditioned" on) some fact or feature of those individuals' lives, in particular. That is, God's election of those who would be saved was not conditioned on something they would do, some choice they would make, how good or bad they might be, or anything else specifically true about them in contrast to others also enslaved to sin and deserving God's just condemnation. Rather, God elected some to be saved according to the good pleasure of his will without respect for their individual qualities, characters, actions, or choices. His election, then, was "unconditional" as it pertains to particulars of the elect persons themselves, while it is also clearly conditioned and dependent on God's own good pleasure and will.

"Individual election" asserts that God did more than (but not less than) choosing that the nation of Israel as a whole would be called out to be his people and that he did more than (but not less than) choosing that there would some day be a group or company of the saved including both Jews and Gentiles. Without doubt God did choose the nation of Israel to be a special nation of his (Deut. 7:6; 14:2), and he did determine that there be a "chosen race" (1 Pet. 2:9 HCSB), his church comprising all true believers in Jesus Christ, his bride made up of those men and women purified for his Son. But more than this, God also elected those individuals who make up the church, or who constitute the bride of Christ. Individual election, then, affirms that each individual saved person—man, woman, boy, or girl—was loved and favored by God before the creation of the world so that God specifically chose him or her from condemnation and ruin to be made his holy and blameless child (Eph. 1:4–5), conformed to the likeness of his Son (Rom. 8:29).

"Infralapsarian election" relates to the question of the moral condition of the whole of humanity whom God considered in his mind's eye and out of whom he selected those whom he would save. Did God view all of humanity as (merely) created but not yet fallen (i.e., lapsed),[1] and hence, as neither sinful nor deserving of condemnation? Or did he view humanity as the total number of all who would ever live, considered as fallen sinners, corrupted and deserving of condemnation due to their connection to Adam and his fall into sin? One thing that all sides have agreed on through the history of the church (an agreement that open theism, sadly, chooses now to dispense with, despite Scripture's clear and direct teaching) is that from "before the foundation of the world" God had in mind exactly those whom he would save (Eph. 1:4 HCSB; cf. Matt. 25:34; 2 Tim. 1:9; 1 Pet. 1:20; Rev. 13:8).

But the question here is when God chose "the elect," though he had not as of yet created the world or any of the human beings who

---

1. The term "lapsarian" comes from the Latin *lapsare,* "to fall," so supralapsarianism means "before (or above) the fall" and infralapsarianism means "after (or below) the Fall."

would populate it, did he choose these elect ones from the "pool" of humanity considered as unfallen (as argued by supralapsarianism) or considered as fallen (as argued by infralapsarianism)? The position argued here is that God considered humanity as already fallen when he chose those whom he would save. That is, he looked upon the human race in his mind's eye as those who live after ("infra") the fall ("lapse"), and so God's election truly is an election of lost, fallen, and condemned people whom he surely and certainly will save in Christ. In short, divine election is infralapsarian.

In what follows, we shall consider each of these three main characteristics (unconditional, individual, and infralapsarian) of the salvific election taught in Scripture. While some attention will be given to a historical overview of various aspects of our discussion, since other fine overviews exist,[2] we will devote most of our attention to the Scripture's own teaching on these matters. In each case positive arguments will be set forth defending the position argued here, and where appropriate, the strongest and most compelling objections will be considered and responses will be given. Throughout this discussion my hope and prayer is that the wonder of God's gracious and saving election of sinners may be seen more clearly, that we may cherish this doctrine as we ought, and that God may be honored as he ought. In his election and salvation of sinners, to him alone belongs all glory and praise.

Unconditional Election

Definition and Explanation of Unconditional Election

Unconditional election to salvation may be defined as God's gracious choice, made in eternity past, of those whom he would save by faith through the atoning death of his Son, a choice based not upon anything that those so chosen would do, or any choice that they would make, or on how good or bad they might be, or on anything else specifically true about them (i.e., their qualities, characters, decisions, or actions) in contrast to others, but rather based only upon God's own good pleasure and will. In particular, and in light of the long-standing debate over this doctrine between Calvinists and Ar-

---

2. For brief but helpful overviews of the history of the doctrine of election, see Bruce Demarest, *The Cross and Salvation: The Doctrine of Salvation,* in the Foundations of Evangelical Theology series, gen. ed. John S. Feinberg (Wheaton, Ill.: Crossway, 1997), 50–69, 97–118; and Paul K. Jewett, *Election and Predestination* (Grand Rapids: Eerdmans, 1985), 5–21.

minians, unconditional election specifically denies that God elects persons based upon his advanced knowledge, in eternity past, of their future decision of whether to receive Christ or not when presented the gospel. That is, divine election is not based upon or conditioned by the "foreseen faith" of those who will, in time, believe in Christ.

At its heart, the doctrine of unconditional election assures the believer that salvation, from beginning to end, is *all* of God. From God's electing in eternity past of those whom he would save, of those whom he would make "holy and blameless" (Eph. 1:4 HCSB), to the final perfection in holiness of those same elect persons who are, in time, effectually called, justified, and then glorified as they are renewed into the likeness of Christ (Rom. 8:29–30), the whole of "salvation is from the Lᴏʀᴅ" (Jon. 2:9 HCSB). To God alone, then, belongs all glory and honor, and no one may boast before the Lord of any manner of contribution to his salvation (1 Cor. 1:26–31; Eph. 2:8–9).

For if God's election of those whom he will save is conditional— conditioned upon "foreseen faith" as is often asserted and believed in the classic Arminian tradition—then there is one ultimate action relating to our salvation that we do and God specifically does not do and cannot effect. For these Arminians, while it is true that God must provide grace (prevenient grace) for any to be enabled to believe in Christ, as both Arminius[3] and Wesley[4] believed, yet it remains entirely up to the individual whether he will believe. By necessity, in light of the supposed libertarian freedom of the individual, God cannot ensure that any person will believe. God does all that he can do, but the choice, in the end, is up to us. Therefore, conditional election asserts human choice and action as that which is ultimately decisive in personal salvation. Put differently, at its most crucial moment (the moment of belief or disbelief), salvation is *of us,* not of the Lord.

But because "salvation is from the Lord" in every respect, from start to finish, and because to God alone belongs all glory and boasting for the gracious saving work he accomplishes and applies to sinners'

---

3. See Jacob Arminius, *The Works of James Arminius,* 3 vols., trans. James and William Nichols (London: 1825), 1:589–90, where he asserted that by God's foreknowledge, God knew "from all eternity those individuals who would through his preventing [i.e., prevenient] grace, believe, and through his subsequent grace would persevere . . . and he likewise knew who would not believe and persevere."

4. See John Wesley, *The Works of John Wesley,* 14 vols., ed. T. Jackson (1831; reprint, Grand Rapids: Baker, 1979), 6:509, where Wesley states, "Salvation begins with what is usually termed (and very properly) preventing [i.e., prevenient] grace; including the first wish to please God, the first dawn of light concerning his will, and the first slight transient conviction of having sinned against him."

lives (1 Cor. 1:26–31; Eph. 2:8–9), therefore the unconditional nature of God's election is highly valued by its advocates. Both the rightful glory of God and the proper humility of sinners are secured in salvation only when the work of salvation, from beginning to end, is grounded in God's unconditional elective purposes. With the psalmist, we proclaim, "Not to us, LORD, not to us, but to Your name give glory" (Ps. 115:1 HCSB). Only if God's election of those whom he determines to save is grounded on the good pleasure of God and not at all on any quality, decision, or action that will one day be true of those persons whom God creates can we proclaim, without qualification, that salvation is altogether from the Lord, and to him alone belongs exclusive glory.

Support for Unconditional Election

While it is clear that God's election as unconditional matters much to those of the Reformed tradition, what are the strongest reasons set forth in support of this doctrine?

Key passages teaching unconditional election. First, the clearest and most compelling understanding of many passages of Scripture indicate that God's election of those whom he will save is unconditional. Consider with me some of the main texts and the rationale for unconditional election that they provide.

John 17:2, 6, 9, 24. Jesus' high priestly prayer in John 17 is peppered with a phrase and concept that can only be accounted for rightly by appeal to God's election as unconditional. Consider Jesus' statement in John 17:1b–2: "Father, the hour has come. Glorify Your Son so that the Son may glorify You, for You gave Him authority over all flesh; so He may give eternal life to all *You have given Him*" (HCSB; italics added). As one reads John's Gospel, one becomes familiar with the need to stop and ponder deeply and at length the profundity of what John writes. This passage is no exception! Here Jesus says that the Father has granted him authority over all people (*pases sarkos,* "all flesh") for a specific purpose (*ina,* "so").

What might this purpose be? Why has the Father granted his Son universal authority? And here Jesus amazes us by indicating the purpose is, "so He may give eternal life to all" whom the Father has "given Him" (*pan o dedokas auto dose autois zoen aionion*). Here is authority over all in order to give eternal life to some. And what identifies those select ones to whom this eternal life is given? Those "given Him" from the Father. The Father's choice of those whom he would save is then made effective as the Son is given these very ones and grants to them his gift of eternal life. The unconditional election of the Father accounts for those who receive eternal life from the Son. As one continues reading John 17, this theme of those "given Him" from the Father continues. Jesus revealed truth about the Father to his own disciples, and these men are identified by Jesus as "the *men You gave Me* from the world" (John 17:6a HCSB; italics added). Jesus continues, "They [his disciples] were Yours, *You gave them to Me,* and they have kept Your word" (John 17:6b HCSB; italics added). A few verses later he prays for his disciples, saying, "I am not praying for the world but for *those You have given Me,* because they are Yours" (John 17:9 HCSB; italics added). And lest we think that Jesus has in mind only the selection of the disciples alone, consider the prayer that Jesus offers for all believers: "I pray not only for these [disciples], but also for those who believe in Me through their message" (John 17:20 HCSB).[5] And who are these subsequent believers? Do they become believers simply on their own, as they hear the gospel message from Jesus' disciples and choose to believe? Instructive here is one of Jesus' concluding statements, "Father, I desire those You have given Me to be with Me where I am" (John 17:24). Clearly, as Jesus' prayer develops, "those who believe in Me" of John 17:20 (HCSB) are the same ones as "those You have given Me" of John 17:24 (HCSB).

Just as the disciples become the disciples because the Father gives these ones to Jesus, so also all future believers come to believe in Christ through the message of the disciples because God has given these to his Son. Belief is necessary, to be sure. But those who believe are those given to Christ by the Father. The unconditional election of the Father, then, accounts for the subsequent faith and salvation of those to whom the Son grants eternal life.

Acts 13:48. In the context just preceding this verse, Paul and Barnabas had preached the gospel in Antioch. When the whole town assembled to hear their message (Acts 13:44), the Jews were filled with jealousy and began opposing and insulting Paul (Acts 13:45). In response, Paul and Barnabas turned from the Jews to the Gentiles, stating to their Jewish opponents, "But since you reject it [i.e., God's message of the gospel], and consider yourselves unworthy of eternal life, we now turn to the Gentiles!" (Acts 13:46 HCSB). They quoted Isaiah 49:6, indicating that their very preaching to the Gentiles fulfilled

---

5. If anyone doubts whether this text has wider reference here, see John 6:37ff.

what Isaiah had prophesied (Acts 13:47). Following this, Luke makes this astonishing comment: "When the Gentiles heard this, they rejoiced and glorified the message of the Lord, and all who had been appointed to eternal life believed. So the message of the Lord spread through the whole region" (Acts 13:48–49 HCSB).

One indisputable aspect of Luke's statement, "All who had been appointed to eternal life believed," is that God's appointment of those who would receive eternal life preceded the belief of these very people.[6] There is, then, a *temporal priority* indicated here. God's appointment precedes in time the belief of the people. But is there not also a *logical priority* indicated in God's prior appointment? If, as many classic Arminians argue, God chooses those whom he knows in advance are going to choose him, then clearly the logical priority must be given to human choice, for God's choice is logically dependent upon and a reflection of this foreseen faith. But if so, why should Luke make this point?[7] If the real reason they believed is that it was up to them whether they believed, and nothing that God had chosen affected what they decided, then the appointment to eternal life loses its significance.

But if one considers the appointment of God to eternal life as not merely temporally prior to the human choice but also as logically prior, now this statement by Luke is filled with significance; and one can understand why he would include it. For, indeed, what Luke is stating is this: even though many Jews have rejected the gospel message, God has ordained that his gospel be spread to the Gentiles (Acts 13:46–47). And, unlike the response among the Jews, encountered by Paul over and again as he visited synagogue after synagogue, in

---

6. F. F. Bruce, *The Acts of the Apostles,* 2nd ed. (Grand Rapids: Eerdmans, 1952), 275, refers to the appointment here as a divine "enrolling" or "inscribing" of their names to eternal life. He comments on this phrase in Acts 13:48, saying, "Those here referred to showed by their believing that *they had been so enrolled,* in contrast to the unbelieving Jews of ver. 46a" (italics added). Notice the logical and temporal priority given to their enrolling (i.e., appointment) that grounds and precedes their subsequent belief.

7. In fact, to make the Arminian understanding work here, it requires, essentially, reversing what the text actually says. Consider this explanation by a leading Arminian theologian, William W. Klein, *The New Chosen People: A Corporate View of Election* (Grand Rapids: Zondervan, 1990), 121: "The Gentiles believed and entered the category of the appointed ones." Notice that here Klein reverses the sequence, viz., their belief grounds and precedes their actual personal and existential appointment to eternal life. Of course, he can only do this by first suggesting that the so-called "category of the appointed ones" is an empty set until people enter it. We will address later the individual nature of God's saving election that will demonstrate that Klein's misreading of this text not only involves his reversing of its order but also includes his (empty) corporate notion of election.

contrast there are many Gentiles who hear the gospel and believe in Christ—so many that Luke observes, "So the message of the Lord spread through the whole region" (Acts 13:49 HCSB).

Now the natural question is this: what accounts for the fact that Jews (as a whole) who hear the gospel reject it, while increasing numbers of Gentiles, hearing the same gospel message, accept it? Answer: God appointed to eternal life those (Gentiles) who believed and were saved (Acts 13:48). So it is not ultimately a matter of human choice that determines who rejects and who accepts the gospel. Although human choice (i.e., belief in Christ) is necessary for any to be saved, what stands prior—both temporally prior and logically prior—to this human choice is the choice of God, which divine choosing is causally linked to and hence accounts for the human choice to believe. In short, these Gentiles believed the gospel, while Jews rejected the same saving message because God had chosen these very Gentiles to believe. Only an unconditional view of election can account for what Luke says here.

Romans 9:10–16. One of the clearest and strongest assertions of the unconditional nature of God's election is given by Paul in Romans 9:10–16. Some[8] have sought to argue that the election spoken of here has nothing to do with salvation but is rather an election to a special service designed by God. This view has been addressed at length by others, and its basis has been shown as lacking either contextual or exegetical support.[9] To see one strong reason for rejecting this view, one need only read carefully the opening verses of Romans 9 to realize that Paul's "intense sorrow and continual anguish" (Rom. 9:2 HCSB) of heart for his people Israel could only be his concern over their salvation (cf. Rom. 10:1–4). The context establishes that Paul's deepest concern for Israel was that so many Jews were not saved. His argument asserts, though, that God has not failed in his promise to save Israel (Rom. 9:6) because God has saved some Jews throughout Israel's history in anticipation of the great and final day in which "all Israel will be saved" (Rom. 11:26 HCSB). In light of this context, and

---

8. See, e.g., J. D. Strauss, "God's Promise and Universal History: The Theology of Romans 9" in *Grace Unlimited,* ed. Clark H. Pinnock (Minneapolis: Bethany, 1975), 190–208; and Roger T. Forster and V. Paul Marston, *God's Strategy in Human History* (Wheaton: Tyndale, 1973).

9. See especially, John Piper, *The Justification of God: An Exegetical and Theological Study of Romans 9:1–23* (Grand Rapids: Baker, 1983, 1993); and Thomas R. Schreiner, "Does Romans 9 Teach Individual Election unto Salvation?" in *Still Sovereign: Contemporary Perspectives on Election, Foreknowledge, and Grace,* eds. Thomas R. Schreiner and Bruce A. Ware (Grand Rapids: Baker, 2000), 89–106.

in view of the fact that the election spoken of here is God's election of some in Israel to salvation, consider what Paul says in Romans 9:10–16.

The element of this text that is clearest of all is this: God's election of Jacob, not Esau, was unconditional. As Paul explains, before the two had been born, and before either had done anything good or bad, God chose Jacob over his older brother Esau. That is, apart from any consideration of what these two future individuals would do, or what works they would perform, God, for his own purposes, chose one over the other. His choosing, then, was not based or conditioned on them; and so this election was, strictly speaking, unconditional. And why does Paul emphasize the unconditional nature of the election of Jacob? Answer: "So that God's purpose according to election might stand, not from works but from the One who calls" (Rom. 9:11–12 HCSB). In other words, God wishes to establish his rightful place and authority as God by being the one who—by rights of his deity—elects one but not another. This is God's prerogative as God, and to deny of God that he elects people unconditionally is to deny something that God here (and elsewhere) establishes about the very godness of his being God.

The correctness of this line of interpretation is confirmed as we consider the rhetorical question that Paul suggests might be raised in light of this assertion of God's unconditional election of Jacob over Esau: "What should we say then? Is there injustice with God?" (Rom. 9:14 HCSB). The question, "Is there injustice with God?" and the moral challenge it raises only make sense if the previous discussion has established that God elects one over the other, not based on what they are or do but exclusively according to the purposes of his will. If instead God had chosen Jacob over Esau due to some quality in Jacob that commended him, or because God knew that Esau would be resistant to God's promptings and desires, then we would all conclude that God's election accorded with some reasonable sense of justice. In this case, God would have demonstrated that his favor shown to Jacob could be justified by the very lives, characters, and actions of the two men themselves—whose lives God would have known in advance when he elected one over the other.

But this is not the case! That is, Paul has specifically ruled out the notion that God's election is based on what Jacob or Esau would be like or what either would one day do. Rather, his election of Jacob specifically disregarded anything about either person and was based only and completely in the hidden purpose and will of God. Therefore, the question, Is there injustice with God?, makes sense! And Paul's continued explanation only serves to confirm yet further that God's election of Jacob over Esau was unconditional. After denying unequivocally that God has been unjust, he explains further, quoting Exodus 33:19, which has God saying, "I will show mercy to whom I show mercy, and I will have compassion on whom I have compassion" (Rom. 9:15 HCSB). Again, what is emphasized is that the will of God—his choice of the ones to whom he will show mercy and have compassion—is the basis for God's election, not the future lives or works or characters of those chosen or not chosen. Thus, Paul concludes this immediate discussion, saying, "So then it does not depend on human will or effort, but on God who shows mercy" (Rom. 9:16 HCSB). In accord with all we have seen previously, God chooses of his own purpose and will the ones for whom he shows mercy. Specifically, his choice "does not depend" on what humans will choose or what humans will do. Rather, *God's choice depends on God.* As God, he elects those upon whom he freely and willingly chooses to shower his mercy. His election, then, is unconditional.

Romans 11:5–7. The discussion in Romans 11 continues much of what we have already seen in Romans 9. Paul argues here that God has not rejected his people, Israel. As he has already asserted, God is being faithful to his promise to save Israel, even though the vast majority of current Israel stands outside of Christ and hence, is not saved (Rom. 10:1–4). Yet God's faithfulness to this saving promise to Israel is demonstrated in part by his salvation of some in Israel throughout history (Rom. 9:1–29; 11:1–7) and ultimately in his salvation of "all Israel" in the end (Rom. 11:26). Here in Romans 11, Paul is establishing the fact that even now (as Paul writes), during a time in which "a partial hardening has come to Israel" (Rom. 11:25 HCSB), nonetheless God is faithful to his promise to save Israelites—albeit only a remnant within Israel during this time of widespread hardening. Nonetheless, God's saved Israelites are testimony to God's faithfulness, and God's faithfulness to his promise is happening only because of God's electing grace.

One of the most striking phrases in Romans 11:5–7 is Paul's reference in verse 5 to the remnant as those "chosen by grace." Grace, of course, refers to unmerited favor, of giving to someone a gift that is fully undeserved and unearned. This is clear in what Paul says here concerning grace: "Now if by grace, then it is not by works; otherwise grace ceases to be grace" (Rom. 11:6 HCSB). Grace can only be grace if what grace gives is unearned, undeserved, and unmerited. If the gift of grace is based upon something that someone has done (i.e., in *quid pro quo* fashion), then grace ceases to be grace. Grace gives only as an expression of kindness and favor that is underserved.

Nearly all evangelicals would agree with what has just been stated about grace. That is, there is no real dispute over the point that grace is unmerited favor. But what is interesting here is exactly what gift Paul specifies that is given by grace. Notice that he does not say (here) that salvation is given by grace. All Arminians in the tradition of Arminius and Wesley affirm that salvation only comes to us by grace, for we are fully undeserving of the gift of salvation offered to us by the Lord. But here it is not salvation but *election* which grace gives. That is, the very choosing of the remnant to be a believing minority among the vast majority of those hardened is itself the gift specified that is granted by grace. Gracious election, in short, is unconditional election.

For this election to be gracious, it cannot depend on something done by the person elected, "otherwise grace ceases to be grace"! No, this gracious election is an election that is unmerited, undeserved, and it is an election that brings these elect persons their salvation. As if to emphasize the very contrast between the elect and nonelect, Paul observes in verse 7 (HCSB), "Israel [i.e., the majority of Jews who are unbelieving] did not find what it was looking for, but the elect [i.e., the remnant of believing Israelites] did find it. The rest were hardened." In other words, were it not for God's gracious choosing of the remnant, they, too, would be counted among the majority who did not find salvation at this time, the majority who have been hardened. But out of the hardened in Israel has come this remnant who encompass God's elect, who by his grace have been chosen to be saved. Their election is gracious because they don't deserve to be elected. Instead, they deserve the punishment that comes to those hardened against God.[10] Here God's grace is not only grace (unmerited favor) that saves but grace (unmerited favor) that elects. Those who other-

---

10. Thomas R. Schreiner, *Romans,* in the Baker Exegetical Commentary on the New Testament series, ed. Moisés Silva (Grand Rapids: Baker, 1998), 582, makes this observation on Paul's use of "chosen by grace" in Romans 11:5: "The only reason some Jews believe is because God has graciously and mercifully chosen them to be part of his people (cf. 9:27–29). The linkage of grace and election also must be observed. Many worry that the choosing of some and not all would be unjust, but this idea overlooks the fact that election is gracious. No one deserves to be elected, and thus the election of any is a merciful gift of God that cannot be claimed as a democratic right."

wise would be hardened in their rebellion are instead saved, and this has happened only because God's grace has elected them to be saved. Election, then, is unconditional.

Ephesians 1:3–6, 11. As I mentioned in the introductory paragraphs of this chapter, it is nothing short of astonishing that when Paul brings to his mind and lips specific reasons for why God should be blessed (1:3), the first and second items he recalls and celebrates are our election in Christ (1:4) and our predestination to be adopted children through Christ (1:5). What is for Paul both primary and central in the praise of God is for many today secondary at best and divisive and destructive at worst. So, what is this election of which Paul speaks?

Clearly, the main thrust that Paul makes in Ephesians 1:3–14 is that all of our salvation is of the Lord. This saving work of God began in eternity past when God elected us to be made holy and blameless through his Son, and it culminates in the future bestowal of our promised inheritance as now guaranteed by the Spirit who seals us for this day. From eternity past to eternity future, salvation is from the Lord.

Could it be, then, that our election in Christ is conditioned on something that renders it uncertain whether God truly will be able to save those whom he otherwise would will to save? Is God's saving purpose and plan subject to contingencies that may keep him from doing the very thing for which Paul here praises God? Is our salvation, in an ultimate sense, conditioned on what *we* do, whether God would will this or not? Any notion of conditional election is so clearly out of step with what Paul asserts that it simply jeopardizes and undermines the praise that is to go to God alone for this glorious saving work (Eph. 1:6, 12, 14).

Rather, it seems clear that Paul's stating that God's election of us took place "before the foundation of the world" (1:4 HCSB) is first and foremost to underscore the unconditional nature of this election. To be sure, this phrase functions as a time marker. That is, it does tell us *when* God's election of us took place—before God had even created the world. But the primary purpose for including this detail, it seems, establishes the fact that election of those whom God will save (i.e., make holy and blameless) is God's choice pure and simple, a choice with which we had nothing to do and could have had nothing to do. Why? We had not even been created! So when God chose us, only God was. Therefore his election of us was based on God's will and purpose and was not based, and could not have been based, on our lives, characters, or choices. In short, God's election of us "before the foundation of the world" is, by necessity, an election that is unconditional.[11] Confirmation for the notion that God's choice of us is based on his will and purpose and not based on us comes in Ephesians 1:11. Here Paul states that we will receive an inheritance since God has predestined us to have it.[12] According to Paul, this predestination was "according to the purpose of the One who works out everything in agreement with the decision of His will" (Eph. 1:11 HCSB). Incredible! God works everything according to his will, but notice that nothing is said here about God working things out according to our wills! In other words, all that God chooses is unconditional, including his predestination and election of us. The God who works everything as he so wills is the God who elects us to be holy in Christ, as he so wills. God's election of us, then, is unconditional.

2 Thessalonians 2:13; 2 Timothy 1:8–9; Ephesians 1:4. As we just observed, in Ephesians 1:4 Paul writes that God made his choice of those whom he would save "before the foundation of the world" (HCSB). In two[13] other passages, likewise, Paul refers to God's elec-

---

11. Molinists may deny the argument presented here, believing that divine election could be conditioned upon what God knew would be true in various possible situations that he might actualize. The Molinist may argue that even if I were never created, there still would exist from the foundation of the world contingent propositions stating what I would freely choose in various situations (i.e., counterfactuals of creaturely freedom). However, it is not clear that such knowledge is logically possible. As the grounding objection inquires, What makes these counterfactuals true? It cannot be *me* since they are true before I exist and even if I never exist. And it cannot be *God* because if so, I wouldn't have libertarian freedom as the Molinist insists. Thus such counterfactuals are groundless in Molinism, and hence, divine election cannot be conditioned upon such counterfactuals of creaturely freedom.

12. Note that Paul speaks of predestination twice in this lengthy sentence (Eph. 1:3–14), the first indicating that we are predestined to be adopted through Christ (1:5), and the second that we are predestined to receive an inheritance (1:11). The connection between these two concepts is clear when one recalls that sons are the ones who rightly receive their fathers' inheritance. So God's predestining us to sonship entails, then, his predestining us to the reception of our inheritance. What sovereign grace this is, that God would choose us, before he created the world, to be his own sons to whom he would give all the riches of his Son.

13. A similar but less explicit statement can also be seen in Titus 1:1–2: "Paul, a slave of God, and an apostle of Jesus Christ for the faith of God's elect and the knowledge of the truth that leads to godliness, in the hope of eternal life that God, who cannot lie, *promised before time began*" (italics added). Notice how parallel the main features of thought are to Ephesians 1:4. God's election leads to godliness, and this promise of eternal life was made before time began. Clearly these are central truths for the apostle Paul, and although they are stated with different nuances in each text, their basic ideas are parallel.

tion of his people occurring in eternity past. In both of these passages, along with Ephesians 1:4, the "time" of God's choosing of us to be saved is placed in eternity past. One must ask the question, Why does the apostle emphasize, as he does in all three texts, that God's election of those whom he would save took place before time began?

It seems clear that the fundamental reason that stands behind these various expressions placing election before the very creation of the world and time is this: we did not yet exist, and so God's election of us simply can have nothing to do with certain truths about us! The impact of these temporal clauses, then, is much like the impact that Paul sought in Romans 9:11. There, because neither Jacob nor Esau had yet been born, because neither had done anything good or bad, therefore Paul drives home the point that God's election of Jacob, not Esau, had to do with God's purposes and good pleasure altogether and could not have been based on something true about them. Why not? Answer: they didn't yet exist! So it is here, in these three texts locating God's election as occurring "before the foundation of the world" (Eph. 1:4 HCSB), "from the beginning" (2 Thess. 2:13 HCSB), or "before time began" (2 Tim. 1:9 HCSB). Because no one existed when God's election took place, God's election of those whom he would save simply could not have to do with something about them. Rather, God's election has to do with what God chooses. In short, these time markers are in these verses precisely to instruct us that God's election to salvation is unconditional.[14]

Effectual calling requires unconditional election. Second, Scripture clearly indicates that the gospel message calling people to put faith in Christ and be saved is meant for all people, throughout all the world. This is sometimes referred to as the "general call" (or *vocatio externa*) to salvation, extended to all people everywhere, that whoever hears the gospel is invited to come to Christ and be saved.[15] But those in the Reformed tradition have also often noted that the "general call" is not the only kind of divine calling to salvation that is taught in Scripture. Another sense of "the call" to be saved is indicated by several texts, but these passages portray not a general but a

14. Discussion of these and additional passages, with independent comment and evaluation, can be found in the recently released and very helpful volume, Robert A. Peterson and Michael D. Williams, *Why I Am Not an Arminian* (Downers Grove: Inter-Varsity, 2004).

15. See, e.g., Isaiah 45:22; 55:1; Matthew 11:28; 22:2–14; John 7:37; and Revelation 22:17. These expressions of the general call accord with Jesus' own commission to his disciples that the gospel be spread to all the nations, as he commands in Matthew 28:18–20 and Acts 1:8.

"special" call because (1) it is a call to salvation directed only to some people, not all, and (2) it is a call that always succeeds in bringing people to saving faith in Christ. Hence, this "special call" is sometimes referred to as the "effectual call" (or *vocatio interna*[16]) since through this call to salvation, God necessarily effects (i.e., certainly and unfailingly brings about) the person's salvation.

In brief, the general call is extended (in principle) to every person everywhere, yet not all of those who are called actually respond to the call and are saved. But the effectual call is extended only to some people (i.e., some of those who hear the general call), and when this effectual call comes to them, all of those so "called" are saved. The effectual call effects the salvation of all of those so called.[17]

Since I have argued elsewhere that the effectual call of God is taught in Scripture and that, rightly understood, it entails the truthfulness of the doctrine of unconditional election,[18] I here will only summarize a portion of both the biblical support for the doctrine of the effectual call and how this doctrine requires unconditional election also to be true. One passage that shows with unmistakable clarity that the "special" or "effectual" call of God is taught in Scripture is Romans 8:29–30. Notice two things about this passage. First, the calling of God to be saved here is *extended only to some* and not to all. Who, according to Romans 8:30, are those called? Answer: "those He predestined" are "also called." Thus, this call is not extended to all people everywhere but only to a certain subset of the whole of humanity, viz., only to the "predestined."

Lest we wonder if in some sense God may have predestined everyone so that when the call goes to those predestined it actually goes to all people (for all are predestined), notice that the predestined are

---

16. For the distinction between the *vocatio externa* and the *vocatio interna*, see Heinrich Heppe, *Reformed Dogmatics,* trans. G. T. Thomson (reprint, Grand Rapids: Baker, 1978), 512–13.

17. Please see also Thomas R. Schreiner, "Does Scripture Teach Prevenient Grace in the Wesleyan Sense?" in *Still Sovereign: Contemporary Perspectives on Election, Foreknowledge, and Grace,* eds. Thomas R. Schreiner and Bruce A. Ware (Grand Rapids: Baker, 2000), 229–46, for a very fine discussion of the Arminian/Wesleyan alternative view of saving grace often called "prevenient grace" where Schreiner demonstrates that this type of grace is simply not taught in Scripture. If in fact Scripture does not support prevenient grace while it does support and teach the effectual call (i.e., irresistible grace), then an Arminian soteriology is undermined while a fundamentally Calvinist understanding of salvation is further established.

18. Bruce A. Ware, "Effectual Calling and Grace," in *Still Sovereign: Contemporary Perspectives on Election, Foreknowledge, and Grace,* eds. Thomas R. Schreiner and Bruce A. Ware (Grand Rapids: Baker, 2000), 203–27.

only those whom God foreknew[19] out of all of humanity. And notice further that all of those whom God foreknew and predestined are ultimately saved—"those He foreknew He also predestined . . . [and] justified . . . [and] glorified." As such, unless one holds to universalism (i.e., the view that all will ultimately be saved—a view already excluded by what Paul taught in Romans 2:5–11), then one must rightly conclude that only some are foreknown, and these same ones are those who are predestined and called.

Second, the calling of God to be saved here is *effectual;* i.e., it succeeds in accomplishing what the call desires by bringing those called surely and certainly to salvation. Notice that throughout these verses a pattern emerges. It begins in Romans 8:29 with "those" foreknown who are "also" predestined. Verse 30 continues the pattern: "those" predestined are "also" called, "those" called are "also" justified, and "those" justified are "also" glorified.[20] In other words, the same people are in view from God's foreknowledge of them to God's ultimate glorification of these same persons. Each step in the process takes them on to the next step so that all who are foreknown are glorified. As this relates to the question of what kind of calling Paul speaks of here, it is clear, then, that Romans 8:30 refers to a calling that effects the salvation of the ones called. In other words, this call works! This call results necessarily in all of those called being saved.

While much more biblical support could be offered,[21] this is sufficient for our present purposes to conclude that the doctrine of effectual calling is biblical. But what relation does this doctrine have to the question of whether God's election of those whom he will save is unconditional or not? Rightly understood, these two doctrines are mutually entailing. That is, if effectual calling is true, it entails the truthfulness of unconditional election, and if unconditional election is true, it entails the truthfulness of effectual calling. Put differently, you cannot have one without the other.

Consider first the entailment if unconditional election is deemed to be true. If God has unconditionally elected just certain specific persons to be saved, and if this election is grounded only in the good pleasure and will of God and does not consider the characters, actions, or choices of these individuals, and if this election of God is certain so

---

19. See discussion on divine foreknowledge under "Objections to Unconditional Election," below.

20. In the Greek text the phrase *toutous kai* is used three times in Romans 8:30, indicating "those/these also."

21. See Ware, "Effectual Calling and Grace," 211–26.

that those individuals cannot fail to be saved, then it follows that God must so work in them particularly such that they, but not others, are surely and certainly saved. We might say that if God has unconditionally elected them to salvation, he must call them effectively to salvation, and this calling, since it actually saves them, can be granted only to those whom he has elected. Unconditional election, then, requires God's effectual call to those elected, so that his elective purposes for them are accomplished.

Now consider the two doctrines in reverse order. If God effectually calls only some to be saved, and if this calling, by its nature, is granted only to some such that all of those called actually and certainly are saved, then it follows that God must select those to whom this calling is extended. That is, God's effectual calling cannot be based on how people respond to the general call since the general call includes no certainty of the salvation of those called. But since the effectual call does include the certainty of the salvation of all those called, then it follows that God must grant the effectual call to specifically selected individuals only, such that when they are called (effectually), they are surely and certainly saved. So, what name shall we give to this "selection" by God of those specific individuals to whom he extends the effectual call? Surely we could rightly speak of these persons as those "chosen" or "elected" by God to be the recipients of the effectual call. Therefore, if the doctrine of the effectual call is true, it follows that God has previously elected just those specific persons to whom he extends this call.[22] Effectual calling, then, entails unconditional election.[23]

---

22. See also John Calvin, *Institutes of the Christian Religion*, Library of Christian Classics, 2 vols., ed. John T. McNeill, trans. Ford Lewis Battles (Philadelphia: Westminster, 1960), 2.964 (3.24), where the chapter title reads, in part, "Election Is Confirmed by God's Call," and is followed by the section heading (3.24.1) that reads, "The call is dependent upon election and accordingly is solely a work of grace."

23. One implication of this argument is that the Arminian notion of foreknowledge in Romans 8:29 falters. As will be discussed further below, many Arminians see foreknowledge in this text as God seeing in advance those who will believe in Christ when presented with the gospel ("foreseen faith," as it is sometimes called). That is, from the vantage point of eternity past, God looks down the corridors of history and sees those who, in time, put faith in Christ when it was in their power to reject Christ. They could have believed or disbelieved, but God saw in advance who would believe. But if this is true, it makes no sense later for Paul to say that those whom God foreknew he then called—if this calling is effectual. For if God's calling of them to salvation is effectual, they *must believe*; but if the foreknowledge of God is what Arminians claim, then those whom God foresees as believing *could instead have not believed*. In short, there is no way to reconcile the Arminian notion of foreknowledge in Romans 8:29 if the calling of Romans 8:30 is effectual. Since the calling of Romans 8:30 is indeed effectual ("those He called, He also justified" HCSB), foreknowledge cannot mean what these Arminians claim.

Regeneration that precedes saving faith requires unconditional election. Third, Scripture indicates that those who believe in Christ only do so because they have been "born again," enabling and eliciting this saving faith. Arminians, of course, dispute this point. They argue that those who believe are regenerated. But most Calvinists[24] understand Scripture to say that since unconverted sinners are dead in their sins (Eph. 2:1), blinded by Satan so that they cannot see Christ's glory (2 Cor. 4:4), and fully unable to do anything pleasing to God (Rom. 8:6–8), therefore God must work in them to open their blind eyes, to enliven their hard hearts, and to grant them the capacity for doing what they simply could not do on their own, viz., believe in Christ so as to be saved. In other words, unbelievers must be born again so that having been given new life by the Spirit of God, they now immediately do what their new natures cry out to do in trusting Christ for their salvation.

Does Scripture indicate that regeneration precedes and grounds saving faith? Consider two passages: 1 John 5:1 and John 1:12–13. The book of 1 John offers several indicators of what the born-again person is like. For example, 1 John 2:29 (HCSB) claims that "everyone who does what is right has been born of Him [God]." The verb for "has been born" (*gegennetai*) is a perfect, passive indicative of "to beget or bring forth" (*gennao*). The perfect tense normally indicates past action that continues into the present. So John is saying that the person who has been and is born again is like this: he does what is right. That is, being born again accounts for doing right. This surely means that the new birth precedes a righteous life; otherwise John would be teaching works-righteousness (i.e., doing "what is right" accounting for being born again)! No, rather, regeneration accounts for the "right" sort of actions and behavior of which John speaks. Similarly, 1 John 4:7 (HCSB) states that "everyone who loves has been born of God and knows God." Again, "has been born" is perfect, passive, indicative, and so the idea is clear: being born of God and knowing God are the basis by which one is able to love.

---

24. Some Calvinist theologians have argued that while regeneration and saving faith are simultaneous, the former is logically dependent on the latter. See, e.g., Millard Erickson, *Christian Theology*, 2nd ed. (Grand Rapids: Baker, 1998), 944–45; and Demarest, *Cross and Salvation*, 289–95. It should be noted, though, that while these Calvinists differ in the order of regeneration and conversion, yet their understanding of effectual calling is such that this calling goes only to the elect, and this calling, that surely will save the elect, awakens in them the faith by which they then are regenerated. So even here it is clear that God's enlivening work in the unsaved person must precede his exercising of faith in Christ.

In light of this clear understanding in John, it is instructive that John also indicates that faith in Christ is likewise the outgrowth of being born of God. That is, just as doing what is right and loving are expressions of being born of God, so also faith itself is an expression of being born of God. First John 5:1 (HCSB) asserts, "Everyone who believes that Jesus is the Messiah has been born of God." Here, as in the other verses just considered, "has been born" is perfect, passive, indicative; and the same logic applies. One expression of being born of God, says John, is that the person born again believes that Jesus is the Messiah. Presumably the opposite, then, is true. If one is not born again, he cannot believe that Jesus is the Messiah, just as if he is not born again, he cannot do what is right and he cannot love. Being born again, then, gives rise to doing right, to loving others; and it gives rise to believing that Christ truly is the Messiah. Faith in Christ, then, flows out of the life of one who has been regenerated.

Second, John 1:11–13 is also important. One might think, from verse 12, that a person becomes a child of God *because* he believes in the name of Christ. But this conclusion would be premature. Notice that John does not say, "He gave them the right to be children of God *because* they believed in His name." Rather, he merely notes that these two things both happen: they are given the right to be children of God, and they believe in his name. What he does not say in verse 12 is that becoming children of God results from their faith.

But when one considers verse 13, now the causal conception and explanation is introduced. John writes of those given the right to be children of God, to those who believe in Christ, that they "were born" *of God*. That is, what accounts for them having the right to be God's children, and what accounts for their believing in Christ's name, is that they had been born of God. The verb "were born" is aorist, passive, indicative, indicating action done previously. So, because a person was born of God, this person now has the right to be God's child; and this person now believes in Christ. Being born of God (1:13), then, precedes and grounds the reality expressed in verse 12.

This is only confirmed by what John says did *not* give rise to this believing in Christ. He says that they were born "not of blood" (i.e., not due to one's physical descent), "or of the will of the flesh" (i.e., not due to one's own personal determination and will), "or of the will of man" (i.e., not because of any other person's determination or will), "but of God" (i.e., God alone is the One who has brought into existence this new life). The regeneration spoken of in verse 13, then, provides the basis for a person's belief in Christ. Such belief could not come from oneself or be given by another. Rather, only God could grant a person the new life by which he could believe. Regeneration, then, precedes and grounds saving faith.[25]

It should be clear, then, that if regeneration precedes and gives rise to saving faith, that regeneration requires unconditional election. As with our previous discussion of the effectual call, since only some are regenerated by the Holy Spirit, and those who are regenerated unfailingly believe in Christ and are saved, then it follows that God must select those particular ones whom he chooses to grant the new birth. That is, God's choice of those whom he will regenerate must precede the actual work of the Holy Spirit accomplishing this regenerating work. And if God must choose the particular persons he will regenerate, and if they cannot believe in Christ apart from his regenerating work, then it must be the case that God's election of those individuals is unconditional.

It simply cannot be the case that God looks ahead in time and sees those who will believe in Christ and so elects them based on his advanced knowledge of their faith. For apart from regeneration, God would see only unbelief as he looked down the corridors of history. But since some do believe in Christ, and since regeneration is necessary for any to believe in Christ, then it must be the case that God grants some individuals the regenerating work by which they then believe. And if so, then God must select those individuals who are granted his regenerating work, and this selection cannot consider some supposed expression of faith they would have, since regeneration is necessary for saving faith to occur. In other words, God cannot choose people to regenerate by looking ahead and seeing them doing what only those already regenerated can do! Therefore, because

---

25. D. A. Carson, *The Gospel According to John* (Grand Rapids: Eerdmans, 1991), 126, suggests that the connection between faith and the new birth are not spelled out in John 1:12–13, disagreeing with previous commentators who have argued either for the logical priority of faith for regeneration (e.g., Barrett), or (as I argue here) for the logical priority of regeneration for faith (e.g., Holtzmann). But just prior to this judgment, Carson has rightly pointed out the parallel nature of the teaching of John 1:12–13 with John 3:6 ("Whatever is born of the flesh is flesh, and whatever is born of the Spirit is spirit"). But does it not stand to reason that the contrast in John 3:6 indicates that what we do in the flesh does not account for our regeneration? And if so, would this not further support the notion that regeneration by the Spirit gives rise to our faith, rather than faith coming from ourselves prior to or apart from this regenerative work of the Spirit? It seems to be John's point, then, in both John 1:12–13 and John 3:6 that regeneration occurs totally apart from our doing, which eliminates "our faith" as the basis for this regeneration. Rather, regeneration happens to us but apart from us, and this gives rise to faith.

regeneration is the enlivening work of God (alone) in the hearts of those dead in sin, and because regeneration gives rise to saving faith, the doctrine of regeneration requires the unconditional nature of God's election to salvation.

Divine sovereignty, rightly understood, requires unconditional election. Fourth, Scripture teaches a strong sense of divine sovereignty, meaning that God exerts and maintains ultimate control of everything that occurs throughout the universe and throughout time. Paul indicates this understanding of divine sovereignty when he says that God "works out everything in agreement with the decision of His will" (Eph. 1:11 HCSB). Everything![26] We are justified, then, in believing that God exerts ultimate control of all that happens since his will and purpose guide history in such a way that everything that occurs happens in agreement with the will and purpose of God.

Nor does this statement stand alone. Rather, Scripture is simply filled with both explicit teachings and examples indicating that God ultimately controls all that occurs in life and throughout human history. I have discussed elsewhere what I have called the several "spectrum texts" of Scripture.[27] These are passages indicating that both good and evil, light and darkness, life and death, health and sickness—both sides of the spectrum, as it were—are ordained and controlled by God. In fact, some texts indicate that God's claim to exclusive deity is grounded on his being the one who alone controls all of life. Consider just one such text. Isaiah 45:5–7 (HCSB) records God as saying, "I am the LORD, and there is no other; there is no God but Me . . . I am the LORD, and there is no other. I form light and create darkness, I make success and create disaster; I the LORD do all these things." One cannot miss the emphasis God here makes, that he alone is God, and that as the true and only Lord of all, he controls darkness as well as light, disaster as well as success. He is the Lord who does "all these things."

---

26. To be sure that Paul really means "everything," consider his use of the very same term and concept in the previous verse. Here he indicates that God's plan is "to bring everything [*panta*] together in the Messiah, both things in heaven and things on earth in Him" (Eph. 1:10 HCSB). Notice that the same word, "everything" (*panta*) is used in both verses 10 and 11, and that in verse 10, "everything" introduces the notion of "things in heaven and things on earth," obviously reinforcing the idea that absolutely nothing is left out! Yes, "everything" in verse 11 should really be understood as "everything"!

27. Bruce A. Ware, *God's Lesser Glory: The Diminished God of Open Theism* (Wheaton, Ill.: Crossway, 2000), 204–7; and *God's Greater Glory: The Exalted God of Scripture and the Christian Faith* (Wheaton, Ill.: Crossway, 2004), 61–78.

Either we believe God, or we don't. As this relates here, either we believe God when he tells us that he has absolute control over all that happens, or we deny that what he says is true. Furthermore, in light of the buildup to these claims—"I am the Lord, and there is no other"—we can only conclude that God means it when he tells us that all things are carried out by his ordination, and that his own rightful claim to deity is attached to this very action. So, while it is true that God possess no "evil" (*ra*), as Psalm 5:4 makes clear, it is also true that God exerts ultimate control over all "evil" (*ra*), as Isaiah 45:7 insists. The same word, "evil" (*ra*), is used in each passage, and the lesson could not be more clear or more important: God, who is wholly good and not evil (Ps. 5:4), is the same God who controls both good and evil (Isa. 45:7). As difficult as this is to grasp, Scripture teaches this grand truth, and we must accept what God, through Scripture, tells us.[28]

Obviously, if God controls all that happens, it goes without saying that he controls who is saved and who is not. Unconditional election is logically required from this strong, biblical definition of divine sovereignty. In Ephesians 1:11 (HCSB) Paul not only indicates that God "works out everything in agreement with the decision of His will" but also that we were "*predestined* according to the purpose of the One who works out everything in agreement with the decision of His will" (italics added). In other words, the connection that we already observed between a strong, biblical understanding of divine sovereignty and unconditional election is rendered explicit and is taught directly here by Paul. Predestination to salvation, for Paul, is one central element within the larger sovereign work of God, a work that encompasses absolutely everything that happens in all of time and space. Because God is sovereign, God controls all that occurs. Within his sovereign control, says Paul, stands our predestination to salvation. A strong understanding of divine sovereignty, then, requires the doctrine of unconditional election.

The only substantive form of election is unconditional election. Fifth, I return to a point made in the introduction of this chapter. When Paul sets his mind to contemplate the reasons for which God is worthy of praise, the first and second items off his lips in Ephesians 1 are "He chose us" (Eph. 1:4 HCSB) and "He predestined us" (Eph. 1:5 HCSB). One reason that seeing God's saving election of sinners in

---

28. For an extended discussion of God's relation to both good and evil that maintains that God is exclusively good and in no respect evil, see Ware, *God's Greater Glory*, chapter 4, "Ruling through Creation: Divine-Human Concurrence," 97–130.

Scripture as unconditional is compelling is this: only election understood as *unconditional* election accounts for why this biblical truth
is elevated, cherished, and commended. Only if the entirety of God's
saving work really does hinge on a decision made by God in eternity
past, a decision that put in motion all the other steps of our salvation
and that guaranteed that those whom he chose would truly and surely
be saved; only if the fact that we are now saved is owing to what God
decided when he chose us to be the recipients of his grace in Christ;
only if election truly is unconditional and is the decision God made
of who he surely would save—only then does it make sense that this
concept would receive the special attention and be given the special
commendation that Scripture affords it. In short, only unconditional
election really and truly is election.

Paul Jewett has expressed this point with eloquence. Writing of
what he calls the *a posteriori* approach to election (i.e., the approach
that sees the election of God based on the choices of men and women
as God looks ahead at the lives they will live and chooses according to
what they will do), he observes that this approach

gives meaning and significance to human history only at the expense of the divine agency and purpose. The emphasis it places on
the human agent's choosing the Savior becomes so basic that the
emphasis on God's choosing the sinner is reduced, for all practical purposes, to mere appearance. In other words, it conceives of
the divine purpose as not a purpose at all but mere prescience,
divine foresight of what will happen by human choice. The only
purpose left that may be described as God's purpose is his decision to accept the foreseen decision of the creature. This really
drains election of all significance, for it is the choice at the human level—belief or unbelief—foreseen, perhaps, but not foreordained, that constitutes the basis of "election." One is not chosen
from "before the foundation of the world"; rather, one's choice of
Christ is foreseen "from before the foundation of the world."[29]

And a few pages later, he comments of this same view,

that such a position is in fact simply a way of saying that God
does not really elect or reject anyone, but that from eternity he
simply resolves to actualize a general redemptive purpose that
incidentally gives rise to a distinction among men and women.
. . . Instead of a free *divine* election *in* Christ, there is a free *human* election *of* Christ. . . . The Scriptures say that God chose

---

29. Jewett, *Election and Predestination,* 66.

us in Christ from before the foundation of the world (Eph. 1:4), not that he saw us from before the foundation of the world as choosing Christ. There is no possible way of reducing these two statements to a common meaning.[30]

If one considers seriously the gravity of this doctrine to biblical writers, it becomes clear that the only conception of election that accords with the weightiness with which it is presented is the astonishing truth that God, before time and creation, chose particular sinful men and women, and that he determined on their behalf that he would do absolutely everything (and oh, how much that is!) that would be required to bring to them their sure and certain salvation. Because God chose them, in time, they would be enlivened so that they would choose him. This election of God—unconditional election—alone accounts for the place and prominence this doctrine has in the biblical record. Election to salvation, then, is unconditional election.

Objections to Unconditional Election

On Sunday morning, April 29, 1739, John Wesley (1703–1791) preached one of the most memorable and impacting sermons of his entire preaching ministry. In this sermon that was soon published under the title, "Free Grace,"[31] Wesley took as his text Romans 8:32 ("He that spared not his own Son"), and as Wesley wrote to James Hutton the next day, he "declared openly for the first hour against 'the horrible decree'"—an obvious reference to Calvin's own comment about the doctrine of divine reprobation, some version of which follows from the doctrine of unconditional election.[32] In his informative discussion of Wesley's sermon and its impact on Methodism,[33] H. B. McGonigle comments, "This sermon was something of a theological *tour de force*. It revealed John Wesley, in his first sermon and publication on predestination, to be dogmatically anti-Calvinist. Although Calvin's name was never mentioned nor that of any other

---

30. Ibid., 72–73.

31. The full text of "Free Grace" is published in John Wesley, *The Works of John Wesley. The Bicentennial Edition,* ed. Frank Baker (Oxford and Nashville: 1975–1996), 3.542–63.

32. Calvin, *Institutes of the Christian Religion,* 2.955 (3.23.7). Here Calvin writes, "The decree is dreadful indeed, I confess. Yet no one can deny that God foreknew what end man was to have before he created him, and consequently foreknew because he so ordained by his decree."

33. Herbert Boyd McGonigle, *Sufficient Saving Grace: John Wesley's Evangelical Arminianism* (Carlisle, UK: Paternoster, 2001), 112–21.

Calvinist writer, it was Calvin's teaching on the 'horrible decree' that was plainly the target."[34]

Wesley enumerated several objections to the Calvinist doctrine of unconditional election, as many Arminians throughout history have done. In what follows, I will express and answer what seem to me to be the most serious and the most oft-repeated of these objections, endeavoring to defend the doctrine of unconditional election in light of them. Because of space limitations, the reader will have to settle for brief and sometimes less than fully adequate explanations. But I hope that the main lines of responses are clear enough to see how this doctrine can rightly withstand these challenges.

Objection 1

Since Scripture declares plainly (Rom. 9:29; 1 Pet. 1:1–2) that divine election is based (or conditioned) on God's foreknowledge, then it is clear that election cannot be unconditional. Both of these texts indicate that God knows from eternity past how each person will act and choose throughout all of history, and this foreknowledge includes God's advanced knowledge of how each person will respond when the gospel is presented, i.e., whether each will believe in Christ or not. Therefore, God's election is conditioned upon God's knowledge of persons' "foreseen faith" and so his election is conditional, not unconditional.

Reply. First, while God's "knowledge" in Scripture can refer simply to God's cognitive and factual knowledge of what occurs, in many instances it has the richer relational meaning of God having a disposition to favor and relate intimately with ("know") certain persons. Consider in the Old Testament, Jeremiah 1:5 (HCSB), "I chose you [lit. "I knew you," from *yada,* "to know"] before I formed you in the womb; I set you apart before you were born. I appointed you a prophet to the nations"; and Amos 3:2a (HCSB), "I have known only you out of all the clans of the earth." And in the New Testament, consider Matthew 7:23 (HCSB), "Then I will announce to them, 'I never knew you! Depart from Me, you lawbreakers!'"; John 10:14 (HCSB), "I am the good shepherd. I know My own sheep, and they know Me"; and Galatians 4:9 (HCSB), "But now, since you know God, or rather have become known by God, how can you turn back again to the weak and bankrupt elemental forces?" As such, "foreknowledge" likewise refers most often not merely to God's factual knowledge of future affairs

---

34. Ibid., 118.

but is rather *God's prior disposition to relate to and favor* ("know") certain persons. That is, before they even exist (e.g., Jer. 1:5 HCSB), God seeks to "know" them, to favor them and relate intimately with ("know") them.[35]

Second, as Jewett points out, a serious problem with the Arminian reading of Romans 8:29 and 1 Peter 1:1–2 is that they read into these passages ideas that simply are not stated. In his own reply to this Arminian objection from these passages, Jewett states, "The answer is simply that these texts do not say, 'Whom God foreknew *would believe,* he predestinated,' nor that we as Christians are 'elect according to the foreknowledge *which God has of our faith.*'"[36] Jewett is correct. Indeed, while these texts clearly say that God foreknew *the people* whom he then elected, they do not indicate something *about them,* or some *future choice of theirs,* that God knew as the basis of his election of them to salvation. Put differently, foreknowledge here is not of some specific *propositional knowledge* about people, but it refers to God's *relational knowledge* of certain people themselves. As Romans 8:29 (HCSB) puts it, "For *those He foreknew* He also predestined" (italics added).

Third, compelling evidence against the Arminian understanding comes from usage of the same term, "foreknowledge," in other texts in Romans and 1 Peter, respectively. Romans 11:2 (HCSB) states, "God has not rejected His people whom He foreknew." Now, if we applied the Arminian notion of foreknowledge here, this text would mean, "God has not rejected His people *whom He knew in advance would choose Him.*" But clearly this is not the case! God chose Israel, from all the nations of the world, even though she was the smallest and weakest of the lot (Deut. 7:6–8; 14:2)! It simply is not the case that God picked Israel to be his people because he knew in advance that Israel would pick him! Rather, what Romans 11:2 (HCSB) is saying is this: "God has not rejected His people whom He *previously had been disposed to be in relationship with and favor.*" Both the usual lexical meaning of "foreknowledge" and the historical facts about God's relationship with Israel indicate that this is what Paul means in Romans 11:2.

---

35. See also S. M. Baugh, "The Meaning of Foreknowledge," in *Still Sovereign: Contemporary Perspectives on Election, Foreknowledge, and Grace,* eds. Thomas R. Schreiner and Bruce A. Ware (Grand Rapids: Baker, 2000), 183–200, where Baugh defends the biblical notion of "foreknowledge" as God initiating "covenant relations" with those yet to be (192–94) or his establishing a "gracious" and "personal commitment" to particular people before he creates the world (194–97).

36. Jewett, *Election and Predestination,* 70.

And consider 1 Peter 1:20 (HCSB), "He [Christ] was destined [literally, "He was foreknown"] before the foundation of the world, but was revealed at the end of the times for you." Again, if the Arminian conception of "foreknowledge" is applied here, we would be led to think Peter meant, "Before the foundation of the world, God *knew that Christ would choose to come,* but He was revealed at the end of the times for you." The problem with this reading is that it conflicts with how Jesus himself explained his own coming to earth, time and time again. We regularly hear Jesus saying things like, "I have come down from heaven, not to do My will, but the will of Him who sent Me" (John 6:38 HCSB); "I came from God and I am here. For I didn't come on My own, but He sent Me" (John 8:42 HCSB); and "I do nothing on My own. But just as the Father taught Me, I say these things" (John 8:28 HCSB). Jesus uniformly credits the Father with sending him to earth, and he seeks always and only to do the will of his Father.

Instead, then, 1 Peter 1:20 must mean something like this: "Before the foundation of the world, Christ was *previously favored by God to be the One Whom He would send to come as Savior,* but was revealed at the end of the times for you." Given that the same term for "foreknowledge" is used in such close proximity to our two key texts, and given that the Arminian understanding fails in both of these parallel texts, it seems highly doubtful that "foreknowledge" means what Arminians claim in Romans 8:29[37] or 1 Peter 1:1–2.

Therefore, the Arminian conception of foreknowledge in Romans 8:29 and 1 Peter 1:1–2 suffers from lexical, conceptual, and contextual objections that show that it cannot be the meaning that the biblical authors intended. Rather, when foreknowledge is understood as God's prior disposition to relate with and favor certain people, now these passages make clear sense. Paul would mean, "For those for whom God had a prior disposition to relate with and favor, He predestined . . . called . . . justified . . . and glorified." Favor, indeed! And Peter would mean, "You were chosen according to the Father's prior disposition to relate with you and favor you, and so you were set apart by the Spirit for obedience, to be sprinkled with the blood of Jesus Christ." And, understood this way, election based on God's foreknowledge is fully consistent with the doctrine of unconditional election. Recall that this doctrine holds that God selects whom he will save, not based on anything about their characters, actions, or choices *but*

---

37. Please also see the difficulty for the Arminian understanding of foreknowledge in Rom. 8:29 as explained in fn. 31, above.

in accord with his own good pleasure and will. Election conditioned on foreknowledge, in this sense then, is fully compatible with and expressive of the doctrine of unconditional election.

Objection 2

The universal, impartial, and equal love of God for all people demonstrates that unconditional election cannot be true. Since God is love, and since God's love is the same for all people whom he has made, it cannot be the case that the reason some are not saved is owing to *God's* choice, ultimately. Rather, some are not saved because *they* choose not to be saved, yet God would gladly (in love) have saved them, too, had they but come. Therefore, the election spoken of in Scripture simply cannot be unconditional election.

Reply. While Scripture clearly teaches God's universal, impartial, and equal love for all people, this is certainly not the only, or the most central, meaning of the love of God. As D. A. Carson has explained so helpfully, the Bible actually speaks of the love of God in five different senses.[38] One of those five senses is God's universal love for all (e.g., as seen in John 3:16). But another sense, one more prominent in Scripture, is God's particular, selective, and discriminate love for his own people. Consider two representative passages, both of which reflect God's special love for his own people, a love that moves him to save them and benefit them in a manner that distinguishes them from all others.

First, Isaiah 43 begins in a manner that believers have often found greatly comforting. "Do not fear," God tells his people, "for I have redeemed you; I have called you by name; you are Mine" (Isa. 43:1 HCSB). Further, God promises, "I will be with you when you pass through the waters, and when you pass through the rivers, they will not overwhelm you" (Isa. 43:2 HCSB). So God establishes the fact that he is the God of his people, and he will be with them to provide for them and to protect them, for as he says to them, "you are Mine."

The true significance of God's special claim upon *this* people, *his* people, is about to be seen more clearly, however. We read on: "For I the Lord your God, the Holy One of Israel, and your Savior, give Egypt as a ransom for you, Cush and Seba in your place. Because you are precious in My sight and honored, and I love [from *aheb*, "to love"] you, I will give human beings in your place, and peoples in place of

---

38. D. A. Carson, *The Difficult Doctrine of the Love of God* (Wheaton, Ill.: Crossway, 2000).

your life" (Isa. 43:3–4 HCSB). Here, then, is the particular, selective, and discriminate love of God for his own. He loves his people Israel by saving them at the expense of ("in the place of") many lives of Egyptians. Clearly this is a reference to the favor shown the Jews at the time of their exodus from Egypt. For, although God could have given the same warning and instruction in Egypt regarding the upcoming angel of death as he did among the Israelites prior to the exodus, he did not. Nor did he intend to do so.[39]

Instead, God warned and instructed only the Jews (Exod. 12:1–13), and since the Jews did as God said and put the blood of a slaughtered lamb over the doorposts of their houses, the angel of death "passed over" their homes. But since the Egyptians knew nothing of this means of being spared, the angel went on into Egypt and killed the firstborn in every Egyptian home and stable (Exod. 12:29–30). Accordingly, Isaiah 43 demonstrates the love of God for his people Israel, a love which is only meaningful in this passage and context by virtue of its selectivity and particularity, with God saving Israel only through the judgment and death brought to Egypt.

Second, consider the significance of this well-known and instructive passage: "Husbands, love your wives, just as also Christ loved the church and gave Himself for her, to make her holy, cleansing her in the washing of water by the word. He did this to present the church to Himself in splendor, without spot or wrinkle or any such thing, but holy and blameless" (Eph. 5:25–27 HCSB). Often what is pointed out from this passage, and rightly so, is the sacrificial nature of Christ's love for the church, an amazing and costly love that is the model for all husbands to endeavor to emulate. But another principle arises when one considers this text: because Christ's love here is likened to a husband's love for his wife, Christ's love, then, is a particular, selective, and discriminate love. That is, Paul tells us that husbands are to love *their wives* as Christ loved *the church*. Without question, a husband's love for his own wife is a selective and particular love; it is a love that seeks the nurture, well-being, protection, provision, joy, and blessing of this *one woman* over all others. And so it must be!

---

39. As early as Exodus 4:21–23, God told Moses that he planned to perform signs in order to demonstrate his power but that he would harden Pharaoh's heart "so that he won't let the people go" (4:21). But, because Pharaoh will refuse to let Israel, God's firstborn, go, Moses is to tell him that God says, "Now I will kill your firstborn son!" (4:23). Clearly God intended from the outset to show his favor on Israel through the means of bringing judgment on Egypt while saving his people.

Just imagine the response a husband would receive from his wife were he to say to her, "Honey, I love you, but I want you to know that the love I have for you is the same love in every respect that I have for all the women I meet, indeed, for all the women of the world!" If the wife responded by saying, "Well then, you don't really love *me!*" she would be right. If a husband's love for his wife is not particular, selective, and discriminate, then it is not really husbandly love. And the parallel truth is made clear and explicit in this passage: Christ loved *the church* and gave himself *for her.*

This love, by definition and necessity, then, is a love for his own bride that is different in kind and content from the general love God (or Christ) has for the world. This love, as we see from verses 26–27, leads Christ to save and purify the church. This love impels Christ to make the church "holy and blameless," fulfilling what the Father had in election chosen for the church to become in his Son (note: Eph. 1:4 and 5:27 use the same phrase, "holy and blameless"). In short, this richest of all the demonstrations of God's love among human beings is, by necessity, a selective, particular, and discriminate love for just some.

Two main problems surface, then, in this Arminian objection. First, it misunderstands the Bible's teaching on the love of God. It "flattens" God's love and so reduces it to only one of the biblical senses of God's love. Theological reductionism is dangerous simply because it errs by telling only partial truths. Arminianism, then, tells a partial truth about the love of God, but because it presents it as the whole, it distorts what Scripture actually says. Second, due to the reductionism just mentioned, the richest and most incredible sense of the love of God for human beings is lost, viz., God's committed, sacrificial, faithful, loyal love for his own people. Just as "husbandly" love is destroyed altogether if a man were only capable of loving all women (including his wife!) equally and exactly in the same way, so here God's love for his own people is lost when the distinctiveness of this greatest of God's loves is denied. As Paul reminds us in Ephesians 1, we should bless and praise God the Father because *"in love* He predestined us to be adopted through Jesus Christ for Himself" (Eph. 1:4b–5 HCSB; italics added). His electing love (Eph. 1:4–5), his saving love (Eph. 5:25–27) is, by necessity, a gracious, selective, and particular love for which God is worthy of the highest praise and honor.

Objection 3

Unconditional election stands directly opposed to God's own desire that all be saved. Out of his universal love for all, God has a universal desire for the salvation of all sinners. Ezekiel 18:23; 1 Timothy 2:4; and 2 Peter 3:9 all teach, in their own ways, that God does not desire the wicked to perish but rather that he wills that all be saved. Since this is taught in Scripture, it simply cannot be the case that God unconditionally wills that he certainly will save only some such that he also wills that others certainly perish. Election, then, must be conditional upon the freewill choices of human beings who reject God's loving desire that all be saved.

Reply. My reply must be far briefer than this objection deserves, but thankfully other fine and more extensive treatments are available.[40] The heart of the answer here is much like what we saw in the previous discussion. On the question of the will of God regarding salvation, the Bible presents God's saving will in two ways, not one. Yes, Arminians are correct to point to passages teaching the will of God that all be saved. And many Calvinists, including myself, will grant that these texts teach the universal saving will of God, much as I also am fully convinced that the Bible teaches the universal love of God for all people. But the Bible's teaching does not stop here. Rather, Scripture teaches also the specific and inviolable will of God that some surely and certainly be saved along with its teaching that God wills the salvation of all.[41] The *particular will of God* surely and certainly to save some (i.e., the elect), stands alongside the *universal will of God*

---

40. See, e.g., John Calvin, *Concerning the Eternal Predestination of God,* trans. and ed. J. K. S. Reid (London: J. Clarke, 1961); Jonathan Edwards, "Concerning the Decrees in General, and Election in Particular," in *The Works of Jonathan Edwards,* 2 vols. (Edinburgh: Banner of Truth, 1974), 2:526–34; Jewett, *Election and Predestination,* 97–101; and especially, John Piper, "Are There Two Wills in God?" in *Still Sovereign: Contemporary Perspectives on Election, Foreknowledge, and Grace,* eds. Thomas R. Schreiner and Bruce A. Ware (Grand Rapids: Baker, 2000), 107–31. Piper's chapter in particular is enormously helpful in thinking through both biblical texts and issues that relate to this question.

41. Jewett notes that many Arminian and Lutheran theologians have also appealed to a version of the "two wills" doctrine since they all agree that God created a world in which *he knew* only some would be saved and others would perish. In this sense, God *willed* to create a world in which some people perish, but he also was *willing* that none perish, i.e., two wills are evident. Jewett states that following Dort (1618–1619), some "sought to resolve the problem of the divine will by assuming that the universal offer of the gospel reflects an antecedent act of the divine will that all *may* be saved, whereas the assurance that some shall infallibly *be* saved reflects a consequent act of the divine will based on foreseen faith in those who accept the gospel offer" (Jewett, *Election and Predestination,* 98).

that all be saved. How can it be both ways? Consider just one pair of passages that illustrates these "two wills" of God, and then I'll offer a few summary comments.

First Timothy 2:3–4 (HCSB) states, "This is good, and it pleases God our Savior, who *wants everyone to be saved* and to come to the *knowledge of the truth*" (italics added), and 2 Timothy 2:24–26 (HCSB) says, "The Lord's slave must not quarrel, but must be gentle to everyone, able to teach, and patient, instructing his opponents with gentleness. Perhaps *God will grant them repentance to know the truth*. Then they may come to their senses and escape the Devil's trap, having been captured by him to do his will" (italics added). One feature common to both of these passages is that for people to be saved, they need to come to the knowledge of, or to know, "the truth." Yet, while they share this in common, they differ insofar as in 1 Timothy 2:4 (HCSB) God "wants everyone to be saved and come to the knowledge of the truth," but in 2 Timothy 2:25 (HCSB), God must "grant them repentance" for them "to know the truth" and be saved.

In other words, God wills that all be saved, but unless God wills to grant repentance they cannot be saved. Or yet again, God wills both that all be saved, and God wills that only those to whom he grants repentance be saved. God's will, then, is both universal and particular, desiring in the first case that all be saved and in the second case that only some be saved.[42]

Perhaps two summary comments are in order. First, whether we can understand fully how it is that God can possess *a universal love for all,* along with a *particular love for his own,* or how God can possess a *universal will that all be saved,* along with a *particular will that elects only some to be saved*—whether we can grasp fully how both can be true—nevertheless, we are bound to the Scriptures! The Arminian view errs on these matters, not fundamentally by falsely teaching what the Bible says but by teaching only part of what the Bible says without accepting other teachings which do not easily fit with what already has been accepted. When half-truths become presented as whole truths, misrepresentation and error are inevitable. We must have a determination to accept all that Scripture teaches, and clearly it teaches both sets of truths on these issues.

Second, I do think we can understand something of how God can genuinely desire the salvation of all yet ordain and determine

---

42. For helpful discussion of several more biblical examples of the two wills of God, see Piper, "Are There Two Wills in God?" 111–19.

the salvation of only some.[43] We can understand something of this because we experience much the same reality at times in our human experience. I recall watching a PBS special many years ago that told the story of an agonizing decision Winston Churchill had to make during WW II. Hitler's messages to his frontline troops and U-boats were sent to them encoded, and the German units possessed decoding machines (called "enigmas") to read and know what he was instructing them. Allied scientists developed their own version of such a decoding machine, and they would intercept Hitler's messages, decode them, and call Churchill, telling him what Hitler had instructed. On one occasion Churchill learned through his scientists' hard decoding work that Hitler had planned, in three days, to send a squadron of bombers over the English channel to bomb the small city of Coventry (a munitions factory lay just outside of the city). Obviously, Churchill wanted to call the mayor of Coventry, have the city evacuated, and save his people. But as recounted in this PBS special, Churchill never made this call. Instead, just as he had been told, German bombers flew over Coventry and bombed it mercilessly, unanticipated by all in the city, resulting in many English lives lost and much property destroyed.

Why didn't Churchill warn the city? The answer is this: if he had called the mayor of Coventry and had the city evacuated, the Germans would have known that Churchill had been able to decode Hitler's instructions. But then this intelligence-gathering advantage would be lost. Churchill believed that the entire war effort was at stake here, that is, that he could save Coventry, but he could not save these people and also win the war. He chose, then, not to save those whom he could have saved—those whom, in one sense, he willed very much to save—because he valued even more highly the fulfillment of the mission that the allied forces win the war.

Clearly all illustrations break down at some point, but where this one helps especially is here: One can possess both the *will and the ability to save certain people,* and this will can be genuine and the ability real. Yet one can also possess, at the same time, a *will not to save those same persons whom one could have saved.* Why would one not save those whom one both could and wants to save? Answer: One would will not to save only if there are *greater values and higher purposes* that could only be accomplished in choosing not to save those whom one could save, those whom one would otherwise want

---

43. See also, ibid., 122–31.

to save. Scripture does give us some indication that this is the case with God.

Consider Romans 9:22–24 (HCSB): "And what if God, desiring to display His wrath and to make His power known, endured with much patience objects of wrath ready for destruction? And what if He did this to make known the riches of His glory on objects of mercy that He prepared beforehand for glory—on us whom He also called, not only from the Jews but also from the Gentiles?" Here, as throughout all of Scripture, the glory of God is the supreme value of God. And so we, his creatures, must simply bow and accept what God in his infinite wisdom, holiness, goodness, and power has determined will bring to expression the greatest glory to his name. That both wrath and mercy, both deserved judgment and undeserved grace, both hell and heaven should be planned from all eternity by the perfect mind and heart of God, we must accept since God has told us that this is his ultimate will and that this alone will manifest the fullness of his matchless glory. In the end we must, in our own minds and hearts, let God be God. And we must honor him both for who he is and for the glorious display of his just wrath against deserving sinners as the backdrop for the manifestation of the splendor of his mercy, shown to others who likewise deserved only his condemnation but are now granted his gracious and glorious salvation in Christ.

Objection 4

If unconditional election is true, then it must be the case that those elected to salvation *must* believe in Christ, and those not elected *cannot* believe in Christ. But if so, this raises two big *moral* problems: (1) human beings cannot really be free in their response to the gospel, since they are not able, when responding, to have chosen otherwise, and (2) God cannot rightly and justly hold the unsaved responsible for rejecting the gospel when, in their rejection, they did the only thing they could do, and it was not in their power to do otherwise. In brief, both human freedom and moral responsibility are undermined by the doctrine of unconditional election.

Reply. First, on the question of human freedom, it simply is not the case that we humans have the kind of freedom that Arminians assert we have. Called "libertarian freedom" or "contra-causal freedom" or "freedom of contrary choice," the Arminian claims that we are only free if, when we choose one thing, we were able—all things being what they are at the moment of our choice—to choose otherwise.

That is, we are free in choosing A if, when we choose A, we could instead have chosen B (where B is an action included in the set of logically possible actions other than A). While this notion of freedom has intuitive appeal, it stands up neither to reason nor to Scripture.

Reason. Suppose (along with libertarians) that when we choose A in a given situation, S, we could have chosen B. This means that any reason (or set of reasons) explaining why we chose A would be the *identical* reason (or set of reasons) explaining, instead, why we would choose B. For after all, since our reason(s) for making the choice are included in S, it follows that there is *no choice specific reason*[44] (or set of reasons) for why we chose A over B. (Note: If our reason(s) were not included in S, then this would mean we were not in identical circumstances in making the choice—yet this is something upon which the libertarian notion of freedom depends.) But if our choice of either A or B stems, then, from the identical reason (or set of reasons), our choosing of A instead of B, or B instead of A, reduces to arbitrariness. This is why many Calvinists have labeled the Arminian notion of freedom a "freedom of indifference." The point is not that when we choose we have no reason. Rather, it is that when we choose, any reason (or set of reasons) we have must be the identical reason (or set of reasons) for why we might instead have made the opposite choice—this makes us indifferent in respect to choosing A *or* B, and thus there is no accounting for why we chose A *and not* B.

The Calvinist notion of freedom, on the other hand, explains fully why we choose A and not B. Our freedom is not a freedom of indifference, but a "freedom of inclination"[45]—that is, we choose and act out of our natures so that we do what we *most want* (i.e., what we are *most inclined*) to do. We are free in our choices if, when we make a choice, we are not constrained or coerced but rather we do exactly what we *most want* to do.[46]

Take an example: suppose a dieter chooses to pass up a piece of chocolate cake. He might say to a friend, "I really want to eat that piece of cake," but if he passes it up, then it is the case that he wanted something more than he wanted to eat the cake, viz., he *wanted most*

---

44. Some might substitute "rationally contrastive reason" for what I refer to here as "choice-specific reason."

45. This is one way Edwards describes the sense of freedom he commends, in Jonathan Edwards, *The Freedom of the Will,* ed. Paul Ramsey (New Haven: Yale University Press, 1957).

46. I develop in greater depth both my criticism of libertarian freedom (i.e., "freedom of indifference") and my defense of compatibilist freedom (i.e., "freedom of inclination") in Ware, *God's Greater Glory,* 78–95.

to stick to his diet. But it stands to reason that if we do what we most want at any given moment, then it cannot be the case that when we choose what we do, we could have chosen otherwise. That is, given the exact conditions that pertain when we make a choice, our wills give expression to the *one thing that we most want in that situation,* so in that situation we do what we have to do, i.e., what we most want to do. In this sense, then, we are not able to do otherwise. Change—perhaps even slightly—the situation, the conditions, the circumstances, and yes, we could (and probably would) do otherwise. But under the particular conditions in which we make a given choice, we do the one thing we most want, and in this sense, we cannot do other than the one thing we want *most* to do.

Scripture. Scripture abounds with examples of how our free acts accord with God's prior will and purpose so that although we do what we most want, and so we act freely, nonetheless we are fulfilling God's plan and so we could not do otherwise. Space permits only one example:[47] Through the prophet Isaiah, God announces, "Woe to Assyria, the rod of My anger—the staff in their hands is My wrath. I will send him against a godless nation; I will command him to go against a people destined for My rage, to take spoils, to plunder, and to trample them down like clay in the streets" (Isa. 10:5–6 HCSB). Amazingly, God states that the nation of Assyria, with its military prowess and might, is actually a tool in his hand, commanded by him to carry out his will. Assyria has no clue that this is the case (see Isa. 10:7, 12–14), but the fact remains that Assyria is the rod of God's anger against his people Israel.

Yet notice how this passage began: *Woe* to Assyria! One might think that if God has raised up Assyria to do his will, if God commands Assyria to bring this devastation upon the people of Israel whom God is hereby judging, that Assyria would not be held morally responsible. But this is not so. Rather, they do God's will, and they are judged for doing the very thing they do. Verse 12 (HCSB) makes this clear: "But when the Lord finishes all His work [i.e., of judgment through Assyria] against Mount Zion and Jerusalem, He will say, 'I will punish the king of Assyria for his arrogant acts and the proud look in his eyes.'" Yes, Assyria does God's express will, and Assyria is held accountable for all the evil they do from the willful arrogance of their hearts.

---

47. See D. A. Carson, *Divine Sovereignty and Human Responsibility* (Atlanta: John Knox, 1981), for extended discussion of biblical passages showing the compatibility of God's prior will being carried out through our free and responsible actions.

And consider one more point: the freedom of Assyria, then, cannot be a freedom of contrary choice; no, they must do the will of God, for God has raised them up for this purpose and commanded them to carry out his will. Rather, their freedom is found in this: *they do exactly what they most want to do.* Notice indications of this in these statements: "But this is not what he [Assyria] *intends*; this is not what he *plans*" (10:7 HCSB); "*My hand seized* the idolatrous kingdoms" (10:10 HCSB), "*I have done this* by my own strength" (10:12 HCSB); "*My hand has reached out,* as if into a nest" (10:14 HCSB; italics added). Although God has willed that Assyria be the tool by which he would bring his judgment on Israel,[48] yet Assyria carries out its evil plans and purposes entirely as it most supremely wants to do. God's sovereign plan is carried out, then, through the free and responsible actions of this wicked people.

Second, if one has followed the previous discussion carefully, one can already detect how the issue of the justice of God in holding people morally accountable for the evil they do may be answered. In particular, how can God rightly and justly hold the unsaved responsible for rejecting the gospel when, in their rejection, they did the only thing they could do and it was not in their power to do otherwise? The answer, in brief, is this: so long as those who reject the gospel act out of their own natures and inclinations, choosing and doing what they most want, then they are fully responsible for their actions. A supposed power of contrary choice is not necessary for God to hold people accountable. Since both reason and Scripture demonstrate that the so-called power of contrary choice is an illusion and does not really exist, obviously God is not bound to make sure people have it before holding them morally responsible for their actions.

Rather, unsaved people have natures that do not seek God (Rom. 3:11), natures dead in trespasses and sins (Eph. 2:1), natures blinded to the truth of the gospel (2 Cor. 4:4), such that they are hostile to God and unable to please him (Rom. 8:6–8). When unsaved people hear and reject the gospel, they do what their natures *most want* to do, and hence they are fully responsible. It is not necessary for them to have had the moral ability to accept the gospel (when they reject it) for God to hold them accountable since this notion (of the so-called

---

48. This is so much the case that God chides Assyria, who thinks that they were doing *only* as they pleased, with these words, "Does an ax exalt itself above the one who chops with it? Does a saw magnify itself above the one who saws with it?" (Isa. 10:15 HCSB). So God insists on taking credit for being the ultimate cause of the actions Assyria carried out, even though Assyria did exactly what she wanted most to do.

power of contrary choice) is both contrary to reason and Scripture. Rather, unbelievers do the one thing they most want to do, and so they choose freely and with moral culpability when they hear the gospel of Christ and say, "no."

But allow me to take this one step further. The situation I've just described is the case for all sinful human beings, for all of us share in the sin of Adam and its consequences (Rom. 5:12–19). Were it not for God's effectual call on the lives of his elect, were it not for his giving of irresistible grace to those whom he had chosen to save out of all of humanity deserving destruction, none of us would ever have believed in Christ and been saved. Therefore, those who reject Christ deserve the condemnation they receive, for they did what they most wanted in that choice to say "no" to God's gracious offer of salvation. And those who receive Christ cannot boast at all in their receiving the eternal life that comes by faith (1 Cor. 1:26–31; Eph. 2:8–9), for apart from God's effectual and gracious work in their lives, to open their hearts (Acts 16:14) and their eyes (2 Cor. 4:6), they, too, would never have come. God is sovereign, and yes, we are free and responsible. Both of these truths are taught in Scripture, they are compatible, and those of us who cherish the Scriptures and bow to their authority must accept both as true.

Objection 5

If unconditional election is true, then it must be the case that those elected to salvation *must* be saved, and those not elected *cannot* be saved. But if so, this raises a significant *practical* problem: both prayer for the unsaved and evangelism to reach the unsaved are undermined, since due to God's election, the elect cannot fail to be saved and the nonelect cannot, under any circumstances, be saved. So why pray? Why share the gospel?

Reply. The answer to these related practical questions is the same for each: God not only has ordained the "ends" (i.e., the goals or outcomes or purposes) that he has designed for all of creation, but he also has ordained the "means" that are necessary to occur for the ends to be fulfilled.[49] As this relates to unconditional election, yes it is absolutely true that the elect most surely and certainly will be saved, and that the nonelect are just as certainly left in their sinful condition to experience the consequences of their sin. But again here, we

49. See also J. I. Packer, *Evangelism and the Sovereignty of God* (Downers Grove: InterVarsity, 1961); and John Piper, *Let the Nations Be Glad!* (Grand Rapids: Baker, 1993).

see that Scripture has more to say than this one thing. Scripture is also unambiguous and insistent that people must put faith in Christ to be saved (Rom. 3:22–23; Gal. 2:16). One of the most stirring calls upon Christians to commit themselves to getting the gospel out to people who have not heard comes in Romans 10. Get the significance of this point! Throughout this discussion the reader will no doubt have noticed several references to Romans 9 and Romans 11 in support of unconditional election. Right in the middle of this discussion, in relation to unsaved Jews for whom Paul has a deep and abiding burden, he makes some telling statements in Romans 10:12–15. Here, in the chapter following Paul's declaration on God's behalf, "I will show mercy to whom I show mercy, and I will have compassion on whom I have compassion" (Rom. 9:15 HCSB), Paul now declares, "Everyone who calls on the name of the Lord will be saved" (Rom. 10:13 HCSB).

And of course, both statements are true. Yes, God has elected those upon whom he surely will show mercy, and they will be saved. But how will they be saved? Answer: Only as they hear the gospel proclaimed to all, throughout the world, and only as the Spirit works in them to see the glory of Christ in the gospel and come to saving faith. The means of gospel proclamation are absolutely necessary for the elect to be saved.

Consider two other passages. First, Paul writes, "Keep in mind Jesus Christ, risen from the dead, descended from David, according to my gospel. For this I suffer, to the point of being bound like a criminal; but God's message is not bound. This is why *I endure all things for the elect: so that they also may obtain salvation,* which is in Christ Jesus, with eternal glory" (2 Tim. 2:8–10 HCSB; italics added). The apostle Paul, who celebrates and teaches that God has elected people to be saved, understands this election not as a barrier to evangelism but as an incentive! For Paul, how very wrong it is to think that election undermines gospel witness. Just the opposite is the case. Because God has elected people to be saved and because they will only be saved as they hear the gospel and believe in Christ, therefore Paul says that he endures all the suffering and persecution that he has "for the elect: so that they also may obtain salvation, which is in Christ Jesus, with eternal glory" (2 Tim. 2:10 HCSB). Gospel witness to the unsaved is empowered, not hindered, by the realization that God has chosen people out there who, upon hearing the gospel of his Son, will come. But hear they must, and come they will.

Second, Jesus said, "I am the good shepherd. I know My own sheep, and they know Me, as the Father knows Me, and I know the Father. I lay down My life for the sheep. But *I have other sheep* that are not of this fold; I must bring them also, and *they will listen to My voice.* Then there will be one flock, one shepherd" (John 10:14–16 HCSB; italics added). Jesus has already made clear that the true mark of his own sheep is that they hear his voice and they follow him (John 10:4–5). Now he indicates that there are other sheep of his but sheep who have not as yet heard his voice and so they are not now following him. They *are* his sheep, though, for he says, "I *have* other sheep that are not of this fold," not, "I will seek to acquire other sheep." So they are his sheep, but they have not yet come to him, and so they are not now of his fold. How then will they come? How will these sheep belonging to Jesus become part of his fold? Answer: they must hear his voice! And when they hear the voice of the Good Shepherd, because they are his sheep, "they *will* listen" to his voice, and they *will* become part of "one flock" with "one shepherd."

Gospel proclamation, then, may be thought of as speaking forth the voice of the Good Shepherd through the voice of the evangelist or missionary. As we bear witness to Christ and his saving death, through our voices the Spirit brings the voice of Jesus to the hearts of the elect. Those sheep that belong already to Jesus but are not yet part of his fold will hear, and they will come. Such is the confidence and joy of gospel proclamation that accords with the glorious doctrine of unconditional election. And such is the conviction that propelled the fathers of the modern missions movement—William Carey, Hudson Taylor, and Adoniram Judson, for example—to take the gospel to foreign lands. The elect will come, they were convinced. But they will come and be saved *only* as they hear and believe the gospel. So missionaries must go!

Both of these passages have focused on evangelism, but the same principles apply to prayer in regard to the unsaved. We must pray for the Lord of the harvest to send forth workers into his harvest (Matt. 9:38), pray that doors are opened for the proclamation of the gospel (Col. 4:3), pray that we and others remain alert in the midst of spiritual warfare (Eph. 6:10–18), pray for those witnessing to have boldness to speak as they should (Eph. 6:19–20), and pray that the word of the Lord would spread rapidly and be glorified (2 Thess. 3:1). In all these ways and more, we are to pray in order for the purposes of God in saving the elect to occur. Both prayer and evangelism, then, are *necessary* in the outworking of God's purposes so that while the ends that God has designed surely will be accomplished, they will only come to pass as those means, ordained by God as necessary to the completion of his work, are carried out. Both prayer and evangelism, then, are empowered activities for the Christian through the realization that God has ordained these as the necessary means to accomplish the glorious and gracious saving work he has designed.

Individual Election

Definition and Explanation of Individual Election

Individual election to salvation may be defined as God's gracious choice, made in eternity past, of the specific individual persons whom he would save by faith through the atoning death of his Son. That is, Scripture teaches not only that God the Father chooses to save "a people" or "the church" or "a bride" for his Son but also that those particular persons who comprise the saved people of God, or the church, or the bride of Christ, are themselves unconditionally elected by God to be saved.

Support for Individual Election

Key passages teaching individual election. First, many of the passages examined earlier in support of seeing election as unconditional also indicate that this unconditional election by God is of individuals whom God, in time, then saves. Consider some passages supporting the individual election to salvation.

John 6:37, 39; 17:2, 24. John 6:37 is helpful on the question of whether election to salvation is corporate only or specific individuals are in view. Here, Jesus tells those who have refused to believe in him, "Everyone the Father gives Me will come to Me, and the one who comes to Me I will never cast out." And in verse 39 (HCSB), he says, "This is the will of Him who sent Me: that I should lose none of those He has given Me but should raise them up on the last day." Two things are clear. First, Jesus declares that *specific persons* are given to him by the Father. The point of Jesus saying what he does in verse 37 was so that the Jews who rejected Jesus would conclude that they have not been given to him. If they had been, they would have come. But their disbelief and hardness of heart are evidence that they have not been given to Jesus by the Father. In contrast, Jesus tells them,

"Everyone the Father gives Me will come to Me." Therefore, some specific ones are given to Jesus by the Father, and other specific ones are not.

Second, that all of those given to Jesus by the Father are saved further confirms that *specific persons* are given to Christ by the Father. This is clear from both verses ("The one who comes to Me *I will never cast out,*" and, "I should *lose none* of those He has given Me but should *raise them up on the last day*"). Accordingly, those given to Jesus from the Father cannot be understood as the Father giving the Son the whole world (so that the Father has no control over who actually chooses to come and be saved) or as the Father giving Jesus some unspecified but empty "group" of the saved. Rather, here *each and every one* of those given to the Son is saved; he will lose *none* of them but will raise each one up on the last day. Since only some are saved in the end and since all that the Father gives the Son are saved, it follows that the Father gives the Son specific individual persons whom the Son then surely and certainly saves.

Jesus' prayer to the Father in John 17 indicates his desire and longing to give eternal life "to all You have given Him" (John 17:2 HCSB) and to bring to glory "those You have given Me" (John 17:24 HCSB). For this to be a meaningful request requires that Jesus understand the Father to have given him certain specific individuals whom he would save. The alternative, it seems, is senseless. Could the Father have given Jesus an empty set of "ones saved by Jesus," which set was then filled by whoever chose to become a part of this set through their own personal faith in Christ but of whose constituents the Father exerted no control? If this is the case, then the Father gave the Son no one at all, and there is no point in speaking of the Father giving these to the Son. Instead, the Father would only have given the Son the mandate to save, but whoever actually is saved depends on whoever comes. Of course, this is a logical possibility, but it is not a possibility that accords with the statements in John 17:2 and 24 (and many similar texts). Rather, the only meaningful way of understanding Jesus' statements in these verses is in affirming that the Father gave specific persons to the Son, for whom he prays, and to whom he longs to grant eternal life.

John 10:16. When Jesus states, "*I have other sheep* that are not of this fold; I must bring them also, and they *will listen* to My voice" (John 10:16 HCSB; italics added), surely this means that there are other specific individuals who are already his, specific ones who surely will be saved ("They will listen to My voice"), but as yet they have not been saved. If, instead, it was possible for any and all of the sheep of the world to hear his voice and follow him, then this statement would make no sense. In that case he doesn't presently have any other sheep, but he would hope to be able to gain some more in time. Rather, here he indicates that specific sheep, among all the sheep of the world, are already his. When these specific sheep hear his voice, what marks them as his sheep is that they *will* hear his voice and come. Specific and individual election is required to make meaningful sense of what Jesus says.

Acts 13:48. "When the Gentiles heard this, they rejoiced and glorified the message of the Lord, and all who had been appointed to eternal life believed" (HCSB). The individual nature of election is clear from the fact that many Jews had just heard the gospel and had rejected it (Acts 13:44–46). But, in turning to the Gentiles, Paul encountered a different response with many Gentiles believing. But when Luke records this phenomenon, he does not say, "Unlike the Jews who rejected the gospel, many Gentiles believed unto eternal life." This surely would not have been wrong or inaccurate, but it would have left out one of the main points Luke built in. What Luke wants to get across is just why these specific Gentiles believed when the response previously had been so distressing. Luke underscores the point that "all who had been appointed to eternal life believed." In light of the fact that the gospel was spread widely among many, yet only some came, it is significant here that "all" (or some translations have "as many as," still indicating a set number of persons) of some category are saved. Who are these? All whom God appointed are saved. It simply won't work to import the notion of corporate election of an empty set of "the saved." This cannot account for the fact that all those appointed are saved. Individual election to salvation is the only reasonable reading of what Luke records here since "all" (or "as many as") must refer to the specific persons appointed by God to believe in Christ in contrast to others who are not saved.

Ephesians 1:4–5; Romans 8:29–30. These important and familiar texts also support the individual election of specific persons to salvation. In both cases, persons, not categories or classes, are said to be "elected" or "predestined." Notice that Paul says, "God chose *us* " in Christ (Eph. 1:4 HCSB), "He predestined *us* " to be adopted (Eph. 1:5 HCSB), and *"those* He foreknew He also predestined . . . and *those* He predestined, He also called; and *those* He called, He also justified; and *those* He justified, He also glorified" (Rom. 8:29–30 HCSB). Granted, Paul has in mind many persons. But many persons making up a category (i.e., those chosen) is different from an empty category to be filled however others see fit. These verses indicate that the election of persons accounts for the presence of the category, and not the reverse. Why is there a church? Why is there a people of God? Why is there a saved community? The answer is that God chose *us,* he predestined *us,* i.e., he called *those* individuals who would make up the company of the redeemed. Individual election is called for by these glorious texts, and what joy to think of God's eternal plan of salvation that had in mind each and every specific person whom he chose to save through the liberating work of his Son.[50]

Effectual calling requires individual election. It simply is impossible to deny individual election to salvation if the means by which each and every saved person comes to faith in Christ is the Spirit's effectual call, a call that necessarily moves each one to saving faith. Now, it is true that if the only kind of divine calling taught in Scripture were the general call, a corporate rather than individual notion of election would work well. The general call, then, is compatible with a corporate notion of election.

But if all who are saved are actually called by God also through the effectual call (as argued above), then the discriminating and selective nature of this call—of who is called in this way and who is not—indicates that God's choice of who to save is made on the individual level. The effectual call, then, by nature of its being selective, requires that the choice of those to whom this call is extended is individual, not corporate.

Unconditional election requires individual election. As we have seen, the doctrine of unconditional election asserts that God chooses whom he will save, not based on any fact or feature of people's lives but according to his good pleasure and will. Upon hearing this, some might think, then, that such an election could not be individual, since God does not consider features of individuals' lives in deciding whether to choose them to be saved. This misses the point, however, that he still chooses the individuals who will be saved although nothing about their choices, actions, or character figures into the "why" of

---

50. Due to space considerations and because other excellent discussions are available, I've not included a discussion here on Romans 9 and individual election. See John Piper, *The Justification of God;* and Thomas R. Schreiner, "Does Romans 9 Teach Individual Election unto Salvation?" in *Still Sovereign,* 89–106, for defenses of Romans 9 as teaching individual (e.g., Jacob) as well as corporate (e.g., Israel) election and salvation.

his choice. God still chooses each person who is saved but not because of the person himself or herself.

Perhaps the example in Romans 9 of Jacob and Esau will help bring this point home. You'll recall that Paul says of them, "For though they had not been born yet or done anything good or bad, so that God's purpose according to election might stand, not from works but from the One who calls, she was told, the older will serve the younger" (Rom. 9:11–12 HCSB). Clearly the unconditional nature of election is emphasized in verse 11. Yet, while nothing particular about them was the basis of God's election, their identities as "Jacob" and "Esau" were established clearly so that God specifically chose one, not the other. Unconditional election, then, does not undermine individual election, but it does ensure that none who are elected may rightly take credit, in any respect, for their being elected by God. So, while unconditional election assures us that the *basis* of God's election is devoid of any quality or choice or action in our own lives, it also instructs and amazes us that the *subjects* of God's election are indeed specific, individual persons. Unconditional election, rightly understood, requires that our election to salvation is individual.

God's exhaustive definite foreknowledge requires individual election. There is a sense in which any Arminian who attempts to understand election as merely corporate (i.e., God chooses the "empty set" of the "saved," which set is filled only by the free choices of people in time) can only do so by ignoring or denying the exhaustive definite foreknowledge of God. That is, since God knows everything about the future of the world he will create "before" he ever takes the first step in creating it, it stands to reason that he must know, as part of this exhaustive knowledge of all that will transpire, exactly and particularly who will come to Christ and be saved and who will reject Christ and be condemned. That is, God's exhaustive foreknowledge, as understood by all Christian denominations throughout all of history, requires that God know precisely the constituents that make up "the saved" at the same "instant" that he chooses, in fact, to save. Individual election, then, is logically required when one holds to exhaustive definite foreknowledge.

One further comment is in order in light of the openness rejection of exhaustive definite foreknowledge. Obviously because open theism denies that God can know the future free choices of his moral creatures, God cannot know from eternity past any of the individuals who will be saved. More precisely, he cannot know whether any individuals will be saved or who they are, if in fact they are saved. Furthermore, God cannot know which individuals will actually live, what any of them will do, how long they might or might not live, or anything else about human life on the planet he seeks to populate with his free moral human beings. It is clear, as one contemplates seriously the openness proposal, that the ignorance of God regarding the future of human history is vast indeed.[51]

One implication of the openness denial of exhaustive definite foreknowledge for the doctrine of election, then, is that it places God in the position of considering the idea of saving fallen human beings as a mere contingency plan, at best. Since he cannot know that the fall will occur (though he may, contrary to John Sanders,[52] consider that the fall is likely), he certainly cannot know that he will need to save anyone. And, since he cannot know who will need to be saved (indeed, he cannot know that there will be any actual persons living who need to be saved), he cannot plan on anyone's salvation, in particular. The result of all of this is to make the eternal plan of God to save sinners both speculative and impersonal, and this stands in direct conflict with the Bible's own portrayal of God's plan of salvation, from eternity past, as both definitive and personal—even individual. How ironic that a model of God that attempts to show God as more, not less, personal, requires a view of his saving purposes (one of the most important things God does!) as abstract and altogether impersonal.

Infralapsarian Election

Definition and Explanation of Infralapsarian Election

Infralapsarian election to salvation may be defined as God's gracious choice, made in eternity past, of those whom he would save by faith through the atoning death of his Son, a choice which considered all of humanity as fallen, sinful, and guilty in Adam, fully deserving of eternal condemnation while fully undeserving of the bestowal of any

---

51. For consideration of further implications of the openness denial of exhaustive definite foreknowledge, see Bruce A. Ware, "Defining Evangelicalism's Boundaries Theologically: Is Open Theism Evangelical?" *Journal of the Evangelical Theological Society* 45/2 (June 2002): 193–212, and reprinted in Ware, *God's Greater Glory*, 215–41; and for a broader descriptive and critical discussion of open theism, see Ware, *God's Lesser Glory*.

52. See John Sanders, *The God Who Risks: A Theology of Providence* (Downers Grove: InterVarsity, 1998), 46–69, where Sanders argues that when sin occurs in the garden of Eden, "the implausible happens."

favor or kindness, according to which God elected out of the whole of this fallen and guilty humanity some particular sinners to be granted eternal life in Christ, by grace, and through faith.

Historians of the Reformed tradition have uniformly noted that the infralapsarian view has been the dominant position held by the inheritors of Calvin's predestinarianism. Clearly all the major Reformed confessions and creeds reflect either a straightforward infralapsarian view, or they speak in ways that leave the issue indefinite so that advocates of both infra- and supralapsarianism may subscribe. But no major Reformed creed has espoused a strict supralapsarian view that intentionally and explicitly excluded infralapsarians. Berkhof comments that

> the Reformed Churches in their official standards have always adopted the infralapsarian position, even though they have never condemned, but always tolerated, the other view. Among the members of the Synod of Dort and of the Westminster Assembly there were several Supralapsarians who were held in high honour. . . . but in both the Canons of Dort and the Westminster Confession the infralapsarian view finds expression.[53]

In more recent times the preference for the infralapsarian view continues among most in Reformed theology, yet there is also a greater sense expressed by some today that this debate may be misdirected. John Feinberg, for example, considers the disagreement between infra- and supralapsarians over the order of the divine decrees "fundamentally wrongheaded." He continues:

> It is so because it treats God's decree as sequential—granted, it contains a logical rather than a temporal sequence, but it is sequential nonetheless. However, individual actions are not disjoined from one another so that God can pick and choose specific items as he constructs the decree for our world. Instead, as God deliberated, he was confronted with an infinite set of possible worlds. He first (logically) decided whether to create at all, and then, having chosen to do so, he chose which of the many worlds he would actualize. But in choosing any given possible world he

---

53. Louis Berkhof, *Systematic Theology* (London: Banner of Truth, 1939, 1958), 123. See also B. B. Warfield, "Predestination in the Reformed Confessions," in *Studies in Theology* (New York: Oxford, 1932), 228, who writes regarding the Reformed confessions of faith: "Some are explicitly Infralapsarian, and none exclude much less polemically oppose, Infralapsarianism. None of them are [sic] explicitly Supralapsarian: many, however, leave the question between Supra- and Infralapsarianism entirely to one side, and thus open the door equally to both; and none are [sic] polemically directed against Supralapsarianism."

would already see Adam and everyone else as sinners or not, and either as saved or not. In worlds with sin which is paid for by Christ's atonement, God would see at once all the sinners, saved and unsaved, along with Christ's sacrifice. There simply is no logical sequence of choices to construct when what God chooses is a whole world, not individual events, actions, etc. Hence, it is wrong to ask whether God decreed first (logically) to create human beings, to save the elect, or whatever.[54]

Peterson and Williams also register their complaint that with Beza[55] (not Calvin), Reformed theology took a turn back toward a fundamentally scholastic orientation with its insistence on fully developing all logical extensions of doctrines and providing complete explanations in areas that involved some degree of speculation. They write:

> The return to pre-Reformation scholastic theological method enabled a more precise definition and more central place given to the notion of divine decrees and the doctrine of predestination in the thought of such Reformed theologians as Beza, Vermigli and Zanchi than they had enjoyed in Calvin's more exegetically driven theology. . . . Augustine's asymmetric understanding of predestination, in which God causes belief in the elect but does not cause the unbelief of the unregenerate, is replaced by a doctrine of double predestination. The decree of God relates to belief and unbelief in the same manner. Even though Beza sought to soften the harshness of the doctrine of double predestination by emphasizing the role of secondary causes, human responsibility for sin, and the notion of divine permission in relation to human sin and unbelief, it is difficult to imagine how God escapes culpability for human sin in his thought.[56]

Still others in the Reformed tradition are working at providing what might be viewed as a synthesis of the infra- and supralapsarian models of the divine decree. Robert Reymond, for example, has endeavored to put something of a "new face" on supralapsarianism.[57] He suggests that while the supralapsarian view has rightly held that God's particu-

---

54. John S. Feinberg, *No One like Him: The Doctrine of God,* in the Foundations of Evangelical Theology series, gen. ed. John S. Feinberg (Wheaton, Ill.: Crossway, 2001), 535–36.

55. See Peterson and Williams, *Why I Am Not an Arminian,* 96, where they identify Beza as a supralapsarian who argued that "the elective work of God precedes the fall into sin within the eternal counsel of God."

56. Ibid., 94–96.

57. Robert L. Reymond, *A New Systematic Theology of the Christian Faith,* 2nd ed. (Nashville: Thomas Nelson, 1998), 479–502.

larist and redemptive purposes stand ultimately behind the entirety of the creation and all it involves, nonetheless supralapsarianism has suffered by seeing God's ultimate discrimination between elect and reprobate as occurring among men *as men,* not among men *as sinners.* His proposal,[58] then, incorporates what might be called the "infralapsarian insight" that God's election to salvation is of *sinful men,* yet it upholds the "supralapsarian insight" that the discriminating decree of election and reprobation is prior (logically) to the Fall, being best seen, in fact, as first in the order of the decrees.[59]

The intramural debate among Calvinists over infra- versus supralapsarianism, then, has never been fully resolved. Reflection and revision continue, and concern is rightly registered over avoiding theological speculation, especially where the moral integrity and purity of God may in any way be jeopardized. Still the predominant position advocated among most Reformed communities continues to be some version of infralapsarianism.[60] Why in Reformed circles is the preference normally granted for this way of understanding the elective plan and purpose of God?

Support for Infralapsarian Election

Key passages teaching that divine election is to salvation support infralapsarian election. First, many passages of Scripture that speak of God's election indicate that it is an election *to salvation.* It stands to reason, if this is the case, that God must have in view persons needing to be saved who are consequently chosen by him for that gracious

---

58. Reymond (ibid., 489) acknowledges that the revision of supralapsarianism he advocates has been advanced previously, with variations, by theologians such as Jerome Zanchius, Johannes Piscator, Herman Hoeksema, and Gordon Clark.

59. Reymond (ibid.) puts forth the following order of the decrees as his proposed alternative either to the infralapsarian or more common and traditional Supralapsarian orders:

1. the election of some sinful men to salvation in Christ (and reprobation of the rest of sinful mankind in order to make known the riches of God's gracious mercy to the elect),
2. the decree to apply Christ's redemptive benefits to the elect sinners,
3. the decree to redeem the elect sinners by the cross work of Christ,
4. the decree that men should fall, and
5. the decree to create the world and men.

60. This is even evident in Feinberg (*No One like Him,* 536), where after calling debates over the order of the divine decrees "fundamentally wrongheaded" nonetheless suggests a logical order of "God's choices" which places the divine choice to elect some to be saved after the choice to have a world in which creatures sin. Hence, it is clear that Feinberg affirms the basic infralapsarian insight that election and reprobation have as their objects sinners who deserve condemnation. Hence, election surely can be gracious and undeserved, while reprobation is, correspondingly, righteous and just.

saving work. But of course, if God's election is of persons needing to be saved, then it follows that those persons elected are viewed as sinners. Only as sinners would they need salvation, and clearly their election is for this very purpose. Put differently, in eternity past and before the creation of the world, God must have had in mind that the fall into sin had already occurred when he contemplated the totality of humanity out of which he elected some to be saved. Divine election to salvation, then, is infralapsarian. Consider the following passages:

Acts 13:48. "When the Gentiles heard this, they rejoiced and glorified the message of the Lord, and all who had been appointed to eternal life believed" (HCSB). The appointment of these who believe is "to eternal life." Therefore, their previous election considered them needing the gift of eternal life, hence they were considered sinners.

Romans 8:29–30. Here the goal of predestination includes several elements which indicate that those predestined are sinners chosen to be saved. First, they are predestined to be conformed to the image of Christ. One might question if this could relate to unfallen human beings. But the reference to Christ as the "firstborn among many brothers" is unmistakably to Christ as risen from the dead and glorified (cf. Col. 1:18 HCSB). Hence, those predestined need to be raised with Christ, which entails that they deserve, outside of Christ, death and condemnation. Sinners, then, are predestined to be conformed to the likeness of Christ, the risen One. Second, those predestined are later justified, also indicating that their state, as viewed from eternity past, is as sinners needing forgiveness, not as unfallen creatures who have no sin to be forgiven. Finally, glorification is the ultimate goal of predestination (which accords, of course, with being conformed to the image of Christ), and this, too, indicates the culmination and perfection in holiness they will receive as God's saved ones. Those foreknown and predestined by God, then, are sinners.

Ephesians 1:4. If those elected are chosen *to be* holy and blameless, then presumably, they are not viewed as holy and blameless already at the "time" of their choosing. No, rather, they are viewed as sinners who need to be made what they currently are not, as sinners who are made "holy and blameless" only by the saving work of Christ (Eph. 5:25–27 HCSB). This is confirmed by the fact that election only begins the listing of reasons for praising God that Paul offers in verses 4–14, and among the other reasons he gives is that in Christ we have received "redemption through His blood, the forgiveness of our trespasses" (Eph. 1:7 HCSB). Our election to be holy requires also the shed blood of Christ to bring to us forgiveness. Surely, then, it follows that "when" God elected us, he viewed us as sinners needing forgiveness and sinners whom he determined to make holy.

2 Thessalonians 2:13. Paul here gives perhaps the most explicit statement in Scripture that God chose those who needed to be saved.[61] It follows, then, that God chose sinners since only sinners need the salvation for which they are chosen.

2 Timothy 1:9. Although less explicit than the previous reference, this text also indicates that God chose sinners "before time began" (HCSB). How else could it be, since God's saving us and calling us with a holy calling are linked together, as that which God has given to us in Christ before the creation of the world? Since the gift given to us is that, in Christ, we are viewed as those saved and called to be holy, it must be the case that outside of Christ we are viewed as sinful and deserving condemnation. Confirmation also comes in the reference to grace, not works, by which we receive this salvation and holy calling. If grace must be given, then the one to whom it is given is undeserving. Sin, then, stands in the background as what God overcomes despite our inability to merit or achieve our own holiness. "Before time began," then, God determined to save and call to holiness those who only by grace could be granted such favor. God's election of us in eternity past, then, views us as sinners.

1 Peter 1:1–2. Here Peter links their being chosen with their being set apart *"for* obedience" and *"for* the sprinkling with the blood of Jesus Christ" (HCSB). Clearly both of these references indicate that the state of these persons, when viewed by God "prior" (logically) to his choosing them and setting them apart, was of those who were *not* obedient, as those who *needed* to be sprinkled with the blood of Christ. God chose sinners, in other words, and his grace is manifest in that they were chosen *as sinners* to become obedient and pure.

Our election "in Christ" supports infralapsarian election. Recall that Paul specifically indicates that our election, decided by God in eternity past, was an election "in Christ." Again, Ephesians 1:4 reads, "For He chose us *in Him,* before the foundation of the world, to be holy and blameless in His sight" (HCSB). Similar language is found in 2 Timothy 1:9, where God's calling and grace are "given to us *in Christ Jesus* before time began" (HCSB). One must ask in what sense our election is "in Christ." Surely we cannot reduce this to Christ as

---

61. The text variant ("first fruits") mentioned earlier makes no difference to the point that is being made here from this passage of Scripture.

the elect One only, as Barth has done.[62] As indicated previously, the object of the verb, "He chose," is "us," not Christ. And surely this cannot mean merely that God chose the possibility that some undefined number and constituency of persons would one day be "in Christ," as Klein is prone to suggest.[63] This view neither accounts for the "us" as the object of God's choosing (indicating these specific individuals as elect ones), nor does it account for why Paul would celebrate the truth of election as he here does. Klein's conception of corporate election in Christ reduces election itself to a mere formality in which God simply ratifies our choices exactly as we make them. With Klein's position, God certainly is praiseworthy for redemption (Eph. 1:7), but there really is no reason to extol God either for election (Eph. 1:4) or predestination (Eph. 1:5).

Rather, our election "in Christ" must refer to the fact that the Father intended, from the beginning, that there be a people who are saved by his Son and who are united with his Son in newness of life. Surely our being chosen "in Christ" establishes the means, in the plan and purpose of God, by which we will be made "holy and blameless in his sight." This is confirmed by Paul's later reference to the same "holy and blameless" conception, where he declares that Christ has so loved the church and given himself for her that he might present the church to himself, without spot or wrinkle, "but holy and blameless" before him (Eph. 5:27 HCSB). To be chosen "in Christ," then, is to be selected to the unspeakable privilege of sharing in the character and the image of the risen and glorified Christ so that we become like him (holy and blameless) through the purifying work done by him (cf. Rom. 8:29 where we are predestined "to be conformed to the image of His Son"). "In Christ," then, is the destiny of those chosen before the foundation of the world (Eph. 1:4), much as our adoption by God through Christ is the intended goal of our predestination (Eph. 1:5).

All of this argues, then, that as God looked upon us in eternity past as those as-of-yet unchosen, God had to have seen us as those needing to be saved, i.e., as sinners in need of a Savior. And, in his grace and love, he chose us sinners for the most incredible joy imaginable, viz., that we be united with his Son to experience the fullness and joy of his own character reproduced in us. When choosing us, then, he viewed us as sinners. God's election of the "us" in Ephesians

---

62. See Karl Barth, *Church Dogmatics,* ed. Geoffrey W. Bromiley and Thomas F. Torrance, trans. Geoffrey W. Bromiley, et. al. (Edinburgh: T. & T. Clark, 1955), 2/2.51–58.
63. See Klein, *The New Chosen People.*

1:4 is of sinners destined to be united with his Son, to the praise of his glorious grace.

God's asymmetrical relationship between election and reprobation aligns best with infralapsarian election. Besides the biblical evidence just discussed, the other most compelling line of argument for the infralapsarian position is that it establishes, more clearly and unambiguously than its supralapsarian counterpart, that God relates to election differently from the way in which he relates to reprobation. *Reprobation* (to eternal condemnation) is based on the just judgment of God in which unrepentant and unbelieving sinners are rightly and justly given the punishment that they deserve. But in contrast, *election* (to eternal life) is based on the mercy of God by which he sends his Son to pay sin's full penalty and thereby forgives all the elect as they are called effectually and so are saved by grace, through faith in Christ. In brief, *reprobation is conditional,* i.e., based on what sinners have done and deserve, whereas *election is unconditional,* i.e., based on the unmerited grace and favor of God despite what sinners have done and deserve.

Romans 6:23 expresses the heart of this contrast nicely: "For the wages of sin is death, but the gift of God is eternal life in Christ Jesus our Lord" (HCSB). Now, because it is the case that in reprobation, *sinners* receive what they deserve ("wages . . . death"), and in election, *sinners* receive what they do not deserve ("gift of God . . . eternal life"), what is common to those in both categories is that both are understood as sinful. God's just judgment comes to sinners, and God's gracious gift of eternal life also comes to sinners. Therefore, it must be the case that when God elected those to be saved, he had in view the totality of humanity in its sin and chose from among all who deserved condemnation some to be saved in order to bestow on them (and them alone) his gracious gift of eternal life, in his Son. What the infralapsarian view makes clear, then, is *both* that God's reprobation of sinners is fully in accord with his justice and that God's election to salvation of sinners is fully and gloriously gracious. The fundamental asymmetry of Romans 6:23 is upheld in the infralapsarian position.

None of what has been argued above mitigates against the fact that God has ordained both evil and good, both sin and obedience, both reprobation and election (Deut. 32:39; Isa. 45:5–7; Eph. 1:11). But God's relationship and manner of control with regard to each of these opposite moral poles is necessarily different. Because *God is good,* all good can extend directly and immediately from his very nature; but because *God is not in the slightest respect evil,* evil simply cannot extend from him as good does, but rather his control of evil occurs through his meticulous permission and prevention of all the evil that is produced within the created order. So, while God ordains both reprobation and election with the same degree of certainty, his means of rendering each certain, or of controlling just how each is expressed, is asymmetrical both morally and operationally.

In speaking of the certainty of reprobation in the divine plan, Berkhof provides a helpful word of caution:

> We should guard against the idea, however, that as election and reprobation both determine with absolute certainty the end unto which man is predestined and the means by which that end is realized, they also imply that in the case of reprobation as well as in that of election God will bring to pass by His own direct efficiency whatsoever He has decreed. This means that, while it can be said that God is the author of the regeneration, calling, faith, justification, and sanctification, of the elect, and thus by direct action on them brings their election to realization, it cannot be said that He is also the responsible author of the fall, the unrighteous condition, and the sinful acts of the reprobate by direct action on them, and thus effects the realization of their reprobation. God's decree undoubtedly rendered the entrance of sin into the world certain, but He did not predestinate some unto sin, as He did others unto holiness. And as the holy God He cannot be the author of sin.[64]

Berkhof's comment near the end of this statement ("He did not predestinate some unto sin, as He did others unto holiness") helps us see how the infralapsarian view contrasts with its supralapsarian counterpart. In its endeavor to understand the order of the divine decrees in an *a priori* fashion, following what Reymond calls "the teleological principle,"[65] supralapsarians most commonly understand the decree of election and reprobation as discriminating among human beings who are created but not as yet fallen. What compels supralapsarians in this direction is the conviction that since God's ultimate goal is the glory of his name through the means of both condemnation and salvation (e.g., Rom. 9:22–24), from the very first God had in mind and planned the election of some in Christ and the reprobation of all others.

---

64. Berkhof, *Systematic Theology,* 117.
65. Reymond, *New Systematic Theology,* 488.

But while there is a clear logical force to this argument, it entails that both election and reprobation be seen as directed toward those who are unfallen and not sinful. But if so, then God's decree of *reprobation* of those not yet sinful (logically) would seem to entail the predestination of these persons not only to their assigned judgment but also to the sin for which they are judged. It is difficult to see, in this case, how God can escape the charge of being the author of sin. And the decree of *election,* also of those not yet sinful (logically), would seem to entail both (1) the undermining of grace (since they are chosen when they are neither guilty nor deserving of judgment), and (2) their predestination, with the reprobate, to the sin out of which they are to be saved. Therefore, in the end both clear biblical teaching and deep moral concerns have led most in the Reformed community to follow the infralapsarian understanding of election and reprobation as directed toward those comprising fallen, sinful humanity.

John Gerstner discusses Jonathan Edwards's strong and persistent opposition to supralapsarianism as expressed in both his sermons and *Miscellanies.* Gerstner writes that:

Edwards was clearly and explicitly infralapsarian in his view of the decrees. First of all, he refutes the fundamental argument of the supralapsarians. They contended that the last thing in execution was always the first in intention. That is, the actual reprobation and salvation of some proved that this was the original intention behind the creation, fall, salvation and damnation. Edwards critiques this. That principle, he contends is true "with regard to the end and all the proper means, but not with regard to every prerequisite condition"—but only with regard to the "ultimate end." . . . Even more explicitly . . . he states that "God's decree of the eternal damnation of the reprobate is not to be conceived of as prior to the fall."[66]

Robert Reymond offers an alternate supralapsarian model in which God's first decree is to elect some *sinful* men to salvation in Christ, yet it is not until the fourth decree that men would actually *fall* in Adam.[67] Obviously, Reymond wishes to escape the force of the moral objection just discussed by ensuring that the decree of election and reprobation is directed to men as sinners, but it is questionable

66. John Gerstner, *The Rational Biblical Theology of Jonathan Edwards,* vol. 2 (Powhatan: Berea Publications, 1992), 161–62. Gerstner quotes here from Edwards's *Miscellanies* 292 and 704.

67. Reymond, *New Systematic Theology,* 489, 494–96. See also note 65, above.

whether this alternative approach, taken as a whole, can succeed. Consider two observations. First, it simply is not clear to me how it is coherent to speak in the first decree of "sinful men" who do not actually fall in Adam and hence *become sinners* until the fourth decree. This has something of the feel of sleight of hand, though I am confident that this proposal is offered in full sincerity. But the obvious problem is that in order for the first divine decree (i.e., that God elects *sinful* men) to have integrity and be genuine, it requires that an implicit reality be envisioned as true, viz., that mankind be contemplated as having fallen into sin. And yet this very fall into sin is not supposed to be in view literally and really in the mind of God until the fourth decree. It simply is not clear how one can have it both ways. It is a noble attempt to find a synthesis of the infra- and supralapsarian positions, but it appears to lack coherence.

Second, I do think that John Feinberg's concern[68] about this whole discussion, quoted above, has validity. Is it possible that we are trying to line up things with a kind of precision and logical sequencing beyond what God's revelation rightly should lead us to do? Should we not understand that God sees at once the whole of the world he plans to create so that our attempts to provide logical sequencing beyond what Scripture clearly indicates may only lead to some degree of speculation? It seems to me that there is abundant and clear biblical evidence that when God elected persons in Christ, he chose those who needed to be saved (2 Thess. 2:13), that his election of them was itself a gracious and unmerited work (Rom. 11:5), that he elected them to be forgiven of sin and made holy in his Son (1 Pet. 1:1–2; Eph. 1:4), and that through their election they would be justified and glorified since they had been appointed to eternal life (Rom. 8:29–30; Acts 13:48).

Given this evidence, it seems entirely right to conclude that Scripture teaches the election, in eternity past, of fallen sinners to salvation. And perhaps this is as far as we can go. Yes, God does all for the glory of his name, and clearly God has control over all that occurs, just as certainly over the evil of this world as the good (Rom. 9:20–23). But if Scripture teaches that God elects those who are considered, in his mind's eye, as living after the fall and in their state of sin, then perhaps it is best to see that God views the whole picture at once, as Feinberg helpfully observes. Understood this way, we can (and should) affirm what Scripture says—which requires a fundamentally

---

68. Feinberg, *No One like Him*, 535–36.

infralapsarian view since God's election is to salvation of those possessing the sin and guilt incurred in the fall of Adam—while leaving to rest questions for which Scripture provides no basis for answering. One fears that the supralapsarian proposal seeks to tie some loose ends together and provide a full order of the decrees in areas where Scripture is, at best, unclear. But unfortunately it does so at the expense of what is clear in the teaching of Scripture.

That God has chosen his elect "for salvation" (2 Thess. 2:13 HCSB) shows that the elect both need to be saved and hence that they are viewed as sinners. Perhaps wisdom would encourage us to resist speculation and rather to embrace humble celebration of the grace of God manifest in God's choice of fallen and undeserving sinners to be saved.

Conclusion

Through the depth of thought and studied reflection required to navigate the issues of the doctrine of election, may God grant greater clarity and vision for what makes this doctrine so glorious to Paul, Peter, John, and Jesus. May God favor his people with ever-increasingly open eyes to behold their salvation as *all of God* and *all of grace*. And may we see and embrace the truth that the fullness of this glorious saving work of God commenced when God looked, in his mind's eye, on the fallen human race and determined to choose some whom he certainly and surely would save in his Son, to the glory of his name. Indeed! For it is true: God has chosen us in Christ, before the foundation of the world, and because of this we will one day be holy and blameless before him. We will receive his promised gift of eternal life. We will be conformed to the likeness of his own Son. This God will do because he chose us in Christ. May God alone be praised![69]

---

69. I would like to express my sincere thanks to several who read an earlier draft of this chapter and offered helpful suggestions and encouragement. In certain cases I chose (perhaps foolishly) not to follow their advice, but many parts of this chapter have been enriched by their insight and suggestions. My appreciation is extended to Gregg Allison, Wayne Pickens, Tom Schreiner, David Steele, Ashton Wilkins, and Shawn Wright.

CHAPTER 2

Responses to Bruce A. Ware

Response by Jack W. Cottrell

In many ways Ware's essay is exactly what I expected, i.e., heavy emphasis on biblical exegesis with a typical Calvinist spin. My critique will thus begin by examining the key texts used by Ware to undergird his view. We will see that they are not as straightforwardly Calvinist as they have been made to appear.

The first passage is John 17. Ware emphasizes Jesus' references to *those whom the Father has given him* (vv. 2, 6, 9, 24), who are taken to be all those who are unconditionally elected to salvation, those to whom the Son "may give eternal life" (v. 2). They are taken to be not just the apostles but all believers, based on verse 20. Ware asserts that *"each and every one* of those given to the Son is saved."

In reply, first of all, I believe it is clear that Jesus' references to "those whom the Father has given him" apply to the twelve apostles, not to the totality of saved individuals. Verse 20 clearly makes this distinction. Also, verse 20 clearly applies only to the prayer in verses 17–19, and perhaps verse 21.

Second, even if John 17 does refer to *unconditional* election, it is election to *apostolic service,* not to salvation. This applies also to John 15:16, "You did not choose Me but I chose you." God unconditionally gave the Twelve to Jesus as apostles, and Jesus *also* desires that they be saved—he *wants* to give them eternal life (vv. 2, 24; see

John 6:39), but their salvation is not assured simply because they have been "given" to Jesus by the Father. This is shown in this chapter, in verse 12 (a verse Ware understandably does not mention). In this verse Jesus refers again to "those which You have given Me," and he says that "not one of them perished but the son of perdition," i.e., Judas. God gave Judas to Jesus, but Judas was lost.

In summary, those *given* and *chosen* are the apostles, not believers in general; and they are given or chosen for service, not salvation. That they are unconditionally so chosen is irrelevant for the "predestination to salvation" issue.

The second passage is Acts 13:48, a verse almost uniformly translated in a way that pleases Calvinists: "As many as had been appointed to eternal life believed." How can this be reconciled with the Arminian view? There is no need to invoke an implied foreknowledge here or to seek some esoteric meaning for the verb *tasso*. The key is to understand that the verb form (*tetagmenoi*) should be taken as *middle* (reflexive) voice, not passive. "As many as arranged themselves unto (*eis*) eternal life believed," or, "As many as turned themselves toward eternal life believed."

The third text is Romans 9:10–16, which Ware says is "one of the clearest and strongest assertions of the unconditional nature of God's elect." I agree with that; but as I argue in my own essay in this book, the point is unconditional election to *service,* not to *salvation.* Ware thinks he has refuted this approach to Romans 9 in part by pointing out that the Jews' salvation definitely *is* in Paul's mind as he writes this chapter (see 9:1–3; 10:1–4). This argument is fallacious, however, because the issue is not whether the *passage* is about salvation but whether the *election* to which the passage refers is about salvation, as I have noted in my own chapter.

The fourth passage is Romans 11:5–7, where Paul refers to the remnant within Israel (see 9:6) that has been elected or chosen by grace. Ware interprets this as unconditional election because he assumes that it is the *same* election as in chapter 9, which is indeed unconditional election. He then uses the reference to grace (*eklogen charitos,* "election of grace") as further proof that the election of the remnant to salvation is unconditional.

This argument fails for two reasons. One, this is *not* the same election as in chapter 9. As I explain in my chapter, chapter 9 *is* about unconditional election, but to service not salvation. In 11:5 the election of the remnant *is* unto salvation. Two, it is simply false to assume that election according to grace must be unconditional. The error here is to equate *unconditional* and *undeserved*.

The fifth and last passage for discussion is Ephesians 1, to which Ware gives the usual Calvinist spin. In this passage Paul declares that God chose us in Christ before the foundation of the world (v. 4); that he predestined us to adoption as sons according to the good pleasure of his will (v. 5); that he purposes to bring all things under the headship of Christ (vv. 9–10); and that we have been predestined according to the purpose of God, who works all things according to the counsel of his will (v. 11).

All of this, according to Ware, must refer to unconditional election. This is true, he says, because this election was "before the foundation of the world" (v. 4); thus it cannot have anything to do with our choices because we did not even exist at that point (vv. 10–11). "We did not yet exist, and so God's election of us simply can have nothing to do with certain truths about us!" This is an extremely weak argument, though, in view of God's "exhaustive definite foreknowledge," the reality of which Ware himself argues for.

Ware's other argument based on Ephesians 1 is that Paul says *everything* is done according to *God's* will (v. 11). But if election is conditional, then in an ultimate sense this would be according to *our* wills, not God's. "God works everything according to his will, but notice that nothing is said here about God working things out according to our wills!" In response to this, however, if we conclude that God's original creative will was to make a world of freewill beings whose final destiny *does* ultimately depend upon their own choices, then both election and reprobation based on his foreknowledge of our free choices *is*—repeat, *is*—working all things out according to his will.

Regarding Ephesians 1 as a whole, I am not at all convinced that verses 4, 5, and 11 are referring to individual election in the first place. I believe a strong case can be made for an entirely different approach, namely, that Paul is speaking of the predestination of the two different categories of the human race as commonly distinguished in his day, i.e., the *Jews* and the *Gentiles*. I base this case on two facts: (1) the sudden shift from first person plural to second person plural in 1:13; and (2) the underlying theme of the letter as expressed in 2:11–3:21, i.e., God's "eternal purpose" (3:11) of uniting Jews and Gentiles together through Jesus Christ into a single body, the church.

I should think that if one is proceeding through his interpretation of Romans 9, using the Calvinist template of unconditional election and reprobation of individuals as his guide, by the time he gets to 9:22–24 and finds himself forced to draw such conclusions as the above, he would immediately say, "Something is wrong with this picture! Something is wrong with this concept! Something is wrong with this system!" Indeed there is. That "something" is Calvinism.

Response by Clark H. Pinnock

Ware offers us a fine exposition of the doctrine of election unto salvation as it is understood (and sometimes believed) in the Reformed churches. Together with Reymond's work, the reader is provided with a rich banquet of theological feasting. An important point of difference in my view of election compared with these two is that I understand election in the Bible to be a social concept—as in God electing Israel to be his servant. This means that much of this debate which assumes otherwise is irrelevant. The foundational teaching of the Old Testament is that God has chosen a nation to be his priestly people. God wants this unlikely tribe to be a light to the nations. She was not chosen for salvation in heaven—she was chosen to serve the nations.

Election then is not about a favoritism shown to some individuals in contrast to the rejection of others. On the contrary, Israel's election is for the sake of the nations that they might be gathered unto God. In Romans 9–11 (for example), a text taken up by several of our authors because of its importance, Paul speaks about groups and nations, not about individuals as such, wanting to explain to them how God's purposes will be fulfilled in a world of sin and disobedience. So much of the debate around election assumes that election is an individualistic category when it is not. Believing that has fostered a conversation among Arminians also. For example, Cottrell also accepts this idea, but I do not. Talbott and I are singing from the same page.

Strong Calvinist though he is, Ware knows that most Christians are not going to be able to stomach the harsh (if logically rigorous) version of the Reformed faith as set forth by Reymond. He rightly fears they will abandon Calvinism altogether (which is what happened to me) unless they are introduced to a more intelligible rendition of it. Ware is sensitive to such realities and is known for his ability to ease some of the pressures that paleo-Calvinism can exert. He knows that most people, even in the Reformed churches, are ill informed in their thinking about election, if they think about it at all. But he has an idea which he thinks will help, drawing upon the infralapsarian tradition.

Ware's idea is that, while election remains unconditional, reprobation must not be seen in that way. Even though the elect and the nonelect are who they are by the predetermination of God, the non-elect are rejected, not arbitrarily, but on account of their sins. Most people would feel a lot better if they could believe that. It puts God in a better light by introducing a measure of conditionality into the God-human relation (as Reymond is quick to notice). It allows one to say that the nonelect are responsible for their plight, not God. Thus it clears God of the charge that he sends the nonelect to hell for no other reason than his own glory and good pleasure.

Ware senses how wrong this would be and how untenable, and so, without doing anything to help us understand unconditional election, he does make an effort to represent the divine reprobation as an act of justice and not an arbitrary decision to bypass the nonelect. Ware wishes us to see that, although election may be unconditional, reprobation is not but is based on what sinners deserve. It introduces into this highly abstract debate about the divine decrees a welcomed historical and relational element. It also has the odor of an Arminian way of thinking in allowing for a human contribution to the salvation drama, even if it's only for the fall into sin.

But frankly it's hard to see how this works, given the fact that Ware also believes that God predestines the nonelect to be condemned before the foundation of the world and therefore abandons them and passes them by in his decree when he could as easily have saved them. We have to remember that, in the context of Calvinism, God determines the fall along with everything else. At no time could the nonelect have done other than perish. Given his adherence to determinist freedom (he calls it compatibilist because it sounds better), people are only doing what they have been programmed to do. There is no moral credibility in this move—the reprobate are set up to perish. Sure they are doing what they "want" to do—that is, sin—but this just happens to coincide with divine predestination.

There is another way to attempt this point. One might think of Adam having libertarian freedom, that is, being able to sin or not to sin before the fall. And one might put on the table the strange concept of federal headship, whereby all mankind is reckoned to have sinned in Adam's act. One difficulty is that this would involve a heavy reliance on a single act of libertarian freedom on Adam's part to give moral credibility to the idea that all sinners are to blame even though they cannot do otherwise than sin. It also brings the Calvinist perilously close to the Arminian notion that there is no moral guilt unless there is at least a degree of libertarian freedom, however slight.

Response by Robert L. Reymond

Because Bruce Ware is the other Calvinist contributing to this volume, naturally I deeply appreciate almost everything that he has written. I rejoiced at his careful, detailed exposition of Scripture as he made the case for unconditional and individual election to salvation. I even found myself agreeing with much that he criticized about classical supralapsarianism since I too differ with classical supralapsarianism in one major respect in order to make it more consistent. It is only with his infralapsarianism that I take exception. Consequently, what I have to say in this "intramural" debate between us will be fairly short.

Just as Ware found it necessary to address classical supralapsarianism as he made his case for infralapsarianism, so also I found it necessary in my essay to set forth my problems with classical infralapsarianism as I made my case for a consistent supralapsarianism that does not forsake the principle that "in planning the rational mind passes from the end to the means in a retrograde movement, so that what is first in design is last in accomplishment" and what is last in design is first in accomplishment.

To state the matter succinctly, the all-wise God is all knowing. At every moment he is cognizant of everything that ever was, now is, or ever shall be. He necessarily knows his own uncreated essence exhaustively, his own eternal purpose exhaustively, and his created universe exhaustively—and he knows them intuitively, instantaneously, simultaneously, and everlastingly. His knowledge of himself and of all created things, as I said earlier, is absolutely comprehensive and eternally "intuited"—that is to say, he never had to learn anything through the learning process because he already knows everything there is to know. He "never receives from some other source or from his own inventive genius an idea he never previously had" (Gordon H. Clark). Nothing escapes his notice; nothing is hidden from him, nothing happens without his awareness, which means, of course, that no one has ever had a private conversation with someone else!

But while the church of Jesus Christ has always believed and confessed that the one living and true God is infinitely wise and all knowing, it is the Reformed church alone that includes within its exposition of God's wisdom and knowledge a serious study of God's "eternal purpose" (Eph. 3:11). Reformed theology, which it is our happy lot to inherit, emphasizes that God's "eternal purpose" reflects his infinite, eternal, and unchangeable wisdom that devised perfect ends and achieves those ends by perfect means. God in his infinite wisdom had wise reasons for determining all the ends and all the means to those ends that he did for his creation even though these ends and means for the most part, if not totally, are inscrutable and hidden to most, if not to all, of his rational creatures.

All this means—and now we return to Ware's concern—that there was also *never a moment* in the divine mind when God's unitary, complete, and total purpose was not entirely "literally and really in the mind of God"—*never a moment* when his eternal purpose's end was not "literally and really in the mind of God," *never a moment* when the Spirit's application of Christ's saving benefits was not "literally and really in the mind of God," *never a moment* when Christ's atoning work was not "literally and really in the mind of God," *never a moment* when fallen mankind was not "literally and really in the mind of God," and *never a moment* when our unfallen first parents and his "very good" created universe were not "literally and really in the mind of God." This also means, if a certain measure of distortion occurs, as I said in my essay, when we Calvinists arbitrarily stop at five or six or seven aspects of the eternal purpose and do not continue to enumerate all the particulars of the unitary decree, that there is an equal risk of a measure of distortion that we Calvinists open ourselves up to, if we let the italicized fact above slip from our minds, when we even split the one eternal purpose of God at all! We can unwittingly begin to think of God's eternal decree as having a chronological element in it after all.

Therefore, while it is true as I stated in my essay that the fall and the prior creation of human beings were not yet elements in the *purposing* order at the point in that order where they are viewed as elected or reprobated or for that matter where their existence is determined, yet, *since God's decree is eternal with no chronological antecedence or subsequence in it,* there was *never a moment* when people, viewed as fallen and created people, did not certainly exist as well in it. In fact, the first decree as the final "end" decree because it had to do with mankind viewed both as sinful people and as created people, rendered the fall and creation aspects of the eternal decree teleologically necessary. Accordingly, their existence as fallen and created people was as decretally "literal and real" in the divine mind at the point of the first decree as it was at the point of the fourth and fifth.

When Ware states, however, that in order for my first decree (that is, that God elects *sinful* men) to have integrity and be genuine, "it requires that an implicit reality be envisioned as true, viz., that mankind be contemplated as having fallen into sin. And yet this very fall into sin is not supposed to be in view literally and really in the mind of God until the fourth decree"—when he says this, I say—it appears to me that he has not grasped, first, what I said above as he should have, namely, that there was *never a moment* in the divine mind when God's unitary, complete, and total purpose was not entirely before him, and, second, that I hold that the one unitary decree of God has no chronological element in it at all, that is to say, there is no temporal "before" and "after" in it. What I am urging by my suggested order of the decrees is simply that God, as a rational planner, has eternally had before him the myriad aspects of his one eternal purpose, each viewed as a means (with the exception of the end), in the order that requires each aspect as logically *necessitating* the next, thereby bringing *purposive* unity to the one entire eternal purpose of God.

While Ware declares that he is confident that I offer my proposal in full sincerity, for which expression of brotherliness I am deeply grateful, I regret that he thinks this representation of the order of the decrees has "something of the feel of sleight of hand" about it. Perhaps we can talk together about this matter some time, and perhaps I can remove his reticence concerning my proposal. In any event I deeply appreciate his personal commitment to the Reformed faith and his making the effort to interact with my adjustment to classical supralapsarianism.

Response by Thomas B. Talbott

Like Robert Reymond, Bruce Ware defends a doctrine of limited election; and like Reymond, Ware pretty much assumes, without supporting argument, that universalism is false. Perhaps that is because his main target in this discussion is Arminianism, and his argument against Arminianism does include a few strands of argument against universalism as well.

In his discussion of Romans 8:29–30, for example, Ware argues that, according to this text, "God foreknew and predestined and called only some, not all." Why? Because "there is no point," he claims, "in Paul's saying, 'For those he foreknew,' if he has in mind all of humanity." But that is not true at all. You might as well argue that there is no point in saying, "For those God loves he also chastens," if one believes that God loves all people. The point of the latter remark would most likely be to offer a word of assurance during a time of hardship, not to sow doubts concerning the universality of God's love, and that was precisely the point of Paul's remark as well. His was a word of assurance that all will be well in the end (see 8:28) because God will guarantee it; in no way was he trying to frighten his readers with the thought that perhaps some of them—or, worse yet, perhaps some of their own loved ones—may never have been foreknown at all.

Ware goes on to write, "Unless one holds to universalism (a view already excluded by what Paul taught in Rom. 2:5–11), then one must rightly conclude that only some are foreknown." But surely Ware could have anticipated the obvious counterclaim of similar form: "Unless one holds to Calvinism (a view already excluded by what Paul taught in Rom. 5:12–21), then one must rightly conclude that all, not merely some, are foreknown." At least Romans 5:12–21 contains the explicit statement that Jesus Christ brings "justification and life to all" humans. Romans 2:5–11, by way of contrast, carries no implication that those "storing up" wrath for themselves will suffer unending punishment and hence will *never* be reconciled to God. So how, I wonder, would Ware defend his own claim in light of the obvious counterclaim?

Misunderstanding the Nature of Love

Ware's contention that God suffers from a conflict of will in the case of the nonelect also carries important implications for Ware's understanding of the divine nature. For not only is God's justice in conflict with his mercy; given Ware's view, God also experiences an inner conflict between one kind of love, which expresses itself in grace and mercy, and another so-called "love," which does not express itself in grace and mercy but instead permits an eternity of torment to befall its objects. Ware thus distinguishes between "God's universal love for all (e.g., as seen in John 3:16)," on the one hand,

and his "particular, selective, and discriminate love for his own people," on the other.

But this entire line of argument seems to me misguided, to say the least. First, a married man may properly love many women—his mother, his sisters, his daughters, and others who are not blood relatives—every bit as much as he loves his own wife. Did not Jesus himself command that we love our neighbor, who just might be a woman, even as we love ourselves? And is that not exactly the same love that in Ephesians 5:33 Paul instructed husbands to have for their wives? Second, not only does a man's love for other women not detract from his love for his own wife; the latter actually *requires* that he love other women—his wife's mother, for example—even more, not less. For a man could hardly love his wife properly and, at the same time, refuse to love and respect her own loved ones, and neither could God love Isaac properly without also loving Isaac's beloved Esau every bit as much as he loves Isaac himself (see "the Paradox of Exclusiveness" in my original essay).

Third, as human beings with limited time and energy, we are all no doubt incapable, as a practical matter, of cultivating the same degree of emotional intimacy with everyone we meet, not to mention those we never meet. For time and energy devoted to one relationship is time and energy taken away from another. But God faces none of the *practical* difficulties that prevent us from including too many in our circle of intimacy. Fourth, exclusiveness in marriage and sexual relationships—which, if we take Jesus' remarks in Luke 20:34–36 seriously, may be a concession to the human condition—has nothing to do with exclusiveness in love. For wherein lies the sin of adultery? Does it lie *only* in the fact that the man is acting in an unloving way toward his own wife? Not at all. It also lies in the fact that he is acting in an unloving way toward another woman whom he is obligated to love every bit as much as he is obligated to love his own wife. The point is that husbandly love, like parental love, brotherly love, sisterly love, etc., should illustrate our *oneness* in Christ without any implication of excluding someone else from that *spiritual* oneness.

A Confusion about Moral Responsibility

We thus approach the most basic weakness in Ware's understanding of Reformed theology. According to Ware, the nonelect are morally responsible for rejecting the gospel even though it was causally determined long before they were born that they would do so. "So long as those who reject the gospel," he writes, "act out of their own natures and inclinations, choosing and doing what they most want, . . . they are fully responsible for their actions." But according to this quotation, doing what one most wants is a *sufficient condition* of being morally responsible for one's actions, and not even a sophisticated compatibilist (someone who believes that a thoroughgoing determinism is compatible with moral responsibility) would make that claim. A lion that devours a man and a paranoid schizophrenic who goes off his medication and kills his loving mother may both be doing what they most want at the time, but it hardly follows that they are morally responsible for their actions.

In the end, moreover, Ware's version of compatibilism undermines entirely the New Testament doctrine of salvation by grace and the traditional Christian asymmetry between *merited* blame and *unmerited* favor. For both the damned and the sanctified simply do what they most want to do; in that respect, they both meet Ware's stated sufficient condition of being morally responsible for their actions. And according to Ware, "those who reject Christ deserve the condemnation they receive, for they did what they most wanted in that choice to say 'no' to God's gracious offer of salvation." But if that is true, then, by parity of reasoning, so also is the following: "Those who accept Christ *deserve* the reward they receive, for they did what they most wanted in that choice to say 'yes' to God's gracious offer of salvation."

Similarly, the sanctified should receive (and even take) moral credit for their righteous actions. For if the damned deserve moral condemnation for actions caused by a sinful nature over which they have no control, then the sanctified likewise deserve moral credit for actions caused by their regenerated hearts and renewed minds. In the next sentence, however, Ware writes: "And those who receive Christ cannot boast at all in their receiving the eternal life that comes by faith, . . . for apart from God's effectual and gracious work in their lives, to open their hearts . . . and their eyes, . . . they, too, would never have come." But you simply cannot have it both ways. You cannot sensibly say *both* that all credit for salvation goes to God because he graciously regenerates the hearts of the elect, causing them to repent, *and* that none of the blame for damnation goes to God even though he brings the nonelect into their earthly existence with a sinful nature over which they have no control, blinds them to the truth, and causes them to be hard of heart.

CHAPTER 3

The Classical Arminian View of Election

JACK W. COTTRELL

Arminianism as such, in its broadest sense, is simply non-Augustinianism or non-Calvinism. It has many variations, "from the evangelical views of Arminius himself to left-wing liberalism."[1] What holds them all together is the rejection of the Augustinian concept of true total depravity (bondage of the will), and a belief in significant free will, at least in relation to the ability to accept or reject the gospel offer of salvation.

It is actually a misnomer to call this view "Arminianism" since it existed long before James Arminius (A.D. 1560–1609). It was the consensus belief in Christendom prior to Augustine (A.D. 354–430),[2] and was affirmed by even Augustine, especially but not exclusively in his earlier years.[3] For example, Augustine declared in A.D. 412 that the Creator gave human beings free will as "an intermediate power, which is able either to incline towards faith, or to turn towards unbelief. . . . God no doubt wishes all men to be saved, but yet not so as to

---

1. Millard J. Erickson, *Christian Theology,* 2nd ed. (Grand Rapids: Baker, 1998), 931.
2. See Roger T. Forster and V. Paul Marston, *God's Strategy in Human History* (Wheaton: Tyndale, 1974), 243–57.
3. See Eugene Portalie, *A Guide to the Thought of Saint Augustine,* trans. Ralph J. Bastian (Chicago: Henry Regnery Co., 1960), 196–98; Norman Geisler, *Chosen but Free* (Minneapolis: Bethany, 1989), 150–51.

take away from them their liberty of will."[4] Catholic thinking in the Middle Ages was mixed but from the time of the Reformation,[5] official Roman Catholic teaching has been in line with Arminianism.[6] In the sixteenth century the Anabaptists and most of the Radical Reformation taught a doctrine of (restored) free will, contrary to the main Reformers.[7]

When Arminius himself made the transition from Catholicism to Protestantism, he was exposed to strict Calvinist views, especially those of Beza in Geneva; but he personally rejected both the supralapsarian and the sublapsarian forms of Calvinism.[8] Though he acknowledged the Adamic legacy of total depravity and affirmed the necessity of grace to enable faith,[9] he denied the practical significance of such depravity by declaring that such enabling grace is universal and resistible.[10] Thus as to whether sinners have the ability to accept or reject the gospel, Arminius was certainly an Arminian. Some, such as C. Gordon Olson, Robert Picirilli, and Stephen Ashby, refer to Arminius's overall view, and that of his early Remonstrant followers, as "Reformed Arminianism."[11] Picirilli and Ashby espouse and expand this view. F. Leroy Forlines calls Arminius's view "Classical Arminianism" and identifies his own view with it.[12]

Many who have continued in the general freewill tradition, and who are thus Arminian in this broad sense, fall outside the pale of orthodox,

---

4. Aurelius Augustine, "On the Spirit and the Letter," 58, in *The Works of Aurelius Augustine,* ed. Marcus Dods, vol. IV, *Anti-Pelagian Works,* vol. I, tr. Peter Holmes (Edinburgh: T. & T. Clark, 1872), 219–20.

5. E.g., Desiderius Erasmus, *Discourse on Free Will* (New York: Ungar, 1961).

6. "Arminianism also includes conventional Roman Catholicism" (Erickson, *Christian Theology,* 932). See "The Canons and Dogmatic Decrees of the Council of Trent," in Philip Schaff, *The Creeds of Christendom,* vol. II (New York: Harper and Brothers, 1919), 92, 111.

7. George H. Williams, *The Radical Reformation* (Philadelphia: Westminster, 1962), 839; Carl Bangs, *Arminius: A Study in the Dutch Reformation* (Nashville: Abingdon, 1971), 169–70.

8. Bangs, *Arminius,* 138, 141.

9. James Arminius, "Public Disputations," XI:7, in *The Writings of James Arminius,* 3 vols. (Grand Rapids: Baker, 1956), I:526.

10. Arminius, "A Declaration of the Sentiments of Arminius, on Predestination," IV, in *Writings,* I:253–54. See Bangs, 343.

11. C. Gordon Olson, *Beyond Calvinism and Arminianism: An Inductive, Mediate Theology of Salvation* (Cedar Knolls, N.J.: Global Gospel Publishers, 2002), 30; Robert E. Picirilli, *Grace, Faith, Free Will, Contrasting Views of Salvation: Calvinism and Arminianism* (Nashville: Randall House, 2002), i, ii; Stephen M. Ashby, "A Reformed Arminian View," in *Four Views on Eternal Security,* ed. J. Matthew Pinson (Grand Rapids: Zondervan, 2002), 137–43.

12. F. Leroy Forlines, *The Quest for Truth: Answering Life's Inescapable Questions* (Nashville: Randall, 2001), xvii.

conservative Christendom. This includes groups such as Socinians and Unitarians;[13] Quakers;[14] some cults, such as Jehovah's Witnesses; and what Erickson generally calls "left-wing liberalism."[15]

The most common form of post-Arminius Arminianism is that formulated by John Wesley and embraced by his followers in the Methodist, holiness, and pentecostal denominations. It is similar to Arminius's own view but includes a more complete and consistent view of the prevenient grace of God that restores to Adam's race the freewill ability to accept or reject the gospel. This view is usually called "Wesleyan Arminianism," or "evangelical Arminianism."[16]

Other modern groups in the general freewill tradition include some Baptists (e.g., the Free Will Baptist Church, represented by For-lines and Picirilli), and the Restoration (Stone-Campbell) Movement fellowships (Christian churches; Churches of Christ), of which I am a part.

With the exception of Catholics and nonorthodox groups such as those named above, the view espoused by most of those mentioned in this brief historical survey can be thought of as "classical Arminian-ism" in the broadest sense. I know that Forlines uses this title (with a capital "C") in a more specific sense that includes the doctrines of prevenient grace and substitutionary atonement.[17] Nevertheless I am going to apply this title (with a small "c") to all those who believe in man's significant free will to accept or reject the gospel, however the presence of this ability is explained.

How, then, does the classical Arminian doctrine of *predestination* fit into this picture? As I am using the term, it is the view that before the world ever existed God conditionally predestined some specific individuals to eternal life and the rest to eternal condemnation, based on his foreknowledge of their freewill responses to his law and to his grace. For most of those described here as classical Arminians, the key idea is that God predestines according to foreknowledge (prescience) of future human free-will decisions. Jewett calls this the oldest view

---

13. Geoffrey F. Nuttall, "The Influence of Arminianism in England," in *Man's Faith and Freedom: The Theological Influence of Jacobus Arminius,* ed. Gerald O. McCulloh (Nashville: Abingdon, 1962), 50.

14. Ibid., 48.

15. Erickson, *Christian Theology,* 931.

16. Olson, *Beyond Calvinism and Arminianism,* 30; Paul K. Jewett, *Election and Pre-destination* (Grand Rapids: Eerdmans, 1985), 17.

17. Forlines, *Quest for Truth,* x, xvii, xviii.

of predestination, traceable to the early Greek Fathers, and "the most widely held view" today "among lay students of Scripture."[18]

Some may be surprised to hear that Arminians believe in *predestination* at all. This is because many associate the word with Calvinism, and assume that only Calvinists accept such a doctrine. This is not the case, however. As Forlines says,[19] the doctrine of predestination is just as essential for Arminians as it is for Calvinists, and we in the former category need to reclaim the word as well as the concept, along with all the blessings entailed thereby.

I will now present four things: (1) a more complete explanation of the Arminian view of predestination; (2) a brief history of the Arminian view; (3) a statement of the general theological presuppositions of this view; and (4) a brief exposition of Romans 9 as a crucial text relating to this subject.

The Arminian View of Predestination

As just defined, predestination is the view that before the world ever existed God conditionally predestined some specific individuals to eternal life and the rest to eternal condemnation, based on His foreknowledge of their freewill responses to his law and to his grace. In unpacking this definition we shall explore the meaning, the objects, the end, and the manner of predestination.

The Meaning of Predestination

The term *predestination* refers to God's decision to perform a particular future act or fulfill a certain purpose, or his prior determination to cause something to come to pass. God's predetermining activity is not limited to his decisions concerning the final destiny of individuals; it also includes other aspects of his eternal purposes. For example, as applied to persons God has not only predestined some to *salvation* but has also predestined some to roles of *service* whereby he uses them as instruments to carry out his purposes as related to salvation. Discerning the difference between the two is crucial for a

---

18. Jewett, *Election and Predestination,* 68–69. In my sections of this book, unless otherwise specified, when I use the words *Arminian* and *Arminianism,* they will refer to what I am calling "classical Arminianism"; and when I use the word *predestination,* it will refer to the classical Arminian view as defined here.

19. Forlines, *Quest for Truth,* 394.

correct understanding of what it means to say God has predestined some to salvation.

Terminology

The Greek verb translated "to predestine" is *proorizo*, which combines *orizo*, "to limit, to fix, to appoint, to determine"; and *pro*, "before, prior to." *Proorizo* thus literally means "to determine beforehand, to predetermine, to foreordain." Predestination is thus God's predetermination or decision to do something, to cause something, to bring about a certain event or state of affairs at a future time. The word occurs six times in the New Testament (Acts 4:28; Rom. 8:29, 30; 1 Cor. 2:7; Eph. 1:5, 11); the four uses in Romans and Ephesians refer specifically to persons. The English word *predestine* suggests the nuance "to predetermine the final destiny of," but a reference to final destiny is not inherent in the Greek term.[20] It is an appropriate word nevertheless since the uses in Romans and Ephesians do seem to refer to the predetermination of personal destinies. In these cases the prefix *pro-* ("pre-") indicates that the determination took place before the world was created (see Eph. 1:4; Rev. 17:8).

In reference to eternal destinies, predestination includes both election and reprobation.[21] Regarding salvation *election* is God's choice of certain individuals for the specific purpose of giving them eternal life, whereas, *reprobation* is God's decision to assign the non-elect to eternal damnation. Our main focus here is on the former.

Divine election in general is God's determination to choose or select one person or group from among others for a specific role or purpose in his plan. The New Testament terms for this are the verb *eklegomai*, "to choose, to select, to elect"; the noun *ekloge*, "choice, election"; and the adjective *eklektos*, "chosen, elect." These terms appear much more frequently than *proorizo* and have a broader range of application. In 1 Timothy 5:21 Paul refers to elect or chosen angels; in all other cases divine election refers to human beings.

Regarding the latter, it is of supreme importance to note that many of the passages about election have nothing to do with predestination to salvation but refer instead to God's choosing of certain individuals or groups for *service*, i.e., to fill a certain role in the

---

20. Olson (*Beyond Calvinism and Arminianism,* 165) emphasizes this and suggests the word should be translated "preappoint" and not "predestine."
21. See Picirilli, *Grace,* 48. The term is never actually used of the latter.

historical accomplishment of salvation. To be chosen for service is a totally different issue from being chosen for salvation.

Chosen for service. Those predestined for specific roles in the accomplishment of redemption include the Redeemer himself, Jesus of Nazareth. The election of Jesus is the central and primary act of predestination. In Isaiah 42:1 the Lord speaks of Jesus as the elect one: "Behold, My Servant, whom I uphold; My chosen one in whom My soul delights."[22] Matthew 12:18 quotes this passage and applies it to Jesus. At the transfiguration God announced the election of Jesus in these words: "This is My Son, My Chosen One; listen to Him!" (Luke 9:35 NASB). (See also Luke 23:35; 1 Pet. 2:4, 6.)

The election of Jesus was part of the divine plan even before the worlds were created. Foreknowing both the obedience of the Redeemer and the disobedience of his enemies, God predetermined the accomplishment of redemption through Jesus of Nazareth (Acts 2:23; 1 Pet. 1:20). Jesus was foreordained to die for the sins of the world (Acts 4:28).

At times other individuals were chosen for special roles in order to facilitate God's purposes. To create the nation of Israel God chose Abraham, Isaac, and Jacob (Neh. 9:7; Acts 13:17; Rom. 9:7–13).[23] He chose Moses (Ps. 106:23) and David (Ps. 78:70; 139:16) among others. He even chose certain Gentile rulers to help carry out His purpose for Israel, e.g., Pharaoh (Rom. 9:17[24]) and Cyrus (Isa. 45:1).

As instruments for establishing the church, another group of individuals was chosen, namely, the apostles. From among His disciples Jesus "chose twelve of them, whom He also named as apostles" (Luke 6:13). Later He asked them, "Did I Myself not choose you, the twelve?" (John 6:70 NASB). Christ says to the apostles, "You did not choose Me but I chose you, and appointed you that you would go and bear fruit" (John 15:16 NASB; see 13:18; 15:19; Acts 1:2). Likewise chosen for service as an apostle were Matthias (Acts 1:24) and Paul (Acts 9:15; Gal. 1:15–16).

That such election was for service and not salvation is seen from the fact that even Judas is among the chosen twelve (Luke 6:13; John 6:70), though his predetermined role was that of the betrayer of Jesus (John 6:71). God did not *cause* Judas to fulfill this role but rather

---

22. All quotations from Scripture, unless otherwise noted, are from the New American Standard Bible (1995).

23. See Jack Cottrell, *The College Press NIV Commentary: Romans,* 2 vols. (Joplin, Mo.: College Press, 1996, 1998), II:73–97.

24. Ibid., II:97–106.

foreknew what he would do as an apostle (Acts 2:23). In other words, Judas did not betray Jesus because he was chosen to do so; he was chosen because God foreknew that he would betray Jesus.

One of the most important of God's acts of predestination for service applies not to an individual but to a group, namely, the nation of Israel: "For you are a holy people to the LORD your God; the LORD your God has chosen you to be a people for His own possession out of all the peoples who are on the face of the earth" (Deut. 7:6; see Deut. 14:2; 1 Chron. 16:13; Acts 13:17). This election of Israel was the election of the nation in general, not the election of specific individuals. The nation was chosen specifically to prepare the way for the coming Messiah. The nation could serve its purpose of preparing for the Messiah even if the majority of individual Jews were lost.[25]

Since Israel was chosen specifically to prepare the way for the Messiah's appearance, her purpose was accomplished and her destiny fulfilled in the incarnation, death, and resurrection of Jesus (Acts 13:32–33; Rom. 9:3–5). Thus the nation of Israel is no longer God's elect people. In the new covenant age God has a new elect body, a new Israel, the church. While not strictly parallel to Old Testament Israel, in this age the church as a body is now God's chosen people (1 Pet. 2:9); and this election is in part an election to service. When Peter describes the church as a "chosen race," he adds this purpose for the choosing: "that you may proclaim the excellencies of Him who has called you out of darkness into His marvelous light" (1 Pet. 2:9 NASB). Thus in terms of service, whereas Israel was elected for preparation, the church is elected for proclamation.

Chosen for salvation. The language of election does at times refer to predestination to salvation. The verb is used for this purpose infrequently (e.g., Eph. 1:4); most often the adjective *eklektos* is used to describe those whom God has saved, either individually (Rom. 16:13) or collectively. In the collective sense sometimes it refers to "the elect" as the general company of the saved (Luke 18:7; Rom. 8:33; Rev. 17:14), as the church in general (2 Tim. 2:10; Titus 1:1; 1 Pet. 1:1; 2:9), or as specific churches (2 John 1, 13). In 1 Thessalonians 1:4 the noun *ekloge* is used in this last sense. In Romans 11:5, 7 it is used for the saved (the "remnant") within the nation of Israel.

---

25. The Bible's main teaching on Israel's election for service is Romans 9, which will be discussed in detail in part 4, below.

While the terms *predestination* and *election* are not always used interchangeably in Scripture,[26] they are certainly closely related in meaning. Without question those who will be in heaven with God for eternity are both elected and predestined for it. The only shade of difference between the two concepts seems to be this, that election is God's act of choosing or selecting certain individuals rather than others from a larger group, while predestination is God's act of preappointing those so chosen to their final destiny. The two go hand in hand, and a reference to one implies the other.

The Objects of Predestination

The next question is the objects of predestination. According to Arminians, where matters of eternal destiny are concerned, specifically *who* are the objects of God's predestining activity? Two issues arise here. First, does predestination apply to the lost as well as to the saved? Second, does predestination apply primarily to individuals or to groups?

The lost are predestined, too. Arminians agree that some are predestined to eternal salvation; the elect are chosen for eternal life. As with Calvinism, though, there is no universal agreement as to how predestination applies to the lost. Defining it only in a Calvinistic sense, John Miley absolutely rejects the concept of reprobation.[27] Others, however, understand that reprobation according to foreknowledge works in exactly the same way as election according to foreknowledge, and thus have no difficulty accepting it as a doctrine parallel to election. Pointing out that Arminius accepted both, Picirilli affirms that "reprobation is corollary to election" and that they are "essentially parallel (although as opposites)."[28]

I accept the latter view, though it is mostly an inference from what we know of the relation between foreknowledge and election. There are few specific biblical references to this doctrine. Careful exegesis of Romans 9:22 shows that the unbelieving Jews *prepared themselves* (middle voice) for destruction through their own unbelief;[29] thus this text is not relevant here. Two texts that may be relevant, though, are 1 Peter 2:8 and Jude 4.

---

26. Contra Dave Hunt, *What Love Is This? Calvinism's Misrepresentation of God* (Sisters, Oreg.: Loyal, 2002), 126.

27. John Miley, *Systematic Theology*, vol. 2 (Peabody, Mass.: Hendrickson, 1989 reprint of 1893 edition), 263–66.

28. Picirilli, *Grace*, 48, 59.

29. Cottrell, *Romans*, II:126.

Jude 4 speaks of certain ones who long ago were marked down or branded for condemnation; but it is their *condemnation* that is prerecorded,[30] not their foreseen unbelief. Peter (1 Pet. 2:6–8) refers to those who through unbelief and disobedience stumble over the "stone of stumbling and rock of offense." Then he adds, "unto which indeed they were appointed." If we assume that those appointed are the unbelievers, it is not clear unto what they were appointed. A reasonable explanation is that they were appointed ("destined," NIV) to stumble over the Rock, i.e., be brought down unto eternal ruin and death by the very Stone they rejected, namely, Jesus. They were not appointed or destined to unbelief and rejection of Jesus but to the "stumbling" as the natural and deserved consequence of their unbelief and rejection.[31]

Another possibility in 1 Peter 2:8 is that the ones "appointed" are not the unbelievers but the "precious corner stone" of verse 6 and the "stone of stumbling and rock of offense" themselves. The verb for "appointed" in verse 8 is *tithemi,* which in verse 6 is used for "laying" the stone. That is, this is one of the purposes for which the stones were laid or appointed: to be the source of judgment and downfall for unbelievers. The verb in verse 8 (*etethesan*) is plural because it refers both to the "precious corner stone" in verse 6 and the "stone of stumbling" in verse 8 (both of which refer, of course, to Jesus). If this is the proper interpretation, then 1 Peter 2:8 would not refer to any kind of reprobation.

Predestination refers primarily to individuals. The next question regarding the objects of predestination—whether it applies primarily to individuals or to groups—is not argued among Calvinists, who understand it to be of individuals. But Arminians have some disagreement over this issue. Some emphasize group or corporate election, while others see it as primarily individual.

Those taking the former view assert that God in his precreation counsels predetermined that all who later would fall into a certain category of people would be chosen for eternal salvation. That is, God determined that he would give salvation to anyone who would fulfill certain conditions; "all who meet the specified conditions" are thus predestined to be in heaven. The act of predestination applies not so much to the concrete individuals who would later become a part of

---

30. The word is *prographo,* "written down beforehand."
31. See Cottrell, *Romans,* II:150–54.

this group, as it does to the abstract group or category itself. "God predestines the plan, not the man" is a common contention. H. Orton Wiley is an example. He has stated, "I hold, of course to *class* predestination." He finds it objectionable to say "that God has determined beforehand whether some should be saved or not, applied to individuals."[32] Another example is Robert Shank, who explains election as "primarily corporate and only secondarily particular." He says, "The election to salvation is corporate and comprehends individual men only in identification and association with the elect body."[33] This applies even to the passages which connect predestination with foreknowledge: "Whether God has actively foreknown each individual—both the elect and the reprobate—may remain a moot question."[34]

C. Gordon Olson agrees, declaring that the letter to the Ephesians "militates for corporate, not individual, election."[35] He says that 1 Peter 2:9 indicates "that the Church's election, like Israel's, was corporate."[36] After presenting several arguments for corporate election, he says, "We can see how Paul could well be referring to the corporate church as that which God chose in eternity past to become His choice people." Thus "the corporate nature of election is so clear in enough contexts to lead to the probability that all should be taken corporately."[37] Olson does allow for individual election but says that "if we may speak about it at all," it is "secondary and ancillary."[38]

In his *Christian Theology* Alister McGrath leaves the impression that all Arminians understand predestination corporately,[39] but this simply is not true. In fact, Arminian defenders of individual election are abundant, beginning in modern times with Arminius himself, who declares that his own sentiment on predestination includes the "decree, by which God decreed to save and damn particular persons. This decree has its foundation in the foreknowledge of God," by which from all eternity he knew which individuals would believe

---

32. H. Orton Wiley, et al., "The Debate over Divine Election," *Christianity Today* (Oct. 12, 1959), 4:3, 5.

33. Robert Shank, *Elect in the Son: A Study of the Doctrine of Election* (Springfield, Mo.: Westcott, 1970), 45, 48; see 45–55, 131.

34. Ibid., 154–55.

35. Olson, *Beyond Calvinism and Arminianism*, 38.

36. Ibid., 182.

37. Ibid., 193–95.

38. Ibid., 189.

39. Alister E. McGrath, *Christian Theology: An Introduction*, 2nd ed. (Cambridge, Mass.: Blackwell, 1997), 454.

and persevere and the ones who would not.[40] In the early nineteenth century Richard Watson, granting the election of individuals to service and of nations and groups to special privileges, affirms that a "third kind of election is personal election; or the election of individuals to be the children of God."[41] Forlines strongly affirms that the elect "were chosen *individually*. I think Paul makes clear that election is *individual*."[42] In my judgment this is correct, and I agree with Picirilli that "the Arminian doctrine of election" is "personal and individual."[43] This view is more consistent with the overall theology of classical Arminianism and with biblical teaching itself.

Without question, when the Bible speaks of predestination to salvation, it refers to persons and not to an impersonal plan (e.g., Rom. 8:29–30; 1 Pet. 1:1–2). In 2 Thessalonians 2:13 (NASB) Paul says that "God has chosen you," the Christians at Thessalonica, "for salvation." In Romans 16:13 Rufus is called an elect person. Revelation 17:8 implies that specific names have been written in the book of life from the foundation of the world. What can this be but individual predestination? As we shall see below, a distinctive feature of the Arminian view of predestination is that it is based on literal divine foreknowledge (Rom. 8:29; 1 Pet. 1:1–2). True foreknowledge is foreknowledge of *individuals*. One cannot believe in predestination according to foreknowledge and at the same time deny individual predestination. Thus a consistent Arminian theology affirms the predestination of individuals.

Some biblical references to election may indeed be corporate. This is especially the case when the collective group of living, saved individuals are called "the elect" (e.g., Col. 3:12; 2 Tim. 2:10; Titus 1:1). The New Testament church as a group is God's "chosen race" (1 Pet. 2:9), and when one is added to the church he becomes one of "the elect." But this does not mean that predestination to salvation in no way applies to individuals. In fact, the reality of an elect group presupposes individual election. That is, contrary to Shank and Olson, individual or personal election is primary, and corporate election is secondary.

---

40. James Arminius, "Declaration of Sentiments," I.5.iv, in *Writings*, I:248.
41. Richard Watson, *Theological Institutes* (New York: J. & J. Harper, 1830), 337.
42. Forlines, *Quest for Truth*, 400.
43. Picirilli, *Grace*, 48, 51.

The Goal of Predestination

The next question concerns the objective or goal of predestination: *to what specific end* are individuals predestined? How this question is answered constitutes a key difference between Calvinists and Arminians. For Calvinists everything about an individual's salvation is predetermined by God—not just the final gift of eternal life but also the required means by which the gift is received. God chooses from among the mass of unbelievers the ones he wants to save, then he predestines the chosen ones *to become believers* and thereby to receive eternal salvation. The ones he does not choose are predestined to remain in their unbelief and thereby to be eternally lost.

Arminians insist, however, that God predestines only the ends and not the means. He predetermines to give salvation to all believers, but he does not predestine certain unbelievers to become believers and the rest to remain in their unbelief. Those who accept Christ through faith do so of their own free choice. Their choice of Jesus Christ is not predestined. That choice, however, is foreknown; and as a result the choosing ones become the chosen ones, who are then predestined to receive the full blessings of salvation.

Scripture itself says nothing about individuals being predestined to believe. As Watson says, "We have no such doctrine in Scripture as the election of individuals *unto* faith." He adds, "This predestination, then, is not of persons '*unto* faith and obedience,' but of believing and obedient persons *unto* eternal glory."[44] As Forster and Marston put it, predestination "does not concern who should, or should not, *become* Christians, but rather their destiny *as* Christians."[45] They point out that Ephesians 1:4 says God chose us *in* Christ, not *to be put into* Christ.[46]

The same is seen in 2 Thessalonians 2:13, where Paul says that "God has chosen you [Thessalonian believers] from the beginning for salvation through sanctification by the Spirit and faith in the truth." The goal of the election is salvation itself; the means by which the salvation is actualized—sanctification and faith—are themselves not predestined. In 1 Peter 1:1–2 this actualized salvation is seen to include the double cure of grace: a life of good works and justification by the blood of Jesus ("chosen . . . to obey Jesus Christ and be sprinkled with his blood"). Baugh tries to equate this obedience to Christ

---

44. Watson, *Institutes*, 340, 344.
45. Forster and Marston, *God's Strategy*, 101.
46. Ibid., 97.

with faith itself, which would mean that Peter is saying that we are indeed chosen "unto faith" or chosen to become believers.[47] However, there is no good reason to think this obedience is anything other than the Spirit-driven sanctification of 2 Thessalonians 2:13 or the "good works" of Ephesians 2:10 (NASB).

Romans 8:29 states clearly that those whom He foreknew were "predestined to become conformed to the image of His Son, so that He would be the firstborn among many brethren." Some mistakenly take this to be a reference to the sinner's spiritual re-creation in the moral image of Jesus or perhaps to the "coming of age" at which a child is given the status of full sonship (as in Gal. 4:1–7).[48] But the context of Romans 8 shows that this predestined conformity to Christ's image is a reference to our final inheritance, the redeemed and glorified body we will receive at the final resurrection (Rom. 8:11, 23). "The image of His Son" refers to the fact that our resurrection bodies will be like that of Christ (Phil. 3:21; 1 Cor. 15:29; 2 Cor. 3:18). Thus we as believers are chosen to become God's glorified children (Rom. 8:30), with Christ being the "firstborn among many brethren" because he was "the firstborn from the dead" (Col. 1:18; Rev. 1:5), i.e., the first to be raised in a glorified body (Acts 13:34; 26:13; Rom. 6:9; 1 Cor. 15:20).[49]

Predestination to glory is likewise the point of Ephesians 1:5 (NASB), which says, God "predestined us to adoption as sons," as well as the point of Ephesians 1:4 (NASB), which says, "He chose us in him before the foundation of the world, that we would be holy and blameless before him." Both "adoption as sons" and "holy and blameless" refer to our state of future glory (see Col. 1:22).

This, then, is the end or goal of predestination: "our adoption as sons, the redemption of our body" (Rom. 8:23 NASB). "This is the *only predestination* taught in these passages," says Kirk; and trying to make them teach "the predestination of some to be converted, is most hopeless indeed." Rather, we find in them that the believer "is predestinated to stand in the glorified body of the resurrection, and to share the glory of his blessed Lord. This is the doctrine of predestina-

---

47. S. M. Baugh, "The Meaning of Foreknowledge," in *Still Sovereign: Contemporary Perspectives on Election, Foreknowledge, and Grace,* ed. Thomas R. Schreiner and Bruce A. Ware (Grand Rapids: Baker, 2000), 196.
48. For example, see Picirilli, *Grace,* 67; Forlines, *Quest for Truth,* 393–94.
49. See Cottrell, *Romans,* II: 481, 487–488, 502–03. See also Forster and Marston, *God's Strategy,* 102.

tion as taught in the Bible."[50] In other words, God predestines believers to go to heaven, just as he predestines unbelievers to go to hell. But he does not predestine anyone to become and remain a believer or to become and remain an unbeliever. This choice is made by each person, and as foreknown by God it is the factor that conditions the predestination of an individual's eternal destiny.

The Manner of Predestination

We now turn to the *manner* in which God predestines the elect to salvation. How does it happen? Why are certain ones predestined to heaven and the others to hell? Herein lies one of the most pronounced differences between the Calvinist and the Arminian views. The key concepts are that predestination is conditional and that it is based on the foreknowledge of God.

Predestination is conditional. The Calvinist view is summed up in the phrase "unconditional election." This means that God's selection of certain ones for salvation is purely a matter of his sovereign and unconditional good pleasure; there is nothing whatsoever within the ones so chosen that influences God to choose them rather than others. The classical Arminian view says otherwise, affirming that election is conditional because it is based on God's foreknowledge of who will freely meet the conditions designated by God for receiving salvation. Hunt says that unconditional election is "the heart of Calvinism," and Picirilli declares that the view of conditional election "is the Arminian's main point of departure from Calvinism."[51] These judgments may be a bit extreme, but they truly reflect the seriousness of the choice between unconditional and conditional election.

The concept of conditionality applies to both election and predestination, and in this discussion both are included even if at times only one is specifically mentioned. There is indeed a technical difference between them. That is, in *election* God chooses some specific individuals rather than others for salvation; those thus chosen are then *predestined* to receive the blessings of salvation. Both, however, are acts of God, and both are conditional since only those who meet the announced conditions will be chosen and predestined. They are the result of foreknowledge since by nature God foreknows prior to the event of creation who will and who will not meet the conditions.

---

50. John Kirk, *The Cloud Dispelled: or, the Doctrine of Predestination Examined* (New York: N. Tibbals & Co., 1860), 253.

51. Hunt, *What Love Is This?*, 190; Picirilli, *Grace*, 53.

For Calvinists predestination (like every act of God) is not and cannot be conditioned on anything in the creature/sinner. For Arminians, though, God's act of predestination is conditioned upon the freewill choices made by creatures/sinners in response to God's law and God's grace. That is, it is conditioned upon human decisions, first of all the decision to sin against God's law, and then the decision either to accept or reject God's offer of salvation. Those who make the right decisions are chosen by God to be a part of his family and are predestined to eternal life; those who make the wrong decisions are rejected by God and are predestined to eternal damnation.

The reason predestination is conditional is because salvation itself is conditional.[52] Those who accept the reality of significant free will have no difficulty accepting such conditionality; indeed, it is inconsistent for any Arminian to speak of "unconditional grace" or "unconditional salvation." God's saving grace is conditional. He has freely and unconditionally made it available through Jesus Christ, but he will bestow it only upon those who meet certain sovereignly specified, gracious conditions. Likewise, whether God predestines a particular individual to heaven is conditioned upon his foreknowledge of whether that person will meet these conditions. Election is thus conditional.[53]

Predestination is the result of foreknowledge. The second key element in the Arminian concept of the manner of predestination is the role of foreknowledge. God elects and predestines as the result of his precreation foreknowledge of the future freewill choices of all human beings.[54] Of course, in theory, salvation could be *conditional* totally apart from foreknowledge and predestination. Prior to creation God could have specified certain conditions for receiving salvation, planning to save anyone who would ultimately meet those conditions (as in the corporate predestination view). He then could have just waited to see what decisions would be made and then sealed each person's eternal destiny with a *post facto* decree. Then after the entire course

---

52. See Jack Cottrell, *What the Bible Says about God the Redeemer* (Joplin, Mo.: College Press, 1987), 389–99.

53. While predestination to salvation is always conditional, predestination to certain roles of service in God's historical plan of salvation may be either conditional or unconditional.

54. The semantics of the relationship between foreknowledge and predestination is not a crucial issue (contra Geisler, *Chosen but Free*, 52–53, 68). It is acceptable to say that predestination is the result of, is contingent or dependent upon, is based on, or is according to foreknowledge.

of history has been run, the final lists of the saved and the lost could be posted.

But this is not how it has happened. In fact (figuratively speaking) the entire lists of the saved and the lost are already posted and have been since before the world began. Indeed, given the biblical teaching concerning how God's knowledge transcends the flow of time, it could not have been any other way. Foreknowledge is a necessary result of God's infinite nature. Before he created this world, he knew—*fore*knew—every human decision, including those related to each individual's salvation. As a result of this foreknowledge, "from all eternity" he predestined some to heaven and the rest to hell.

Erickson rightly observes that "the role of foreknowledge in the election of persons to salvation" is a basic concept of Arminianism.[55] It is the heart of the classical Arminian view of predestination. Arminius himself declared that God's decree to save and damn certain persons "has its foundation in the foreknowledge of God, by which he knew from all eternity" who would believe and persevere and who would not.[56] As Dave Hunt affirms, God "gives foreknowledge as the reason for predestination. Election/predestination is always explained in the Bible as resulting from God's foreknowledge."[57]

This straightforward view of predestination based on foreknowledge is directly affirmed in two New Testament texts. Romans 8:29 (NASB) says, "For those whom he foreknew, he also predestined to become conformed to the image of His Son." In his first epistle Peter writes to those "who are chosen according to the foreknowledge of God the Father" (1 Pet. 1:1–2 NASB). These verses say only that God foreknew certain *persons*; they do not say specifically *what* he foreknew about them. But in view of the Bible's teaching about the conditional nature of salvation as such, Arminians reasonably infer that what God foreknows is our decision to meet these conditions, especially the condition of faith.[58] As Godet says of Romans 8:29, "In what respect did God thus *foreknow* them? . . . There is but one answer: foreknown as sure to fulfil the condition of salvation, viz. *faith*; so: foreknown as His *by faith*."[59] Forlines agrees: "Based on his

---

55. Erickson, *Christian Theology*, 933.

56. Arminius, "Declaration of Sentiments," I.5.iv, in *Writings*, I:248.

57. Hunt, *What Love Is This?*, 197.

58. We may identify other specified conditions for receiving salvation, but this issue need not be explored here. See Cottrell, *The Faith Once for All: Bible Doctrine for Today* (Joplin, Mo.: College Press, 2002), 346–74.

59. F. L. Godet, *Commentary on the Epistle to the Romans*, trans. A. Cusin and T. W. Chambers (Grand Rapids: Zondervan, 1956 reprint of 1883 edition), 325.

foreknowledge He knows who will believe in Christ and has chosen them in Christ (Eph. 1:4)."[60] The reference to calling and justifying in Romans 8:30 may imply that faith is the object of the foreknowledge on which predestination is based. In the New Testament both calling and justifying are linked to the decision to believe: God's call must be answered by faith, and justification is given only to faith.

One often overlooked object of divine foreknowledge possibly intended by Romans 8:29 is suggested by Romans 8:28 itself, namely, love for God.[61] We must not overlook the connection between these two verses, as if verse 29 exists apart from any context. Verse 29 begins (after the conjunction) with the relative pronoun "whom" (or "those"). The antecedent for this pronoun is in verse 28, namely, "those who love God." God foreknew those who would love him, i.e., he foreknew that at some point in their lives they would come to love him and would continue to love him unto the end. See the parallel in 1 Corinthians 8:3, "But if anyone loves God, he is known by him."[62] This is exactly the same idea as Romans 8:29, the former referring to knowledge and the latter to foreknowledge.

We should also note that Romans 8:29 begins with the causative conjunction *hoti,* "for, because." This most likely goes with "we know" in verse 28. Thus the thought is simple: We know that God works all things for the good of those who love him and are called into his eternal family according to his purpose. How do we know this? Because, having foreknown from eternity that they would love him, he has already predestined them to this state of eternal glory! Thus we can be sure that the temporary trials of this life are not able to nullify what Almighty God himself has already predestined will occur! Rather, he uses them in ways that prepare us to enjoy eternity even more.

Calvinists reject this simple connection between foreknowledge and predestination, of course. At issue, they say, is the meaning of the word *foreknow.* Since *ginosko* means "to know," and *pro* means "before," it would seem obvious that *proginosko* means "to know beforehand" in the sense of prior cognitive awareness. God certainly has such precognition. Because of his unique relation to time, his

---

60. Forlines, *Quest for Truth,* 374.
61. Watson (*Institutes,* 344) highlights the connection between these two verses and says, "Those 'whom he did foreknow,' are manifestly the believers of whom he speaks in the discourse; and who are called in chap. viii.28, 'them that love God.'"
62. Compare John 14:21, "He who loves Me will be loved by My Father, and I will love him."

knowledge is not limited to the now; he knows the past and the future as well as he knows the present.[63] The verb *foreknow* is used in Romans 8:29 and in four other places in the New Testament: Acts 26:5; Romans 11:2; 1 Peter 1:20; 2 Peter 3:17. (The noun is used twice: Acts 2:23; 1 Pet. 1:2.) Everyone agrees that in Acts 26:5 and 2 Peter 3:17, where it refers to human foreknowledge, it has this simple meaning of precognition or prescience.

But Calvinists argue that in the texts where God is the subject, both the verb and the noun have connotations that are altogether different from prescience. The basic nuance, they say, is that of love and affection: "whom he foreloved."[64] As Murray explains, since the word *know* itself at times is "practically synonymous with 'love,' to set regard upon, to know with peculiar interest, delight, affection, and action," foreknowledge in Romans 8:29 (and 1 Pet. 1:1–2) must mean "whom he knew from eternity with distinguishing affection and delight," or "whom he foreloved."[65]

Another connotation Calvinists include in *proginosko* in the context of predestination is the idea of selecting or choosing. As noted above, Murray calls it God's "distinguishing affection." The Greek word, he says, "is not the foresight of difference but the foreknowledge that makes difference exist. . . . It is sovereign distinguishing love."[66]

The key word here is *distinguishing*. For Calvinists God's foreknowledge is the act by which he (unconditionally) makes distinctions among people, *choosing* some out of the mass of future mankind to be the sole recipients of his saving grace. Foreknowledge is the same as election. As Moo sums it up, "The difference between 'know or love beforehand' and 'choose beforehand' virtually ceases to exist."[67] For Romans 8:29 one Greek lexicon defines *proginosko* as "choose beforehand."[68] Erickson agrees that "foreknowledge as used in Romans 8:29 carries with it the idea of favorable disposition or selection as well

63. See Cottrell, *What the Bible Says about God the Creator* (Joplin, Mo.: College Press, 1983), 255–59, 279–89.

64. See Baugh, "The Meaning of Foreknowledge," 191–95. He suggests that *proginosko* in Romans 8:29 may be translated, "Those to whom he was previously devoted" (194).

65. John Murray, *The Epistle to the Romans*, vol. 2 (Grand Rapids: Eerdmans, 1965), 317.

66. Ibid., 318.

67. Douglas J. Moo, *The Epistle to the Romans* (Grand Rapids: Eerdmans, 1996), 533.

68. William F. Arndt and F. Wilbur Gingrich, *A Greek-English Lexicon of the New Testament and Other Early Christian Literature*, 3rd ed., revised and edited by Frederick William Danker (Chicago: University of Chicago Press, 2000), 866.

as advance knowledge."[69] It has the "connotation of electing grace," says F. F. Bruce.[70] It can mean "He chose," says Baugh,[71] or "whom he chose beforehand," says Jewett.[72]

As many Calvinists see it, then, in the final analysis God's fore-knowledge is actually equivalent to predestination itself. As Jewett says, "We are elect according to the *fore*knowledge (*fore*ordination) of God the Father."[73] Baugh approves of translating *proginosko* [*pro-egno*] as "he predestinated."[74]

What evidence do Calvinists give for this peculiar definition of foreknowledge? They refer mainly to a few selected biblical uses of the verbs for "to know," in which they attempt to find the connotations of "choose" and/or "love." These include the places where "know" is a euphemism for sexual intercourse, plus a few other Old Testament uses of *yada* (Hebrew for "know"), usually Genesis 18:19; Exodus 2:25; Jeremiah 1:5; Hosea 13:5; and Amos 3:2. Also cited are these New Testament texts: Matthew 7:23; John 10:14; 1 Corinthians 8:3; 13:12; Galatians 4:9; and 2 Timothy 2:19. Since "know" in all these passages allegedly means much more than simple cognition, they conclude that "*fore*know" in Romans 8:29 and elsewhere also means much more, namely, "distinguishing love bestowed beforehand." Thus, "whom he *chose* beforehand, he also predestined."

How may we respond to this? Primarily, by a thorough analysis of how the Bible uses the words for "know" and "foreknow." Such an analysis may be summarized as follows. First, noncognitive connotations for *ginosko* are virtually nonexistent in secular Greek. Moo admits that the Calvinist definition of foreknowledge sounds "somewhat strange against the background of broad Greek usage."[75]

Second, the use of "know" as a euphemism for sexual relations contributes nothing toward this Calvinist view since it refers specifically to the sexual act and not to any love that might be associated with it. Also, the act of sexual "knowing" in no way includes the connotation of choosing but rather presupposes that a distinguishing choice has already been made (via marriage). Finally, the use of "know" for

---

69. Erickson, *Christian Theology*, 383.
70. F. F. Bruce, *The Epistle of Paul to the Romans* (Grand Rapids: Eerdmans, 1963), 177.
71. Baugh, "The Meaning of Foreknowledge," 191.
72. Jewett, *Election and Predestination*, 38, 70.
73. Ibid., 109.
74. Baugh, "The Meaning of Foreknowledge," 191.
75. Moo, *Romans*, 532.

this act is much closer to cognition than either loving or choosing; it connotes cognitive knowing at the most intimate level.

Third, biblical texts where "know" and "foreknow" seem to have a connotation of love or affection (e.g., Exod. 2:25; Hos. 13:5) prove nothing because they usually do not specify the *reason* for God's love knowledge, and they certainly do not suggest that it was unconditional. In fact, 1 Corinthians 8:3 (NASB) seems to say it is conditional: "The man who loves God is known by God."

Fourth, an analysis of the New Testament texts where the words for "know" have persons as their objects, i.e., where the action of knowing is specifically directed toward persons and not facts as such, shows that in such cases these words never have the connotation of "choosing" or "imposing a distinction." This applies to *ginosko* (used about fifty-two times in this way), *epiginosko* (about fifteen times), and *oida* (about forty-three times).

Such an analysis yields helpful insights into the meaning of God's foreknowledge. In order of increasing specificity, the three basic connotations of "know a person" are as follows.

Recognition. In this case "to know" means to recognize someone, to know who he is, to know his identity or his true identity, to be able to identify him for who he is, to be acquainted with him, to be familiar with him, to understand him, to know his true nature. This is by far the most common connotation.[76] It is a purely cognitive act. It does not impose an identity upon someone but perceives that identity. This includes the idea of recognizing someone as belonging to a particular group as distinct from those who do not. This is the sense in which Jesus "knows" his sheep (John 10:14, 27), even as his sheep know him (John 10:14; see 2 Tim. 2:19). This is the connotation of "know" that applies to "foreknow" in Romans 8:29 and 1 Peter 1:1–2.

Acknowledgment. Here "to know" means not only to have a cognitive knowledge of someone's identity but also to acknowledge that identity. As such it is an act of will, though it presupposes an act of cognition. The most important thing is that this acknowledging does not impose a particular identity upon anyone but simply confesses it. See Mark 1:24, 34; Acts 19:15; 1 Corinthians 1:21; 16:12; 1 Thessalonians 5:12.

---

76. "Know" with a person or persons as its object occurs in this sense at least eighty times. A few examples are Matthew 11:27; 14:30; 17:12; 26:72, 74; Luke 7:39; 10:22; 13:25, 27; 24:16, 31; John 1:10, 26, 31, 33, 48; 7:27–28; 14:7, 9, 17; Acts 7:18; Romans 1:21; 1 Corinthians 13:12; Hebrews 10:30; 1 John 4:2, 6.

Experience. The third and most intense connotation of "to know" when a person or persons are its object is to know experientially, to experience a relationship with someone. Again, it presupposes cognition but goes beyond it. Most significantly, such knowing is not an act that initiates a relationship but simply experiences it. This connotation is found especially in 1 John.[77] Matthew 7:23; 1 Corinthians 8:3; and Hebrews 8:11 could be either (1) or (3).

In each case the act of knowing does not create a person's identity or his distinction from other people. It rather presupposes an already existing identity or distinction; the act of knowing perceives and in some cases acknowledges that identity or distinction. These connotations for knowing fit the term *foreknowledge* well as it is used in Romans 8:29 and elsewhere. Those whom God from the beginning recognized and acknowledged as his own, he predestined to be members of his glorified family in heaven. (The connotation of experiencing a relationship does not transfer well to the concept of *fore*knowledge since foreknowledge as such precedes the existence of its object, precluding an experienced relationship.)

In any case, an analysis of all the uses of "know" with persons as the object undermines the notion that it means "predestine" or "choose," and thus fails to support the Calvinist idea that foreknowledge is the same as election or choosing beforehand. Olson is adamant about this: "It is my proposition that a lexical study of the uses of *yada, ginoskein,* and *proginoskein* uncovers not the slightest scintilla of hard evidence that there is such a selective connotation."[78] Forster and Marston concur, declaring that they have found no biblical text where "the sense intended by the writer would not be radically changed by putting 'chosen' instead of *yada* or *ginosko.*"[79] Olson rightly notes that if foreknowledge is basically the same as predestination, then Paul's use of both terms in Romans 8:29 makes no sense: "Thus any definition of *proginoskein* which would make it in any way synonymous with *proorizein* would absolutely destroy the logic of Paul's (and the Spirit's) sequence. This would reduce it to a mere redundancy and totally undo the symmetry of the development. I believe this is the final refutation of any pregnant connotation for *proginoskein.*"[80]

---

77. Examples are John 17:3; Philippians 3:10; 2 Timothy 1:12; Titus 1:16; 1 John 2:3–4, 13–14.
78. Olson, *Beyond Calvinism and Arminianism,* 464 (see 464–70).
79. Forster and Marston, *God's Strategy,* 190.
80. Olson, *Beyond Calvinism and Arminianism,* 170. See similar arguments in Miley, *Systematic Theology,* 2:261; and Hunt, *What Love Is This?,* 226.

The fifth conclusion from our analysis is that the various New Testament uses of "foreknow" and the two uses of "foreknowledge" do not comfortably bear the connotations of "forelove" and "choose beforehand." Acts 26:5 and 2 Peter 3:17 do not refer to God's foreknowledge, but they clearly refer to precognition. Romans 11:2 refers to God's foreknowledge of Israel as a nation and not to any individuals within it and not even to the saved remnant within the ethnic nation as a whole. The context suggests that God's precognition of Israel included a foreknowledge of their persistent rebellion and idolatry, as well as a foreknowledge that a remnant would remain faithful. Because he foreknew there would always be an abiding remnant identified as the true spiritual Israel (Rom. 9:6), he did not abandon his ethnic people, even though he foreknew most of them would never respond to his offer of grace (Rom. 10:21).

The cognitive connotation of *proginosko* is found also in other New Testament texts using the term. In 1 Peter 1:20 Christ is the one foreknown from the foundation of the world; and in the context precognition, not choosing, is the preferred meaning. The contrast is between the hidden and the revealed. Even though the Father knew from the foundation of the world that Christ the Son would be our Redeemer, he did not reveal it until the last days.

The use of the noun *foreknowledge* in 1 Peter 1:1–2 is consistent with the non-Calvinist understanding of "foreknow." This text speaks of those who are *chosen* according to *foreknowledge*. Thus a clear distinction is made between foreknowledge and choosing, and there is no reason to see in foreknowledge anything other than its basic meaning of precognition. Thus the relationship between foreknowledge and election here is exactly the same as that between foreknowledge and predestination in Romans 8:29.

Acts 2:23 also refers to the foreknowledge of God the Father; its object is Jesus Christ and the circumstances of his death. Jesus was delivered up "by the predetermined plan and foreknowledge of God." "Predetermined plan" is equivalent to predestination. God had already determined from eternity that Christ would die for our sins. That he was delivered up "by foreknowledge" means that God foreknew all the human acts of participation in Christ's betrayal and death, such as those of Judas and Herod. God did not predetermine these acts, but he knew them in advance and therefore could work his plan along with them and through them.

Sometimes Calvinist exegetes try to equate the foreknowledge and predetermined plan in Acts 2:23 by invoking a rule of Greek grammar. Here is how MacArthur[81] argues: "According to what Greek scholars refer to as Granville Sharp's rule, if two nouns of the same case (in this instance, "plan" and "foreknowledge") are connected by *kai* ("and") and have the definite article (the) before the first noun but not before the second, the nouns refer to the same thing. . . . In other words, Peter equates God's predetermined plan, or foreordination, and His foreknowledge." Wuest[82] puts it almost exactly the same way, that in such a case the second noun "refers to the same thing" as the first; therefore Acts 2:23 shows that predestination and foreknowledge "refer to the same thing."

This argument, however, is seriously flawed. Both MacArthur and Wuest misquote Sharp's rule. The rule does not say that the two nouns in the construction described above "refer to the same thing." It says only that in such a case the second noun "always relates to the same person that is expressed or described in the first noun." There is a huge difference between *relating* to the same person (or thing) and *referring* to the same person (or thing). Carson says it is an exegetical fallacy to assume that the latter or strict form of Sharp's rule has universal validity. He says, "If one article governs two substantives joined by *kai,* it does not necessarily follow that the two substantives refer to the same thing, but only that the two substantives are grouped together to function in some respects as a single entity."[83] Also, Sharp states his rule as applying only to persons, not to things. As one Greek scholar says, "Non-personal nouns disqualify the construction"; he cites Acts 2:23 as a specific example of this.[84]

The preponderance of evidence thus shows that "foreknowledge" is not equivalent to election or choosing and that in Romans 8:29 and 1 Peter 1:1–2 it refers to nothing more than the cognitive act by which God knew or identified the members of his family (as distinct from all others) even before the foundation of the world. He identified them by the fact that they were (would be) the ones who met (would meet) the required conditions for salvation. Knowing through his divine omniscience who these individuals would be, even at that

---

81. John MacArthur, *Romans,* vol. 1 (Chicago: Moody, 1991), 496.

82. Kenneth S. Wuest, *Romans in the Greek New Testament for the English Reader* (Grand Rapids: Eerdmans, 1955), 143–44.

83. D. A. Carson, *Exegetical Fallacies* (Grand Rapids: Baker, 1984), 84–85.

84. Richard Young, *Intermediate New Testament Greek: A Linguistic and Exegetical Approach* (Nashville: Broadman & Holman, 1994), 62.

point he predestined them to be part of his glorified heavenly family through resurrection from the dead after the pattern established by the firstborn brother, Jesus Christ.

Though a biblical basis is lacking for it, attaching an element of affection to the concept of foreknowledge[85] is not destructive to the Arminian view, as long as these cautions are observed: (1) the element of affection must never be equated with choosing or foreordaining,[86] and (2) the primary meaning of *proginosko* must always be understood to be *prescience* or *cognitive knowing*. Hunt is probably right: "To foreknow is simply to know in advance and can't legitimately be turned into anything else."[87] But if one wants to think, as Picirilli does, that in the Bible foreknowledge "is, at least some of the time, something more than mere prescience"—such as "previously loved and affectionately regarded as his own"[88]—he must remember that such "foreloving" is secondary to and actually the *result* of foreknowledge as prescience, which is the primary and only solidly grounded meaning of the word. The bottom line is found in this statement: "Predestination to eternal life is plainly conditioned upon the foreknowledge of God. . . . What ever else 'foreknow' may mean, it means foreknow."[89]

In summary, the Bible teaches that God predestines or chooses by name certain individuals to eternal salvation, but he does so only on the basis of his foreknowledge or precognition that these individuals will meet the conditions for salvation as set forth in his Word.[90]

History of the Arminian View

The classical Arminian view of predestination, in essence, says that the omniscient God foreknew all who would of their own free choice trust in his saving grace; and on the basis of that foreknowledge, he

---

85. As in Forlines's "affectionate foreknowing" (*Quest for Truth*, 399).

86. Contra Erickson's interchangeable use of "favorable disposition or selection," (*Christian Theology*, 383).

87. Hunt, *What Love Is This?*, 226.

88. Picirilli, *Grace*, 56, 78.

89. E. H. Johnson and H. G. Weston, *An Outline of Systematic Theology*, 2nd ed. (Philadelphia: American Baptist Publication Society, 1895), 247.

90. As suggested earlier, a right understanding of the relationship between foreknowledge and predestination completely rules out the concept of corporate election as the only or even primary form of predestination. Shank's virtual dismissal of foreknowledge as a factor in predestination, in his effort to defend corporate election, seems based on an unfortunate confusion between foreknowledge-based election and unconditional election. See Shank, *Election in the Son*, 153–55.

predestined them to eternal life. He likewise foreknew all who would not trust him for salvation and justly predestined them to eternal condemnation. Though this is called "the Arminian view," it has actually been present in Christian thought almost from the beginning.

Philip Schaff observes that up until Augustine, all the Greek fathers "had only taught a conditional predestination, which they made dependent on the foreknowledge of the free acts of men."[91] Some second-century fathers acknowledged God's foreknowledge,[92] with "The Shepherd of Hermas" relating it to predestination in a general way. In explaining why all do not repent, he says that to those whose hearts God "saw were about to become pure, and who were about to serve him with all their heart, he gave repentance; but to those whose deceit and wickedness he saw, who were about to repent hypocritically, he did not give repentance."[93] At about the same time Justin Martyr speaks of the end times as the time when "the number of those who are foreknown by him as good and virtuous is complete."[94] Equating Scripture with the mind of God, Justin says, "But if the word of God foretells that some angels and men shall be certainly punished, it did so because it foreknew that they would be unchangeably [wicked], but not because God had created them so."[95]

In the third century Origen strongly defends God's foreknowledge in reference to predictive prophecy, saying that it does not affect free will since it is not causative and implies only the simple futurity of an event, not its necessity.[96] He says that Romans 8:29 shows "that those whom God foreknew would become the kind to conform themselves to Christ by their sufferings, he even predestined them to be conformed and similar to his image and glory. Therefore there precedes a foreknowledge of them, through which is known what ef-

---

91. Philip Schaff, *History of the Christian Church*, vol. III, *Nicene and Post-Nicene Christianity* (Grand Rapids: Eerdmans, 1960), 852.

92. See "An Ancient Christian Sermon Commonly Known as Second Clement," 9:9, in *The Apostolic Fathers*, 2nd edition, trans. J. B. Lightfoot and J. R. Harmer, ed. and rev. Michael W. Holmes (Grand Rapids: Baker, 1989), 72: "For he is the one who knows everything beforehand." The same language is found in "The Shepherd of Hermas," Mandate 4.3.4 (*The Apostolic Fathers*, 219).

93. "The Shepherd of Hermas," Similitude 8.6.2 (*The Apostolic Fathers*, 257).

94. Justin Martyr, "First Apology," 45, in *The Ante-Nicene Fathers*, vol. I, *The Apostolic Fathers, Justin Martyr, and Irenaeus*, ed. Alexander Roberts and James Donaldson (New York: Charles Scribner's Sons, 1913), 178.

95. Justin Martyr, "Dialogue with Trypho," 141 (*The Ante-Nicene Fathers*, I:270).

96. Origen, "Against Celsus," II.xx, in *The Ante-Nicene Fathers*, vol. IV, *Fathers of the Third Century*, ed. Alexander Roberts and James Donaldson (New York: Charles Scribner's Sons, 1913), 440.

fort and virtue they will possess in themselves, and thus predestination follows, yet foreknowledge should not be considered the cause of predestination."[97]

Fourth-century writers affirming this view include Ambrosiaster, who says, "Those who are called according to the promise are those whom God knew would believe in the future."[98] Concerning Jacob and Esau in Romans 9:11 Ambrosiaster says, "Therefore, knowing what each of them would become, God said: *The younger will be worthy and the elder unworthy.* In his foreknowledge he chose the one and rejected the other."[99] Also, "Those whom God foreknew would believe in him he chose to receive the promises."[100] Another fourth-century writer, Diodore of Tarsus, says that God does not show mercy to one and harden another "by accident, for it was according to the power of his foreknowledge that he gave to each one his due."[101]

As Harry Buis notes,[102] even Augustine in his earlier writing shares this thinking before he arrived at what would become known as the Calvinist view. Pelagius and his disciples continue to emphasize the predestination-by-foreknowledge view. Pelagius says, "Those whom God knew in advance would believe, he called."[103] He says Romans 9:15 means, "I will have mercy on him whom I have foreknown will be able to deserve compassion."[104] In the years following the rift between Augustine and Pelagius, the semi-Pelagians rejected Augustine's new deterministic view of predestination and continued to emphasize "a predestination to salvation conditioned on the foreknowledge of faith."[105] For example, John Cassian taught that "God's predestination must be in the light of what He foresees is going to be the quality of our behaviour," as Kelly summarizes it.[106] Commenting on Romans 8:29–30, Theodoret of Cyrrhus (d. 466) says, "God

---

97. Origen, *Commentary on the Epistle to the Romans, Books 1–5*, trans. Thomas P. Scheck, vol. 103, *The Fathers of the Church* (Washington, D.C.: Catholic University of America, 2001), 65–66.

98. Ambrosiaster, *Commentary on Paul's Epistles*, cited in *Ancient Christian Commentary on Scripture, New Testament*, vol. IV, *Romans*, ed. Gerald Bray (Downers Grove: InterVarsity, 1998), 233.

99. Ibid., 250.

100. Ibid., 235.

101. Diodore, *Pauline Commentary from the Greek Church*, in Bray, *Romans*, 261.

102. Harry Buis, *Historic Protestantism and Predestination* (Philadelphia: Presbyterian and Reformed, 1958), 9.

103. Pelagius, *Pelagius's Commentary on Romans*, in Bray, *Romans*, 237.

104. Ibid., 255.

105. Schaff, *History*, III:858.

106. J. N. D. Kelly, *Early Christian Doctrines*, 2nd ed. (New York: Harper and Row, 1960), 371.

did not simply predestine; he predestined those whom he foreknew," i.e., "Those whose intention God foreknew he predestined from the beginning."[107]

Throughout the Middle Ages this view was held alongside the Augustinian view; it "reappears again and again," as Buis notes, for example in Duns Scotus, and in William of Occam and the Occamists.[108] Though the major Reformers sided with Augustine, most of those identified with the Radical Reformation either abandoned or revised that view and taught the restoration of free will through universal prevenient grace.[109]

Though the classical Arminian view of predestination obviously did not begin with Arminius, it is clear that he held to this view. He sums up his doctrine of predestination thus, that from eternity

God decreed to save and damn certain particular persons. This decree has its foundation in the foreknowledge of God, by which he knew from all eternity those individuals who *would,* through his preventing grace, *believe,* and through his subsequent grace *would persevere,* according to the before described administration of those means which are suitable and proper for conversion and faith; and by which foreknowledge, he likewise knew those who *would not believe and persevere.*[110]

"*This doctrine of Predestination,*" he says, "*has always been approved by the great majority of professing Christians,* and even now . . . it enjoys the same extensive patronage."[111]

Concerning God's foreknowledge Arminius is quick to admit that he does "not understand the mode in which He knows future contingencies, and especially those which belong to the free-will of creatures."[112] But God does have such foreknowledge, in its true sense of prescience. Some of his decrees are occasioned by "the foreseen free act of rational creatures," e.g., the decree to send Christ into the world "depends on the foresight of the fall."[113] Likewise "God by his own prescience, knows who, of his grace, will believe, and who, of their own fault, will remain in unbelief."[114] Just as God predetermines

---

107. Theodoret of Cyrrhus, *Interpretation of the Letter to the Romans,* in Bray, *Romans,* 236–37.

108. Buis, *Historic Protestantism,* 16, 21, 29.

109. Williams, *Radical Reformation,* 839–40.

110. Arminius, "Declaration of Sentiments," I.5.iv, in *Writings,* I:248.

111. Ibid., I:250.

112. Arminius, "A Friendly Discussion between James Arminius and Francis Junius, Concerning Predestination," in *Writings,* III:66.

113. Arminius, "An Examination of the Treatise of William Perkins," in *Writings,* III:283.

114. Ibid., III:479.

to punish some because of "the foresight of future sin,"[115] so does he predestine to salvation those who are foreseen to believe, according to these three assertions: "(1) 'Faith is not an effect of election.' (2) 'Faith is a necessary requisite in those who are to be elected or saved.' (3) 'This requisite is foreseen by God in the persons to be elected.'"[116]

The bottom line, as Bangs says,[117] is that "Arminius has reversed the relationship of foreknowledge to predestination" that was characteristic of the Augustinian view which he learned from the main Protestant Reformers and has returned to the view of the ancient church fathers.

Arminius and his followers had considerable influence. This was especially the case in England where the Arminian doctrine ultimately affected the beliefs and teachings of John Wesley.[118] In a sermon on predestination based on Romans 8:29–30 Wesley asserts that "God *foreknew* those in every nation who would believe, from the beginning of the world to the consummation of all things." For God it is not a literal foreknowledge, since all things are present before him in an eternal now; but from our perspective it is a true foreknowledge. "In a word, God, looking on all ages, from the creation to the consummation, as a moment, and seeing at once whatever is in the hearts of all the children of men, knows every one that does or does not believe, in every age or nation. Yet what he knows, whether faith or unbelief, is in no wise caused by his knowledge. Men are as free in believing or not believing as if he did not know it at all."[119] The next step after foreknowledge is predestination. "In other words, God decrees, from everlasting to everlasting, that all who believe in the Son of his love, shall be conformed to his image."[120] Wesley says, "As all that are called were predestinated, so all whom God has predestinated he foreknew. He knew, he saw them as believers, and as such predestined them to salvation, according to his eternal decree, 'He that believeth shall be saved.'. . . Who are predestinated? None but those whom God foreknew as believers."[121]

Wesley specifically explains Romans 8:29 thus: "'For whom he did foreknow' *as believing,* 'he also did predestinate to be conformed

---

115. Arminius, "A Friendly Discussion," in *Writings*, III:147.
116. Arminius, "The Apology or Defence," IV.i, in *Writings*, I:285.
117. Bangs, *Arminius*, 352.
118. See Buis, *Historic Protestantism*, 89–98.
119. John Wesley, "Sermon LVIII, On Predestination," in *The Works of John Wesley*, 10 vols. (Grand Rapids: Zondervan, n.d.), VI:226–27; see VI:230.
120. Ibid., VI:227.
121. Ibid., VI:229.

to the image of his Son.'"[122] This aptly sums up the view of most Arminians today, whether they be Wesleyan or non-Wesleyan in their general theology.

Thus it is clear that the view of predestination known today as classical Arminianism has a long and consistent history.

Theological Presuppositions of the Classical Arminian View of Predestination

The classical Arminian view of predestination does not exist in a vacuum; it is one element of a consistent doctrinal system. The purpose of this section is to summarize the theological presuppositions that constitute the general framework for it. That is, the classical Arminian view of predestination presupposes a certain interpretation of the following concepts.

God's Will or Purpose

Calvinism's view of God's will or purpose is set forth in its doctrine of the eternal, efficacious, comprehensive, and unconditional decree. Arminians also believe that God has an eternal decree, but they usually speak of it as his eternal purpose. More importantly, Arminians do not believe that this eternal purpose is comprehensively efficacious and unconditional.

Scripture certainly teaches that God has a purposive will by which he decrees that certain things will absolutely occur. This efficacious purpose is represented by the Greek terms *boule* (Acts 2:23; 4:28; 13:36; Eph. 1:11; 6:17), *boulomai* (1 Cor. 12:11; James 1:18), *thelema* (Matt. 26:42; John 6:40; Eph. 1:5, 9, 11; Rev. 4:11), *thelo* (Rom. 9:18), *prothesis* (Rom. 8:28; 9:11; Eph. 1:11; 3:11), and *protithemi* (Eph. 1:9).

Contrary to Calvinism, however, the Bible itself clearly shows that God's purposive (efficacious) will does not include all things. It is not comprehensive; it does not include "whatsoever comes to pass." This is seen in the fact that sometimes the above words that speak of God's determinative purpose are used to represent God's *desire* for certain things to happen which in fact do not happen. Jesus wanted the inhabitants of Jerusalem to come to him, but they refused (Matt. 23:37). God desires all men to be saved and to come to know the truth

---

122. John Wesley, "Predestination Calmly Considered," 25, in *Works*, X:218. Italics added.

(1 Tim. 2:4), but this does not happen. The same words at times refer to contingencies that occur *contrary* to God's own desire and will. Some little children will be lost, even though it is not the Father's will (Matt. 18:14). Though it is contrary to God's purpose, some will never repent and therefore will perish (2 Pet. 3:9).

The most fundamental aspect of God's purposive will is that he has certain *general* purposes which he will infallibly accomplish through his sovereign power. For example, it is God's eternal purpose to glorify himself, to share his goodness with other personal beings, and to provide salvation for sinners. Then, in order to accomplish these general purposes, God has also determined to cause whatever *specific means* are necessary to bring them about. In order to manifest his glory, God determined to create all things (Rev. 4:11); in order to share his goodness, he created personal, freewill beings who are able to honor him and give him thanks (Rom. 1:21).

Having foreknown the entrance of sin into his creation, in order to provide salvation for sinners God determined to become incarnate as Jesus of Nazareth and to die for the sins of mankind (Acts 2:23; 4:27–28; Eph. 1:4–10; 1 Pet. 1:20; Rev. 13:8). In order to accomplish his purpose through Jesus of Nazareth, God determined to use a specific nation (Israel) to prepare the way for his coming. Much of the biblical teaching about God's purposive will refers to his creation and use of Israel as a nation (Deut. 7:6–8), his use of other nations related to Israel (Isa. 14:24–27; 37:26; 46:9–11), and his election and use of individuals within and related to Israel (e.g., Abraham, David, Cyrus, Pharaoh; see Rom. 9:7–18). Once his purpose for Israel and his initial redemptive purpose for Jesus had been accomplished, it was God's eternal plan, through the preparatory work of chosen apostles (John 15:16; Gal. 1:15), to bring the church into existence by combining believing Jews and believing Gentiles together into his new "chosen people" (Rom. 11:17–24; Eph. 3:1–11). It was then his predetermined plan to use the church as the locus of salvation and the means of evangelism until the end of the age (Eph. 1:10).

In all of these matters God's will or purpose is efficacious, causative, or determinative. Since the divine determination to bring them about occurred prior to creation, God's purposive will is in essence equivalent to predestination. The main difference between the Arminian's purposive will and the Calvinist's eternal decree is that the latter is comprehensive while the former is not.

The Nature of Created Reality

The main reason Arminians do not see God's purposive will as comprehensive is because they have a certain view of the nature of created reality. By God's own sovereign decision, the kind of world he chose to create is able to operate and progress in such a way that God does not need to be the direct cause of all things. In fact, most specific things that happen in the world are not caused by God.

God could surely create many different kinds of reality, but in our case he did in fact choose to create a world endowed with *relative independence*.[123] Our world includes two major forces with their own relatively independent power to initiate events, i.e., two *causal* forces besides God himself: natural law and free will. The existence of these causal forces is a part of God's own purposive decree.

Especially important is the existence of beings who possess a significantly free will. This kind of free will (which is the only kind that is genuinely free) is sometimes called the power of opposite choice. As Geisler says, "At a minimum, freedom means the power of contrary choice; that is, an agent is free only if he could have done otherwise."[124] Also, a will is significantly free only if the choices it makes are not caused or determined, either directly or indirectly, by an outside force. Thus we can say that truly free will is the ability to choose between opposites without that choice's being fixed or determined by some power outside the person's own will. This applies especially to the sinner's ability either to believe or to reject the gospel. As Forlines says, "In Arminianism there is agreement that human beings have freedom of choice. This includes the freedom to place their faith in Christ upon hearing the gospel, or conversely they can refuse to place their faith in Christ."[125]

Calvinists and other determinists usually are reluctant to abandon the concept of free will altogether; but if they retain it, they usually redefine it so that it is compatible with the comprehensive, efficacious decree. According to such compatibilism, the will is considered to be free because its decisions are directly determined by one's own inner motives and desires. That is, one is conscious of choosing to do whatever he wants to do. The reason this is not truly free will, though, is that (according to compatibilism) God implants within us the specific motives and desires that will inevitably cause us to make

123. See Cottrell, *What the Bible Says about God the Ruler* (Joplin, Mo.: College Press, 1984), 105–11, 191–95; Cottrell, *The Faith Once for All,* 115.
124. Geisler, *Chosen but Free,* 44.
125. Forlines, *Quest for Truth,* 322.

only the choices that God has determined we shall make. Nevertheless in this view the will is still called "free" since it is *not conscious* of being caused or compelled to make those choices. The person is only doing what he wants to do, says Feinberg, even though he "could not have done otherwise, given the prevailing causal influences." Therefore this is "a genuine sense of free human action, even though such action is causally determined."[126]

Arminians rightly reject this as a counterfeit or spurious concept of free will. The psychological feeling of freedom cannot replace the true inward ability to make a genuine choice between opposites.

At the same time Arminians rightly reject all Calvinist caricatures of truly free will, such as the so-called "liberty of indifference" according to which all choices are seen as arbitrary, unpredictable, capricious, and random.[127] An example is Erickson's description of Arminian free will as "total spontaneity, random choice."[128] This is hardly a responsible characterization. The ability of the will to choose between opposites does not require equal influence toward both sides; sometimes the will opts for a certain choice against overwhelming influences in the opposite direction (see Amos 4:6–11; Hag. 1:1–11).

The reality of truly free will is a key ingredient in the Arminian system and a necessary presupposition of the Arminian view of predestination. Such free will is inconsistent with the concept of a comprehensively efficacious decree or an all-inclusive purposive will of God. In fact, a world that contains forces with the built-in ability to independently initiate ("create") events makes it necessary to speak of "the will of God" in two other senses besides his purposive will.[129] One is God's *permissive* will, according to which God simply allows to happen most physical events produced by natural law and most decisions produced by freewill beings. He may of course decide to *prevent* any planned or projected event from happening (James 4:15), which would be an instance of his purposive will. God's purposive and permissive wills together are comprehensive (though only the former is efficacious), encompassing "whatsoever comes to pass." We must not allow these two kinds of divine will to overlap, however—a Calvinist error that results in the loss of genuine permission.[130]

126. John S. Feinberg, "God Ordains All Things," in *Predestination and Free Will*, ed. David Basinger and Randall Basinger (Downers Grove: InterVarsity, 1986), 21, 24.
127. See Cottrell, *God the Ruler*, 193.
128. Erickson, *Christian Theology*, 386.
129. See Cottrell, *God the Ruler*, ch. 8, "The Will of God," 299–329.
130. See Cottrell, "The Nature of the Divine Sovereignty," in *The Grace of God, the Will of Man*, ed. Clark H. Pinnock (Grand Rapids: Zondervan, 1989), 105–6.

The third sense in which we may speak of "the will of God" has to do not with actual events but with potential events. These are the choices and actions that God wills or desires for his freewill creatures but which can be rejected or left undone by them. This is sometimes called God's *preceptive* will because it includes God's precepts or commands which we will either obey or disobey (e.g., Matt. 7:21; 12:50; Rom. 2:18; 1 John 2:17). This aspect of God's will also includes God's *desires* for us, especially his desire that no one should be lost but that all should be saved (e.g., Matt. 18:14; 1 Tim. 2:4; 2 Pet. 3:9). God's will in this sense is not always realized (Matt. 23:37; Luke 7:30). Thus this aspect of God's will is not efficacious; our conformity with it is the choice of our free wills. This is simply the nature of the reality God himself freely chose to make.

God's Sovereignty in Dealing with Creation

How one understands the sovereignty of God directly relates to his view of predestination. If one begins with a concept of sovereignty that requires God to be the ultimate cause of all things and does not allow anything about God to be conditioned by anything outside of God, he cannot avoid the Calvinist concept of unconditional predestination. Arminianism, however, rejects such a concept of sovereignty as arbitrary and unbiblical. For Arminians the key words for divine sovereignty are *control*, not causation; and *conditionality*, not unconditionality.

God could have created a universe in which he would be the sole cause of all events, but he chose instead to create freewill beings who themselves have the power to choose and initiate events. As a result God is *not* the sole cause of whatsoever comes to pass in this universe. As Picirilli notes, "Man is therefore an *actor* in the universe."[131] This in no way contradicts God's sovereignty because he freely and sovereignly chose to make this kind of world. This is not a limitation imposed upon God from outside himself; it is a freely chosen self-limitation, an *expression* of his sovereignty.[132]

But how can God maintain his sovereignty in such a universe if he himself does not cause everything? The answer is in the word *control:* through his infinite power and knowledge God maintains complete control over everything that happens. The word *control* should not be equated here with causation as if God were operating a univer-

---

131. Picirilli, *Grace,* 42.
132. See Cottrell, *God the Ruler,* 187–90.

sal control panel that manipulates and micromanages every event. Rather, God controls all things in the sense that he is "in complete control of" every situation: he monitors, supervises, plans, permits, intervenes, and prevents as he pleases through his infinite knowledge and power.

God exercises his sovereign control especially through his permissive will, which presupposes divine foreknowledge of future free-will choices. Such foreknowledge gives God the genuine option of either permitting or preventing men's planned choices, and prevention is the ultimate control. James 4:13–15 chastises the man who blithely says, "Today or tomorrow we will go to such and such a city, and spend a year there and engage in business and make a profit." But wait a minute, says James, you are not taking account of God's sovereignty. "Instead, you ought to say, 'If the Lord wills, we will live and also do this or that'" (NASB). In other words, it is not wrong to have plans, but we should always acknowledge God's power to veto them (as in Luke 12:19–20). This is the significance of Proverbs 19:21, "Many plans are in a man's heart, but the counsel of the LORD will stand" (see Prov. 16:9 NASB).

This highlights the fact that having free will gives human beings only a *relative* independence since the sovereign God maintains the right and power to intervene in the world's circumstances in whatever way he chooses. Through his special providence he can intervene in and influence the laws of nature without actually violating them and thus use natural events to influence human decisions.[133] The reality of free will means that such influence can be resisted (Amos 4:6–11; Hag. 1:1–11); thus God sometimes exercises his right to intervene in natural and human events in a direct way. This means he sometimes suspends natural law and performs miracles;[134] it also means that he is able to suspend free will itself if his purposes require it (as with Balaam, Num. 23–24).[135]

That God has such sovereign control means that although the creation has been endowed with independence, such independence is only relative. True control does not require causation,

---

133. See Forlines's explanation of the "influence and response" model of divine sovereignty, as an alternative to the "cause and effect" model of Calvinism (*Quest for Truth*, 336–38). See Cottrell, *God the Ruler*, 187–217.

134. Cottrell, *God the Ruler*, 244–61.

135. Baugh's inexcusable caricature of my statements on this subject, alleging that I make God out to be "an unpredictable tyrant" who operates according to "eccentricity" and "whimsy" ("The Meaning of Foreknowledge," 197), shows that he should have read my complete treatment of it in *God the Ruler*, 196–97.

predetermination, or foreordination of all things; but it does entail causative intervention when necessary. Free creatures are usually allowed to go their own way, but God can and will intervene when his purposes require it.

The other key word for the Arminian concept of sovereignty is *conditionality*. Such a concept is contrary to the Calvinist doctrine of an unconditional decree, which says that nothing God does can be conditioned by the creature. God cannot react or respond to anything outside himself and be sovereign at the same time. A. A. Hodge says it clearly: "A conditional decree would subvert the sovereignty of God."[136]

The idea that sovereignty demands unconditionality, however, is an unwarranted presupposition, one which necessitates the unacceptable compatibilist redefinition of "free will." This presupposition stands in direct contradiction to God's sovereign choice to create beings with a genuinely free will. If we are truly free, then God's own decisions and actions are sometimes *reactions* to, i.e., are *conditioned* upon, circumstances initiated by creatures.

In fact, most of God's works in this world are his reaction or response to foreknown human acts. This is the way the Bible pictures it. Virtually every major action of God recorded in the Bible after Genesis 3:1 is a response to human sin. The Abrahamic covenant, the establishment of Israel, the incarnation of Jesus, his death and resurrection, the establishment of the church, the Bible itself—all are part of the divine reaction to man's sin. Likewise God's act of bestowing salvation upon individuals, and the act of predestining that this will happen, are God's response or reaction to human faith-decisions. In like manner God's act of condemning some to hell is conditioned upon their sin and their refusal to repent.

Some of the concepts most crucial to God's sovereign control over his creation are in fact *reactive* in nature. This is true of genuine permission of particular events, as well as any divine preventive intervention to preclude such events. Such permissive and preventive decisions are conditioned by creatures' intentions as foreknown by God. Calvinists attempt to absolve God from responsibility for sin by declaring his eternal decree regarding sin to be permissive rather than efficacious. But this contradicts the Calvinist concept of sovereignty, the essence of which is unconditionality ("God always acts; he never

---

136. Archibald Alexander Hodge, *Outlines of Theology* (New York: Robert Carter, 1876), 168. See Cottrell, "The Nature of the Divine Sovereignty," 102–3.

reacts"). As Erickson describes it, Calvinism declares that the nature of God's sovereign decree means that "humans have had no input into what God has planned"; "God is not dependent on what humans decide."[137] That is, God's dealings with man are unconditioned. Real permission, however, is simply incompatible with such unconditionality; and those Calvinists who understand this are forced to speak oxymoronically of "efficacious permission."[138]

Another crucial concept that is conditional by its very nature is foreknowledge itself. The content of the mind of God which is called "foreknowledge" is conditioned by the events that take place in the world as foreseen by God before they even exist. Calvinists reject such a notion of passive knowledge, declaring it to be unworthy of God and contrary to his sovereignty. Conditioned knowledge, says Chafer, "places God in the unworthy position of being dependent upon his creatures."[139] If God's foreknowledge is not thus dependent upon his creatures, what does cause it? "His foreknowledge of future things . . . rests on his decree," says Berkhof.[140] One problem with this idea, of course, is that such unconditional knowledge is not true foreknowledge of what creatures will do; it is rather God's simple knowledge of what he himself plans to do.

All of these unnatural and strained concepts within Calvinism (compatibilist "free" will, efficacious permission, nondependent foreknowledge) can be avoided by simply rejecting the arbitrary notion that divine sovereignty demands unconditionality, as Arminianism does. Arminians freely assert that much of God's knowledge and many of God's actions are conditioned by his creatures, but they insist that this in no way impinges on his sovereignty since this is the kind of universe he sovereignly chose to make. An arrangement where God reacts to man's choices would be a violation of sovereignty only if God were forced into it, only if it were a necessity imposed upon God from without. But this is not the case. It was God's sovereign choice to create a universe inhabited by freewill beings whose decisions would to a great extent determine the course of his own actions. It is arbitrary and false to say that such a situation negates divine sovereignty when the situation itself is the *result* of his sovereignty.

137. Erickson, *Christian Theology*, 378, 381.
138. See Cottrell, *God the Ruler*, 219–21; Cottrell, "The Nature of the Divine Sovereignty," 105–6.
139. Lewis S. Chafer, *Systematic Theology*, vol. I (Dallas: Dallas Theological Seminary, 1947), 230.
140. Louis Berkhof, *Systematic Theology* (London: Banner of Truth, 1939), 67–68.

The point is that a truly sovereign God does not *need* to cause or predetermine all things in order to maintain complete control over his creation; his sovereignty is *greater* than that! Nor does God's freely chosen universe in which his actions are sometimes conditioned by his creatures diminish his sovereignty; it does in fact *magnify* it! What is at stake here is not just man's freedom but God's freedom also. A sovereign God is a God who is free to limit himself with regard to his works, a God who is free to decide *not* to determine if he so chooses, a God who is free to bestow the gift of relative independence upon his creatures without losing control over them. This is true sovereignty.

God's Foreknowledge

The fourth presupposition of the Arminian view of predestination is a particular concept of divine foreknowledge. It is affirmed that God had a complete foreknowledge of the entire history of the created universe, prior to the act of creation itself. Some speak of such foreknowledge as *eternal:* God "foresaw the future from all eternity," says Forlines.[141] "From eternity past God has known all that would happen in the universe and in the minds and affairs of men," says Hunt.[142] Whether this foreknowledge has been present in the mind of God literally for eternity is not the crucial point; what matters is that it was there before any part of this universe had come into existence.

The biblical affirmations of divine foreknowledge are abundant and unassailable. God tells us that the sure mark of deity is the ability to declare what is going to take place, to announce what is coming (Isa. 41:21–23). This is exactly what God has done: "I am God, and there is no other; I am God, and there is no one like me, declaring the end from the beginning, and from ancient times things which have not been done" (Isa. 46:9–10; see Isa. 42:8–9; 44:7–8; 45:20–21; 48:3–7). In all these texts God asserts his exclusive possession of knowledge of the future.

The whole possibility of predictive prophecy depends largely upon God's genuine foreknowledge. The mark of a true prophet, says the Lord, is if the thing he predicts comes true (Deut. 18:20–22). After Daniel interpreted Nebuchadnezzar's dream about the statue, he said, "The great God has made known to the king what will take place in the future" (Dan. 2:45 NASB). Just before Moses died, God told him

---

141. Forlines, *Quest for Truth*, 335.
142. Hunt, *What Love Is This?*, 229; see 143.

about the future apostasy of the Israelites (Deut. 31:16–21). In these and other cases God is not just declaring what he himself plans to do in the future but is also foretelling what human beings will be doing of their own free will.

Other specific references to foreknowledge include Romans 11:2, which says that God foreknew his people Israel. Also, he foreknew the justification of the Gentiles (Gal. 3:8). In Psalm 139:4 David mentions how God knows his words before he (David) even speaks them; in verse 16 he says that God knew all the days of his (David's) life before they had even begun. God knew Jeremiah before he was formed in the womb (Jer. 1:5). He knew that Cyrus, king of Persia, would release Israel from Babylonian captivity and help them rebuild Jerusalem (Isa. 44:28–45:13). The fact that names have been written in the Lamb's book of life from the foundation of the world is a clear indication of God's foreknowledge (Rev. 13:8; 17:8).

Of greatest importance is the fact that the New Testament specifically relates foreknowledge to the predestination of individuals to salvation (Rom. 8:29; 1 Pet. 1:1–2). The death of Jesus likewise involved a combination of foreknowledge and predestination (Acts 2:23; 1 Pet. 1:18–20).

We should not be surprised that the Bible so freely and abundantly affirms divine foreknowledge; this is simply one aspect of the omniscience of God, who "knows all things" (1 John 3:20 NASB). "He knows what will happen because he is all-knowing and therefore the future is as plain to him as the past."[143]

Acceptance of this biblical testimony to God's foreknowledge is one of the main things that distinguishes classical Arminianism from openness theology. The latter's rejection of foreknowledge is not new in Arminian ranks. In 1890 the Arminian D. Fisk Harris, in his polemical work against Calvinism, called attention to a number of fellow Arminians who "deny this divine foreknowledge on the ground that its acceptance necessitates the denial of human freedom and responsibility."[144] But Harris himself, like contemporary classical Arminians, found the Bible's testimony conclusive. He rightly asserted, "It is this firm adherence to the Bible that has compelled me to disagree so emphatically with that class of Arminian thinkers who deny the divine foreknowledge."[145]

---

143. Ibid., 144.
144. D. Fisk Harris, *Calvinism Contrary to God's Word and Man's Moral Nature* (n.p.: published by author, 1890), 248.
145. Ibid., 291.

Regarding foreknowledge, classical Arminians also differ from Calvinism in two distinct ways. First, Arminians believe that much of what God predestines is in a real sense based on his foreknowledge of certain things. This is especially true of his predestination of some individuals to heaven and others to hell. Because he foreknew that some would freely accept the free offer of grace and meet the conditions for receiving it, God predestined them to eternal life (Rom. 8:29). In contrast to this, Calvinism consistently says that God's foreknowledge of all things is based upon his predestination or foreordination of all things through his efficacious, unconditional decree. In fact, according to this view, the only way God is able to know the future is *because* he has predestined it—a limitation upon God's omniscience on which Calvinists and openness theologians strangely agree.

Calvinists clearly affirm this alleged dependence of foreknowledge upon predestination. Shedd says, "The Divine decree is the necessary condition of the Divine foreknowledge. If God does not first decide what shall come to pass, he cannot know what will come to pass."[146] Strong agrees: "No undecreed event can be foreseen." Thus "God cannot foreknow actualities unless he has by his decree made them to be certainties of the future. . . . He foreknows the future which he has decreed, and he foreknows it because he has decreed it."[147] Pink says emphatically, "Is it not clear that God foreknows what will be *because he has decreed what shall be?* . . . Foreknowledge of future events then is founded upon God's decrees, hence if God foreknows everything that is to be, it is because he has determined in himself from all eternity everything which will be."[148] Commenting on Acts 2:23, Baugh says "that God had clear prescience of all that surrounded Christ's death . . . because he had determined to bring it about." Also, "it was certain and foreknown because God had determined to accomplish it."[149]

There could hardly be a sharper contrast between Calvinism and Arminianism than this. For the former, predestination always precedes foreknowledge; for the latter, at least regarding human deeds and destinies, foreknowledge precedes predestination.

146. William G. T. Shedd, *Dogmatic Theology,* vol. I (Grand Rapids: Zondervan, 1969 reprint of 1888 edition), 396–97.

147. Augustus H. Strong, *Systematic Theology* (Valley Forge: Judson, 1907), 357.

148. A. W. Pink, *The Sovereignty of God,* rev. ed. (London: Banner of Truth, 1961), 74–75.

149. Baugh, "The Meaning of Foreknowledge," 189, 191.

The second way in which the Calvinist and Arminian views of foreknowledge differ is in its definition. For Arminians foreknowledge is almost always understood in a cognitive sense, i.e., it is primarily *prescience,* an actual prior knowledge or mental awareness of future events. Calvinists, however, usually insist that "foreknowledge" is something other than knowledge as such. In a general sense "foreknowledge" *is* predestination. "'God's foreknowledge' is of such a character that its object is foreknown with absolute certainty, and then it is identical with predestination."[150] As Harris perceptively observes, "The Calvinistic doctrine of God's foreknowledge is no foreknowledge. It is simply foreordination."[151]

Also, in a more specific sense, when the foreknowledge of human beings is cited in Scripture as the basis for their predestination to salvation (Rom. 8:29; 1 Pet. 1:1–2), the Calvinist almost always redefines it as foreloving or forechoosing (as discussed earlier in this chapter). This strained reinterpretation of foreknowledge is necessary in order to reconcile it with Calvinism's efficacious, unconditional decree.

One of the most common objections to the Arminian understanding of God's foreknowledge as a real and simple prescience of man's future freewill choices is that such a notion is actually incompatible with free will. The claim is that if God has foreknown from precreation time every choice that everyone will ever make, then all human choices are fixed or certain and therefore cannot be free. Foreknowledge thus rules out free will.

This is a common Calvinist criticism. Baugh calls it "an Achilles' heel for Arminianism. If God infallibly foreknows the free choices of humans, then these choices must be certain in a way that excludes the Arminian (libertarian) conception of free will."[152] As Westblade put it, "Infallible foreknowledge of an event presupposes the necessity of that event and therefore precludes its real freedom."[153] Openness theologians usually make the same point. Richard Rice declares, "In spite of assertions that absolute foreknowledge does not eliminate freedom, intuition tells us otherwise. If God's foreknowledge is infallible, then what he sees cannot fail to happen. . . . And if the future is inevitable,

---

150. Herman Bavinck, *The Doctrine of God,* ed. and trans. William Hendriksen (Grand Rapids: Eerdmans, 1951), 377.
151. Harris, *Calvinism,* 279.
152. Baugh, "The Meaning of Foreknowledge," 183.
153. Donald J. Westblade, "Divine Election in the Pauline Literature," in *Still Sovereign,* 71.

then the apparent experience of free choice is an illusion."[154] As Hunt sums up the problem, "If God knows what every person will think or do, and if nothing can prevent what God foreknows from happening, then how can man be a free moral agent?"[155]

Classical Arminianism has always denied the validity of this criticism and has always taken great care to show that foreknowledge in no way negates the contingency or freeness of freewill choices. This view "affirms that the future is perfectly foreknown by God and yet is, in principle and practice, 'open' and 'undetermined.'"[156] Foreknowledge does not cause or determine any of the events so foreknown, any more than an observer's witnessing of present events that are unfolding before him has any causative influence on those events. On the contrary, it is the events that cause the knowledge, whether it be present knowledge or foreknowledge.

Also, once an event has occurred, it becomes a past event and thus becomes "fixed" or "certain" in the sense that it cannot be changed. But this does not mean that any freewill choices involved in that event are somehow robbed of their freeness, just because the event has taken on the characteristic of certainty. As Harris (citing Moses Stuart) correctly asks, "'Does the certain knowledge we now have of a past event, destroy the free agency of those who were concerned in bringing about that event? Did any previous knowledge of the same necessarily interfere with their free agency?'"[157] The answer is obviously no. Therefore, as R. A. Torrey concludes, "Foreknowledge no more determines a man's actions than afterknowledge. Knowledge is determined by the fact, not the fact by the knowledge."[158]

It is true, then, that all future events, including freewill choices, are certain to happen as foreknown; but the foreknowledge is not what *makes* them certain. Raymond says, "All that foreknowledge does is to *prove* the certainty of future events, and that must be admitted without proof; all things will be as they will be, whether known or not, whether decreed or not; the future history of the universe will be in one single way and not two."[159] But if this is true, then how is foreknowledge different from foreordination? It differs with respect

---

154. Richard Rice, "Divine Foreknowledge and Free-Will Theism," in *The Grace of God, the Will of Man*, 127.

155. Hunt, *What Love Is This?*, 160.

156. Picirilli, *Grace*, 60.

157. Harris, *Calvinism*, 309.

158. R. A. Torrey, *Practical and Perplexing Questions Answered* (New York: Revell, 1898), 61.

159. Miner Raymond, *Systematic Theology*, vol. I (Cincinnati: Walden and Stowe, 1877), 502.

to that which *makes* man's future acts certain. What makes them certain? The foreknowledge itself? No, it does not *make* them certain; it only means that they *are* certain. Then what makes them certain? *The acts themselves,* as viewed by God from his perspective of eternity. All would agree that past events are certain. What makes them so? The simple fact that they have already happened the way they happened. The acts themselves have made them so. This same principle establishes the certainty of foreknown future events.

But still the critic asks, "If future choices are certain, how can they be free?" The source of the confusion seems to be that both Calvinism and openness theology are reading too much into the concept of *certainty,* wrongly equating it with *necessity.* Westblade and others are incorrect in thinking that "infallible foreknowledge of an event presupposes the *necessity* of that event."[160] Long ago Augustine argued that foreknowledge does not negate free will, calling such an idea "strange folly!" That foreknowledge makes our choices *necessary,* he said, is a "monstrous assertion."[161] Arminius also distinguished between certainty and necessity: "Certainty pertains to the knowledge of God; the necessity of an event, to the will and decree of God."[162] Again he says, "For the word '*certainly*' is used in respect to the divine prescience; but '*necessarily*' in respect to the decree of God."[163] Harris says, "With the great body of Arminians I readily grant that the foreseen actions of free agents are absolutely certain in the sense that they will occur as God foresees them: but this does not prove that they must so occur."[164]

The proper distinction is between "will certainly occur" and "must occur." As Forlines correctly notes,[165] Robert Picirilli "has an excellent treatment on this subject" as he explains the relationships among certainty, contingency, and necessity. Picirilli shows that a contingent event can be certain without being necessary: "'shall be' (certain) is not the same as 'must be' (necessary)." "Certainty is not necessity"; it is "simply futurity."[166]

---

160. Westblade, "Divine Election," 71. Italics added.

161. Aurelius Augustine, "On Free Will," III:8, in *Augustine: Earlier Writings,* trans. John H. S. Burleigh (Philadelphia: Westminster, 1953), 175.

162. James Arminius, "A Friendly Discussion," in *Writings,* III:231.

163. Arminius, "An Examination of the Treatise of William Perkins," in *Writings,* III:402.

164. Harris, *Calvinism,* 261.

165. Forlines, *Quest for Truth,* 333.

166. Ibid., 37, 39, 63.

In conclusion, according to Arminians, even before creation God had true foreknowledge (prior knowledge, prescience) of all future events, including all freewill choices. This foreknowledge was neither determined by nor equivalent to predestination but rather in many cases was the basis of the latter (as in Rom. 8:29). Even though this foreknowledge means that every future event was indeed certain to happen as foreknown, in itself the foreknowledge does not render any future event necessary and therefore does not negate free will.

God and Time

The next theological presupposition of the Arminian view of predestination is a certain view of how God is related to time. Arminians believe that predestination is based on true foreknowledge. But this raises the question: how is foreknowledge possible? How is it possible for God, in his precreation existence, to foreknow a future that has not even happened yet? The answer: it is possible because he is infinite or unlimited regarding time; he is "the eternal God" (Rom. 16:26 NASB), the eternal and immortal King (1 Tim. 1:17). As eternal God he transcends the limitations of time in two senses: quantitatively and qualitatively.

Though some deny it, the biblical data support the concept of God's eternity in the sense of beginningless and endless quantitative duration: he has always existed in the eternal past and will always exist in the eternal future. He has existed "from everlasting" (Ps. 93:2 NASB), and he "lives forever" (Isa. 57:15 NASB; see Rev. 4:9–10; 10:6; 15:7). He is "from everlasting to everlasting" (Ps. 41:13 NASB). "Before the mountains were born or you gave birth to the earth and the world, even from everlasting to everlasting, you are God" (Ps. 90:2 NASB; see Ps. 102:25–27). God is the one "who is and who was and who is to come" (Rev. 1:4, 8; 4:8 NASB). He is the first and the last, the Alpha and the Omega, the beginning and the end (Isa. 44:6; Rev. 1:8; 21:6). This is why "with the Lord one day is as a thousand years, and a thousand years as one day" (2 Pet. 3:8 NASB; see Ps. 90:4). This does not mean that all moments of time are the same or simultaneous for God. It just means that to one who is eternal, one finite period of time is no more significant than any other finite period.

This linear, quantitative sense of God's eternity is not the crucial point for foreknowledge, though. What makes foreknowledge possible is that God is also eternal in a qualitative sense. That is, in a significant way he is outside the flow of time and is not bound by its limitations. This does not mean that God is outside the flow of time in every sense. As indicated above, God *exists* in an eternal duration of successive moments, which means that in some sense the passing of time is part of the divine nature in and of itself, totally apart from creation. This is in effect the denial of the classical theistic concept of the *timelessness* of God, or the eternal simultaneity of the divine nature. The latter is the idea that with God there is no succession of moments or even a consciousness of succession of moments. God's being, all of his acts, and all of his knowledge coexist as one eternal *now,* in a single, simultaneous present. There is no past or future, no before or after, with God. Though his acts appear on a historical continuum from our perspective, for God himself all his acts, as well as the contents of his consciousness, are frozen in a single, unvarying, eternal simultaneity.

In my judgment this idea of God's eternity is an extreme view based on nonbiblical philosophy rather than on biblical teaching. Everything Scripture tells us about God indicates that he does experience the passing of time in an everlasting succession of moments. He exists and acts in the present moment. From God's own perspective some of his acts (such as the creation) are in the unalterable past, while some (such as the final judgment) are yet to come, and even God must wait for their time to arrive.

What *does* it mean, then, to say that God is eternal in a qualitative sense? In what sense *is* he outside the flow of time and therefore not bound by its limitations? Biblical teaching shows that this is true in the sense that his *consciousness* (his knowledge) is not bound by time. Though he exists and acts in the ongoing present (not in a single eternal present), and though he is conscious of existing and acting in this ongoing present, in his consciousness he stands *above* the flow of time and *sees* the past and the future of his creatures just as clearly and certainly as if they were present. This is how his foreknowledge is possible.

It is important to see that the reality of foreknowledge does not require the classical theistic view of divine timelessness or simultaneity. This is contrary to theologians such as Geisler, whose whole theology is based on classical theism and who defends foreknowledge on the basis of divine timelessness: *"nothing is future to God."*[167] Geisler says that this "classical view of God" has been held by all "traditional

---

167. Geisler, *Chosen But Free,* 107; see 50–53.

Arminians";[168] but this is questionable. Some contemporary classical Arminians do accept such a view. Hunt, for example, says that God is "by very definition outside of time and thus time is unrelated to Him"; "God, being timeless, lives in one eternal now"; "for God there *is* no time"; everything is "one eternal present" to him.[169] On the other hand, not all contemporary classical Arminians accept this view of God. Forlines, for example, says that the consistent "eternal now view . . . cannot stand"; it is "without merit."[170] I agree with Forlines.

Classical Arminianism says that God's predestination of individuals to salvation is based on his foreknowledge of their future free-will choices; it says that such foreknowledge is possible because the eternal God's knowledge or consciousness is not limited by time; he sees the future *as if* it were present. But how is it *possible* for God to see the future if it has no objective reality? We may never know the answer to this question simply because of the qualitative difference between the nature of the transcendent, infinite Creator and us finite creatures. True piety has long affirmed that "the finite cannot contain the infinite"; finite minds cannot grasp all the implications of God's unlimited existence.[171]

Thus Forlines is right to leave the "how" of foreknowledge in the realm of inscrutable mystery.[172] We cannot deny God's foreknowledge simply because we do not understand it. Long ago John Kirk warned us not to try to reduce God's knowledge to our human level. He declares that "had not man presumed to limit and pare down the power of Jehovah's knowledge to the level of the standard of our own, he would never have asserted that God could not foreknow an event which is in its nature perfectly *contingent*."[173] We should simply accept what Kirk calls "the divine glory of foreknowledge"[174] without declaring that it must either be explained or be denied. We must accept it as true simply because the Bible affirms it. As Harris says, the Bible "clearly teaches that God does know the future free actions of men without explaining the *modus operandi*." The inability to understand the "how" does not give us the right "to invent a theory which

---

168. Ibid., 51, 54.
169. Hunt, *What Love Is This?*, 145, 160, 193.
170. Forlines, *Quest for Truth*, 68, 330.
171. As Hunt says, "We are finite and God is infinite; therefore, we could not possibly understand *how* He knows the future" (*What Love Is This?*, 145).
172. Forlines, *Quest for Truth*, 332–33.
173. Kirk, *Cloud Dispelled*, 34.
174. Ibid., 37.

shall unequivocally conflict with the plain teachings of the Word"; nor do we want to have a God who can be fully comprehended.[175] In the final analysis Harris is right: "To say that it can not be true because we can not see how God can thus foreknow, is to substitute ignorance for argument."[176]

God's Plan for Salvation

The Arminian view of predestination also presupposes a certain view of the nature of salvation. This is true because all the elements of God's plan of salvation had to be in place from the moment he determined to create this world of freewill beings and consequently foreknew that all would fall into sin and need redemption. Thus even prior to creation God had already determined how he would infallibly work out his plan of salvation in the context of our freewill universe. This redemption plan is the heart of God's "eternal purpose" or purposive will; everything associated with it was from the beginning predestined to occur. Exactly what did God predetermine to do?

How salvation would be accomplished. The first thing God predestined regarding salvation was the manner or method by which it would be accomplished and made available to sinners. Here is an unconditional element of predestination: God purposed to accomplish salvation through the incarnation of the second person of the Trinity as Jesus of Nazareth and through the incarnate One's own atoning death and resurrection. He purposed this in conjunction with his foreknowledge of the actions of the human participants in the drama, but the essential events were sure to happen according to God's "predetermined plan" (Acts 2:23); those who crucified Jesus were only doing what God's hand and purpose had "predestined to occur" (Acts 4:28). In this sense Christ as our redemptive sacrifice "was foreknown before the foundation of the world" (1 Pet. 1:20) with a foreknowledge that was indeed based on predestination.

In predetermining how salvation would be accomplished, the primary object of predestination was Jesus Christ himself. But in order to bring his saving work to pass, it was necessary for God secondarily to foreordain all the essential *means* of accomplishing this. This refers mostly to the selection (election) of certain nations and individuals to be used as instruments for bringing Christ into the world and then for beginning the process of applying the saving results of his

---

175. Harris, *Calvinism*, 277, 291.
176. Ibid., 264.

redemptive work to the world. This is predestination to *service*, not to salvation.

The most obvious example of this predestination to service is God's unconditional choice of the nation of Israel to be the context for bringing the Savior into the world. For this purpose God chose the Jews "to be a people for His own possession out of all the peoples who are on the face of the earth" (Deut. 7:7 NASB). To this end he said to them, "You are My servant, I have chosen you and not rejected you" (Isa. 41:9 NASB). As a result the nation of Israel was blessed in abundance with manifold special privileges (Rom. 3:2; 9:4–5). Such predestination for service did not include, however, a similar election to salvation (see the next main section).

In like manner God in the person of Jesus Christ chose certain individuals to be apostles who would help to lay the foundation for the church—also a role of service, not guaranteeing salvation (Luke 6:13; John 6:70; 13:18; 15:16, 19). As Olson says, none of these texts "says anything about a doctrine of election to salvation,"[177] and the fact that Judas was among those so chosen shows that the purpose for this choice was not salvation (John 6:70).

Much of the biblical data about predestination and election (e.g., Rom. 9) refers to this utilitarian predestination, which is part of God's eternal purpose regarding how salvation would be accomplished, not how it would be applied to individuals. A main source of Calvinism's error on this subject is failure to distinguish properly between utilitarian and redemptive predestination. See, for example, Erickson's misapplication of Romans 9 and John 15:16. Amazingly he applies the latter text to Jesus' initiative "in the selection of his disciples to eternal life."[178]

How salvation would be applied. God's predetermined redemptive plan included not only his predestination of the way in which salvation would be *accomplished* but also his predestination of the way in which it would be *applied*. From beginning to end the *way* of salvation is decided and specified by God alone. This preserves God's sovereignty in the matter of salvation without his having unconditionally to choose which individuals will actually receive it.

First of all, in his eternal purpose God predetermined to apply salvation *conditionally*.[179] As Miley explains it, "The actual salvation of the soul is not an immediate benefit of the atonement, nor through

177. Olson, *Beyond Calvinism and Arminianism*, 181.
178. Erickson, *Christian Theology*, 383, 929.
179. See Cottrell, *The Faith Once for All*, 346–74.

an irresistible operation of divine grace, but is attainable only on a compliance with its appropriate terms." That is, "our actual salvation" is "a conditional benefit of the atonement."[180] The essence of such conditionality is clearly seen in God's lament over Israel in Isaiah 65, "I permitted myself to be sought by those who did not ask for me; I permitted myself to be found by those who did not seek me. I said, 'Here am I, here am I,' to a nation which did not call on my name. I have spread out my hands all day long to a rebellious people" (vv. 1–2 NASB). God is so anxious to welcome sinners back that he in effect jumps into their path, waves his arms, and yells, "Here I am!" But the people ignore him; thus he declares, "I will destine you for the sword, and all of you will bow down to the slaughter. *Because I called, but you did not answer; I spoke, but you did not hear*" (v. 12 NASB, emphasis added).

That God's way of salvation is conditional is consistent with our nature as freewill beings. Human free will and the conditionality of salvation go together. Miley rightly points out that many New Testament texts offer salvation to sinners on the basis that certain specified conditions must be met and on the other hand exclude from salvation those who refuse to meet the conditions. He cites Mark 1:15; 16:15–16; John 3:16, 18, 36; and Acts 2:38.[181] The fact that salvation is offered conditionally presumes that individuals, even in their sinful state, have the freewill ability to meet those conditions. "If no free personal action of our own has any conditional relation to our salvation why should such action be imperatively required, just as though it had relation?" asks Miley.[182] Jesus' lament over Jerusalem shows that its inhabitants were lost because of an act of their own free will, not God's selective will: Jesus wanted (*thelo*) to receive them, but they were not willing (*ou thelo*).

That God's way of salvation is conditional is also consistent with the sovereignty of God since God himself is the one who determined that it shall be this way and since God himself is the one who determined what the conditions are. No one imposed this plan upon God; it was his own unconditional, sovereign choice. As Picirilli says, "If the sovereign God unconditionally established faith as the condition for salvation (and therefore for election), then His sovereignty is not violated when He requires the condition."[183]

---

180. Miley, *Systematic Theology,* II:249.
181. Ibid., II:250–51.
182. Ibid., II:251.
183. Picirilli, *Grace,* 57.

How does this relate to predestination? The bottom line is that if salvation itself is conditional, then predestination and election to salvation must also be conditional. Conditional salvation would be completely inconsistent with unconditional election. Arminians see conditionality at both levels: God's predestination of some to eternal life is conditioned on his foreknowledge that they will meet the specified conditions for receiving salvation.

In the second place, God's predetermined plan for applying salvation included his decision to bestow it upon individuals only on the basis of *grace*. That is, his eternal purpose is that the event of receiving salvation will be both conditional and gracious. Some think that these two characteristics are incompatible; they assume that grace by its nature must be unconditional. John Murray says, "If grace is conditioned in any way by human performance or by the will of man impelling to action, then grace ceases to be grace."[184] This is a serious error, sometimes based on a false equation of *unconditional* and *unmerited*. Not all conditions are meritorious, however. Sometimes the error of seeing conditions and grace as incompatible is based on a confusion between the accomplishment of salvation and the application of such. God's accomplishment of salvation through Jesus Christ is indeed unconditional, as are the love and grace which motivated him to make this provision in the first place; but the gracious application or bestowing of that salvation upon individuals is conditional. Sometimes the error is simply the product of Calvinism's view of sovereignty as such, which does not allow God to do *anything* conditionally. That is, if the eternal decree is necessarily both comprehensive and unconditional, then there is no way that salvation can be regarded as conditional.[185] But as we have seen, this is a false view of sovereignty.

In the final analysis, there is no reason to think that a gracious salvation cannot be a conditional salvation. The fact that the Bible presents it as both conditional and gracious shows that these characteristics are compatible.

That God's plan for applying salvation is both conditional and gracious means that the *particular* conditions he has specified for receiving salvation are consistent with grace. This is true of course of the primary condition, namely, faith. Paul himself specifically affirms the complementarity of grace and faith in Romans 4:16 and

184. Murray, *Romans*, II:70.
185. See Cottrell, *God the Ruler*, 184–86, 226–27.

Ephesians 2:8.[186] As a condition for salvation, nothing could be more natural than faith and more compatible with the nature of grace as a gift. Since our salvation is accomplished by the work of someone else (Jesus) and since it is offered to us as a free gift, the only thing we can do is accept (believe) God's Word that this is so and hold out an empty hand to receive the gift. Faith is often identified with this empty hand. It is the exact opposite of merit.[187]

To say that faith is the primary condition for salvation does not mean it is the only condition, contrary to the belief of many.[188] Most Arminians would have no problem adding repentance as a condition; and a right understanding of Romans 10:9–10 suggests that confession of faith in Jesus Christ is also a condition since in the text it is parallel in every way with faith itself.[189] Others see baptism as a salvation condition, perfectly consistent with grace.[190] For our present purpose, however, it is not necessary for Arminians to agree on the complete list. Given that salvation is both conditional and gracious, the only issue here is whether the specified conditions are consistent with grace.

To say it another way, we cannot include anything in the conditions for salvation that is a *work* in the Pauline sense of the word (Rom. 3:20, 28; 11:6; Gal. 2:16; Eph. 2:8–9; Titus 3:5). A work in Paul's sense cannot be defined simply as "something you do" since Jesus calls faith itself a work in this generic sense (John 6:28–29). Rather in the Pauline sense a meritorious or nongracious work is specifically a "work of law" (Rom. 3:28 NASB), i.e., an act of obedience to a law-commandment given by God as the Creator to men as creatures. Such meritorious "works of law" do not include the Redeemer's gracious instructions to sinners on how to receive salvation (e.g., Luke 3:3; John 3:16; Acts 2:38; 16:31; Rom. 10:9–10). If an act such as repentance or confession were a meritorious condition (a "work of law") that conflicts with grace, we can assume that God our Redeemer would never have specified it as a condition for salvation in the first place. Whatever conditions God has sovereignly required are gracious conditions.

---

186. See Shank, *Elect in the Son,* 125.
187. See Samuel Fisk, *Divine Sovereignty and Human Freedom* (Neptune, N.J.: Loizeaux Brothers, 1973), 26–29.
188. See Cottrell, *Romans,* I:111–15, 268–71.
189. Cottrell, *The Faith Once for All,* 353–59; Cottrell, *Romans,* II:173–82.
190. Cottrell, *The Faith Once for All,* 360–74.

I am emphasizing this point over against those Calvinists who caricature the Arminian view of conditional election as predestination based on foreseen *works* or foreseen *merit,* as if predestination based on the foreknowledge of man's meeting *any* conditions, even faith itself, would be contrary to grace. Such is the implication of this statement by Calvin: "But it is a piece of futile cunning to lay hold on the term foreknowledge, and so to use that as to pin the eternal *election* of God upon the *merits* of men, which election the apostle everywhere ascribes to the alone purpose of God."[191] Berkouwer likewise asserts that "election does not find its basis on man's works and *therefore* not in his foreseen faith."[192] Such criticism of the Arminian view of predestination is patently unfair and misguided, in view of the biblical teaching on the conditionality of salvation and therefore of election.

In conclusion, God's predetermined plan for accomplishing and applying salvation as described here is part of his eternal purpose, the purpose according to which he predestines, calls, justifies, and glorifies those whom he foreknows will respond to the call (Rom. 8:29–30).

Human Sinfulness

The final theological presupposition for the Arminian doctrine of predestination is a certain view of the nature of man as a sinner. The Calvinist view of unconditional election necessarily follows from the doctrine of total depravity. The essence of total depravity is that a sinner's spiritual nature is so corrupt that he is totally unable to respond positively to the general gospel call. This is why God must choose whom he will save, which he does unconditionally as part of his eternal decree. Then at a time determined by God, he selectively issues to his chosen ones a special inward gospel call, which efficaciously and irresistibly regenerates their sinful natures and implants within them the gift of faith.

Classical Arminianism has a different view of the nature of man as a sinner. While there are variations in the explanation of why this is so, all Arminians believe that at the time of the hearing of the general gospel call, every sinner has the free will either to accept or to reject it. This is in essence a denial of the Calvinist doctrine of total deprav-

---

191. John Calvin, "A Treatise on the Eternal Predestination of God," in *Calvin's Calvinism,* trans. Henry Cole (Grand Rapids: Eerdmans, 1956), 48.

192. G. C. Berkouwer, *Divine Election,* trans. Hugo Bekker (Grand Rapids: Eerdmans, 1960), 42. Italics added.

ity. Some Arminians believe that no sinner is ever totally depraved; others believe that all people are initially afflicted with total depravity but that God through a universal preparatory grace mitigates the depravity and restores a measure of freedom. Either way the result is the same: when the moment of choice comes, sinners have a freedom of the will to meet or not to meet the conditions for salvation. This is a prerequisite for the Arminian concept of conditional election.

Thus, for Calvinists, the universal presence of total depravity means that the only gospel call which anyone can answer must be selective and irresistible. For Arminians the universal absence of total depravity (whether by nature or by grace) means that the only gospel call God issues is universal and resistible. For Calvinists total depravity dictates that the final decision of who is saved and who is not must be made by God. For Arminians the final decision belongs to each individual.

In the Arminian system it does not really matter whether this freewill ability to accept or reject the gospel is regarded as *natural* (as in Pelagianism), as *restored* for all at conception via original grace,[193] or as restored for all at a later time through the Holy Spirit's intervention in an act of prevenient grace.[194] What matters is that when the gospel message reaches the sinner, he is *not* in a state of unremedied total depravity and thus of total inability to believe in Jesus without an unconditional, selective, irresistible act of the Spirit. Rather, every sinner is able to make his own decision of whether to believe or not. Erickson has it right, that a "major tenet of Arminianism is that all persons are able to believe or to meet the conditions of salvation. . . . But is there room in this theology for the concept that all persons are able to believe? There is, if we modify or eliminate the idea of the total depravity of sinners."[195]

Some Arminians basically accept the view described above but still claim to believe in total depravity. For example, Fisk says he believes that man is totally depraved but that this does not entail total inability.[196] This is self-contradictory, however, since the latter is the essence of the former. Another example is Picirilli, who says he (like Calvin and Arminius) accepts total depravity, including total inability.[197] But

---

193. See Cottrell, *Commentary on Romans,* I:330–64, 468; Cottrell, *The Faith Once for All,* 179–90, 197–200.
194. See Picirilli, *Grace,* 153–59.
195. Erickson, *Christian Theology,* 932–33.
196. Fisk, *Calvinism Contrary,* 30.
197. Picirilli, *Grace,* i, 35–36, 41–42, 149–51.

when he adds that this total depravity is universally canceled to the point that all who hear the gospel have the ability to resist it,[198] he in effect negates the main consequence of total depravity; it is no longer "total." Though he calls himself a "moderate Calvinist" and claims to believe in total depravity, Norman Geisler similarly strips the doctrine of its essence (total inability).[199] Such approaches as these, I believe, are confusing and misleading. Retaining the term while denying the traditional heart of the doctrine it represents blurs the distinction between Calvinism and Arminianism at a crucial point.

Predestination in Romans 9

This section presents an Arminian interpretation of Romans 9. This is a key passage for our discussion since it usually serves as a main proof text for the Calvinist view of predestination. It is the "bedrock"[200] and "lynchpin"[201] for the concept of the unconditional election of individuals to salvation. Thus it is crucial to show that this doctrine is not taught in this chapter.[202]

The Overall Purpose of Romans 9

There is considerable agreement that the issue being addressed in Romans 9 is the righteousness of God, as stated in the question Paul raises in Romans 9:14 (NASB), "There is no injustice with God, is there?" Specifically, has God been unjust in his dealings with Israel? This question was raised in Paul's day by the conjunction of three interrelated states of affairs. First is the unquestioned fact that God had chosen Israel to be his special people beginning with Abraham and had showered them with unparalleled supernatural blessings from that point on (Rom. 9:4–5). Second is the Jews' own assumption that their special relationship with God included an implicit promise of salvation for practically every individual Israelite. Their attitude seemed to be, "God chose us to be his own special people; therefore he is obligated to save us." As Picirilli says, "Those Jews would contend that God had unconditionally promised to save all Israel and would

---

198. Ibid., 153–58.
199. Geisler, *Chosen but Free*, 56–58, 116.
200. Forlines, *Quest for Truth*, 345.
201. Olson, *Beyond Calvinism and Arminianism*, 72.
202. For a detailed exposition of Romans 9–11 see Cottrell, *Romans*, II:23–203.

therefore be unrighteous if He failed to keep that promise."[203] The third state of affairs is Paul's emphatic teaching in Romans 1–8 that most Jews were in fact lost (e.g., Rom. 3:9). This fact was the source of "great sorrow and unceasing grief" for Paul (Rom. 9:2 NASB), but to the Jews themselves such a claim implied that God was dealing unfairly with them. If masses of Jews are unsaved, surely God's promises to them have failed, and he is therefore unrighteous.

Paul knows that in view of these three facts, the question of God's righteousness in his treatment of the Jews will arise. Is God unrighteous when he does not automatically save the Jews? How can God reject those whom he has elected? Does the nonsalvation of the Jews mean that he has broken his covenant promises to them? "May it never be!" Paul emphatically says (Rom. 9:14 NASB). Indeed, "it is not as though" the word of God has failed" (Rom. 9:6 NASB).

Though most agree that everything Paul is doing in Romans 9–11 is designed to establish this point, there is strong disagreement concerning *how* these chapters show that God's promises to Israel have not failed. All agree that the theme of divine election is the main point, but the disagreement is over the *nature* of this election. Specifically, is Paul talking about election to *salvation* or election to *service*?

The Calvinist approach is that in Romans 9 Paul is teaching the unconditional election of some individuals to salvation (and for many, the unconditional reprobation of all others to hell). The question is framed thus: why are some (Jews) saved and others lost? The answer is that it is simply a matter of God's sovereign, unconditional choice. An example of this is John Piper, who asks, "Does election in Rom. 9:1–23 concern nations or individuals? And does it concern historical roles or eternal destinies?" His answer: "The evidence is overwhelmingly in favor of the view that Paul's concern is for the *eternal* destinies of those *within* the nation of Israel who are saved and who are accursed."[204] Thomas Schreiner agrees: "Calvinists typically appeal to Romans 9 to support their theology of divine election. In particular, they assert that Romans 9 teaches that God unconditionally elects individuals to be saved."[205]

---

203. Picirilli, *Grace*, 72. See C. E. B. Cranfield, *A Critical and Exegetical Commentary on the Epistle to the Romans*, 2 vols., The International Critical Commentary, new series (Edinburgh: T. & T. Clark, 1975; 1990 corrected printing), 1:172, note 1.

204. John Piper, *The Justification of God: An Exegetical and Theological Study of Romans 9:1–23*, 2nd ed. (Grand Rapids: Baker, 1993), 15, 71.

205. Thomas R. Schreiner, "Does Romans 9 Teach Individual Election unto Salvation?" in *Still Sovereign*, 89.

Some Arminians actually agree with this view up to a point. They, too, understand Paul to be explaining why some (Jews) are saved and some are lost. That is, they see Paul as speaking of election to salvation. For example, Picirilli says of Romans 9, "The purpose of verses 14–24 is to argue that the sovereign God is the one who determines who will be saved. . . . God still saves whom He wills and damns whom He wills, Jews or otherwise."[206] How is this different from the Calvinist view? It differs in that the Arminians who read Romans 9 in terms of election to salvation assume and assert that this election is conditional, or corporate, or according to foreknowledge. In my judgment, though, such qualifications are difficult to sustain in view of the teaching of Romans 9 itself. But this is not a problem since in the final analysis it is not necessary for Arminians to attempt to apply such qualifications to this election since it is not an election to salvation at all but an election to service.

Whether it be presented by Calvinists or Arminians, this soteriological interpretation of the election in Romans 9 is wrong because it does not really address the question of God's righteousness but rather intensifies it. It does not address the question because it does not deal with the role of ethnic Israel as a whole, which is really what the problem is all about. In the minds of the Jews, the problem was simply this: "Why are so many Jews lost, when God has promised to save them all?"

According to most Calvinists, Paul's answer to this question goes something like this: "It's true that God made a covenant with Abraham and with Israel that includes salvation promises. So why are not all Jews saved? Because God never intended to give this salvation to *all* Jews in the first place. All along he had planned to make a division within Israel, unconditionally bestowing salvation on some and unconditionally withholding it from the rest."

But how does this answer the charge that God is unrighteous or unfair in his dealings with the Jews? In my judgment this is *no answer at all* to the main question! If this is all Paul can say, then God is made to appear even more unrighteous and unfair than ever.

The only approach to Romans 9 that truly addresses the issue of God's righteousness as it relates to ethnic Israel is that the election spoken of in verses 7–18 is election to service. Paul's thesis is that God's word of promise to Israel has not failed (Rom. 9:6a). Why not? The answer is Romans 9:6b (NASB), "For they are not all Israel who

---

206. Picirilli, *Grace*, 72.

are descended from Israel." Here Paul is not distinguishing between two groups *within* Israel, the saved and the lost, with the ensuing discussion focusing on how God unconditionally makes the distinction. Rather, the contrast is of a different sort altogether. There *are* two groups, but they are not completely distinct from each other. One is actually *inside* the other, as a smaller body within a larger body. Both groups are called Israel, but they are different kinds of Israel. The larger one is ethnic Israel, the physical nation as a whole; the smaller belongs to this group but is also distinguished from it as a separate entity, i.e., as the true spiritual Israel, the remnant of true believers who enjoy the blessings of eternal salvation.

But the contrast between these two Israels is not that one is saved while the other is lost. This cannot be, since the smaller (saved) group is also a part of the larger body. What is the difference between these two Israels, and why does Paul even bring it up here? The key difference is that *God's covenant promises to these two groups are not the same.* The promises God made to ethnic Israel are different from the promises he has made to spiritual Israel. Paul is saying, in effect, "You think God has been unfair to ethnic Israel because all Jews are not saved? Don't you know there are *two* Israels, each with a different set of promises? You are actually *confusing* these two Israels. You are taking the salvation promises that apply only to the smaller group and are mistakenly trying to apply them to Israel as a whole."

Here is the point: there are two "chosen peoples," two Israels; but only remnant Israel has been chosen for salvation. Contrary to what the Jews commonly thought, ethnic Israel as a whole was *not* chosen for salvation but for service. God's covenant promises to physical Israel as such had to do only with the role of the nation in God's historical plan of redemption. Their election was utilitarian, not redemptive. God chose them to serve a purpose. The Jews themselves thought that this election involved the promise of salvation for individuals, but they were simply mistaken. This same mistake lies at the root of the Calvinist view that the election in Romans 9 is election to salvation. This is Piper's root exegetical error, as he strains mightily to read salvation content into the blessings described in Romans 9:4–5.[207] He concludes that "each of the benefits listed in 9:4, 5 has saving, eschatological implications for Israel,"[208] and then proceeds to try to explain why such benefits were not enjoyed by all Jews. His

---

207. Piper, *Justification of God,* 21–44.
208. Ibid., 49.

answer is that God makes a distinction within Israel, unconditionally choosing to apply these saving benefits to only some Jews. Schreiner takes a similar approach, saying that Paul's thesis in Romans 9–11 as stated in Romans 9:6—that "the word of God has not failed"—refers to God's promises to save his people Israel.[209]

Even Forlines, an Arminian, interprets God's covenant promises to Abraham and his seed (as in Gen. 13:14–15; 17:8) as including "the promise of eternal life."[210] But this is simply not true. The terms of the covenant God made with Abraham and later with Israel as a whole did not include a promise to save *anyone* simply because he or she was a member of the covenant people. The key promise God made to Abraham and his seed was this: "In you all the families of the earth will be blessed" (Gen. 12:3 NASB), a promise that was fulfilled when "the Christ according to the flesh" ultimately came from Israel (Rom. 9:5 NASB). All the other promises and blessings were subordinate to this one and were designed to bring about its fulfillment. None involved a promise of eternal salvation for the individual members of the covenant people. The blessings listed by Paul in Romans 9:4–5 do not include salvation content.[211]

The *main point* of Paul's discussion in Romans 9 is that God has the sovereign right to make this distinction between election for service and election for salvation and to choose individuals or nations to fill certain roles in his plan without also saving them. This is exactly what God has done with ethnic Israel. This nation was unconditionally chosen for service, but this election did not at the same time unconditionally bestow salvation upon all so elected. Jesus' choosing of the twelve apostles (John 15:16) is almost an exact parallel, as is the choosing of Pharaoh (Rom. 9:17–18). The fact that God used Pharaoh for his redemptive purposes did not require the latter to be saved, and the same is true of Israel. If God wants to use the Jews in his service yet deny them salvation because of their unbelief, that is perfectly consistent with his righteous nature and his covenant promises.

Where does salvation enter the picture? Salvation is bestowed upon spiritual Israel only—the "vessels of mercy" (Rom. 9:23 NASB) or the remnant (Rom. 9:27–29; 11:5), those Jews who met the gracious faith conditions for receiving it as spelled out in Romans 1–8 and 9:30–10:21. Schreiner is seriously wrong when he claims that the election-to-service view of Romans 9 does not address the question of

209. Schreiner, "Romans 9," 91.
210. Forlines, *Quest for Truth*, 363.
211. See Cottrell, *Romans*, II:49–59.

THE CLASSIC ARMINIAN VIEW OF ELECTION — **127**

Israel's salvation.[212] The issue with which Paul is dealing is the question of why *all* Israelites are not saved. His answer has nothing to do with a supposed unconditional election to salvation but with the fact that the promise of salvation was never made to the *nation* in the first place. The whole point of Romans 9 is that one must not equate election to service with election to salvation.

The Structure of Romans 9 and 10

The above interpretation of Romans 9 is clearly borne out by the overall structure of Romans 9 and 10. After posing the problem and his basic answer to it (9:1–6), Paul first discusses unconditional election for service (9:7–18), then conditional election to salvation (9:19–10:21).

Romans 9:7–18. In this first section Paul asserts God's sovereign right to choose and use (for service) anyone he pleases on his own terms. He is free to elect individuals or groups to serve his purposes without saving them. The point Paul is establishing in these verses applies to ethnic Israel, not spiritual Israel.

Verses 7–13. A common understanding of these verses is that they show how God unconditionally chose to save *some* Israelites but not others. For example, Baugh says these verses show that "saving grace depends upon predestination."[213] As Forlines sees it, just as God distinguished between Isaac and Ishmael, and between Jacob and Esau, so "there is no reason to believe that all of the Covenant Seed of Abraham (those who descended from Abraham through Jacob) are saved."[214] Such an explanation assumes that these verses are about how God chooses remnant Israel for salvation and rejects the rest for damnation, i.e., about *how* the smaller group in Romans 9:6b is set apart from the larger group. My understanding, though, is that verses 7–13 are talking about the larger group itself, i.e., ethnic Israel as a whole and how it came into being in the first place.

The progression of thought is thus: Not all members of physical Israel are also members of spiritual Israel (9:6b); *neither* are they called the children of Abraham just because they are physically descended

---

212. Schreiner, "Romans 9," 90–98.

213. Steven M. Baugh, "'God's Purpose According to Election': Paul's Argument in Romans 9," accessed at the following: alliancenet.org/pub/mr/mr98/1998.06.NovDec/mr9806.smb.romans.html , 3.

214. Forlines, *Quest for Truth,* 359. Picirilli likewise sums up these verses thus: God "never promised, unconditionally, to save all the fleshly descendants of Abraham, Isaac, or Israel" (*Grace,* 71).

from Abraham (9:7a). Thus verse 7 begins a separate thought. The paragraph through verse 13 focuses on the origin and role of ethnic Israel as such, explaining the manner in which God called them into his service. The main point is that this is *different* from the way he calls individuals to salvation. Only when the two are confused do questions about God's faithfulness to Israel arise.

Calvinists are right that the election described in 9:7–13 is unconditional; they are wrong to assume it is election to salvation rather than election to service. The main reason Paul cites the "divine distinguishing" between Isaac and Ishmael, and between Jacob and Esau, is to emphasize the sovereign, unilateral way in which God established the nation of Israel and enlisted it into his service. Isaac and Jacob thus represent ethnic Israel as a whole, not the elect within the nation. Ethnic Israel existed only by God's gracious choice and promise. God alone controls the selection process and the terms of selection. The ones *not* chosen (Ishmael and Esau) are not thereby condemned to hell; they are simply excluded from having a part in the working out of God's redemptive plan.

All of this was done so that "God's purpose in election" (Rom. 9:11 NIV) would not fail, namely, his purpose to bring "the Christ according to the flesh" (Rom. 9:5 NASB) into the world. God made clear from the beginning that he was going to accomplish this purpose through this particular family regardless of their individual decisions and the direction of their personal piety. He showed this in the way he chose Isaac over Ishmael and Jacob over Esau, and this is the purpose according to which he chose and dealt with the Israelite nation as a whole. Just as "God's purpose in election" did not depend upon the spiritual status of the twins he chose from Rebekah's womb, so it did not depend upon the salvation status of the Jews in Paul's day.

The overall main point of this section is God's sovereign freedom to set up his plan of redemption as he chooses. He can choose whomever he pleases, whether individuals or nations, to carry out his redemptive purposes, apart from their own choice or cooperation, if necessary. His chosen servants do not have to be a part of spiritual Israel to be of service to him, and he is not obligated to reward them with eternal life just because they have played their part in the messianic drama. There is no inherent connection between service and salvation.

Verses 14–16. Next Paul explicitly raises the question of God's righteousness or faithfulness and implicitly relates it to his treatment of ethnic Israel as a whole: "What shall we say then? There is no injustice with God, is there? May it never be!" (verse 14 NASB). God has the sovereign right to choose for service without an accompanying promise of salvation. But one might ask, how do we know that God has this right? Here is the point of Paul's citation of God's declaration to Moses, "I will be gracious to whom I will be gracious, and will show compassion on whom I will show compassion" (Exod. 33:19 NASB; see Rom. 9:15). That is, Paul does not give some logical or rational defense of God's right to choose for service as he pleases; rather, he establishes this right by the simple quoting of the authoritative words of God as recorded in inspired Scripture.

The common understanding of these two verses (Exod. 33:19 and Rom. 9:15) is that they must refer to salvation because of the terms used: grace, mercy, compassion. This is not the case, however. The terms used in these verses do not inherently signify *saving* grace and mercy, in the sense of eternal salvation; in fact, they are often used for nonsoteriological grace or favor and temporal mercy and compassion. The first verb used in Exodus 33:19 is *chanan,* which often refers to God's temporal blessings. Basically it means "to do someone a favor, to show favor, to be merciful and kind, to bestow a blessing." For example, in Genesis 33:11 Jacob says to Esau, "God has dealt graciously with me," i.e., in giving him material wealth. Also, in 2 Samuel 12:22 (NASB) David says, "The LORD may be gracious to me, that the child may live." That is, God may grant my request to spare the life of Bathsheba's child. In the Psalms David often prayed for God to "be gracious" to him by giving him the strength to overcome his physical enemies (e.g., Ps. 31:9; 41:10; 56:1).

The second verb used in Exodus 33:19 is *racham,* which along with its cognates often refers to the attitude of compassion, mercy, or pity upon someone in any kind of need. When used of God's compassion, these words usually refer to his temporal blessings upon national Israel. For example, because God is compassionate, he will not destroy his people (Deut. 13:17; Ps. 78:38). A common idea is that because of his compassion God restores his people from captivity. For example, "Therefore thus says the Lord GOD, 'Now I will restore the fortunes of Jacob and have mercy on the whole house of Israel'" (Ezek. 39:25 NASB). "I will . . . have compassion on his dwelling places" (Jer. 30:18 NASB). (See also Deut. 30:3; Isa. 14:1; 49:10, 13; 54:7–8, 10; Jer. 31:20; 33:26; Zech. 10:6.)

As in Exodus 33:19, these two words (*chanan* and *racham*) and their cognates are often combined in the Old Testament to describe the nature of God's dealing with his people as a nation. They are the basis for God's decision to bless his people, to spare them, to deliver them, to keep them intact as the people through whom he would work out his plan of redemption. For example, "The LORD was gracious to them and had compassion on them" and did not allow Syria to destroy them (2 Kings 13:23 NASB). (See also 2 Chron. 30:9; Isa. 30:18; Ps. 102:13.)

Paul's quotation from Exodus 33:19 in Romans 9:15 is taken directly from the Septuagint, which uses the Greek words *eleeo* and *oiktiro,* which are close in meaning. The verb *eleeo* ("have mercy, be merciful"; cf. the noun *eleos,* "mercy") is used in Romans 9:15, as well as in 9:16 and 9:18. At times it refers to God's saving mercy (e.g., Rom. 9:23; 1 Tim. 1:13, 16; 1 Pet. 2:10); but more often it is used in the temporal sense of showing compassion to the poor, sick, or needy (Rom. 12:8; Philem. 2:27). Thus it is used as a prelude to a request for such mercy: "Have mercy on me, and help me" (e.g., Matt. 9:27; 15:22; 17:15; 20:30–31; Luke 16:24). Most significantly, it is sometimes used to refer to God's choosing or calling someone for service, specifically, Paul's call to be an apostle: 1 Corinthians 7:25; 2 Corinthians 4:1.

In view of the broad array of meanings for all the words involved here, including many that are not related to salvation, it is presumptuous to assume that Paul is using them in Romans 9:15 to refer to election to salvation. In view of the many uses of the Hebrew terms to refer to God's preservation of Israel as a nation, and Paul's use of *eleeo* to refer to his calling to be an apostle, it is reasonable to interpret the terms here in 9:15 as referring to God's choice of the nation of Israel to play a crucial role in his covenant purposes. The words imply that when God chooses anyone for service, such as Israel, he is bestowing great favor upon that person or nation, whether that person or nation is saved or not.

Thus far we have shown that the words *mercy* and *compassion* in Exodus 33:19 and Romans 9:15 do not *necessarily* refer to saving mercy since they have other legitimate uses compatible with election to service. But how do we know that the latter is the connotation intended here? The only way to decide this is to analyze them in reference to their contexts, especially the context of Exodus 33:19 (cf. the narrative from 32:9 to 34:10). Such an analysis shows that, when God says in this text that he will be gracious to and show compassion upon whomever he chooses, his statement has nothing to do with choosing anyone for salvation, temporal or eternal. Rather, he is declaring *his right to do as he chooses with the nation of Israel*. In this case he is exercising this right by sovereignly choosing to spare them as a nation and to continue to use them in his redemptive plan.[215]

Paul is applying this statement in a similar way in Romans 9:15. That is, it is a matter of God's sovereign mercy that he has chosen this nation for his purposes in the first place, and certainly even more so that he has spared and preserved them even this long, allowing them finally to be the physical source of the Savior's presence in the world (Rom. 9:5).

Romans 9:16 does, I think, express the concept of unconditional election; but Paul is applying it only to election for service and not to election for salvation.

Verses 17–18. How does the example of Pharaoh fit into the progression of Paul's argument? The apostle has shown that God's treatment of the Jews is not unjust because he has complete sovereignty in the way he chooses those who will serve his purposes. The way he chose Isaac and Jacob demonstrates this by example, and this is further confirmed by the citation of the general principle from Exodus 33:19. All of this together shows that God is free to choose whomever he pleases for roles of service.

But this in itself does not fully address the issue of the Jews. The question specifically is whether God is unjust because he called the nation of Israel into his service while at the same time condemning many if not most individual Jews to hell. If God is going to use them, is he not thereby obligated to save them? This is the point addressed in verses 17–18. Here Paul shows from the Old Testament that God's sovereignty in election for service includes the prerogative of choosing and using people without saving them. His premiere example is Pharaoh. Not only was he chosen via God's sovereign mercy, but he was also hardened or confirmed in his unbelief.

It is common to take verse 18 as referring to election to salvation and rejection to hell, with the former applying to Moses and the latter to Pharaoh. Nothing could be further from the truth. In the first place, there is nothing in this verse about eternal destinies, either heaven or

---

215. See Forster and Marston, *God's Strategy,* 65–66.

hell. "Mercy" here means the same as the mercy and compassion of verse 15, i.e., the favor God shows when he bestows on someone the privilege of playing a role in the drama of redemption. Second, there is no reference to Moses in this verse at all. Paul has said nothing specifically about Moses in this passage except that God revealed to him the great principle in Romans 9:15. At most that principle applied to him in context in the sense that God chose to answer his prayer. But he is not set forth here as Pharaoh's counterpart, as the object of God's mercy in contrast to Pharaoh as the object of God's hardening.

Rather, the whole of verse 18 refers to Pharaoh. In this context Paul has deliberately chosen to introduce him as an example because he is a perfect paradigm for God's treatment of Israel as one chosen for significant service in God's redemptive plan. In this sense God "had mercy" on Pharaoh just as he had mercy on Israel by choosing Abraham, Isaac, Jacob, and the entire nation to fulfill his covenant purposes. But God not only exercised his sovereign right to raise Pharaoh up for a specific purpose (v. 17); he also chose to use him for this purpose without saving him. In this sense Pharaoh is exactly parallel with Israel regarding the key point of this whole chapter: God's right to choose for service ("have mercy") without also choosing for salvation.

It is important to note that verse 18b ("he hardens whom he desires," NASB) does not mean that God hardened Pharaoh's heart in such a way that he was thereby caused to be an unbeliever. The Old Testament account of the events preceding the exodus from Egypt make clear that Pharaoh had already hardened his own heart against God. The main senses in which God hardened his heart were in extending or protracting Pharaoh's own self-caused hardness and in focusing it upon a particular situation. By doing this God thus caused Pharaoh to prolong his ultimate and inevitable decision to let the people go until all the plagues could be inflicted (cf. Exod. 4:21; 7:3; Rom. 9:17). In this way God used Pharaoh both in spite of his lost state and because of his lost state but without in any way causing his lost state.

This is the exact pattern of God's dealings with ethnic Israel as a whole. In his mercy he chose them for service, and he used them for his purpose both in spite of the fact that many (most) of them were lost and even *because* they were lost. As in the case with Pharaoh, the Jews who had hardened their own hearts toward God were in turn hardened by God early in the new covenant era in such a way that God accomplished a specific purpose through that very hardness (Rom. 11:7–11, 25).

The bottom line is that God's treatment of Israel is perfectly fair and just. He unconditionally chose and used them for his purposes, but this does not mean that they thereby had any claim on God's saving grace. They were both *chosen* and *hardened* at the same time. Thus there is no inherent connection between service and salvation, as the example of Pharaoh shows.

Romans 9:19–10:21. In Romans 9:19–10:21 Paul does turn to the subject of salvation, as he discusses what distinguishes the saved remnant within Israel from the unsaved Jews. Here it is clear that God's choice of the remnant is conditional, in accordance with the already established principle of justification by faith. God does separate spiritual Israel from the unsaved mass (9:19–29), but the agent of separation is faith, not election (9:30–10:21). In the latter section there is no hint of unconditional election to salvation or damnation; rather, it is clear that the separation between the lost and the saved Israelites is the result of their own choices, either to believe or to disbelieve. The Jews who were lost had no one to blame but themselves and their own stubborn wills. God himself is pictured, not as sovereignly deciding in his own secret will who will be saved and who will be lost, but as a loving God who invites all to be saved: "But as for Israel he says, 'All the day long I have stretched out My hands to a disobedient and obstinate people'" (10:21).

This is how this main section ends. Is Israel's lost state a reflection on God, evidence of his unfaithfulness, an indication that his word has failed (9:6)? No, God has faithfully kept his word to Israel in every way. He kept every promise he made to the nation relating to their covenant purposes and privileges (9:1–29). He has sent the Messiah and given them every opportunity to trust in him for personal salvation (9:30–10:21). Their refusal to accept him is their own fault.

Conclusion

In conclusion we shall note two ways in which a proper understanding of Arminian conditional predestination should affect us. First, it should give us a keen sense of personal responsibility. It respects our God-given free will and our ability to come to our own decision regarding faith in Christ. It makes the blame rest solely upon us if we do not meet the gracious conditions for election to glory. It relieves God of the apparent awful stigma of somehow being arbitrary and unjust for choosing some and rejecting others. It forces the unbeliever to face the problem of his own destiny squarely and without excuse. He cannot say, "What's the use? My fate is sealed anyway." Conditional election also warns the believer that he must give diligence to make his calling and election sure (2 Pet. 1:10 KJV).

Second, the doctrine of conditional predestination should give us a sense of personal peace. Usually it is Calvinists who make such a claim. To know, they say, that our salvation in no way depends on our own sinful and fickle selves but wholly upon the sovereign grace of God should give the believer great peace of mind. But in reality the idea of unconditional election has been the source of great anguish to many. "Since I can do nothing but wait," they say, "how can I know whether God has chosen me?" If the reason for choosing one person and not another lies wholly within the secret counsels of God, a person may *always* be uncertain of his status. Even if he knows himself as a believer, he may always wonder if his faith is a genuine gift of God or a temporary and ineffective imitation conjured up by his own deceptive will (see Matt. 13:5–7, 20–22).

The classical Arminian view of conditional election, however, is a source of great comfort. How can one be assured that he is among God's elect? Because God has revealed the conditions we must meet to be given this status, and everyone can know whether he or she has met the conditions. There is no mystery. If a person has not met the conditions, then he must be warned that the doctrine of predestination is not intended to be a comfort for unbelievers. If he has met them and is continuing to meet them, then he can confidently sing, "Blessed assurance, Jesus is mine; O what a foretaste of glory divine!"

CHAPTER 4

Responses to
Jack W. Cottrell

Response by Robert L. Reymond

It is evident from the length and detail of his essay that Jack Cottrell has taken seriously his assignment for this volume, and I honor him for his hard work. His essay sets forth the "classical Arminian view" of predestination, a brief history of the Arminian view,[1] a statement of the general theological presuppositions of this view, and a brief exposition of Romans 9 as a crucial text relating to this subject. I will only address what I regard are the central points of his (and Arminianism's) representation.

With reference to the Arminian doctrine of predestination, Cottrell defines it as "the view that before the world ever existed God conditionally predestined some specific individuals to eternal life and the rest to eternal condemnation, based on his foreknowledge of their freewill responses to his law and to his grace." That is to say, election

---

1. Cottrell apparently sees some value in the antiquity of the doctrine of conditional predestination. This means absolutely nothing to me, for whom the Scriptures alone are my sole doctrinal authority, beyond the fact that this is just one more error of the ancient fathers. I could fill pages documenting other errors that the ancient fathers held and espoused. Indeed, from the apostolic fathers onward the church immediately fell more and more into serious soteric error with grace and faith giving way to legalism and the doing of so-called good works as the announced way of salvation. An unevangelical nomism runs virtually unabated through the writings of the early church fathers; they saw Christianity as simply a "new law" (see my *The Reformation's Conflict with Rome—Why It Must Continue* [Ross-shire, Scotland: Mentor, 2001], 67–77, for documentation). Therefore I will not say anything more about this irrelevancy in this response.

to salvation is ultimately contingent on the human creature's *free* exercise of repentance and faith in Christ (which if not full-blown Pelagianism is certainly semi-Pelagianism), which repentance and faith God foresees and therefore he elects the sinner who believes in Christ.

Problems with the Arminian Understanding of "Free Will"

Cottrell (along with Arminianism in general) claims that men have free will, understood as the ability or power to choose any one of numerous incompatible courses of actions. The problem here is that there simply is no such thing as a will that is detached from and totally independent of the person making the choice—suspended, so to speak, in midair and enjoying some "extra-volitional vantage point" from which to determine itself. The will is the "mind choosing" (Jonathan Edwards). Therefore, men choose the things they do because of the complex, finite persons that they are. They cannot will to walk on water with any success or to flap their arms and fly. Their choices in such matters are restricted by their physical capabilities.

Similarly, their moral choices are also determined by the total complexion of who they are.[2] And the Bible informs us that men are not only finite but are now also sinners to boot, who by nature *cannot* bring forth good fruit (Matt. 7:18), by nature *cannot* hear Christ's word that they might have life (John 8:43), by nature *cannot* accept the Spirit of truth (John 14:17), by nature *cannot* be subject to the law of God (Rom. 8:7), by nature *cannot* discern truths of the Spirit of God (1 Cor. 2:14), by nature *cannot* confess from the heart Jesus as Lord (1 Cor. 12:3), by nature *cannot* inherit the kingdom of God (1 Cor. 15:50), by nature *cannot* control the tongue (James 3:8), and

---

2. For this reason one should never answer the question, "Do human beings have free will?" with a simple yes or no. The answer one gives should always take into account the specific state of humankind that the inquirer has in mind. In his state of innocence, Adam "had freedom, and power to will and to do that which was good and well pleasing to God; but yet, mutably, so that he might fall from it" (*posse non peccare et posse peccare*). In the state of sin, humankind has "wholly lost all ability of will to any spiritual good accompanying salvation; so as, a natural man, being altogether averse from that good, and dead in sin, is not able, by his own strength, to convert himself, or to prepare himself thereunto" (*non posse non peccare*). In the state of grace, the converted sinner, freed by God from his natural bondage to sin, is able "freely to will and to do that which is spiritually good; yet so, as that by reason of his remaining corruption, he doth not perfectly, nor only, will that which is good, but doth also will that which is evil" (*posse non peccare sed non prorsus et posse peccare*). Finally, in the state of glory, the will of the glorified saint "is made perfectly and immutably free to good alone" (*non posse peccare*). See Westminster Confession of Faith, "Of Free Will," IX/ii–v; see also Thomas Boston, *Human Nature in Its Fourfold State* (London: Banner of Truth, 1964 reprint of the 1850 edition).

by nature *cannot* come to Christ (John 6:44–45, 65). In order to do any of these things, they must receive powerful aid coming to them *ab extra*. So there simply is no such thing among men as a free will that can always choose the right if it wants to.

There is yet another problem implicit in Arminianism's quasi-deistic description of God's relationship to human actions as being that of bare "permissionism." Gordon H. Clark has correctly noted that permission to do evil, as opposed to positive causality, does not relieve God of involvement in some sense in mankind's sin inasmuch as it was God after all who made the world and people with the ability to sin in the first place.[3] On grounds that the Arminian demands for him,[4] God could have made both the world and mankind differently, or on these grounds, at the very least he could have made mankind with the freedom to do only good as is the condition of the glorified saints in heaven. It is transparently clear, then, that if the Creator God simply permits a man to sin, as Arminians contend is the case, he is still not totally unrelated to the event when that man does sin.

One other problem with free will must be addressed before we turn to our last topic. It is this: If one grants to God the attribute of omniscience, then it follows by impeccable logic that he infallibly knows all the future acts of men. And if he infallibly knows all the future acts of men, then those acts are not only certain to occur but also necessary to the accomplishment of his purpose. And if they are certain to occur and necessary to his purpose, then men do not have the freedom to choose other future acts. Arminians, asserting that "certainty is not necessity" and that this world has the built-in ability *independently* to create events have struggled to avoid this conclusion by employing semantic distinctions and to save for mankind free choice. But their semantic exercises only prop up their "house of cards" and fail to convince logical minds.

Cottrell's Treatment of Predestination in Romans 9

Cottrell believes that the election spoken of in Romans 9 is election to service, not to salvation. He declares that "the *main point* of Paul's discussion in Romans 9 is that God has the sovereign right to

---

3. Gordon H. Clark, *Religion, Reason and Revelation* (Nutley, N.J.: Craig Press, 1961), 205.

4. I say, "On grounds that the Arminian demands for him" here because, according to the Calvinistic Westminster Confession of Faith, III/I, "God, from all eternity, did, by the most wise and holy counsel of his own will, freely, and *unchangeably* ordain whatsoever comes to pass" (emphasis supplied). By the way, by "freely" here, the confession intends to say that God decreed what he did willingly with no external coercion.

make this distinction between election for service and election for salvation."

When it comes to responding to Cottrell's handling of Romans 9, I feel much like C. H. Spurgeon apparently did, who, when commenting for his students and for "ministers of average attainments," on C. H. Terrot's *Romans, with Introduction, Paraphrase, and Notes,* simply wrote: "Anti-Calvinistic. Why do not such writers let Romans alone?"[5] After reading Cottrell's treatment, I wonder what is the use of responding to such widespread mishandling of the text. I almost despair in thinking that anything I say will persuade him and his Arminian friends of their error, but I will try to make Paul's intention in Romans 9 plain to them!

I begin by laying down the principle that behind every other reason that can be given for a person's salvation ultimately stands God's sovereign, unconditional election. Without this feature of biblical salvation all of the other so-called *ultimate* reasons that might be advanced for one's salvation lack any final ground, certainty, and assurance. This truth is so patent on the face of biblical teaching that it is not too much to say that the person who rejects it as being inimical to human freedom perceived as the real ultimate and distinguishing cause of salvation has not yet learned the ABCs of biblical soteriology.

The divine rejection of Pharaoh and Egypt. God arranged every detail of the exodus event in order to highlight the great salvific truth that it is he who would have to take the initiative and deliver his chosen people if they were to be delivered at all because they neither desired Moses to deliver them nor were they capable of delivering themselves.[6] During his conversation with Moses leading up to Israel's exodus from Egypt, God declared that he would harden Pharaoh's heart throughout the course of the ten plagues precisely *in order to* "multiply" his signs and wonders and thereby to place his sovereign power in the boldest possible relief and this in order that both Egypt and Israel would learn that it was his power that effected the nation's deliverance (see the Song of Moses in Exodus 15). This signal demonstration of his sovereign power, the text of Exodus 3–14 informs us, God accomplished through the means of repeatedly hardening Pharaoh's heart.

---

5. C. H. Spurgeon, *Commenting and Commentaries* (New York: Robert Carter, n.d.), 244.

6. God ordained that Moses would unsuccessfully attempt to deliver his people from Egypt by his own prowess and leadership (see Exod. 2:11–15; Acts 7:23–29) before he sent him to Pharaoh with the rod of God in his hand.

The divine election of Moses and elect Israel. In Romans 9, in view of Israel's high privileges as the Old Testament people of God and the lengths to which God had gone to prepare them for the coming of their Messiah, Paul addresses the naked anomaly of Israel's official rejection of Christ. He addresses this issue at this point in Romans for two reasons: First, he is aware, if justification is by faith alone as he had argued earlier, with the racial connection of a person accordingly being irrelevant to his justification (see Rom. 2:28–29), that one could ask: "What then becomes of all of God's promises made to Israel as a nation? Have they not proven to be ineffectual?" Paul knows that, unless he can answer this inquiry, the integrity of the Word of God would be in doubt, at least in the minds of some. This in turn raises the second reason: "If the promises of God to Israel proved ineffectual, what assurance does the Christian have that those divine promises implicit in the great theology laid out in Romans 3–8 will not also prove to be finally ineffectual for him?"

An arbitrary or purposive God? For Arminians the teaching of unconditional election to salvation raises the question of arbitrariness in God. Even Geerhardus Vos, commenting on Romans 9:11–13, acknowledges "the risk of exposing the divine sovereignty to the charge of arbitrariness"[7] that Paul was willing to run in order to underscore the fact that the *gracious* election of Jacob (and the corresponding reprobation of Esau) was decided before (indeed, *eternally* before) the birth of the brothers, before either had done anything good or bad. Arminian theologians, of course, would spare their readers Vos's words "risk of exposing" and simply charge that the Reformed understanding of election does in fact expose God to the charge of arbitrariness in his dealings with mankind. What may be said in response to this charge? Does the Reformed doctrine of unconditional election (that we are insisting is the Pauline understanding of election as well) impute arbitrariness to God when it affirms that God discriminated between man and man before they were born, completely apart from a consideration of any conditions or causes (or the absence of these) in them?

With Paul (Rom. 9:14) we respond to these questions simply and tersely: "Not at all"—and for two reasons! First, Paul affirms precisely what these criticisms are intended to call into question: he declares that God discriminated between Esau and Jacob before they were born; he asserts that God's discrimination was made completely apart

---

7. Geerhardus Vos, *Biblical Theology* (Grand Rapids: Eerdmans, 1954), 109.

from a consideration of the moral conditions present within Esau and Jacob (see his "before either had done good or bad" and his "not by works"). Second, whether God's dealings with people are arbitrary depends entirely on the meaning of the word *arbitrary* that one is employing. If Arminians mean by the word to choose or to act this way at one time and that way at another with no rhyme or reason, that is to say, willy-nilly or inconsistently, or to choose or to act without regard to any norm or reason, in other words, capriciously, such choosing or acting Reformed thinkers steadfastly deny that they impute to God. They insist that God always acts in a fashion consistent with his prior, settled discrimination and that his prior, settled discrimination among mankind, as Paul informs us, was wisely determined—now note—*in the interest of* the grace principle (see Rom. 4:16; 9:11–12; 11:5).

As Vos states, because Paul recognized that the degree, however small, to which an individual is allowed to intrude himself as the decisive factor in receiving and working out the objective benefits of grace for his transformation "detract[s] in the same proportion from the monergism of the divine grace and from the glory of God,"[8] he calls his readers' attention to God's "sovereign discrimination between man and man, to place the proper emphasis upon the truth, that *His grace alone* is the source of all spiritual good to be found in man."[9] This is just to say that if God chose the way he did, out of the infinite depths of the riches of his wisdom and knowledge (Rom. 11:33), *in order to manifest his grace* (Rom. 9:11), that is to say, if he did so *for a purpose,* then *he did not choose arbitrarily or capriciously.* One may not approve of his purpose, but if God acted *purposively,* then he did not act arbitrarily.

I have attempted to show that if the Scriptures are given their due, a person's theology will be God centered. I have also shown that the sovereign God has foreordained whatever comes to pass, particularly the predestination of his elect, for his own glory, and that he providentially governs all his creatures and all their actions in order to accomplish his wise and holy ends. Though people make choices and initiate actions that either honor God or violate his revealed *preceptive* will, never is his *decretive* will thwarted, his wise design frustrated, or his eternal purpose checkmated. And all of his elect will be

---

8. Ibid., 108.
9. Ibid., 110 (emphasis added).

irresistibly drawn by his grace to eternal life and ultimate salvation, all to the praise of his glorious grace.

I sincerely hope that Jack Cottrell and his Arminian friends will face squarely the inherent problems I have noted with their doctrine of free will. I hope they will become Calvinists. They will do so if logic means anything to them, for I believe with Gordon Clark that if Arminians had a keener sense of logic they would not be Arminians! I would like very much the opportunity to speak to him directly about his views sometime.

Response by Thomas B. Talbott

Once a certain picture of God captures our imagination and we learn to put biblical ideas together in a certain way—or once we begin operating from a given theological paradigm, if you will—we almost naturally assume that we are reading the Bible just as it is, whereas our opponents are ignoring important parts of its clear message. According to Bruce Ware, for example, Arminians teach "only part of what the Bible says without accepting other teachings which do not easily fit with what already has been accepted."[10] And, of course, we non-Calvinists would say the same thing about the Calvinists. In defense of the Arminian view, for example, Jack Cottrell writes: "Contrary to Calvinism, . . . the Bible itself clearly shows that God's purposive (efficacious) will does not include all things. . . . This is seen in the fact that sometimes the . . . words that speak of God's determinative purpose are used to represent God's *desire* for certain things to happen which in fact do not happen."[11]

So the Calvinists, Cottrell argues, are ignoring important parts of the total biblical message. Similarly, I hold that both the Calvinists (or Augustinians, as I prefer to call them) and the Arminians reject some of the clear teaching in Romans 5, Romans 11, and 1 Corinthians 15 and do so because this teaching does not fit with "what has already been accepted" about divine judgment. And my four colleagues in this discussion no doubt believe the same sort of thing about me: As they no doubt see it (and will no doubt argue in their criticism of

---

10. See Ware's chapter in this volume.

11. See Cottrell's chapter. In a similar vein, Clark Pinnock writes: "Although Calvin's view claims to be based on the Bible, it is not. In teaching that grace is given only to a limited group and that God passes over the rest of mankind, it is at odds with Scripture. It fails to do justice to the teachings of the Bible in which God's will for the salvation of mankind is expressed." See Pinnock's chapter.

my chapter), I reject some of the clear teaching in Matthew 25:46; 2 Thessalonians 1:9; and Revelation 20 because it does not fit with my understanding of Paul's universalism.

Still, it continues to bewilder me that the Augustinians and the Arminians should both accept a doctrine of everlasting separation, without even questioning it, and do so in a context where one party limits the extent of God's redemptive love and the other limits the scope of his ultimate victory over sin and death; it bewilders me that so many should reject Paul's clear, systematic, and all-pervasive teaching concerning the extent and triumph of God's redemptive love even as they insist upon a dubious interpretation of texts lifted from contexts of parable, hyperbole, and great symbolism.

Determinism and the Bible

In any event, Cottrell and the Arminians are surely right about this: If God wills or desires for many "things to happen which in fact do not happen," then the best explanation for this is that God chooses not to exercise direct causal control over all events and, in particular, chooses not to exercise such control over all human choices. So Cottrell is also right to emphasize the reality of libertarian freedom, as it is sometimes called, and the power of contrary choice. In his own words, "a will is significantly free only if the choices it makes are not caused or determined, either directly or indirectly, by an outside force."[12] And though the exact meaning of "outside force" is by no means easy to specify in the present context, conditions that lie either in the distant past before the choosing agent is born or in eternity itself surely are external to that agent; hence, no free choice can be causally determined by such conditions as these.

A point to bear in mind here is that ordinary causal language, particularly when applied in certain personal and historical contexts, rarely excludes all causal contingency. Neither the expression, "The coach *molded* a group of individuals into a winning team," nor the expression, "The father *raised up* his son in the fear of the Lord," carries any implication of a rigorous overarching determinism. Or consider Exodus 9:16, where the Lord declared to Pharaoh: "But this is why I *have let you live*: to show you my power, and to make my name resound through all the earth" (my emphasis). In Romans 9:17, Paul actually quoted Exodus 9:16, replacing the words "this is why I have

---

12. See Cottrell. Strictly speaking, however, the will does not make choices; we make choices.

let you live" with the words "I have raised you up," as if the two expressions were virtually synonymous. When Paul said that God raised Pharaoh up for a given purpose, in other words, he simply meant that God created Pharaoh and permitted him to live and to achieve power for a given purpose. Not even the idea of a predestined or foreordained end carries any implication of a rigorous determinism.

In fact—and this is the really important point—we can know in advance that no one can validly deduce a rigorous determinism from the teachings of the Bible. All we need to know in this regard is that the Bible employs ordinary causal verbs, not the technical language of sufficient cause. When ordinary people speak of a cause, they rarely have in mind either a *sufficient* causal condition or even a *necessary* causal condition (concepts that many could not even explain); instead, they have in mind something very different, namely, the most significant part of an explanation, given a particular set of interests. Because the Bible is not a systematic philosophical treatise, moreover, and does not even try to provide the conceptual apparatus necessary for a precise statement of determinism, we can be utterly confident that, though the Calvinists may read determinism *into* the text, they cannot validly deduce a rigorous determinism from any teaching in the text.

The Power of Contrary Choice

But if Cottrell's understanding of free will is safe from Ware's argument from Scripture, what should we say about Ware's so-called argument from reason? The latter argument at least has the virtue of appealing to a true premise. For if, as Ware points out, I make a choice in a situation where I could have chosen otherwise, then "there is *no choice specific reason* (or set of reasons)" that determines my choice [his italics]. And we can illustrate the point in the following way. Suppose that I have a reason to do A (it seems like a thrilling or pleasant thing to do) and a reason to refrain from A (I believe that doing A would be morally wrong). If I have the power of contrary choice in this situation, then the weight of the reasons will not determine my choice for me; to the contrary, in making up my mind and finally arriving at a decision, I will thereby *determine* the weight of the reasons. Part of choosing freely, in other words, is choosing which reason will be decisive and deciding (not *discovering* but *deciding*) what I most want to do. But where does the argument go from there? How does anything said so far demonstrate that such free choices do not exist?

The Arminians, then, have misconstrued, I believe, the essential role that free will plays in the process whereby God reconciles sinners to himself. We no more manufacture for ourselves belief or trust or faith in God (or in Christ) than we manufacture for ourselves true beliefs about the nature of fire; instead, our free choices enable us to make discoveries of various kinds, to learn the lessons we need to learn, and to experience the consequences of acting upon false beliefs and various illusions where such exist.

Nor is the case of our relationship with God, whatever the additional complexities, essentially different from this. For if, as Christians have traditionally believed, separation from God can bring only greater and greater misery into our lives and union with him is the only thing that can satisfy our deepest yearnings and desires—or if, as C. S. Lewis once put it, separation from the divine nature is an objective horror and union with it eternal bliss—then anyone who understands all of this would have the strongest possible motive to unite with God and no intelligible motive whatsoever to reject him. So if such a person should reject God nonetheless, choosing an objective horror over eternal bliss, then this person's choice would simply be too irrational to qualify as a free choice for which the person is morally responsible.

In this life, of course, we rarely, if ever, choose in a context of full clarity. We all emerge and start making choices in a context of ambiguity, ignorance, and illusion, where God remains at least partly hidden from us. But that merely makes matters worse for Arminian theology, not better. For insofar as God remains hidden from us and we do not fully understand the true nature of God or the consequences of separating ourselves from him, we are in no position to reject the true God at all. We may reject a caricature of God, as frequently happens in a context of ambiguity, ignorance, and misperception; but we are in no position to reject the *true* God until our ignorance has been removed and our misjudgments have been corrected.

Response by Clark H. Pinnock

When it comes to the tradition in theology called Arminian, many draw a complete blank. Some suppose it to be the work of Armenian people with names like Alexanian and Bilezikian! Yet it is a contribution to theology with a lasting legacy, which, in the post-Reformation era, amounts to a reforming of Reformed thought. In opposition to Calvinism, it upholds the universal salvific will of God and the genuine freedom of humans to receive or reject the gift of salvation. It bears the name Arminian because it came to expression in the thinking of this important Protestant figure, who represented this understanding in post-Reformation times. Historically (however) this view predates the Augustinian innovation on the subject, though Augustine held it himself in his earlier years.

Arminians mostly view election as conditional upon faith, which in turn is corroborated by the foreknowledge of God. My own essay presents a nonclassical but still Arminian view of the matter and a variation upon it. It arises out of the fact that I have difficulty believing that God's foreknowledge is exhaustive and definite. Let me explain. First, the Scriptures speak not only of certainties when it comes to the future but of possibilities as well. They speak not only of what will be but also about what may be. In other words, it seems that the future is partially open even from God's point of view. Precisely who will be saved in the end (for example) is one of those things still being decided. I believe that God predestines, in the sense of "intends as their destiny," the salvation of all and assists them toward salvation without forcing it upon them. Our names may be written in the book of life, but it is up to us in part whether they remain there.

Second, I have difficulty grasping the ontological grounding for exhaustive and definite foreknowledge. How could God have a complete foreknowledge of that which has not yet been completely decided? If I have the freedom (for example) to decide tomorrow what I will do tomorrow, then I have it in my power to render false anyone's beliefs now held about what I shall do tomorrow. No one, not even God, can know for sure and completely what I will do, or so it seems to me. How can God know the future comprehensively when much of that future will be constituted by future free choices of moral free agents? Third, in terms of human freedom, how can decisions be free if it is already known and certain what the decisions will be? They will have to be precisely what God foresees them to be, or else God would be wrong in his forecast. So there can be no changing them now. Comprehensive foreknowledge and libertarian freedom appear to clash.

This is how I understand the foreknowledge of God. God possesses an infinite intelligence and (therefore) can anticipate and prepare for all possibilities of the future as perfectly as he can anticipate and prepare for all future definite facts. God deals with every possibility that might arise as if it were the only possibility needing consideration. Thus, even though God faces a future consisting partly of possibilities, he is never caught off guard and never fails in his anticipation. Even when something unlikely occurs, it is correct to say that God has been anticipating it from the foundation of the world, as if he had nothing else to do. The nice thing about this way of looking at reality is that, whereas the standard view of foreknowledge only affirms God's knowledge of what will be, this view takes into account what might be also, that is, it takes into account "might counterfactuals." That makes a more complete foreknowledge than the alternatives.

Response by Bruce A. Ware

I always enjoy reading whatever Jack Cottrell writes. His argumentation is regularly saturated with biblical analysis, and his writing style is clear and compelling. One would have to look far and wide to find a more able explanation and defense of the classical Arminian view of election than what one finds in this excellent essay. I commend Cottrell for his careful and capable work. In its overall thesis, and in many of its particular arguments, however, I find myself in substantial disagreement. Consider with me, then, a few of these points of disagreement.

First, it puzzles me why Cottrell opens his essay the way he does. His main point seems to be that the Arminian view has predominated in the history of the church as the dominant view that is set alongside the minority position of Augustinianism or Calvinism. But does he really want to say that "Arminianism as such, in its broadest sense, is simply non-Augustinianism or non-Calvinism"? Surely he is aware of the long history of both Pelagianism and semi-Pelagianism that were rejected by both Arminius and Wesley. Surely he is aware of the current movement of open theism with its Arminian roots but its rejection of the exhaustive definite foreknowledge of God. Surely he understands that process theology likewise holds a nonnegotiable commitment to libertarian freedom, yet in no stretch could it rightly be thought of as Arminianism. I appreciate the rhetorical value of presenting one's own view as the prevailing or majority position, but it seems to me that Arminianism is a bit narrower than Cottrell indicates.

Second, a major plank in Cottrell's argument has to do with the nature of God's foreknowledge and its relation to divine election to salvation. I agree fully with Cottrell, and against open theism, that God possesses exhaustive knowledge of the past, the present, and the future. Cottrell is rightly critical of the openness denial of God's exhaustive foreknowledge, in this sense. And of course, one of the reasons this matters so much to Cottrell is that foreknowledge really is the key to understanding election in the classical Arminian model. He writes, "Those who accept Christ through faith do so of their own free choice. Their choice of Jesus Christ is not predestined. That choice, however, is foreknown; and as a result the choosing ones become the chosen ones, who are then predestined to receive full blessings of salvation." But is it the case that God's election of those whom he will save is based on his (logically) prior foreknowledge of their belief in Christ?

Third, Cottrell upholds the centrality of foreknowledge also for his broader understanding of divine providence, within which election fits. He rejects the notion of God's comprehensive control, or meticulous providence, and argues that God grants free creatures a measure of control so that he does not and cannot violate their choices and actions performed with libertarian freedom. But, he argues, this does not leave God without recourse. Cottrell writes, "God exercises his sovereign control especially through his permissive will, which presupposes divine foreknowledge of future free-will choices. Such foreknowledge gives God the genuine option of either permitting or preventing men's planned choices, and prevention is the ultimate control."

But how can this be? If God in fact has "fore*knowledge* of future freewill choices," this means that he knows with certainty exactly what these free choices *will be*. Notice, this is not knowledge of what might be; it is foreknowledge of every single future free choice and action that God's moral creatures *will* bring about throughout human history. But if this is *knowledge* of what *will take place,* then there is no way God can influence or prevent those choices or actions to be different from what he knows they will be. The sobering conclusion is this: God's providence, in the classic Arminian model, is fully negated.

Fourth, because I have dealt in my own essay with libertarian freedom, I will not rehearse here its inherent problems. Let me just affirm the truthfulness of what Cottrell writes when he says, "The reality of truly free will [i.e., libertarian or contra-causal freedom] is a key ingredient in the Arminian system and a necessary presupposition of the Arminian view of predestination." Indeed, it is! So, as goes libertarian freedom, so goes Arminianism (and all other versions of "freewill theism," all of which uphold libertarian freedom and do so necessarily). I have concluded that libertarian freedom is nonexistent, though its advocacy is broad and impressive.

Last, I am unconvinced by Cottrell's understanding of God's election of Israel in Romans 9. Cottrell distinguishes between ethnic Israel and spiritual Israel, the latter of which is constituted by the believing remnant. Perhaps this quotation gets at the heart of Cottrell's position on what it means when Paul says that Israel will be saved:

> What is the difference between these two Israels, and why does Paul even bring it up here? The key difference is that *God's covenant promises to these two groups are not the same.* The promises God made to ethnic Israel are different from the promises he has made to spiritual Israel. Paul is saying, in effect, "You think God has been unfair to ethnic Israel because all Jews are not saved? Don't you know that there are *two* Israels, each with a different set of promises? You are actually confusing these two Israels. You are taking the salvation promises that apply only to the smaller group [i.e., spiritual Israel] and are mistakenly trying to apply them to Israel as a whole [i.e., ethnic Israel]" (emphases his).

I'll mention here two significant problems with this understanding, as I see it. First, covenant promises for Israel's future and ultimate salvation are unmistakably made to the whole of ethnic, national Israel. For example, listen to how God's promise to put his Spirit within them "and cause" them to "follow in" his statutes and "carefully observe" his ordinances (Ezek. 36:27) is introduced: "Therefore say to the house of Israel: This is what the Lord God says: It is not for your sake that I will act, house of Israel, but for My holy name, which you profaned among the nations where you went" (Ezek. 36:22 NASB). Both God's address to "the house of Israel" and his indicating that they are fully undeserving of the mercy he will show them since they have profaned his name among the nations—both of these features make clear that this covenant promise, of the outpouring of the Spirit on Israel, is made with the whole ethnic, national body of Israel. Likewise and famously, the new covenant of Jeremiah 31 is made "with the house of Israel and the house of Judah" (Jer. 31:31). And what will God do for these, his covenant people? He will write the law on their hearts, so that no one must teach another to know the Lord, "for they will all know Me, from the least of them to the greatest of them" declares the Lord (Jer. 31:33–34 NASB). Therefore, it simply is incorrect, and sadly so, to suggest that God has not promised the whole of the nation of Israel her day of salvation.

Second, Cottrell's interpretation of Romans 9 in this fashion conflicts directly with Paul's development in chapters 10 and especially 11. Recall in Romans 10:1 that Paul expresses his deep heartbreak over the fact that Israel is not saved. They know the law, he says, but they don't understand that only by faith in Christ, not by keeping the law, can they be saved. If we ask of whom Paul speaks here, surely he has in mind not those currently saved (i.e., *not* the believing remnant) but the full nation of Israel. This is confirmed in chapter 11 when he describes the natural branches of an olive tree as first broken off (Rom. 11:17) but then grafted on again (Rom. 11:24), followed immediately with these words: "So that you will not be conceited, brothers [i.e., Gentile believers] I do not want you to be unaware of this mystery: a partial hardening has come to Israel [i.e., the breaking off of the natural branches] until the full number of the Gentiles has come in [i.e., the grafting in of the unnatural branches]. And in this way all Israel will be saved [i.e., the grafting back in of the natural branches" (Rom. 11:25–26)].

In light of the Old Testament prophetic refrain announcing the future salvation of rebellious Israel, and in light of Paul's own usage of Israel in Romans 9–11, it seems clear that the promise of God which Paul is concerned to defend in Romans 9–11 is precisely what Cottrell denies, viz., Paul anticipates a day in the future when God will supernaturally save "all Israel." This will be by his grace that effectually turns masses of hearts of Jews to recognize and savingly trust their Messiah, Jesus Christ of Nazareth (note: libertarian freedom fails miserably here to account for this!). What a glorious day this will be, and what praise will be given to God for keeping his word: he will save Israel as a nation, as a whole ethnic people, just as he said.

CHAPTER 5

A Consistent Supralapsarian Perspective on Election

Robert L. Reymond

In this essay I will argue over against Arminianism, Amyraldianism, infralapsarianism, and inconsistent supralapsarianism the case for consistent supralapsarianism, the view of the order of decretal elements in God's plan of salvation that contends that, because the biblical God as a God of eternal purpose was governed in everything he planned by the purposive principle, to bring glory to himself as the God of grace, he placed the salvation of certain particular fallen men by Christ at the forefront of everything else in the plan as its end and arranged all the means to achieve that end in a retrograde order.

Of course, when the average Christian today hears the phrase, "God's plan of salvation," most likely he will think of the three or four things that a gospel tract he has read declares that the sinner must do in order to be saved, such as: (1) "You must acknowledge that you are a sinner and need to be saved," (2) "You must believe that Jesus died on the cross to save you from your sins," (3) "You must ask Christ to forgive you of your sins," and (4) "You must put your trust in Jesus as your Savior and Lord."

While these are things that the sinner must surely do in order to be saved, they hardly constitute the content of God's "plan of salvation." And it is only a debased theological perception, but one quite current in our time, that would suggest that it is. What the expression has more properly designated since the days of the Reformation is "the order of the decrees"[1] in the mind of the one living and true God of eternal purpose (Eph. 3:11).

Of course, most Christians today have given little or no thought to the subject even though only slight reflection should lead any Christian to conclude that it would be an irresponsible if not an irrational God who would create the world and direct its course of events with no prior plan or purpose behind such activity—or who would not direct the world he created at all. The Bible, however, has a great deal to say—much more than one might suppose at first blush—about the divine purpose standing behind and governing this world and the men who inhabit it. Benjamin B. Warfield has justly remarked about God's plan:

> That God acts upon a plan in all his activities is already given in Theism. On the establishment of a personal God, this question is closed. For person means purpose: precisely what distinguishes a person from a thing is that its modes of action are purposive, that all it does is directed to an end and proceeds through the choice of means to that end. . . . If we believe in a personal God, then, and much more if, being Theists, we believe in the immediate control by this personal God of the world he has made, we must believe in a plan underlying all that God does, and therefore also in a plan of salvation. The only question that can arise concerns not the reality but the nature of this plan.[2]

This being so, our present purpose will be to guide the reader through the labyrinth of intricate issues and details of what I believe is one of the most important (and surely one of the most fascinating) topics that Scripture would give any man warrant to study—what Warfield describes as the *nature* of the eternal plan of salvation or more technically the specific order of the elements in the plan.

That God from all eternity freely and unchangeably decreed whatever comes to pass in earth history is a given in Reformed Christian theism. That he did so by the most wise and holy counsel of his own will, yet so that neither is he the author of sin, nor is violence

---

1. John Murray, "The Plan of Salvation," in *Collected Writings of John Murray* (Edinburgh: Banner of Truth, 1977), 2:124, explains this term this way: "The distinct elements comprised in the design or plan have often been spoken of as the distinct decrees. If this term is adopted, then the expression 'the order of the decrees' means the same as the order that the various elements of salvation sustain to one another in the eternal counsel of God."

2. Benjamin B. Warfield, *The Plan of Salvation* (Grand Rapids: Eerdmans, n.d.), 14–15.

done to the will of the creature, nor is the liberty or contingency of second causes taken away but rather established, is also a given of Reformed Christian theism. In sum, for Reformed Christianity God is the absolute sovereign of the entire universe, both providentially and soteriologically.

Accordingly, Reformed Christians believe that every Christian should have a God-centered theology. And if he gives the Bible its due, not only will his theology be God-centered, but the gospel he espouses will uphold the sovereign grace of God in all its purity. He will reject every suggestion that men contribute anything ultimately determinative to their salvation. He will have discovered from his study of holy Scripture that just as the chief end of man is to glorify God and to enjoy him forever, so also the chief end of God is to glorify and to enjoy himself forever. He will have learned from Scripture that God loves himself with a holy love, that he loves himself with "all his heart, soul, mind, and strength," that he himself is at the center of his affections, and that the impulse that drives him and the goal he pursues in everything he does is his own glory!

To illustrate, the biblically informed Christian will know that God created all things for his own glory (Isa. 43:7, 21). More specifically, he will know, in order that God might show forth through a redeemed community, that is, his church, his "many-splendored" wisdom to the principalities and powers in heavenly realms (Eph. 3:9–10), that in the Old Testament he chose Israel for his renown and praise and honor (Jer. 13:11), that it was for his name's sake and to make his mighty power known that he delivered his ancient people again and again after they had rebelled against him (Ps. 106:7–8), and that it was for the sake of his name that he did not reject them (1 Sam. 12:20–22), spared them again and again (Ezek. 20:9,14, 22, 44), and had mercy upon them and did not pursue them with destruction to the uttermost (Isa. 48:8–11). He will have learned from holy Scripture that it was for his own glory that God did all these things (Ezek. 36:16–21, 22–23, 24–32). He will know too that Jesus came the first time to glorify God in doing his Father's will and work (John 17:4, 6), that every detail of the salvation that Jesus procured and that he himself enjoys God arranged in order to evoke from him the praise of his glorious grace (Eph. l:6, 12, 14), and that Jesus is coming again "to be glorified in his saints on that day, and to be marveled at among all who have believed" (2 Thess. 1:9–10 NASB).

Recognizing this—that according to holy Scripture God in all his activity in the world is ultimately concerned to glorify himself in all that he does—the biblically informed Christian, standing in the tradition of the great Reformers of the sixteenth century, will not hesitate to declare that this same concern—to glorify himself—is central to God's eternal plan. Accordingly, he will not hesitate to declare, in the words of the Westminster Confession of Faith, that "God from all eternity did, by the most wise and holy counsel of his own will, freely and unchangeably ordain whatsoever comes to pass" (III/i),[3] and that by the decree of God, "for the manifestation of his own glory, some men and angels are predestinated unto everlasting life, and others foreordained to everlasting death" (III/iii)—without controversy, surely one of the "deeps" of the divine wisdom.[4]

Concerning those of mankind predestinated unto life, the biblically informed Christian will joyously proclaim that "God, before the foundation of the world was laid, according to his eternal and immutable purpose, and the secret counsel and good pleasure of his will, hath chosen [them], in Christ, unto everlasting glory, out of his mere free grace and love, without any foresight of faith, or good works, or perseverance in either of them, or any other thing in the creature, as conditions, or causes moving him thereunto; and all to the praise of his glorious grace" (III/v).

---

3. God's purpose and his providential execution of his eternal purpose determine all things. This is why Calvin wrote in his *Institutes of the Christian Religion,* III.23.2: "God's will is, and rightly ought to be, the cause of all things that are. For if it has any cause, something must precede it, to which it is, as it were, bound; this is unlawful to imagine. For God's will is so much the highest rule of righteousness that whatever he wills, by the very fact that he wills it, must be considered righteous. When, therefore, one asks why God has so done, we must reply: because he has willed it. But if you proceed further to ask why he so willed, you are seeking something greater and higher than God's will, which cannot be found."

4. While we must insist on the equal ultimacy of election and reprobation in the divine decree, we must not speak of an exact identity of divine causality behind both. For while divine election is alone the root cause of the sinner's salvation, divine reprobation takes into account the reprobate's sin apart from which his condemnation must never be conceived and for which God is in no way the chargeable cause (see *Westminster Confession of Faith,* III.vii). Although this is the case, nevertheless, as John Murray cautions in his review of G. C. Berkouwer's *Divine Election* in *Collected Writings of John Murray* (Edinburgh: Banner of Truth, 1982), 4:330, emphasis original: "The necessary distinctions which must be observed, in respect of *causality,* between election unto life . . . and 'reprobation' unto death . . . do not in the least interfere with the truth which is the real question at issue, to wit, the pure sovereignty of the differentiation inhering in the counsel of God's will. . . . The 'equal ultimacy' is here inviolate. God differentiated between men in his eternal decree; *he* made men to differ. And, ultimately, the only explanation of the differentiation is the sovereign will of God."

Concerning "the rest of mankind," the biblically informed Christian true to God's Word will solemnly yet faithfully preach and teach that "God was pleased, according to the unsearchable counsel of his own will, whereby he extendeth or withholdeth mercy as he pleaseth, for the glory of his sovereign power over his creatures, to pass by; and to ordain them to dishonor and wrath for their sin, to the praise of his glorious justice" (III/vii).

Of course, these two groups making up the totality of mankind, he will also teach, do not arrive at their divinely determined destinies arbitrarily with no interest on God's part with respect to what they would believe or how they would behave before they got there, for he is aware that "as God hath appointed the elect unto glory, so hath he, by the eternal and most free purpose of his will, foreordained all the means thereunto" (III/vi), such as the Son's atoning work, the Father's effectual calling of the elect through the Spirit's regenerating work, by which work repentance and faith are wrought in the human heart, the Father's act of justification and the Spirit's work of sanctification.

And the biblically informed Christian is also aware, while it is true that God's determination to pass by the rest of mankind (this "passing by" theologians designate "preterition" from the Latin *praeteritio*) is grounded solely in the unsearchable counsel of his own will, that his determination to ordain those whom he passed by to dishonor and wrath (condemnation) took into account the condition which alone deserves his wrath—the fact of their sin.

This eternal plan or purpose (Eph. 3:11), the biblically informed Christian will affirm, God began to execute by his work of creation (*Westminster Shorter Catechism,* question 8). He will also affirm that from the creation of the world to this present moment God has continued to execute his eternal purpose to bring glory to himself through his providential exercise of his almighty power, unsearchable wisdom, and infinite goodness, this his providence extending itself to all his creatures and all their actions, "even to the first fall, and all other sins of angels and men; and that not by a bare permission, but such [permission] as hath joined with it a most wise and powerful bounding, and otherwise ordering, and governing of them [all the sins of angels and men], in a manifold dispensation, to his own holy ends" (Westminster Confession of Faith, V/iv).

Adam's sin, he will affirm, "God was pleased, according to his wise and holy counsel [which counsel in its perfection eternally existed before the creation of the world], to permit, having purposed to order it to his own glory" (Westminster Confession of Faith, VI/i). By his sin Adam fell from his original state of righteousness (*status integritatis*)—a state in which it was possible for him to sin or not to sin (*posse peccare aut posse non peccare*)—and so "became dead in sin, and wholly defiled in all the parts and faculties of soul and body" (*status corruptionis*) (Westminster Confession of Faith, VI/ii)—a state in which it was not possible for him not to sin (*non posse non peccare*). And he will declare that, because Adam was the covenantal (federal) representative head of his race by divine arrangement, his first sin was imputed and his corruption conveyed to all mankind descending from him by ordinary generation (Westminster Confession of Faith, VI/iii).

Accordingly, all mankind (with the sole exception of Christ who did not descend from Adam by ordinary generation) God regards as sinners in Adam. And because of their covenantal representation in Adam's sin (their "original sin") as well as their own sin and corruption, all men are continually falling short of the ethical holiness of God and the righteous standards of his law (Rom. 3:23) and thus are under his sentence of death.

But in accordance with his gracious elective purpose, God, the biblically informed Christian with great delight will also preach and teach, is pleased to save his elect, and to save them forever, by Christ's atoning death in their behalf and in their stead and by the Holy Spirit's application of the benefits of Christ's redeeming virtues to them. And though the elect do assuredly trust in Christ to the saving of their souls, yet they contribute nothing ultimately determinative of that salvation since even their trust in Christ is a saving gift (Eph. 2:8). All that they bring to their salvation is their sin and moral pollution from which they need to be saved. Salvation from beginning to end belongs ultimately and wholly, then, to the Lord (Jon. 2:10), to the praise of his glorious grace (Eph. 1:6, 12, 14).

All of these articles of faith the biblically informed Christian will hold to be true to the teachings of holy Scripture. He will, in short, espouse the Reformed faith that is in turn simply the faith of holy Scripture itself. And all this, I say, is a given of Reformed theism.

Before we address the order of the elements in God's eternal plan of salvation, however, it is important that we first set forth the significant biblical evidence for the *fact* of his eternal plan of salvation itself and the central aspects of its content.

The Fact and Central Elements of God's Eternal Plan

The advanced student of theology may be tempted to skip this section and go directly to the discussion of the order of God's decrees, but a review of the pertinent New Testament material will be beneficial to him if it does nothing more than remind him of the fullness of Scripture's witness to the fact of God's eternal plan. As for the reader who may have a certain reticence, if not total resistance, toward any such discussion of God's decrees, even were it conducted by the saintliest man among us, that would seek to understand the logical order in which God planned what he did, a simple rehearsal of some of the basic biblical material about the plan should help to ease his suspicions that men who do so are "rushing in where angels fear to tread."[5] For what God has revealed concerning his plan he surely desires people to attempt to understand.

With regard to the fact itself, for the mind informed by Scripture there can be no question. As Warfield has noted, for the Christian mind "the only question that can arise concerns not the reality but the nature of this plan." And once the reticent reader clearly sees that the eternal plan of God has several major elements that pertain to him and begins to reflect upon the discussion that follows this section, he may even become convinced that it is imperative that he subscribe to a particular order for the several elements of the plan.

God's "Eternal Purpose"

Perhaps it will reassure the theological student for whom this entire subject is new if we begin by considering a general term found in Ephesians 3:11 (NIV). Here Paul speaks of God's *"eternal purpose*

---

5. Many Christians today desire to suppress all study of the eternal plan of God out of fear that the doctrine of election will destroy the Christian's certainty of salvation (on the contrary, it actually grounds his certainty), and because it is, they say, both divisive and detrimental to the "free will" of man. John Calvin warned against such suppression: "Scripture is the school of the Holy Spirit, in which, as nothing is omitted that is both necessary and useful to know, so nothing is taught but what is expedient to know. Therefore we must guard against depriving believers of anything disclosed about predestination in Scripture, lest we seem either wickedly to defraud them of the blessing of their God or to accuse and scoff at the Holy Spirit for having published what it is in any way profitable to suppress. . . . But for those who are so cautious or fearful that they desire to bury predestination in order not to disturb weak souls—with what color will they cloak their arrogance when they accuse God indirectly of stupid thoughtlessness as if he had not foreseen the peril that they feel they have wisely met? Whoever, then, heaps odium upon the doctrine of predestination openly reproaches God, as if he had unadvisedly let slip something hurtful to the church" (*Institutes of the Christian Religion,* III.21.3, 4).

which he accomplished in Christ Jesus our Lord."[6] Five brief comments are in order here.

First, the Greek word translated quite properly here as "purpose" (it may also be translated "plan" or "resolve"[7]) is in the singular: God has one overarching purpose or plan. This plan, of course, has many elements, as we shall see.

Second, Paul describes God's purpose or plan as his *"eternal* purpose," literally, "purpose of the ages," intending by the Greek adjectival genitive[8] that there was never a moment when God had a blank mind or a time when God's plan with all of its parts was not fully determined. He never "finally made up his mind" about anything. This is just to say that God has *always* had the plan and that within the plan itself there is no chronological factor *per se.* The several parts of the plan must be viewed then as standing in a teleological rather than a chronological relationship to one another.

Third, the person and work of Jesus Christ are clearly central to God's "eternal plan" because Paul says that God "accomplished" or "effected" it "in the Christ, Jesus our Lord." The closely related earlier statement in Ephesians 1:9 echoes the same truth: Paul states there that "the mystery of [God's] *will,* according to his *good pleasure"* he *purposed* to put into effect in Christ—that "purposed good pleasure" being "to bring all things in heaven and on earth under one head in Christ." Here we learn that God's eternal plan that governs all his ways and works in heaven and on earth, he purposed to fulfill in Christ. Clearly, Christ, as God's Alpha and Omega, is at the beginning, the center, and the end of his eternal purpose.

Fourth, this eternal purpose or plan, directly and centrally concerned as it is with Jesus Christ, is accordingly directly and centrally concerned with soteric issues as well. In the verses immediately

6. When Paul speaks of God's "purpose," he is simply echoing Isaiah's words in Isaiah 14:24, 27: "Surely, as I have planned (*dmt*), so it will be, and as I have *purposed* (*yatst*), so it will stand. . . . For the Lord Almighty has purposed (*yats*), and who can thwart him?" Note also Isaiah 46:10–11: "I make known the end from the beginning, from ancient times what is still to come. I say: My purpose (*atst*) will stand, and I will do all that I please. . . . What I have said, that will I bring about; what I have *planned* (*ytsrt*), that will I do." See also Proverbs 19:21: "Many are the plans in a man's heart, but it is the *Lord's purpose* that prevails."

7. W. Bauer, F. W. Danker, W. F. Arndt, and F. W. Gingrich (BDAG), *"prothesis," A Greek-English Lexicon of the New Testament and Other Early Christian Literature* (Cambridge: Cambridge University Press, 1957), 713, 2.

8. Theoretically, these "ages" could be any ages, but since they are in no way circumscribed, that is to say, since they are indeterminate of duration, *aionon* here should be construed to mean "of eternity," hence "purpose of eternity," which is just to say, "eternal purpose."

preceding this reference to God's "eternal purpose which he accomplished in the Christ" Paul declares that God "created all things in order that through the [redeemed] church, the manifold wisdom of God should be made known to the rulers and authorities in the heavenly realms" (3:9–10). He then follows this statement with the words of 3:11 to the effect that the indicated activity in 3:9–10 was *"according to* his eternal purpose which he accomplished in the Christ, Jesus our Lord." The church of Jesus Christ—God's redeemed community— also clearly stands in Jesus Christ, then, at the beginning, the center, and the end of God's eternal purpose.

This soteric feature of the divine purpose receives support from the other passages in the Pauline corpus where he refers to God's "purpose." In Romans 8:28 (NASB) Paul declares that Christians were effectually "called [to salvation] *according to* [his] *purpose."* In Ephesians 1:11 he says that Christians were made heirs of God, "being predestined *according to* the *purpose* of Him who works all things according to the *counsel* of His will" (NKJV). And in 2 Timothy 1:9 Paul affirms that "God saved us and called us with a holy calling, not according to our works but *according to his own purpose* and grace which was granted us in Christ Jesus from all eternity" (NASB).

Finally, we learn from Romans 9:11–13 that the elective principle in God's eternal purpose serves and alone comports with the grace principle which governs all true salvation. Here we see the connection between God's grace and his elective purpose dramatically exhibited in God's discrimination between Jacob and Esau, which discrimination, Paul points out, occurred *"before* the twins were born or had done anything good or bad" (NIV; see Gen. 25:22–23). Paul elucidates the *rationale* standing behind and governing the divine discrimination signalized in the phrase, "in order that God's *'according to* election purpose' might stand [that is, might remain immutable]," in terms of the following phrase—"not *according to* works but *according to* him who calls [unto salvation],"[9] which is equivalent to saying, "not according to works but according to grace."

Paul teaches here that God's elective purpose is not, as in paganism, "a blind unreadable fate" which "hangs, an impersonal mystery, even above the gods," but rather that it serves the intelligible purpose of "bringing out the gratuitous character of grace."[10] In fact, Paul will

---

9. See BDAG, *Greek-English Lexicon*, 235, 3, I, for this rendering of *ek*.
10. Geerhardus Vos, *Biblical Theology* (Grand Rapids: Eerdmans, 1954), 108, 110.

refer two chapters later specifically to "the election of grace" (Rom. 11:5 NKJV).

From just this much data we can conclude that God has a single eternal purpose or plan at the center of which is Jesus Christ and in him his church, and which entails accordingly also at its center such soteric issues as God's election, predestination, and effectual call of sinners to himself for salvation in order to create through them the church, which in turn serves as the vehicle for showing forth, not the glory of man (see Rom. 9:12; 2 Tim. 1:9), but the "many sides" of his own infinite grace and wisdom (Eph. 3:10), this latter term a synonym for the plan itself.

Christ's Cross Work in the Plan

In Luke 22:22 (AT) Jesus taught his disciples that "the Son of Man is going [to the cross] *in accordance with the [divine] decree.*" Echoing the same truth later, in Acts 2:23 (AT) Peter proclaimed: "This one [Jesus], *by the determining purpose* and *foreknowledge* of God, was handed over, [and] you with wicked hands put him to death by nailing him to the cross." In both Jesus' and Peter's statements, the church finds indisputable reason for believing that the cross of Christ was central to the eternal plan of God. Accordingly, in Acts 4:24–28 (AT) the entire church affirmed that Herod and Pontius Pilate, with the Gentiles and leaders of Israel, had done to Jesus "what your hand and your will *predestined* should happen."

And while one cannot dogmatize here, it is possible that it is God's eternal plan of salvation in and by Christ's cross work to which Hebrews 13:20 (NASB) refers when it speaks of "the blood of the *eternal* covenant." If this is its referent, then again Christ's cross work is represented as a central aspect of God's eternal purpose. One learns from these verses that not only Christ but also his cross work (that is, his sacrificial death in the stead of others) was an integral part of the divine decree.

God's Foreknowledge and Predestination in the Plan

From Romans 8:29–30 we learn of other aspects of God's eternal purpose or plan. Paul tells the Christian that "[the ones] whom [the Father] *foreknew* (that is, set his heart upon in covenantal love), he also *predestined* to be conformed to the image of his Son, . . . and whom he *predestined,* those he *called,* etc." Two things are clear from this.

First, we learn that in his eternal plan (note the *pro*-prefixes ["before"] attached to the first two verbs) God "foreknew" (that is, "set his heart upon") certain people in covenantal love and "predestined" their conformity to his Son's likeness. And in this context (Rom. 8:33) Paul designates those whom God has always so loved as "God's elect."

Why have we interpreted the first verb "foreknew" (*proegno*) as we have? Reformed theologians have uniformly recognized that the Hebrew verb *yda* ("to know"—see its occurrences in Gen. 4:1; 18:19; Exod. 2:25; Pss. 1:6; 144:3; Jer. 1:5; Hos. 13:5; Amos 3:2) and the Greek verb *ginosko* ("to know"—see its occurrences in Matt. 7:22–23; 1 Cor. 8:3; 2 Tim. 2:19) can mean something on the order of "to know intimately," "to set one's affections upon," or "to have special loving regard for" and that the verb *proegno* intends something approximating this meaning rather than the sense of mere prescience in Romans 8:29.[11]

Reformed theologians also understand Paul to mean here that God did not set his love upon the elect from all eternity because of foreseen faith or good works or perseverance in either of them or any other condition or cause in them moving him thereunto. To assert that he did, they insist, not only intrudes circumstances and conditions into the context which are absent from it but also flies in the face of the teachings of Romans 9:11–13 that election is according to grace and not according to works, of Ephesians 1:4 that God chose us before the creation of the world "that we should *be* holy" (NKJV) and not because he saw that we *were* holy, and of 2 Timothy 1:9 that he saved us and called us to a holy life, not because of anything we have done but because of *his own* purpose and grace.

Second, we learn also from the tight grammatical construction between the verbs "predestined" and "called" that what God planned in eternity, he executes in this created world. So there is a clear connection between his plan and his execution of his plan. He is the author of both. The former is the "blueprint" of the latter. The latter is the "historical construction" of the former.

God's Election of Some Men in the Plan

In Ephesians 1:4–5 (AT) Paul tells us that God the Father "chose us in him [Christ] *before* the creation of the world, that we should

---

11. For an excellent discussion of the meaning of "foreknow" in Romans 8:29, see David N. Steele and Curtis C. Thomas, *Romans: An Interpretive Outline* (Philadelphia: Presbyterian and Reformed, 1963), Appendix C, 131–37.

be holy and without blame before him, in love *having predestinated* us unto sonship by adoption through Jesus Christ unto himself, according to the good pleasure of his will." Here in this great doxology to God the Father, Paul avers in no uncertain terms that from all eternity God has chosen the Christian to holiness and predestinated him to sonship. And he did so, Paul writes, "according to the good pleasure of his will" (see also in this same regard Eph. 1:9, 11). And here, writes Murray,

> it is to trifle with the plain import of the terms, and with the repeated emphasis, to impose upon the terms any determining factor arising from the will of man. If we say or suppose that the differentiation which predestination involves proceeds from or is determined by some sovereign decision on the part of men themselves, then we contradict what the apostle by eloquent reiteration was jealous to affirm. If he meant to say anything in these expressions in verses 5, 9, and 11, it is that God's predestination, and his will to salvation, proceeds from the pure sovereignty and absolute determination of his counsel. It is the unconditioned and unconditional election of God's grace.[12]

In 2 Thessalonians 2:13 (AT), the last verse that we will consider in this connection, Paul informs his readers—whom he describes as "brothers who have been loved by the Lord"—that "God chose you from the beginning unto salvation." This verse, in addition to the previous verses cited, underscores the truth that from all eternity God had determined upon a course of salvific activity for himself that would result in the salvation of his beloved children from sin and death.

From all this it should be clear that no Christian can legitimately doubt the fact or reality of God's eternal plan of salvation. When Reformed theologians speak, then, of God's eternal purpose or God's eternal plan of salvation, they refer to this eternal salvific decision-making on God's part concerning Christ and his cross work and the election and predestination of men to salvation in him. With this scriptural data before us, we may now turn to a discussion of the nature of God's eternal plan.

The Nature and Governing Principle of God's Eternal Plan

Among Reformed thinkers one may find essentially three basic perceptions of the nature of God's eternal plan of salvation: the

---

12. Murray, "The Plan of Salvation," in *Collected Writings*, 2:127.

Amyraldian, the infralapsarian, and the supralapsarian. I will discuss each of these in turn, anticipating that the reader will see by the time we reach the end of our discussion both the biblicity and the logic in the supralapsarian perception.

The Amyraldian Perception (the Inconsistent Governing Principle)

While all Reformed Christians are committed to the particularistic principle, that is to say, to the discriminating or electing element, in God's eternal purpose, some Reformed theologians designated "Amyraldians" after Moise Amyraut (Amyraldus) (1596–1664) of the theological school of Saumur in France who developed the scheme (also known as "hypothetical universalists," "post-redemptionists," "ante-applicationists," and "four-point Calvinists" for reasons which will become clear later) depart from classic Reformed particularism and unite with Arminians in their view of Christ's cross work. They maintain that the Bible teaches that Christ died for all men without exception.[13] Here, they maintain, is at least one aspect of the divine activity looking toward the salvation of everyone that is universal in its design. In other words, Amyraldians maintain that while the Bible does indeed declare that in his eternal plan of salvation God discriminates among men and chooses an elect who alone will be saved, yet Christ died savingly not just for God's chosen elect but for all men without exception.[14] But how can this universalistic aspect of the

13. See Roger R. Nicole, "Amyraldianism," in *The Encyclopedia of Christianity* (Wilmington, Del.: The National Foundation for Christian Education, 1964), I:184–93. Moise Amyraut's view goes back to his tutor, John Cameron (1580–1626), minister of the Reformed church at Bordeaux, who served in a professorial capacity in the schools of Saumur and Montauban and finally in the University of Glasgow. In his *Eschantillon de la doctrine de Calvin touchant la predestination* (1636), Amyraut contended that Calvin espoused universal atonement. Contemporary Amyraldians also contend that their view is essentially that of John Calvin. I will contend in the next footnote that in this they are in error.

14. Contemporary Amyraldians such as R. T. Kendall maintain that John Calvin did not teach the doctrine of particular atonement and that their position is essentially Calvin's. While Calvin did not write an explicit treatment of the extent of the atonement, as far as we know, he never took issue with the contemporary advocates of particular atonement. That he did hold to particular atonement seems clear, however, from certain of his statements. For example, commenting on "who wants all men to be saved" in 1 Timothy 2:4, he expressly denies that Paul speaks here of individual people and states rather that he "simply means that there is no people and no rank in the world that is excluded from salvation." Commenting on 2:5, Calvin writes: "The universal term *all* must always be referred to classes of men, and not to persons, as if he had said, that not only Jews but Gentiles also, not only persons of humble rank, but princes also, were redeemed by the death of Christ."

Commenting on John's clause "and not for ours only" in 1 John 2:2, Calvin states: "Though . . . I allow that what has been said [by the schoolmen to the effect that Christ

divine activity be adjusted to the particularistic aspect of the divine activity that, after all, is the hallmark of the Reformed (or Calvinistic) soteriological vision?

Amyraldian theologians resolve for themselves the tension between soteric particularism on the one hand (which they are convinced the Bible teaches) and the universalistic design of Christ's cross work on the other (which they are equally convinced the Bible also teaches) by analyzing God's eternal plan of salvation and by positing a specific arrangement or order for its several parts or elements. This order, they claim, justifies their soteric vision.

The Amyraldian arrangement of the several major elements or decrees of God's eternal plan of salvation is as follows: First, the decree to create the world and (all) men; second, the decree that (all) men would fall; third, the decree to redeem (all) men by the cross work of Christ; fourth, the election of some fallen men to salvation in Christ (and the reprobation of the others); fifth, the decree to apply Christ's redemptive benefits to the elect.

A cursory analysis of the Amyraldian scheme will show, because they postpone the discriminating decree to the fourth position, that the first three decrees are necessarily universal with respect to their referents since God has not yet introduced any discrimination into the plan (which explains my insertion of the word "all" in parentheses in each of them), with only the last two being particular in regard to their referents, namely, the discriminating decree to elect some men to salvation that comes immediately after the decree to redeem men (hence the scheme's name "post-redemptionism") and immediately before the decree to apply Christ's redemptive benefits (hence its name "ante-applicationism") and the particularistic application decree itself.

---

suffered sufficiently for the whole world but efficiently only for the elect] is true, yet I deny that it is suitable to this passage; for the design of John was no other than to make the benefit common to the whole Church. Then under the word *all* or *whole,* he does not include the reprobate, but designates those who should believe as well as those who were then scattered through various parts of the world."

Here Calvin explicitly excludes the reprobate from Christ's propitiation and represents the "whole world" as referring to all throughout the various parts of the world, without distinction or race or time, who through faith partake of salvation. Finally, in his reply in *Tracts and Treatises* (Beveridge's edition, 2:527) to Tilemann Heshusius, a Lutheran defender of the corporeal presence of Christ in the Lord's Supper, Calvin writes: "I should like to know how the wicked can eat the flesh of Christ that was not crucified for them, and how they can drink the blood which was not shed to expiate their sin?" For a fuller treatment of Calvin's view in this regard, see Roger R. Nicole, "John Calvin's View of the Extent of the Atonement," in *Westminster Theological Journal* 47 (Fall 1985): 197–225; and Paul Helm, *Calvin and the Calvinists* (Edinburgh: Banner of Truth, 1982).

In other words, Amyraldians postulate that in the one "eternal purpose" of God, his first decree pertains to the creation of the world and of all men who would populate it. His second decree pertains to the fall of Adam and in him of all mankind descending from him by ordinary generation. The third decree pertains to the cross work of Christ, and since no "distinguishing decree" yet appears in the order, the referent of its work is all men without exception or distinction. Amyraldians contend that the biblical passages that ascribe a universal reference to Christ's cross work (see "all men" in John 12:32; Rom. 5:18; 8:32; 11:32; 2 Cor. 5:14–15; 1 Tim. 2:5–6; Titus 2:11; Heb. 2:9; and "world" in John 3:16; 1 John 2:2; 2 Cor. 5:19) must be taken seriously and reflect an order of the decrees in which the decree to save mankind by Christ's cross work necessarily precedes the decree to discriminate among people.

Because, however, some biblical passages also clearly mention the fact of election, Amyraldians acknowledge that the election factor must also be taken seriously and given a place in the eternal plan of salvation. Therefore, they willingly include it in their conception of the plan of salvation, placing the electing decree that discriminates among men *after* the "cross work decree" (which conception, they contend, preserves the cross's "unlimited" design and justifies the presence of the biblical passages that speak of Christ's cross work in universal terms) and *before* the decree concerning its application. The upshot of the Amyraldian arrangement is that the actual execution of the divine discrimination comes not at the point of Christ's redemptive accomplishment which is universal in intent but at the point of the Spirit's redemptive application which is limited to the elect.[15]

---

15. R. T. Kendall, a contemporary Amyraldian, in his *Calvin and English Calvinism to 1649* (New York: Oxford University Press, 1979), 16, puts a different twist on the issue of application, arguing that while Christ died equally for all mankind he intercedes only for the elect: "The decree of election . . . is not rendered effectual in Christ's death but in his ascension and intercession at the Father's right hand." He reasons that without the doctrine that Christ died equally for all there can be no assurance of salvation, for otherwise the sinner could never be sure that Christ died for him: "Had not Christ died for all, we could have no assurance that our sins have been expiated in God's sight" (14). But when Kendall makes not the cross but Christ's intercession at the Father's right hand the decisive point at which the divine election becomes effectual, he not only bifurcates the high priestly ministry of Christ, making Christ's oblation universalistic and his intercession particularistic, but moves the problem of assurance from the area of Christ's cross work to that of his intercessory work. But how can the sinner be any more certain that Christ is interceding for him in heaven? He cannot. The consistent Calvinist, however, knows, first, that the sinner, any sinner, can be assured if he will trust Christ that Christ will save him because the sufficiency of Christ's atonement for all grounds the proclamation of the

While their conception satisfies the Amyraldians and preserves for them the right to regard themselves as "Calvinistic" (since they grant a place in their arrangement of elements for the particularistic principle which is the hallmark of Calvinism), those creedal churches within the Reformed world which have adopted the Belgic Confession, the Heidelberg Catechism, the Canons of Dort, and the Westminster Confession of Faith have uniformly rejected it, and in my opinion quite properly so, for three basic reasons.

First, Amyraldianism is a logically inconsistent form of Calvinism in that its scheme has the persons of the Godhead working at cross-purposes with one another: by decree the Son died with the intention to save all men, and by decree the Spirit savingly applies Christ's saving benefits to only some of those for whom Christ died. Each person's labor cancels out the intention of the other's labor.

Second, Amyraldianism is equally illogical in that it implies, because the Son and the Spirit by their respective labors are both simply executing the Father's "eternal purpose" for them, that an irrational element, which in effect imputes confusion to the divine purpose, resides in God, which in turn assaults the rational character of God and his eternal plan. Warfield rightly asks, "How is it possible to contend that God gave his Son to die for all men, alike and equally; and at the same time to declare that when he gave his Son to die, he already fully intended that his death should not avail for all men alike and equally, but only for some which he would select (which . . . because he is God and there is no subsequence of time in his decrees, he had already selected) to be its beneficiaries?"[16]

He answers his own question:

As much as God is God . . . it is impossible to contend that God intends the gift of his Son for all men alike and equally and at the same time intends that it shall not actually save all but only a select body which he himself provides for it. The schematization of the order of decrees presented by the Amyraldians, in a word, necessarily implies a chronological relation of precedence and subsequence among the decrees [or the other alternative which, as we suggested above, is irrationality within the divine mind— RLR], the assumption of [either of] which abolishes God.[17]

Third, when Amyraldians urge that the Bible teaches that both by divine decree and in history Christ's death, represented by it as un-

gospel to all, and second, that because he is trusting him Christ is interceding for him in heaven because Christ died for him at Calvary.

16. Warfield, *The Plan of Salvation*, 94.
17. Ibid., 94.

restricted regarding its referents, was intended to save all men without exception (the doctrine of unlimited atonement), Amyraldianism must necessarily join forces with Arminian universalism and turn away altogether from a real substitutionary atonement[18] "which is as precious to the Calvinist as is his particularism, and for the safeguard

---

18. Classic Arminianism rejects the substitutionary character of Christ's atoning death in favor of the governmental theory of the atonement. Arminians do this because they recognize that if, as they contend, everything God did looking to the salvation of men he did for all men alike, and if Christ substitutionally atoned for all men's sins, then all men would be saved. Since, however, they recognize that all men are not in fact saved, and since in their thinking no one person must receive any benefit from Christ's work that all other people do not also receive (and those who are finally lost obviously do not receive salvation), they construe the cross work of Christ so that in itself it does not possess, nor was it intended to possess, the intrinsic efficacy actually to save anyone. Accordingly, where there is still talk within the ranks of Arminianism of a substitutionary atonement in the sense that Christ's death paid the penalty for sin, it is—as Arminian theologian J. Kenneth Grider acknowledges in his article "Arminianism" in the *Evangelical Dictionary of Theology*, edited by Walter A. Elwell (Grand Rapids: Baker, 1984), 80—a "spillover from Calvinism": "A spillover from Calvinism into Arminianism has occurred in recent decades. Thus many Arminians whose theology is not precise say that Christ paid the penalty for our sins. Yet such a view is foreign to Arminianism. . . . Arminians teach that what Christ did he did for every person; therefore, what he did could not have been to pay the penalty for sin since no one would then ever go to eternal perdition. Arminianism teaches that Christ suffered for everyone so that the Father could forgive the ones who repent and believe; his death is such that all will see that forgiveness is costly and will strive to cease from anarchy in the world God governs."

This, of course, is the governmental theory of the atonement. Its germinal teachings are in Jacobus Arminius (1560–1609); but it was his student, the lawyer-theologian Hugo Grotius (1583–1645), who expounded the view in his *Defensio fidei catholicae de satisfactione Christi adversus F. Socinum* (1636). The governmental theory of the atonement is not intrinsically substitutionary. This may be shown by the following line of argument:

Calvinists aver that Christ's cross work substitutionally propitiated God's wrath for the elect, reconciled God to them, and redeemed them from their bondage to sin's slavery. But if Christ's cross work, whatever it is (and Arminians must make crystal clear precisely what Christ accomplished by his death if he did not substitutionally propitiate God for the elect, reconcile God to them, and redeem them from sin's bondage, and *then they must square their view with Scripture*), did not do this but was intended for every person alike without exception, and if he did not do for any one particular person anything he did not do for every person distributively, one must conclude (1) that Christ died neither savingly nor substitutionally for anyone since he did not do for those who are saved anything that he did not do for those who are lost, and the one thing he did not do for the lost was save them, and (2) that Christ's death actually procured nothing that guarantees the salvation of anyone but only made all men in some inexplicable way salvable in this world governed by God but whose actual salvation must of necessity be rooted more ultimately in soil other than Christ's cross work, namely, in the soil of the individual person's own will and work.

It should be plain to all that the Arminian construction eviscerates Christ's cross work of its intrinsic saving worth, is essentially Pelagian, and makes salvation turn on the merit of fallen humanity's repentance, faith (but in what?), good works, and perseverance in all of these.

of which, indeed, much of his zeal for particularism is due."[19] But this is to wound Christianity as the redemptive religion of God fatally at its heart, for (unless one is prepared to affirm the final universal salvation of all men) one cannot have an atonement of infinite intrinsic saving value, that is, an atonement that really saves, and at the same time an atonement of universal extension. One can have one or the other but not both. I will explain.

If Christ by his death actually propitiated God's wrath, reconciled God, and paid the penalty for sin (which is what I mean by an atonement of infinite intrinsic value), and if he sacrificially substituted himself *for (peri)*, *on behalf of (huper)*, *for the sake of (dia)*, and *in the stead and place of (anti)* sinners, then it follows that for all those for whom he substitutionally did his cross work he procured their salvation and guaranteed that they will be saved. But since neither Scripture, history, nor Christian experience will tolerate the conclusion that all men have become, are becoming, or shall become Christians, we must conclude that Christ did not savingly die for all men but for some men only—even God's elect.

If, on the other hand, Christ did his work for all men without exception, and if he did not intend its benefits for any one man in any sense that he did not intend it for any and every other man distributively, since again neither Scripture, history, nor Christian experience will allow the conclusion that all men are saved, it necessarily follows that Christ actually died neither savingly nor substitutionally for any man since he did not do for those who are saved anything that he did not do for those who are lost, and the one thing that he did not do for the lost was save them. It also follows necessarily, since Christ by his death actually procured nothing that guarantees the salvation of any man, and yet some men are saved, that the most one can claim for his work is that he in some way made all men salvable. But the highest view of the atonement that one can reach by this path is the governmental view of the atonement that holds that Christ's death actually paid the penalty for no person's sin. What his death did was to demonstrate what sin deserves at the hand of the just governor and judge of the universe and thus preserves the honor of his government of human society when he forgives people.

This means, of course, that the actual salvation of those who are saved is ultimately rooted in and hangs decisively upon something other than the work of him who alone is able to save men, namely, in

---

19. Warfield, *The Plan of Salvation,* 94.

something that those who are saved do for themselves. In spite of this shortcoming, the governmental view insists that Christ's death was intended only as a public display to the world of the suffering that God the just Governor of the universe thinks human sin deserves. While he could have simply bypassed his law's moral demand, "the soul that sins, it shall die," and forgiven mankind had he wanted to, that path would have had no value for human society.

Therefore, in order that society would take seriously the need to be morally governed by him, God, in the place of punishing sinners as he threatened he would do, substituted a great measure that was unpleasant and filled with grief for Christ. This "substitution" may appear on the surface to be redemptive on a universal scale, but it is hardly a substitutionary atonement since it does not save the world and the ground for the sinner's forgiveness shifts to *his* repentance, *his* faith, *his* good works, and *his* perseverance in all of these! But this is just to eviscerate the Savior's cross work of all of its intrinsic saving worth and to replace the Christosoteric vision of Scripture with the autosoteric vision of Pelagianism.

For these three reasons "consistent Calvinism" (Warfield's description) has rejected Amyraldianism and followed two other proposed orders, traditionally known as "infralapsarianism" and "supralapsarianism," in its arrangement of the decrees in the one "eternal purpose" of God. To a consideration of these proposed arrangements we will now turn.

The Infralapsarian Perception (the Historical Governing Principle)

The consentient testimony of consistent Calvinism, acutely aware of the pitfalls inherent within Amyraldianism, is that, regardless of the arrangement of the decrees to which one finally concludes, both the decree to save men by Christ and the decree to apply his saving benefits to them by the Holy Spirit must appear in the order of the decrees logically (not chronologically) after the distinguishing or electing decree. By this single adjustment all of the difficulties lurking within Amyraldianism are swept away. For now Christ dies for the elect, and the Spirit applies his benefits to the elect, and both are working consistently together to fulfill the Father's single redemptive purpose—to save the elect. Accordingly, all consistent Calvinism raises God's discriminating decree from the fourth position, the position where Amyraldians insert it, at least to the third position in the order of decrees (as we shall see, supralapsarianism raises it even higher), as follows: First, the decree to create the world and (all) men; second, the decree that (all) men would fall; third (the discriminating decree), the election of some fallen men to salvation in Christ (and the reprobation of the others); fourth, the decree to redeem the elect by the cross work of Christ; fifth, the decree to apply Christ's redemptive benefits to the elect.

The instructed Christian will immediately recognize in this proposed arrangement the Calvinistic scheme known as "sub-" or "infralapsarianism." The terms literally mean "below [*sub*] or after [*infra*] the fall [*lapsus*]" and denote the position in the order of the decrees that the discriminating decree sustains to the lapsarian (fall) decree. As its name implies, this scheme contends that the discriminating decree must be inserted immediately *after* the decree that man would fall. Admittedly, in agreement with the Canons of Dort,[20] most consistent Calvinists espouse this scheme because it represents God as distinguishing among men as sinners, which, they contend, represents God as both gracious and tender toward the elect sinner as well as holy and just toward the reprobated sinner. To advance the discriminating decree to any position *before* the decree respecting the fall, they argue against the supralapsarian ("before [*supra*] the fall [*lapsus*]"), depicts God as discriminating among men as men rather than as sinners (we will suggest later that there is a way to avoid this

---

20. The Canons of Dort, while practically and substantially infralapsarian, are not so framed, however, as to make it impossible for supralapsarians to subscribe to them honestly and intelligently, as is evident from the fact that Franciscus Gomarus and Gisbertus Voetius, members of the Synod of Dort and both staunch supralapsarians, did subscribe to the canons. The Westminster Confession of Faith is noncommittal.

For a discussion of this feature of the *Westminster Confession of Faith,* see Benjamin B. Warfield who writes in his article, "Predestination in the Reformed Confessions," in *Studies in Theology* (New York: Oxford University Press, 1932), 228–30: "Supralapsarianism . . . receive(s) no support from the [Reformed] Confessions. Yet all the Confessions are not Infralapsarian. . . . Some of them are explicitly Infralapsarian, and none exclude, much less polemically oppose, Infralapsarianism. None of them are explicitly Supralapsarian: many, however, leave the question between Supra- and Infralapsarianism entirely to one side, and thus open the way equally to both; and none are polemically directed against Supralapsarianism. . . . In view of these facts, it is hardly possible to speak of the Reformed creeds at large as distinctly Infralapsarian. . . . Some Reformed Confessions explicitly define Infralapsarianism: none assert anything which is not consonant with Infralapsarianism. On the other hand, nothing is affirmed in the majority of the Confessions inconsistent with Supralapsarianism either; and this majority includes several of the most widely accepted documents" (such as, according to Warfield, the *Heidelberg Catechism,* the *Second Helvetic Confession* and the *Westminster Confession of Faith*).

See also John Murray for a similar opinion in "Calvin, Dort, and Westminster on Predestination—a Comparative Study," in *Crisis in the Reformed Churches: Essays in Commemoration of the Great Synod of Dort, 1618–1619,* edited by Peter Y. De Jong (Grand Rapids: Reformed Fellowship, 1968), 154–55.

charge), which in turn makes God appear to be arbitrary, to say the least, if not also the author of sin.

Supralapsarian Calvinists have raised the following objections against the infralapsarian scheme: First, the infralapsarian scheme cannot account for the election and reprobation of angels. There are "elect angels" (1 Tim. 5:21 NIV), but they were not elected out of a totality of their fallen order as the infralapsarian scheme affirms is true of elect men, inasmuch as the elect angels never fell. Moreover, the angels who fell, though they are creatures of God as equally in need of redemption as are fallen men, will know no divine efforts to redeem them (see Heb. 2:16; 2 Pet. 2:4; Jude 6). Apparently, for reasons sufficient to himself, God simply by decree granted the grace of perseverance in holiness to some angels and denied it to the others. If God did so relative to the destiny of angels, did he not do so, to use the infralapsarian's word, "arbitrarily"? And if he did so, is there any reason he should not have done so regarding the destiny of humans? (I personally think the more appropriate, nonpejorative word that should be used here is "sovereignly" rather than "arbitrarily.")

It is true, of course, that the ground of God's dealings toward one order of his creatures (angels) may not be the same for his dealings toward another order of his creatures (humanity), but if any weight is given to it at all, it is a fact that the analogy between the elect angels and elect humans favors more the supralapsarian scheme (to be presented shortly) than it does the infralapsarian scheme.

Second, although the infralapsarian's concern to represent God's reprobation of some sinners as an act of justice (evidenced in his placing the discriminating decree after the decree concerning the fall) issues a proper caution against any depiction of God which would suggest that he acts toward men with purposeless caprice, nevertheless, if he intends by this to suggest that God's reprobation of these sinners is *solely* an act of justice (condemnation alone) which in no sense entails also the logically prior sovereign determination to "pass them by" and to leave them in their sin (preterition), then he makes reprobation solely a *conditional* decree, a position in accord with the Arminian contention that God determines the destiny of no man, that he merely decreed to react in mercy or justice to the actions of men.[21]

---

21. Arminians regularly teach that God does not positively bring about moral evil; rather, he merely permits the sinner to act on his own (see James Arminius, *The Writings of James Arminius* [Grand Rapids: Baker, 1977], 3:450). Unfortunately, John H. Gerstner, though normally uncompromising in his Reformed convictions, in his *A Predestination*

But then, as soon as the infralapsarian acknowledges (as he must if he would distance himself from Arminianism) that sin is not the sole ultimate cause of reprobation and that God who works all things according to the counsel of his will (Eph. 1:11) decreed the fall of man and by his decree of reprobation, which entails both preterition (the "passing by") and condemnation, determined the destiny of the nonelect sinner, his insistence over against the supralapsarian that the discriminating decree must not be advanced to any position prior to the decree concerning the fall lest God appear to be responsible for sin and arbitrary in his dealings with men loses all of its force. Why? Because the infralapsarian also must envision God's preterition regarding the nonelect as ultimately being grounded wholly and solely in his sovereign will, apart from consideration of the fact of their sin.[22]

Primer (Winona Lake, Ind.: Alpha Publications, 1980), 7, also seems to assert this when he writes: "Election is what is called 'a positive decree,' and reprobation is usually regarded as 'a permissive decree.' [By election as a positive decree] we mean to indicate that God from all eternity foreordains that some actions should be unto eternal life by actually initiating, or instigating, or energizing, or empowering, these actions. . . . This is called 'positive' because God actually does something. He actually effects the act in the person. . . . What is meant [by reprobation as a permissive decree]? According to this decree God predestinates the acts of sinful men by ordaining all the circumstances which lead to the sinner's choice of evil without actually inclining, or disposing, or energizing the sinner to do the evil deed. God simply permits the reprobate of himself and his own instigation or inclination to do that which is evil. . . . God, in this instance, refrains from positive action."

In the same vein Gerstner writes later: "It is only the wickedness of the human heart, and not the decree of God, which causes men to reject the overtures of God and his gospel." But this distinction means that, if not elect sinners, at least reprobate sinners do will and act independently of God. The reader is referred to Exodus 4:21; 7:3, Psalm 105:25; and Proverbs 21:1 as a sufficient biblical rebuttal to Gerstner's view of reprobation as a "permissive decree." See also John Calvin, *Concerning the Eternal Predestination of God* (Cambridge: James Clarke, 1961), 174–77, written as a refutation of Albertus Pighius and Georgius of Sicily, for his (and Augustine's) rejection of Gerstner's representation of God's relation to the evil acts of reprobate men.

Gerstner's error here stems at least in part from his insistence that the human will is free: "There is no power with which we are acquainted in this world which can actually force our will. . . . The powers of this world can do virtually anything they want to but this one area is invulnerable and impervious to anybody and anything, namely, the sovereignty of our own will. . . . Not even Almighty God, once he has given me this faculty of choice, can make me, coerce me, force me to choose" (29). Of course, if this were true, God could not "actually initiate, or instigate, or energize, or empower" the elect sinner to choose the way of eternal life. For they too would be "invulnerable and impervious" to God's advances. But Daniel 4:35; John 6:44, and a host of other verses contradict Gerstner's contention.

22. John Calvin in his commentary on Romans 9:11, 30 states that "the highest cause" (*suprema causa*) of reprobation is "the bare and simple good pleasure of God," while "the proximate cause" (*propinqua causa*) is "the curse we all inherit from Adam."

Consequently, the infralapsarian position simply does not relieve the difficulty that it seeks to address. Besides, whether God discriminates among men viewed simply as men (one supralapsarian arrangement admittedly does indeed suggest this) or among men viewed as sinners makes little difference from the perspective of every fallen human objection and consideration not grounded in Holy Scripture. To the rebellious objector a God who determines to leave even one man in his sin when he could save him from it is hardly less arbitrary and cruel than a God who determined some men unto damnation from the beginning.

In other words, from the perspective of bare sinful human considerations, God is still "arbitrary" if he was in a position to determine to save every sinner but determined to save only some sinners and to leave the rest in their sin and then to condemn them for it. Berkhof

---

The Westminster Confession of Faith, III.vii, declares: "The rest of mankind [that is, the nonelect] God was pleased, according to the unsearchable counsel of his own will, whereby he extendeth or withholdeth mercy, as he pleaseth, for the glory of his sovereign power over his creatures, to pass by; and to ordain them to dishonor and wrath for their sin, to the praise of his glorious justice." Concerning this statement, about which he states, "No paragraph in the whole compass of confessional literature excels for precision of thought, compactness of formulation, and jealousy for the various elements of truth in the doctrine concerned," John Murray writes in his article, "Calvin, Dort, and Westminster on Predestination— a Comparative Study," in *Crisis in the Reformed Churches: Essays in Commemoration of the Great Synod of Dort, 1618–1619,* edited by Peter Y. De Jong (Grand Rapids: Reformed Fellowship, 1968), 154–55:

The precision of the formulation is evident in the distinction drawn between the two expressions "to pass by" and "to ordain them." The former is not modified; the latter is. No reason is given for the passing by except the sovereign will of God. *If sin had been mentioned as the reason, then all would have been passed by* [emphasis supplied]. The differentiation [among men] finds its explanation wholly in God's sovereign will and in respect of this ingredient the only reason is that "God was pleased . . . to pass by." But when ordination to dishonor and wrath is contemplated, then the proper ground of dishonor and wrath demands mention. And this is sin. Hence the addition in this case, "to ordain them to dishonour and wrath for their sin." . . . It might be alleged that the *Confession* represents judicial infliction and ill-desert as the only factor [*sic*] relevant to the ordaining to dishonour and wrath, that what has been called "reprobation" as distinct from preterition is purely judicial. The *Confession* is eloquent in its avoidance of this construction and only superficial reading of its terms could yield such an interpretation. The earlier clauses, "God was pleased, according to the unsearchable counsel of His own will, whereby He extendeth or withholdeth mercy, as He pleaseth, for the glory of His sovereign power over His creatures," govern "to ordain them to dishonour and wrath" as well as "to pass by." So the sovereign will of God is operative in ordaining to dishonor and wrath as well as in passing by. And careful analysis will demonstrate the necessity for this construction. Why are some ordained to dishonor and wrath when others equally deserving are not? The only explanation is the sovereign will of God. The ground of dishonor and wrath is sin alone. But the reason why the nonelect are ordained to this dishonor and wrath when others, the elect, are not is sovereign differentiation on God's part, and there is no other answer to this question.

rightly observes: "The Infralapsarian . . . cannot maintain the idea that reprobation is an act of divine justice pure and simple, contingent on the sin of man. In the last analysis, he, too, must declare that it is an act of God's sovereign good pleasure, if he wants to avoid the Arminian camp. . . . [His] language may sound more tender than that of the Supralapsarians, but is also more apt to be misunderstood, and after all proves to convey the same idea."[23]

Third, espousing as the infralapsarian scheme does the view that the *historical* principle governs the order of the decrees and arranging as it does the order of the decrees accordingly in the order that reflects the temporal or historical order of the corresponding occurrences of the events which they determined (as indeed the Amyraldian scheme does also), this construction can show no purposive connection between the several parts of the plan *per se*. In a single, consistent, purposive plan, one may be pardoned if he assumes that any and every single member of the plan should logically necessitate the next member in the order so that there is a purposive cohesion to the whole. The historical arrangement simply cannot demonstrate, for example, why or how the decree to create necessitates the next decree concerning the fall, or why the decree concerning the fall necessitates the following particularizing decree.

Fourth, because the infralapsarian scheme can show no logical necessity between the first two decrees (the creation decree and the fall decree) and the three following soteric decrees, it "cannot give a specific answer to the question why God decreed to create the world and to permit the fall."[24] It must refer these elements to some general purpose in God (such as his general glory as Creator) that has no discernible connection to the central redemptive elements in the "eternal purpose" of God, which severance between creation and redemption could justify the dualism of a natural theology. Berkhof registers this objection in these words:

> The Infralapsarian position does not do justice to the unity of the divine decree, but represents the different members of it too much as disconnected parts. First God decrees to create the world for the glory of his name, which means among other things that he determined that his rational creatures should live according to the divine law implanted in their hearts and should praise their Maker. Then he decreed to permit the fall, whereby

23. Berkhof, *Systematic Theology*, 122–24.
24. Ibid., 121.

sin enters the world. This seems to be a frustration of the original plan, or at least an important modification of it, since God no more decrees to glorify himself by the voluntary obedience of all his rational creatures. Finally, there follows the decrees of election and reprobation, which mean only a partial execution of the original plan.[25]

Fifth, the infralapsarian scheme, by espousing the historical order of the decrees, reverses the manner in which the rational mind plans an action. The infralapsarian scheme moves from means (if, indeed, the earlier decrees can be regarded as means at all, disconnected as they are in purpose from the later decrees) to the end, whereas "in planning the rational mind passes from the end to the means in a retrograde movement, so that what is first in design is last in accomplishment,"[26] and, conversely, what is last in design is first in accomplishment.

Sixth, the infralapsarian scheme does not come to grips with the teaching of certain key Scripture passages as well as the supralapsarian scheme does. In Romans 9:14–18 and 9:19–24 Paul responds to two objections to his teaching on divine election that he frames in question form: (1) "What then shall we say? Is God unjust?"—the question of divine fairness, and (2) "One of you will say to me: 'Then why does God still blame us? For who resists His will?'"—the question of human freedom. Now it seems to the supralapsarian, if Paul had been thinking along infralapsarian lines, that he would have found it sufficient to answer both questions something like this: "Who are you, O sinner, to question God's justice. Since we all fell into sin, God could justly reject us all. As it is, in mercy he has determined to save some of us while leaving the rest to their just condemnation." But this he did not do. As we shall see, in response to both objections he simply appealed to God's absolute, sovereign right to do with men as he pleases in order to accomplish his own holy ends.

In Romans 9:15–18, in response to the first question (divine fairness), contrasting Moses—his example of the elect man in whose behalf God has sovereignly determined to display his mercy (9:15; see also 9:23)—and Pharaoh—his example of the nonelect man whom God has sovereignly determined to raise up *in order to* (*hopos*) show by him his power and to publish his name in all the earth (9:17; see also 9:22), Paul concludes: "Therefore God has mercy on whom he

25. Ibid., 124.
26. Ibid., 119.

wants to have mercy, and he hardens whom he wants to harden" (9:18 NIV). As we just said, here he responds to the question concerning the justice of God in view of his elective and reprobative activity by a straightforward appeal to God's sovereign right to do with men as he pleases in order that he might exhibit the truth that all spiritual good in man is the fruit of his grace alone.

Then in Romans 9:20b–24 (NIV), in response to the second question (human freedom), after his indignant, stinging rebuke, "Who are you, O man, to talk back to God," Paul employs the familiar Old Testament metaphor of the potter and the clay (see Isa. 29:16; 45:9[27]; 64:8; Jer. 18:6) and asks, "Does not the potter have the right to make out of the same lump of clay some pottery for noble purposes and some for common use?" Paul teaches here (1) that the potter sovereignly makes both kinds of vessels, and (2) that he makes both out of the same lump of clay. The metaphor would suggest that the determination of a given vessel's nature and purpose—whether for noble or for common use—is the potter's sovereign right, apart from any consideration of the clay's prior condition. This suggests in turn that God sovereignly determined the number, nature, and purpose of both the elect and the nonelect in order to accomplish his own holy ends, apart from consideration of any prior condition which may or may not have been resident within them (see Rom. 9:11–13). Proverbs 16:4, in my opinion, aptly expresses the intention of the metaphor: "The Lord has made everything for his own purpose, even the wicked for the day of evil."

So here, as earlier, in response to the second objection to his doctrine Paul simply appeals again to God's sovereign right to do with men as he pleases in order to accomplish his own holy ends. And he registers his appeal without qualification even though he fully understands that the "man who does not understand the depths of divine wisdom, nor the riches of election, who wants only to live in his belief in the non-arbitrariness of his own works and morality, can see only arbitrariness in the sovereign freedom of God."[28]

This feature of the metaphor means then, at the very least, that there is no scriptural compulsion to place the discriminating decree in the order of decrees after the decree respecting the fall. Furthermore, it lays stress on the divine will as the sole, ultimate, determinative

---

27. Isaiah goes even further than Paul by actually pronouncing a woe against those who would question their Creator's sovereign right to do with his creatures as he pleases.

28. G. C. Berkouwer, *Divine Election* (Grand Rapids: Eerdmans, 1960), 273.

cause for the distinction between elect and nonelect, one point the supralapsarian scheme emphasizes.

The infralapsarian agrees, of course, that the divine will is the sole determinative cause for the distinction between elect and non-elect, but he insists that the "lump" about which Paul speaks here is mankind already viewed by God as fallen (see, for example, the commentaries by Hodge and Murray, *in loc.*). But if this were the case, God would only need to make one kind of vessel from the lump—the vessels for noble use. He would not need to make the vessels for common use—the "sinful" lump would already represent them. As it is, the metaphor expressly affirms that the potter makes both kinds of vessels from the lump, suggesting that the lump has no particular character beforehand—good or bad—which would necessarily determine the potter toward a given vessel's creation for one kind of use or the other. This feature of the metaphor also favors the supralapsarian scheme.

Then, in Ephesians 3:9–10 (AT) Paul teaches that God "created all things, in order that now through the church the many-sided wisdom of God might be made known to the rulers and authorities in the heavenly realm, according to his eternal purpose which he accomplished in Christ Jesus our Lord." Here supralapsarians urge, Paul teaches that God created the universe, which creative act reflects his prior creation decree, not as an end in itself but as a means to an end. And what end is that? Elsewhere (Rom. 1:20), Paul teaches that by glorifying its maker's power and "architectural skill" (no work of God, simply by virtue of the fact that it is his work, can avoid doing so), creation serves the condemnatory aspect of the particularizing decree by leaving men who would plead ignorance of God in the final judgment *"without excuse."*

But in Ephesians 3:9–10 Paul affirms that the end for which all things were created is not simply the end of glorifying God as maker in order to leave men without excuse when he condemns them, but rather, and more primarily, of providing the arena and all the necessary conditions for God's redemptive activity to manifest itself in order that he might show forth, through the redeemed church, his many-sided wisdom to the rulers and authorities in the heavenly realm.

Further indications that in his "eternal purpose" God integrated the purpose of creation and the creation ordinances into the more primary redemptive plan which he accomplished in Christ are (1) the fact that God's creation rest was the symbol of the Sabbath rest which the redeemed people of God will enter upon at the *Eschaton* (Gen. 2:2; Heb. 4:4–11), (2) the fact that God intended the original marriage ordinance from the beginning as an earthly representation of the relationship between Christ and the redeemed church (Gen. 2:24; Matt. 19:4–6; Eph. 5:30–32), and (3) the fact that God "subjected creation to frustration" specifically because of human sin (Gen. 3:17–18), determining that in empathy with the redeemed all of nature would "groan as in the pains of childbirth right up to the present time," and that, for "its own liberation from bondage to decay," it would have to "wait in eager expectation for the revelation of the sons of God" at the time of their physical resurrection when their bodies will be redeemed, at which time creation too "will be brought into the glorious freedom of the children of God" (Rom. 8:19–23 AT).

In sum, supralapsarians urge, the infralapsarian scheme (1) implies that God originally intended creation to serve some (undefined) purpose other than his final redemptive purpose and history's ultimate end, a theological construction which could be used to justify the erection of an unscriptural natural theology, (2) runs the risk of failing to reflect as clearly as it should that God decreed and grounded the predestination and foreordination of men purely and solely on sovereign considerations within himself, and (3) ultimately, as Berkouwer states, "does not solve anything."[29]

The Supralapsarian Perception (the Teleological Governing Principle)

In light of these difficulties with the infralapsarian arrangement of the order of the divine decrees, supralapsarians, including such eminent Reformed thinkers as Theodore Beza of Geneva, William Whitaker and William Perkins in the sixteenth-century Church of England, Franciscus Gomarus and Gisbertus Voetius in seventeenth-century Holland, William Twisse, first prolocutor of the Westminster Assembly, and in more recent times Geerhardus Vos, offer another arrangement. But most supralapsarians, after placing the discriminating decree in the first position, for some inexplicable reason then abandon their own insight that "in planning the rational mind passes from the end to the means in a retrograde movement" and arrange the remaining decrees not in a retrograde order but in the order in which the events to which they refer occurred historically (the effect of which will become clear as we proceed).

---

29. Ibid., 273.

Thus the more common (though inconsistent) supralapsarian arrangement is as follows: first (the discriminating decree), the election of some men to salvation in Christ (and the reprobation of the others); second, the decree to create the world and both kinds of men; third, the decree that all men would fall; fourth, the decree to redeem the elect who are now sinners by the cross work of Christ; fifth, the decree to apply Christ's redemptive benefits to these elect sinners.

An analysis of this arrangement of the order of decrees will show, because the discriminating decree is placed at the head of all the other decrees with the others then proceeding in the order in which the events to which they refer took place in history, that God at the point of discrimination is represented as discriminating among men simply as men inasmuch as the decree respecting the fall does not come until the third point.

Other supralapsarians, such as (possibly) Jerome Zanchius,[30] Johannes Piscator, Herman Hoeksema,[31] and Gordon H. Clark,[32] have suggested, with minor variations among them, that the decrees should be arranged in an order that more consistently reflects the rational principle in planning:[33] first (the discriminating decree), the election of some sinful men to salvation in Christ (and the reprobation of the others in order to make known the riches of God's gracious mercy to the elect); second, the decree to apply Christ's redemptive benefits to the elect sinners; third, the decree to redeem the elect sinners by the cross work of Christ; fourth, the decree that men should fall; fifth, the decree to create the world and men.

In this latter scheme the discriminating decree stands in the first position with the creation decree standing in the last position. It should also be noted that in this arrangement of the decrees, *unlike in the former*, God is represented as discriminating among men viewed as sinners and not among men viewed simply as men. The election

---

30. See Zanchius's *De praedestinatione sanctorum* and Augustus M. Toplady's translation of this work, *The Doctrine of Absolute Predestination* (Grand Rapids: Baker, 1977 reprint). Richard A. Muller in *Christ and the Decree* (Grand Rapids: Baker, 1986) argues that Zanchius was an infralapsarian (112). Otto Gründler, however, in his *Die Gotteslehre Girolami Zanchis und irhre Bedeutung für seine Lehre von der Prädestination* (Neukirchen, 1965) maintains that Zanchius was indeed a supralapsarian (112). See also L. Leblanc, *Theses Theologicae* (London, 1683), 183.

31. Herman Hoeksema, *Reformed Dogmatics* (Grand Rapids: Reformed Free Publishing Association, 1966), 161–65.

32. Gordon H. Clark, "The Nature of Logical Order," unpublished paper presented at the third annual meeting of the Evangelical Theological Society.

33. One concerned for theological precision should speak, then, of inconsistent supralapsarianism and consistent supralapsarianism.

and salvation of these elect sinners in Christ becomes the decree that unifies all the other parts of the one eternal purpose of God. This revision of the more common supralapsarian arrangement addresses the infralapsarian objection against supralapsarianism *per se* that it depicts God as discriminating among men viewed simply as men and not among men viewed as sinners. And if this revision does in fact overcome this major infralapsarian objection against supralapsarianism, it becomes a significant step in advancing the cause of supralapsarianism over infralapsarianism. So it should be weighed seriously by all infralapsarians and supralapsarians alike. How it is that this revised scheme is able to depict God as discriminating among men as sinners, even as the infralapsarian scheme does (but for an obviously different reason), will become clear as we elucidate now the two principles which govern this revision of the supralapsarian order.

The primacy of the particularizing principle. Persuaded as they are that Scripture places the particularizing grace of God in Jesus Christ, God's Alpha and Omega, at the beginning, the center, and the end of all God's ways and works, those supralapsarians who offer the revised or what may be called the more consistent supralapsarian order make the particularizing principle the central and unifying principle of the eternal purpose of God. (All supralapsarians share this concern, by the way.) Therefore, these supralapsarians believe it both appropriate and necessary so to arrange the decrees that every decree is made to serve this primary principle. Accordingly, they postpone to the fourth and fifth positions respectively, after the explicitly redemptive decrees, the lapsarian decree and the creation decree in order to make the fall and even creation itself serve the particularistic purpose of God.

Contrary to the infralapsarian assertion that "creation in the Bible is never represented as a means of executing the purpose of election and reprobation,"[34] all supralapsarians insist that the created world must never be viewed as standing off over against God's redemptive activity even for a moment, totally divorced from the particularizing purpose of God, which is the ultimate concern of God's "eternal purpose," and fulfilling some general purpose(s) unrelated to the redemptive work of Christ. They insist so on the ground that such a representation of creation shatters the unity of the one eternal purpose of God and provides a base within the eternal decree itself for the development of an unbiblical natural theology. As we have seen, they

---

34. Charles Hodge, *Systematic Theology* (Grand Rapids: Eerdmans, n.d.), II:318.

are persuaded that Ephesians 3:9–11 expressly affirms that creation's purpose is subservient to God's redemptive purpose and that the same subservience is suggested in Romans 1:20; 8:19–23.

In sum, they are persuaded first that God created all things in order that he might show forth through the redeemed community, his church, the glory of his wisdom and grace in accordance with his eternal purpose that he accomplished in Christ Jesus our Lord.[35] Second, they are convinced that he determined that creation by its revelation of his "eternal power and divine nature" would condemn the reprobate. They are also confident that by its reflexive "agony and ecstasy" creation would empathize with the church's agony and ecstasy.

Two exegetical objections to this principle. First, concerning Ephesians 3:9–10 (AT) infralapsarians argue that the *hina* clause commencing verse 10 should not be connected syntactically to the immediately preceding participial clause in verse 9, "[in God] who created all things," but to the penultimate participial clause in verse 9, "[the mystery] which was hidden from the ages in God." By this construction they suggest that Paul intended to teach that God hid the administration of the "mystery" of the church from men in ages past in order that he might reveal it to the rulers and authorities in the heavenly realm *now* in this age through his (and the other apostles') preaching. Infralapsarians marshal to their side in support of this interpretation of Paul's earlier teaching in Ephesians 3:4–6.

Supralapsarians, of course, do not deny that Paul's preaching played a part—indeed, a significant part—in making known through the church "come of age," to a degree to which it could not have been made known by the church "under age" in former times, the many-sided wisdom of God to the rulers and authorities in the heavenly realm. But they insist that infralapsarians commit two errors by rejecting the nearer participial clause in the sentence as the clause to which the *hina* clause of 3:10 should be attached (which participial clause is clearly the closest possible antecedent clause and the one which grammarians ordinarily would recommend when determining a following word's antecedent).

---

35. See Ephesians 1:6, 12, 14; 2:7 (AT) where Paul declares that all that God has done (obviously in accordance with his eternal purpose) for the Christian, he has done "to the praise of the glory of his grace which he has freely given us in the one he loves," and "*in order that* (*hina*) he might show in the ages to come the incomparable riches of his grace in his kindness toward us in Christ Jesus."

First, they reduce the nearer clause, as Gordon H. Clark points out, to a "meaningless excrescence on the verse."[36] Charles Hodge, for example, writes: "The words 'who created all things,' is entirely subordinate and unessential . . . and might be omitted without materially affecting the sense of the passage."[37] But this leaves the phrase serving no intelligible purpose, since it was hardly necessary for Paul to identify the God about whom he spoke as the God "who created all things" or to teach his readers the fact that their God did create all things—surely they would have known these things.

Second, they in effect divorce the creation from God's particularizing purpose in Christ and allow it to have a *raison d'etre* that moves, by implication, in a direction other than the redemptive *raison*. But this implies that God has (or had) two purposes, not directly related to each other: a general purpose that the original creation (which includes unfallen man) was somehow to fulfill (but which purpose had to be abandoned when man, the human part of creation, fell) and a specific redemptive purpose. This in turn implies that God's redemptive purpose was not at first central to his eternal purpose but was even subordinate to the more original general purpose of the creation and man. To avoid these highly questionable implications, supralapsarians urge that it is much better to recognize the presence of the nearer participial clause as the antecedent to the following *hina* clause and to give it its full force as the "lead-in" idea to 3:10.

Third, in their alternative interpretation of Paul's teaching in Romans 8:19–23, infralapsarians contend that supralapsarians make too much of the relationship between creation and the church when they interpret creation's "reaction" to the church's redemptive conditions as a "reflexive" one. But the "reflexive relationship" on creation's part cannot be avoided. Surely there is a divinely imposed reflexive relationship between creation and the changing fortunes of the church—Paul expressly affirms it to be so. And he declares that the church does not await creation's liberation from its bondage to decay, but the other way around: creation awaits what is expressly said to be the church's full and final "redemption" (*apolutrosin*) at the resurrection. In other words, creation's "fortunes" are directly dependent on redemptive considerations. All this being so, how better to describe creation's relationship to the church than as a "reflexive" one?

---

36. Gordon H. Clark, *The Philosophy of Gordon H. Clark* (Philadelphia: Presbyterian and Reformed, 1968), 482.

37. Charles Hodge, *A Commentary on the Epistle to the Ephesians* (Grand Rapids: Eerdmans, 1954), 172.

The purposing principle governing the rational mind. All supra-lapsarians aver as a second consideration (though only those who affirm the revised scheme offer an order of the decrees consistent with this consideration) that in all purposive planning the rational mind is governed by the principle of determining first the end to be accomplished and then the appropriate means to attain that end; and in the case of the means themselves in the plan, each of which becomes an "end" of the immediately following means in keeping with the principle that in planning the end precedes the means, the rational mind determines them in retrograde order from the point of the determined-upon end back through all the means necessary to the accomplishment of the ultimate end. The rational mind recognizes that only in this way is each element of the plan purposive and contributory to the purposive coherence of the entire plan. And God is a purposing planner!

To illustrate: suppose a rational planner decides to buy a car. This is the end that he will pursue. He knows that he must determine the end first, and only then does he determine the appropriate means to achieve the end. (A rational mind is actually capable of doing both instantaneously; by the phrase "only then" we intend a logical or teleological, not a chronological, order.) Never would a rational car buyer first leave home with twenty-five thousand dollars in his pocket, understanding his action to be a means to something, and only then determine the end which his action of leaving home was intended to be a means to. The end always precedes the means in a rational mind.

The rational planner also realizes, if he would achieve his end, that he must actually execute the means he determines are essential to that end in a particular order. For example, suppose the car buyer has determined that between the point where he finds himself—in bed at home and "carless"—and his determined end of purchasing a car stand five means necessary to his becoming a car owner, namely, (1) getting out of bed, (2) leaving home, (3) arriving at the car dealership, (4) agreeing with the car salesman on the purchase price of the car, and (5) arranging a loan for the agreed-upon sum. The rational car buyer realizes with respect to these particular means that he cannot first arrange for the agreed-upon loan, then agree with the car salesman on the purchase price of the car, then get to the car dealership in order to speak with the car salesman, then leave home, and then get out of bed. To attempt to do so would doom to failure at the outset his attempt to reach his desired end. Never would a rational car buyer execute the means to his end in a manner that would only frustrate his plan and lead to failure.

But there is another aspect to rational planning that is not always taken into account, a feature that we have alluded to already. How does the rational mind go about determining the means that are necessary to reach a determined end? Because it recognizes that each means in any purposive chain of means, except for the last one (last, viewed from the point of the determined end), of necessity is the "end" of the means that follows it, and because it is necessary always to pass from the end to the means to the end, the rational mind will not begin from the point where it finds itself and determine from that point the first means to the end. Rather, the rational mind (in the case of men, it may do this at times without even realizing it, while at other times it will be conscious that it is doing so) will begin from the determined end and in a retrograde movement work back in its planning to the point where it finds itself at the moment. Only in this way does each means answer purposively to the need of the former means.

To use our car buyer illustration one more time: The car buyer has determined that he will purchase a car (his ultimate end). But in order to do that (given his present circumstance), he determines, as the first means to his ultimate end (which means becomes the "end" of any second means that he determines would be necessary), that he must arrange a loan for the agreed-upon sum. But in order to do that, he determines, as the second means to his ultimate end (which second means becomes the "end" of any third means that he determines would be necessary), that he must agree with the car salesman on the purchase price of the car. But in order to do that, he determines, as the third means to his ultimate end (which third means becomes the "end" of any fourth means that he determines would be necessary), that he must get to the car dealership. But in order to do that, he determines, as the fourth means to his ultimate end (which fourth means becomes the "end" of any fifth means that he determines would be necessary), that he must leave home. But in order to do that, he determines, as the fifth means to his ultimate end (which means becomes the "end" of any sixth means that he determines would be necessary, but since in our illustration it is the last means it does not become an "end"), that he must get out of bed.

In purposive planning, each element of the plan necessarily answers the need of the preceding element, so that there is purpose in each member and purposive coherence governing the whole plan. This is actually the way the truly rational mind purposes or plans, and one will have no trouble accepting this as so if he will recognize, first, that the purposing mind always determines the end before it determines the means to achieve it, and second, that each means in any plan necessarily is the "end" of the means that follows it in the plan.

One final point: It is exceedingly important to note that when he finally carries out his plan, the rational planner executes the means (if he acts purposively) in the precise inverse order to the order in which the means he determined upon appear in the plan. That which is last in design is first in accomplishment and that which is first in design is last in accomplishment. To use our car buyer illustration a last time: the last means he determined upon in the plan (he must get out of bed) is the first means which he executes in the accomplishment of the plan, and the first means he determined upon in the plan (he must arrange a loan for the agreed-upon sum) is the last which he executes in the accomplishment of the plan.

All supralapsarians take seriously the biblical truth that God is a God of purpose, as we have emphasized, who must necessarily do all that he does purposively just because he is a God of rational purpose. It is inconceivable to them that God would decree to create the world for no purpose or would decree to create it for some purpose unrelated to his one final purpose. Accordingly, in light of their perception of the manner in which the rational mind plans (and who will deny that God is rational, since the only alternative consistent with such a denial is that he is irrational) and then executes its plan, the more consistent supralapsarians urge that the order of God's eternal plan is the precise inverse to the order in which he executes it. Since God initiated the execution of his eternal purpose by first creating the world, the decree to create the world is the last in design, and since God's eternal purpose culminates with redeemed sinners praising him in the *Eschaton* for the glory of his particularizing grace made theirs through the cross work of Christ (see 2 Thess. 1:7–10; Rev. 19:1–8; 21:9–27; 22:1–5), the decree to bring that to pass (the end) is the first in design.

In other words, while the execution of the divine purpose is indeed "infralapsarian" in the sense that God's redemptive activity necessarily follows in history the historical fall, the plan itself behind all this is supralapsarian. But while all supralapsarians share the same basic perception of the principles that govern the order of the decrees, traditional supralapsarians have unwittingly failed to work out the order of the decrees in a manner consistent with their own perception of things and have done a disservice to their cause as a result. By placing the discriminating decree first and then simply arranging the remaining decrees in the historical order, they abandon the purposing principle of arrangement which alone relates the discriminating decree to the fall of man, and accordingly they represent God as discriminating among men as men—since they may be regarded as sinners only after the decree concerning the fall—leaving themselves open thereby to the infralapsarian charge that we have already noted.

The more consistent supralapsarian, however, submits the following order of the decrees, which reflects, it must be emphasized again, not a chronological but a teleological order within the divine plan: First, for the praise of the glory of his grace God elected some sinful men (note: in order to reveal the glory of his grace, he views these men as transgressors of his law from the outset; how it is that they may be so viewed is determined by the fourth decree) to salvation in Christ (Eph. 1:3–14) and for the praise of his glorious justice reprobated the others.[38]

In order to accomplish this end, he determined that, second, the Holy Spirit would apply Christ's accomplished redemptive benefits to elect sinners of the New Testament age and those same redemptive benefits anticipatively to elect sinners of the Old Testament age, the necessary first condition to the consummation of the original determined end.

In order to accomplish this means (which necessarily becomes a second "end"), he determined that, third, Christ would actually redeem elect sinners of both the New and Old Testament ages by his cross work, the necessary second condition if the Holy Spirit was to have Christ's redemptive benefits to apply.

In order to accomplish this means and to provide the context that makes Christ's cross work meaningful (which necessarily becomes a third "end"), he determined that, fourth, men would fall in Adam, their federal head, the necessary third condition if Christ's redemptive benefits were to have any elect referents needing redemption.

---

38. Of course, even here the decree of reprobation is not an end itself; rather, it serves the decree of election. See Paul's teaching in Romans 9:22–23 that the decree of reprobation serves the more ultimate end (*kai hina*—"even in order that") of making known the riches of God's glory (that is, his merciful grace) to the elect, whom he "prepared in advance (*proetoimasen*) for glory."

In order to accomplish this means (which necessarily becomes a fourth "end"), he determined that, fifth, he would enter into a covenant of works with the first man "wherein life was promised to Adam; and in him to his posterity, upon condition of perfect and personal obedience" (Westminster Confession of Faith, VII.ii), making Adam thereby the race's federal head as well, and then providentially "permit" the federal head to fall, but this fall to occur "not by a bare permission, but such [permission] as hath joined with it a most wise and powerful bounding, and otherwise ordering, and governing . . ., in a manifold dispensation, to his own holy ends" (Westminster Confession of Faith, V.iv; see also VI.i), and yet to bind, order, and govern the entire Adamic temptation in such a way that "the sinfulness thereof proceedeth only from the creature, and not from God, who, being most holy and righteous, neither is nor can be the author or approver of sin" (Westminster Confession of Faith, V.iv; see also III.i), all these features of the plan comprising the necessary fourth condition if men were to experience a moral and ethical fall.

In order to accomplish this means (which necessarily becomes a fifth "end"), that is, in order that a moral "lapse" on man's part could occur, he determined that, sixth, he would create Adam in a condition of holiness (*status integritatis*) but also in a mutable condition (*posse peccare et posse non peccare*) "so that he might fall from it" (Westminster Confession of Faith, IX.ii).

In order to accomplish this means (which necessarily becomes a sixth "end"), that is, in order to provide the necessary arena in which all this could take place,[39] and to do so with such an evident display

---

39. The created world as the arena of salvation has, then, a redemptive *raison d'etre* since the redemptive purpose of God ultimately lies behind its creation and providential preservation (see again here Ephesians 3:9–10). John Murray writes in this connection in "Common Grace," *Collected Writings of John Murray*, 2:113, 116: "It is [the] sphere of life or broad stream of history provided by common grace that provides the sphere of operation for God's special purpose of redemption and salvation. This means that this world upheld and preserved by God's [common] grace is the sphere and platform upon which supervene the operations of special [or redemptive] grace and in which special grace works to the accomplishment of his saving purpose and the perfection of the whole body of the elect. . . . Without common grace special grace would not be possible because special grace would have no material out of which to erect its structure. It is common grace that provides not only the sphere in which, but also the material out of which, the building fitly framed together may grow up into a holy temple in the Lord. It is the human race preserved by God, endowed with various gifts by God, in a world upheld and enriched by God, subsisting through the means of various pursuits and fields of labour, that provides the subjects for redemptive and regenerative grace . . . common grace provides the sphere of operation of special grace and special grace therefore provides a [I would say 'the'] rationale of common grace."

of his attributes as to leave fallen men who would eventually even deny his existence without excuse, he determined that, seventhly, he would create and providentially preserve (actually the preserving was determined teleologically prior to the determination to create) the universe (since this is the last means in the plan, it does not become a seventh "end" requiring a following means).

This revision of the more common supralapsarian arrangement, since the first part of the one eternal purpose is teleologically integrated with every element following it, allows God from the first to discriminate among men viewed as sinners and posits for the world a redemptive reason for its creation.

Then, when God put his plan into execution—in inverse order to the order in which the several parts appear in his plan—he created the world and Adam and entered into covenant with Adam, making him the race's federal head. Then Adam fell and all men descending from him by ordinary generation fell in him. Then Christ redeemed the Old Testament elect by his (for them) anticipated cross work and the New Testament elect by his accomplished cross work, with the Holy Spirit applying anticipatively his redemptive benefits to the Old Testament elect and applying his accomplished redemptive benefits to the New Testament elect, all leading to God's finally achieving his determined end—enhanced by the reprobation of the nonelect—even the praise of his glorious electing grace in Christ toward undeserving sinners. Each historical occurrence is purposive because it is the execution of an element of God's one eternal purpose that answers not chronologically but teleologically to the need of the immediately preceding element of the plan.

Four theological objections to this principle. In addition to the two exegetical difficulties already considered, infralapsarians, such as the Reformed Baptist theologian Roger R. Nicole, have certain theological difficulties with this supralapsarian vision (though Nicole acknowledges that this arrangement of the several decrees in the one eternal purpose is "very attractive," possessing a "lucid simplicity" about it).

The first among these objections is the contention that since the decree to create human beings appears here in the distant position from the first, these people—whether viewed as elect and reprobate sinners or simply as elect and reprobate people makes no difference—can be regarded at the point of their election and reprobation in the first position only as "bare possibilities" and not real people, that is to say, as nonexistent entities who can be contemplated not as created but at best only as potential or creatable men. But how, the infralapsarian inquires, can God determine any particular condition for entities that, in the order of the decrees, he has not yet even determined to create?[40] Surely, Charles Hodge, following Francis Turretin, is correct, the infralapsarian urges, when he writes: "Of a *Non Ens* . . . nothing can be determined. The purpose to save or condemn, of necessity must, in the order of thought, follow the purpose to create . . . the purpose to create of necessity, in the order of nature, precedes the purpose to redeem."[41]

The supralapsarian response to this objection is twofold: (1) If the infralapsarian is right when he insists that concerning an entity whose existence God has not yet decreed he can determine nothing, then God could not have even determined to create the world and human beings (the infralapsarian's first decree), since the decree to create them, which entities would necessarily have to possess some characteristics, would necessarily entail the prior determination of these characteristics, which before he decreed to create them, according to the infralapsarian's prescription, are nonentities about which nothing can be determined. Furthermore, (2) if God must determine to create human beings before he can determine any and every further characteristic about them—for example, whether they would be bad or amoral or good, and if the latter whether they would stay good or become bad, and if the latter whether he would punish them or redeem them, and if the latter whether he would redeem all of them or only some of them (the infralapsarian historical order), then it follows that God does not decree his first act with his last in view, which means that he does not purposively decree anything!

Therefore, since the infralapsarian must affirm, for the sake of his own order, that God could determine characteristics for the world and human beings as well as actions on their and his part anticipatory of his decree to create them, then he should be willing to acknowledge that God could determine ultimate ends for people logically prior to his decree to create them. If, however, he persists in his objection that

---

40. Roger R. Nicole highlights this infralapsarian concern in his essay, "Predestination and the Divine Decrees," in *Our Sovereign Savior* (Fearn, Rosh-shire, Scotland: Christian Focus, 2002), 43, in the following words: "We cannot see how people can be saved who are not even viewed as existing. The decree of salvation seems to have no content. And if the decree has no content, then it has no significance either. A decree must be a decision to act, and you cannot decide to act when you do not have a content for the action. The idea of creation seems to be essential for a decree to be rendered."

41. Charles Hodge, *Systematic Theology*, II:318.

God could determine no purpose for the world and mankind until he had first decreed to create them, then he is saying by implication that God decreed the existence of things for no rhyme or reason, which is to ascribe an inherent irrationality to the decrees of God. And this is to fall away from Christian theism altogether.

While it is true that the creation of human beings was not yet decreed at the point in the purposing order where they were elected or reprobated, yet, since God's decree is eternal with no chronological antecedence or subsequence in it, there was never a moment when people, viewed as created people, did not certainly exist in it. In fact, the first decree as the final "end" decree, because it had to do with mankind viewed both as sinful people and as created people, rendered the fall and creation decrees (teleo)logically necessary. Accordingly, their existence as created people was as decretally real and certain in the divine mind at the point of the first decree as it was at the point of the fifth decree.

Second, and again Nicole in particular raises this objection to the view being espoused here, infralapsarians charge that "serious difficulties arise from the attempt to view the order of decrees as the reverse of history." Nicole illustrates his concern this way:

> The relation of the application of salvation by the Holy Spirit to the impetration of salvation by Christ is identical for all the elect. But Abraham and Augustine are not chronologically on the same side of the Cross [his point here is that this would seem to split the decree of application in two, with it appearing both before and after the decree to provide salvation by Christ—RLR]! It would appear, therefore, that the historical order is after all not a precise mirror of the logical relationships in the mind of God.[42]

It is strange that as astute a theologian as Nicole would register this objection against this proposed scheme; for, if nothing more could be said, it applies equally to his infralapsarian order in which the decree to redeem the elect by the cross work of Christ is followed

---

42. Roger Nicole, "The Theology of Gordon Clark," in *The Philosophy of Gordon H. Clark* (Philadelphia: Presbyterian and Reformed, 1968), 397. Also in his essay, "Predestination and the Divine Decree," in *Our Divine Savior*, 44–45, he enunciates this same concern in the following words: "The order in which saving events occur is not as simple as the mere reverse of the order of history. I can show this in terms of the relation of Abraham to the work of Christ on the one hand, and of John Calvin to it, on the other. Historically they are on opposite sides of the cross. Yet in terms of salvation they are related to the cross in exactly the same way. If the supralapsarians are correct in ordering the decrees by a backward unrolling of history, then everybody who is saved should be on the same side of the cross—but this is not the case."

by the decree to apply Christ's redemptive benefits to the elect. Even in this arrangement, if nothing more could be said, the application decree needs to be split in two to effect the salvation of the elect before the cross and the salvation of the elect after the cross. Of course, more can and indeed must be said by both the infralapsarian and the supralapsarian. And it is this: there is a certain measure of distortion in speaking of only five decrees as we have with respect to both representations.

Third, infralapsarians charge that the supralapsarian scheme, in its zeal to place God's particularizing decree at the beginning of all that God planned for men, too severely construes the fall of Adam, which was an act of rebellion on his part against God and which meant the spiritual ruin and misery of some men at least, as a necessary part of the divine plan (indeed, even a "fortunate" event for the elect in that it paved the way for their salvation in Christ). To this objection the supralapsarian responds with a series of questions for the infralapsarian: "Did God, according to your understanding of the order of the decrees, decree the fall?" The infralapsarian knows, as Warfield—an infralapsarian himself—acknowledges, that if he answers this question in the negative he has fallen away not only from Calvinism but also from genuine Christian theism altogether.[43] When he therefore acknowledges that God decreed the fall, the supralapsarian has a second question: "Did he have a purpose in mind for it when he did so?"

Again, the infralapsarian knows, if he answers in the negative, that he has fallen away from Calvinism as well as Christian theism. When he therefore acknowledges that God decreed the fall for a purpose, the supralapsarian asks yet a third question: "Did that purpose play a role in God's redemptive plan or in some other plan?"

Again, the infralapsarian knows, if he answers, "In some other plan," that he must admit, first, that he knows nothing concerning the content of this other plan, and, second, that this other plan (whatever its content) has been frustrated inasmuch as God's redemptive

---

43. Warfield writes in his *The Plan of Salvation,* 111, fn. 81: "It is important to observe that the terms Supralapsarian, Sub- (or Infra-) lapsarian concern the place relatively to the decree of the fall given to the decree of election. A habit has grown up among historians who do not comprehend the matter, of defining Supralapsarianism as the view which holds that God's decree in general is formed before the fall . . . [that is to say,] it makes 'the will of God include the fall of the first man.' That the 'will of God includes the fall of the first man,' no Calvinist (be he Supralapsarian, Sublapsarian, post-redemptionist, Amyraldian, Pajonist) either doubts or can doubt. No theist, clear in his theism, can doubt it."

purpose in Christ directly addresses the fall and the exigencies created by it (which he avers were intended to fulfill a role in another plan). This is plain from the fact that God's redemptive purpose reverses the fall and its effects with regard to elect persons and nature itself (see Rom. 5:12–19; 8:19–23). When he then acknowledges, as he must, that the fall fulfills a purposive role in God's redemptive plan, the supralapsarian finally asks:

Wherein then do we differ, since neither of us believes that sin *per se* is good, and since we both believe that sin is intrinsically evil and proceeds only from the nature of second causes; since neither of us believes that God is the chargeable cause of sin, and since we both believe that God decreed from all eternity that the redemptive aspects of his particularizing purpose would address the Fall and its effects in behalf of the elect? Must we not both acknowledge then that God decreed the Fall and its effects to provide the condition from which Christ would redeem God's elect? And if so, do we not both stand in this respect on precisely the same ground?

The supralapsarian is deeply committed to the belief that the fall has significance as a real event of earth history only as it is allowed to stand in the biblical philosophy of history as a means to an end in relation to God's one eternal plan of redemption, on the ground (along with the others that have already been offered) that *the state of the elect as children of God in Christ by divine grace is ultimately a higher, more glorious, and more praiseworthy end than the state of all men as children of God in unfallen Adam by divine creation.*

Fourth, infralapsarians contend that the supralapsarian scheme is an overly pretentious speculation in its analysis of the manner in which God plans. Better is it, they argue, to be satisfied with the more modest, less pretentious historical order for the decrees. Again the supralapsarian response is twofold: (1) The infralapsarian's charge that the supralapsarian is "pretentiously speculative" because he would attempt to determine the principle which governed the divine mind as God decreed what he did before the creation of the world lacks any real force since the infralapsarian too, after analyzing the divine purpose, offers his order of decrees as the order in the divine mind, thereby tacitly suggesting a governing principle. It is simply a case of determining which of the two is the more likely principle—the historical or the teleological—and the supralapsarian is convinced that his conclusion is more biblical over all and reflects more clearly the purposing character of the mind of God.

The supralapsarian denies that his arrangement is a "pretentious speculation" or "the invention of unaided human intellection."
Rather, he insists that it is simply the result of exegesis of divinely
revealed information about the nature and ways of God (see my many
references to holy Scripture throughout this entire present discussion) and legitimate "sanctified" deductions "by good and necessary
consequence" (Westminster Confession of Faith, I.vi) based upon the
results of that exegetical labor.

Conclusion

While every consistent Calvinist will be either infralapsarian or
supralapsarian, in my opinion the supralapsarian vision of God's eternal plan of salvation holds the exegetical and deductive edge. It certainly satisfies as well as the infralapsarian vision does the demands of
all the pertinent teachings of Scripture, integrates more intelligibly
than the infralapsarian vision does the several parts of the one divine
purpose to magnify the particularizing grace of God in Jesus Christ,
and elucidates better than the infralapsarian vision does the teleological principle which surely governs the whole of the order of the
decrees of God who does everything that he does for a purpose and as
an aspect of his one overarching eternal purpose.

Some readers may be put off by the consistent supralapsarian's
vision and feel that it is lacking in evangelical warmth and not con-
ducive to sincere and earnest gospel preaching. I do not share this
opinion, of course. Not a single feature of this vision prohibits the
supralapsarian from maintaining with infralapsarian Calvinists everywhere that the redemptive activity of God in Christ—the beginning,
the center, and the end of all his wisdom, ways, and works—must be
central to the church's proclamation as well. He glories in the cross
as God's special exhibition of grace to sinful mankind, and he recognizes that the proclamation of the gospel, with the Spirit's enabling,
animating blessing, is the God-ordained means of reaching lost sinners for Christ.

Just as the apostle who wrote Romans 9 and Ephesians 1 could
with no contradiction also declare: "I consider my life worth nothing
to me, if only I may finish the race and complete the task the Lord Jesus has given me—the task of testifying to the gospel of God's grace"
(Acts 20:24 NIV) and could also write: "When I preach the gospel, I
cannot boast, for I am compelled to preach. Woe to me if I do not

preach the gospel" (1 Cor. 9:16 NIV), and, "Although I am less than the least of all God's people, this grace was given me: to preach to the Gentiles the unsearchable riches of Christ" (Eph. 3:8 NIV), so the supralapsarian knows that the same holy burden to be used of God to reach the lost must be his as well. And far from his doctrine of predestination being an impediment to his carrying out the Great Commission, in concert with the infralapsarian he sees it as the guarantee and surety that his ministry will not be in vain. As he preaches the gospel to people everywhere, he knows that God by his Word and Spirit will call his elect to salvation.

Before detractors conclude then that their negative judgment is just, due to some fault in the supralapsarian vision itself, perhaps they should examine themselves to see whether their evaluation may not be due to the fact that they are simply uncomfortable with a soteric vision that places God's sovereignty over the lives and destinies of people so manifestly in the forefront of all of his ways and works with them. No doctrine signalizes the *soli Deo gloria* principle more and no doctrine humbles proud people more than the supralapsarian vision of predestination. It should not surprise even the saintliest Christian to find his heart reacting at first against it.

Whatever one finally decides about the infra/supra debate or about the inconsistent/consistent supra debate (and these debates should not become a basis of party strife among Calvinists), if a Christian upon examination should discover—and this is the more serious matter by far—that his dissatisfaction is with the particularism of the entire Calvinistic vision due to the desire for a doctrinal system that allows room for people to contribute in some ultimate and decisive way to their salvation, then it must be said—said, of course, with all charity and Christian good will but said nonetheless—that he has not yet learned the alphabet of Christianity as the redemptive religion of divine grace.

It only remains to point out in conclusion that this eternal order of the decrees, purposive throughout, Reformed dogmaticians for the most part (for example, Louis Berkhof) have come to designate as the *pactum salutis* or "covenant of redemption" to distinguish it from the concrete, tangible execution of the specifically redemptive aspects of the same eternal decree which they designate the "covenant of grace."[44] There seems to be some justification for this designation,

---

44. The fall of man, occurring in history in accordance with the eternal decree regarding it, is taken up and treated within what Reformed scholars designate the "covenant of works." For example, the Westminster Confession of Faith declares: "The first

first, in the fact that the persons of the Godhead determined before the foundation of the world what role each would fulfill in the redemption of the elect, and second, in the words of Hebrews 13:20 (NIV) where the writer speaks of "the blood of the eternal covenant (*diathekes aioniou*)."

Some Reformed scholars, it is true, have preferred other designations for the order of the decrees. For example, Cocceius spoke of it as the "counsel of peace." Warfield was satisfied to refer to it as "the plan of salvation." Murray preferred the designation, "the inter-trinitarian economy of salvation."[45] The Westminster Confession of Faith speaks of it simply as "God's eternal decree" (see the title of chapter 3). But regardless of what term is finally adopted, Murray is surely correct when he writes,

> The truth concerned is all-important. For it is not only proper, it is mandatory that in the plan of salvation as eternally designed and as executed in time, we discover the grandeur of the arrangements of divine wisdom and love on the part of the distinct persons of the Godhead, and recognize the distinguishing prerogatives and functions of each person and the distinct relations we come to sustain to each person as we become the partakers of God's grace. After all, our study of the plan of salvation will not produce abiding fruit unless the plan captivates our devotion to the triune God in the particularity of the grace which each person bestows in the economy of redemption, and in the particularity of relationship constituted by the amazing grace of Father, Son, and Holy Spirit.[46]

---

covenant made with man was a covenant of works, wherein life was promised to Adam; and in him to his posterity, upon condition of perfect and personal obedience. Man, by his fall, having made himself incapable of life by that covenant, the Lord was pleased to make a second, commonly called the covenant of grace" (VII.ii–iii).

45. Murray, "The Plan of Salvation," in *Collected Writings,* 2:130.
46. Ibid., 2:131.

CHAPTER 6

Responses to Robert L. Reymond

Response by Thomas B. Talbott

Because the dispute between supralapsarians and infralapsarians is essentially a parochial one among those who accept a doctrine of limited election, I am less interested in the details of this particular dispute than I am in an assumption that both parties accept: the assumption that God restricts his mercy to a limited elect. So the question I would pose, right at the outset, is this: Has Robert Reymond provided anything remotely like a strong biblical argument, or even any argument at all, for a doctrine of limited election? And the correct answer, I believe, is that he has not. First, one cannot successfully argue that Paul, for example, held a doctrine of limited election simply by pointing to a few texts in Romans 9 while ignoring Paul's own conclusion in Romans 11 and ignoring, in particular, Paul's explicit statement in verse 32 that God is merciful to all; and second, even if one should restrict oneself to Romans 9, not one word there implies a final and irrevocable rejection of anyone, whether it be Ishmael, Esau, Pharaoh, or Paul's unbelieving kin. You can read the idea of irrevocable rejection *into* Romans 9, but you cannot find anything there that *entails* such an idea.

Now I would have no one interpret these remarks as a criticism of Reymond. None of us can do everything at once, and it is perfectly appropriate for Reymond to construct an argument for supralapsarianism within the context of certain assumptions. By "assumption" here I do not mean something like an absolute presupposition. I mean (roughly) any proposition that one employs as a premise in the context of a given discussion and does so without a supporting argument in the same context. Because none of us can do everything at once, as I said, we all argue from assumptions in this sense; that is, we often employ as a premise some proposition not at issue in a given discussion.

But here is where I think Reymond overplays his hand. In the early part of his essay, he repeats the expression "biblically informed Christian" again and again and repeatedly treats some controversial issue, such as a belief in absolute determinism or the doctrine of reprobation, as if no biblically informed Christian could possibly reject it. He thus concludes that "the biblically informed Christian . . . will, in short, espouse the Reformed faith that is in turn simply the faith of the holy Scripture itself." But this way of speaking, however appropriate it may be for an "in-house" discussion among Calvinists, does nothing to advance a plausible case against either Arminianism or Christian universalism. For in a discussion among Christians with theological differences, such language amounts to little more than the dogmatic assertion, "My interpretation of the Bible is right, and yours is wrong!"

So just how, exactly, are we to interpret Reymond's claim that Scripture (or the Bible as a whole?) will not tolerate a doctrine of universal reconciliation? Perhaps as follows: Whatever such texts as Romans 5:18 and 1 Corinthians 15:20–28 may appear to teach in their own context, other texts, such as Matthew 25:46 or 2 Thessalonians 1:9, exclude the possibility of universal reconciliation. But one could just as easily make essentially the same claim in the reverse direction: Whatever such texts as Matthew 25:46 and 2 Thessalonians 1:9 may appear to teach in their own context, other texts, such as Romans 5:18 or 1 Corinthians 15:20–28 exclude the possibility of an everlasting separation from God.

So which claim, if either, should we accept? One possibility, which Reymond and I both reject, is that the Bible as a whole is simply inconsistent on this matter; another, which Reymond no doubt accepts, is that, contrary to appearances, Romans 5:18 and 1 Corinthians 15:20–28 carry no implication of universal reconciliation; and still another, which seems to me the sober truth of the matter, is that, contrary to initial appearances, Matthew 25:46 and 2 Thessalonians 1:9 carry no implication of unending punishment. But whatever position one adopts, the fact is that *any* interpretation of the Bible as a whole is a far more complex affair than Reymond appears to acknowledge.

One of the best ways, in my opinion, to appreciate some of the complexities in interpreting the Bible as a whole is to reflect upon the following inconsistent set of propositions:

1. God's redemptive love extends to all human sinners equally, and he therefore sincerely wills or desires the redemption of all humans in the sense that, for any two of them, s and s*, God wills or desires the redemption of s in every sense that he wills or desires the redemption of s*.
2. God's redemptive love will triumph in the end and successfully accomplish the redemption of everyone whose redemption he sincerely wills or desires.
3. Some human sinners will never be reconciled to God but will instead be separated from God forever.

Two clarifications are perhaps in order at the outset: First, proposition (1), as I here formulate it, is a bit more complicated than I would like because I want to guarantee that no one who accepts a doctrine of limited election can consistently accept it. For even if, as Bruce Ware insists, God suffers from a conflict of will or desire in the matter of saving the nonelect and therefore does will or desire (in some attenuated or conflicted sense) their redemption and reconciliation, he could not possibly will the redemption of the nonelect *in every sense* in which he wills the redemption of the elect. Second, proposition (2) does *not* merely say that God has *the power* to redeem everyone whose redemption he sincerely wills or desires; it says instead that he will *in fact accomplish* the redemption of everyone whose redemption he sincerely wills or desires. So if someone holds that God has the power to save all but chooses not to exercise it, then this person has already rejected proposition (2). And though Bruce Ware might join the Arminians in rejecting (2), as stated, he would have to accept

2* God's redemptive love will triumph in the end and successfully accomplish the redemption of everyone whose redemption he sincerely wills or desires in every sense in which he wills or desires the redemption of Abraham, Isaac, and Jacob.

Now if the above set of propositions, consisting of (1), (2), and (3), is logically inconsistent, as it surely is, then at least one proposition in the set is false. But which one? Augustinians, such as Reymond and Ware, reject (1); Arminians and open theists, such as Jack Cottrell and Clark Pinnock respectively, reject (2); and we Christian universalists reject (3). The problem, however, is that in each case the rejected proposition is one that other "biblically informed Christians," including some highly competent and highly respected Bible scholars, accept as a clear and obvious teaching of Scripture.[1] So in that respect, all reflective Christians are in the same theological boat, so to speak; they must *either* reject a proposition that other competent scholars accept as a clear and obvious teaching of Scripture *or* simply concede that the teachings of Scripture are logically inconsistent.

My point is not that all three theological positions are equally cogent; far from it. I continue to believe that Christian universalism provides the best and most reasonable interpretation of the Bible as a whole. But I am not so naïve as to expect that every "biblically informed Christian," including Reymond, will automatically agree with me.

Response by Bruce A. Ware

In the broad view, Robert Reymond's position and my own are very close. We both affirm that divine election to salvation is unconditional and individual, and we even agree that by God's election, God purposed "the salvation of certain particular fallen men by Christ." The main place where we differ, then, is quite minor in importance, and this concerns just how one should rightly construe the order of the decrees of God and where his decree to elect stands in relation to other elements.

I must admit to still not comprehending fully just how Reymond can place God's election to "salvation of certain particular fallen men by Christ" as the first of his decrees, when this assumes that God has in mind already both the creation of the whole of the human race with all of its particular people and, more importantly, the fall of that human race into sin. Just how one can make the election of *fallen* men the *first* of the decrees of God eludes me. Implicit in this supposed first decree are two prior decrees, namely, the decree to create them and the decree to permit their fall. But if these "prior"

---

1. For a quick survey of the texts that might initially seem to support each of the three propositions, see Thomas Talbott, "Towards a Better Understanding of Universalism," in Robin Parry and Christopher Partridge, *Universal Salvation? The Current Debate* (Grand Rapids: Eerdmans, 2004), 9–10.

decrees are assumed by the "first" of God's decrees, might it not be better simply to acknowledge that the decree to election comes after these prior implied decrees? And if so, is one not actually articulating an infralapsarian position? So, in short, it seems to me that despite Reymond's noble and able endeavor to propose this modification of supralapsarianism which he calls "consistent supralapsarianism," I cannot see how his position is either consistent or how it is, in the end, supra- and not infralapsarianism.[2]

The portion of Reymond's chapter most directly at odds with my own infralapsarian commitment comes when he states several supralapsarian objections to the infralapsarian view. I'll summarize each of these and give a brief response to each. "First," writes Reymond, "the infralapsarian scheme cannot account for the election and reprobation of angels." Of course this objection assumes that the election of angels and the election of human beings must be parallel, but where are we told this is the case? Rather, it seems that Scripture indicates that election is asymmetrical in relation to these two groupings of moral agents. Holy angels are "elect" (1 Tim. 5:21), to be sure, but since they never did sin, it would seem most natural to understand God's election of these specific angels to be *preserved from sinning* rather than to be saved out of sin. In this sense, it is not technically true that the election of holy angels was supralapsarian—at least, it was not an election that occurred before their fall since their election was precisely to keep them from falling.

Second, if the infralapsarian argues, suggests Reymond, that God's reprobation of sinners is solely an act of divine justice carried out against those justly deserving God's condemnation, and that it does not also include God's logically prior sovereign determination to pass them by, then this makes reprobation conditional. But as Reymond acknowledges, most infralapsarians do not argue this way; rather, they agree that God previously determined that after the fall occurred, he would pass over some and elect others for salvation. But this does not make election supralapsarian simply because the elec-

---

2. A similar point can be seen from Reymond's understanding of the flip side of divine election to salvation, viz., God's passing over others and ordaining their just reprobation. Here, too, God has in mind those fallen and thus deserving of this appointed condemnation. Reymond rightly states, "And the biblically informed Christian is also aware, while it is true that God's determination to pass by the rest of mankind (this 'passing by' theologians designate 'preterition' from the Latin *praeteritio*) is grounded solely in the unsearchable counsel of his own will, that his determination to ordain those whom he passed by to dishonor and wrath (condemnation) took into account the condition which alone deserves his wrath—the fact of their sin."

tion of *those specific individuals* out of their sin for salvation in Christ took place in the mind of God as he considered all of the human race as fallen—and not before.

Third, the infralapsarian scheme does not present each element of the decree as logically necessitating the next element. But is it not often the case that plans for some activity involve many steps, some of which might logically necessitate another, but in other cases particular steps are just necessary as part of the whole plan (e.g., before we leave on vacation, someone be sure to grab the map—this could happen at the beginning, as someone immediately grabs the map and puts it in the glove compartment of the car, or it could happen "last minute" as the car is pulling out of the driveway). This is where my appeal to John Feinberg's notion of seeing the whole of God's creation plan, from beginning to end, as a whole in relation to God's decree is helpful.[3] It just is not the case that each step must be in a logically dependent relationship with another step. What is important—even crucial—is that all the steps necessary for the whole plan to succeed are included, and where necessary, those steps that require other steps are in their proper relation.

Fourth, the infralapsarian scheme, says Reymond, moves contrary to the rational mind, since it moves from means to end, whereas the rational mind moves from end to means. Here, I agree that postulating means without an end in mind is arbitrary at best and irrational at worst. And I understand that the supralapsarian view shows the priority of the final end in a more straightforward way. But it is not the case that the infralapsarian model postulates unrelated means that stand on their own with no end in view until the end finally is stated. Rather, it simply understands that the steps of the decree do not signal from the first instance just what God's ultimate end is. Rather, it is only when one sees the whole of the decree, or the whole of redemptive history in which the decree is played out, that one can determine what the ultimate end was that God had in mind. If a supralapsarian model were applied to the master chess player, it would require that the first move he makes must signal the ultimate end toward which he is moving. But isn't it more the case that we only know that ultimate end as we see the steps unfold?

In the end, the matters on which Reymond and I agree are of such greater significance than these areas of somewhat minor dis-

---

3. John S. Feinberg, *No One Like Him: The Doctrine of God*, Foundations of Evangelical Theology, gen. ed. John S. Feinberg (Wheaton, Ill.: Crossway, 2001), 535–536.

agreement. But because Reymond devoted so much of his chapter to the specific question of his support for supralapsarianism, it may appear that his position and my own are terribly at odds. I respect his view and consider it a viable possibility. What leads me above all to land in the infralapsarian camp are the passages I discussed in my chapter's section defending infralapsarianism: Acts 13:48; Romans 8:29–30; Ephesians 1:4; 2 Thessalonians 2:13; 2 Timothy 1:9; and 1 Peter 1:1–2. That God chose sinners to save, then, upholds both the gospel of grace, and it supports at the same time the infralapsarian election of God.

Response by Jack W. Cottrell

I realize that from Robert Reymond's perspective I am writing as a mere kindergartner, one who "has not yet learned the alphabet of Christianity," yet one who is presuming to critique a wise and learned scholar. We must remember, though, that it was a naive child who pointed out that the emperor had no clothes.

Since Reymond basically dismisses the Arminian view as sub-Christian, he wastes little time in addressing it. He is mainly concerned with defending the supralapsarian version of Calvinism over against infralapsarianism and with clearing up certain inconsistencies that he sees in other versions of the former. Thus his essay addresses the question of the logical order of the various aspects of God's eternal decree. He describes such a study as "one of the most important . . . topics that Scripture would give any man warrant to study." Yet he grants that "infralapsarians contend that the supralapsarian scheme is an overly pretentious speculation in its analysis of the manner in which God plans." If it seems so even to infralapsarians (Calvinists all), then one can imagine how it must seem much more so to us kindergarteners. For example, to an Arminian, to argue whether the order of the decrees is retrograde or historical conjures up images of angels dancing on the head of a pin. It is meaningful only to those who accept the arbitrary concept of omnicausal sovereignty and who deny that God has given a truly free will to any of his creatures.

As the one ultimate purpose of God, the decree to save some sinners to the glory of his grace must have logical priority over all others. It is the one ultimate *end;* all other decrees are simply the *means* of accomplishing it. "Every decree is made to serve this primary principle." To accomplish this ultimate purpose, God determined in his next two decrees to redeem elect sinners through Christ's cross and to apply its redemptive benefits to these sinners through the Holy Spirit.

This means that God has *decreed* the fall of Adam and the ensuing sinfulness of the entire human race so that there would be sinners to redeem. He also decreed the deliberate withholding of salvation from some sinners (preterition) and the condemnation of these nonelect sinners to hell. The preterition and reprobation are "ultimately . . . grounded wholly and solely in his sovereign will, apart from consideration of the fact of their sin." But why has God decreed these things? They are all necessary *means* for accomplishing the one ultimate purpose of glorifying himself by saving some sinners through the grace of Jesus Christ. "God decreed the fall and its effects to provide the condition from which Christ would redeem God's elect," and the reprobation of the nonelect is for the specific purpose of making known the glory of the riches of God's grace to the elect.

To some Calvinists such a view of God and his decrees may sound like pious and glorious mysteries; but to most non-Calvinists it is the height of irrationality and moral contradiction and approaches blasphemy. To say that God deliberately brings about a sinful human race so that he may elect some to salvation, and then deliberately sends the nonelect to hell so that his saving grace may appear all the more glorious, is the *opposite* of grace.

The other implication of the primacy of the particularizing principle is that creation itself—the final decree in Reymond's scheme—is just a means to bring about the redemption of the elect to the glory of God's grace. This "posits for the world a redemption reason for its creation"—that is "creation's purpose is subservient to God's redemptive purpose." The end of creation is to provide "the arena and all the necessary conditions for God's redemptive activity to manifest itself."

All of these concepts together—the primacy of God's elective redemptive purpose, plus the necessity of sin and reprobation and of creation itself as means to accomplish this purpose, are reflected in this statement, "That *the state of the elect as children of God in Christ by divine grace is ultimately a higher, more glorious, and more praiseworthy end than the state of all men as children of God in unfallen Adam by divine creation*" (italics in original).

This may well be the most remarkable statement in Reymond's essay—remarkable for the stark clarity by which it states the ultimate implication of the Calvinist system, remarkable in the absoluteness of its antithesis to the biblical worldview, remarkable in its audacity. To anyone who does not begin his study of the Bible with the arbitrary premise of omnicausal divine sovereignty, the obvious relation between creation and redemption is the opposite of this, i.e., *redemption* is the *means* by which God will accomplish the original purpose of *creation.*

Space considerations do not allow discussion of the reality of free will, whether Ephesians 2:8 teaches that faith is a gift, universal versus limited atonement, or the meaning of foreknowledge. In any case, using the analogy of clothing, these are in a sense accessories, like hats and gloves. I have focused here on the main items, like the suit or robe that covers the torso. And like the child in the story, I find that the emperor has no clothes.

Reply by Clark H. Pinnock

Reymond is what one could call a "voluntarist" theologically. The foundations of voluntarism were laid by Scotus; they led to the nominalism of Occam; and they influenced Luther in (for example) *Bondage of the Will.* According to this view, the will of God is behind everything that occurs. Even the moral good is determined by the absolute will of God. For example, if a man rapes a woman, as Gordon Clark once put it, it is the will of God that he did so. God alone is ultimate and always gets everything he wants. His sovereignty is all determining and all encompassing. He decides everything, including who shall be saved and who shall be lost without reference to anything they have done or will do.

Reymond defends what Calvin called "the horrible decree." This means that even before he decreed that humanity should exist, he made the discrimination between those he would save and those he would damn. The author contends that it is God's prerogative to do so and that it brings glory to his name. Should God decide to damn Reymond himself (for example) which may be the case (who knows?), it would be a self-glorifying action on his part. This is a grim creed. One can only wonder how many, schooled in this ideology, have given up on Christianity when interpreted in this way. I would estimate that many have done so. It would seem that the most important issue here is not the doctrine of election as such but the character of God.

But what kind of gospel is this, one might ask? It is good news (I suppose) for those fortunate enough to be chosen but bad news for those who are left out on purpose. I find in the Bible better news than this. In God's Word we read that God desires all men and women to be saved and come to a knowledge of the truth and that God is not willing that any should perish but that all should come to repentance (1 Tim. 2:4; 2 Pet. 3:9). With Cottrell and Talbott, I hold to the proposition that God's essence is perfect love and that he has compassion for all his creatures. Love is an essential—not an accidental—property of God. It is his nature to love us. God acts lovingly in everything that he does because "God is love" (1 John 4:8).

Reymond may protest that (like it or not) this is what the Bible teaches and resistance to it (like my own) betrays an antipathy to God's sovereignty in redemption. For my part, the system he is defending is profoundly at odds with the central message of the Bible and should be strongly rejected. There is such an obsession here with the absolute power of God that the goodness of God is obscured. It would be better to think in terms of self-limitation when it comes to God's power, such that he allows free creatures to accept or reject his will for them. Reymond is a Calvinistic monergist; I am an evangelical synergist. His view, which was an Augustinian innovation, has never been fully accepted in the Western church and has always been rejected by the Eastern churches. And, although the magisterial Reformers mostly accepted it, Wesley and the free churches have spoken out against it such that today there is a widespread move toward a good news hermeneutic.

Reymond and I both admire the awesome power of God. But he does not understand properly how it expresses itself. It is not the kind of power, spoken of in deterministic theologies, namely, raw power, the power to make everything else surrender. God's power is greater than that. He has created agents with freedom who can be creators and movers in their right. This decision, far from contradicting divine omnipotence, presupposes it because only omnipotence could do such an intricate thing. For who but a most powerful being could create and govern a universe and press on with his plans for it even when creatures disobey him and work against his will? God's power is such that it is able, not only to bring forth the most imposing of things, the world in its totality, but also to contrive the most delicate of things, a creature capable of I-Thou relations with God. God is able not only to lay his hand heavily on the world but also to touch it lightly such that creatures have room to exist and to flourish. As Kierkegaard put it: "It is only a miserable and worldly picture of power to say that it becomes greater in proportion as it compels and makes things dependent."

I believe that this essay misconstrues the glory of God, the very category which it wishes to lift up so highly. I agree that God is certainly the "most" and the "best," but there are different kinds of goodness and greatness. Surely the glory of God consists not in God's all-controlling power but in God's self-sacrificing love. We see the Father when Jesus is lifted up on the cross. God's glory is actually diminished when defined in terms of domination, and it is exalted when it is integrated with his lovingkindness. It is not God's way always to be thinking of himself and contemplating his own excellencies. We worship the triune God who pitched his tent among us and shared in the human condition. It is the devil (is it not?) and not God who wants to exist in solitary glory and be in that sense "absolute." The true beauty of our God lies in his relationality and self-emptying love, not in his distance and aloofness from us.

CHAPTER 7

Universal Reconciliation
and the
Inclusive Nature of Election

THOMAS B. TALBOTT

Christians have traditionally believed that, because they are saved by grace, they can take no credit for their own salvation or even for a virtuous character (where such exists). All credit of this kind goes to God. And understood properly, this doctrine of salvation by grace has three important virtues, among others: it can undermine pride and self-righteous feelings of superiority in the Christian believer; it can encourage the believer to acknowledge his or her solidarity as a sinner with the entire human race, including the most monstrous and deranged criminals; and it can provide the believer with the greatest possible assurance that all will be well in the end.

But once one postulates a final and irrevocable division within the human race between the company of the redeemed in heaven, on the one hand, and the hopelessly lost and eternally damned, on the other, an obvious question arises. Given that we all start out equally as sinners, just what accounts for this final division among us? And no appeal to the mysterious counsels of God can conceal the obvious answer: either the explanation lies in the will of God—that is, in God's freedom to extend his mercy to some and not to others—or it lies in how we humans exercise our own freedom with respect to the mercy that God freely extends to all.

The Augustinians, as I shall call them, take the first alternative, opting for a doctrine of limited election; and the Arminians, as I shall call them, take the second, opting for a doctrine of conditional election. Christian universalists, by way of contrast, insist that election is neither limited in scope nor conditional in nature; election is, after all, an expression of God's love for the world, the whole world, and God's love is neither limited in scope nor conditional in nature. Against the idea that God's love is limited in scope, the New Testament declares that God at least wills or desires the salvation of all humans (1 Tim. 2:4) and is not willing that any of them should perish (2 Pet. 3:9); indeed, it is precisely for this reason that God sent his Son into the world to be "the atoning sacrifice for our sins, and not for ours only but also for the sins of the whole world" (1 John 2:2 NIV). And against the idea that God's love is conditional in nature, St. Paul in particular proclaimed the good news that no failure, no deceitfulness, and no lack of faith on our part can "nullify the faithfulness of God" (Rom. 3:3–4 NASB).

Accordingly, in opposing a doctrine of limited election, Christian universalists stand shoulder to shoulder with their Arminian brothers and sisters who share their view that God, whose essence is perfect love, extends his love and mercy to every person equally; and in opposing a doctrine of conditional election, they also stand shoulder to shoulder with their Augustinian brothers and sisters who share their view that God will eventually accomplish *all* of his will in the matter of salvation. But in opposing the idea of unmitigated tragedy, such as is implicit in any doctrine of everlasting separation from God, they part company from both their Arminian and their Augustinian brothers and sisters.

I shall divide what follows into four parts. In part 1, I shall argue, first, that a doctrine of limited election is inconsistent with the Johannine declaration that God *is* love, and second, that it is riddled with logical impossibilities in any case; in part 2, I shall argue further that a doctrine of limited election flatly contradicts St. Paul's teaching in Romans 11 and also requires an utterly fantastic construal of Paul's statements about all human beings; in part 3, I shall argue that the Augustinians have totally misunderstood Romans 9, in part because they do not interpret this chapter in light of Paul's own conclusion in Romans 11; and finally, in part 4, I shall argue that the Augustinian understanding of unconditional election and irresistible grace, unlike the Augustinian understanding of limited election, accurately reflects Paul's own teaching on the matter.

Part 1: Love and the Nature of God

God is love, and he who abides in love abides in God,
and God in him (1 John 4:16b NKJV).

I begin with the declaration in 1 John 4:8 and 16 that God not only loves but *is* love. How should we interpret this Johannine declaration? Most Christian philosophers writing today would probably interpret these texts, as I do, to mean that love is part of God's nature or essence; using philosophical jargon, we might say that, according to these texts, lovingkindness is an *essential* rather than an *accidental* property of God.

The author of 1 John was not, of course, a philosopher and did not, fortunately, employ philosophical jargon in his writings; nor was he likely even familiar with the philosophical distinction between an essential and an accidental property. But he clearly employed "God" as a proper name (as opposed to a title), the name of a distinct person whom we ought to adore and worship, and he said concerning *this* person that he *is* love. The point, then, hardly seems to be that God just *happens* to love us, as if it were a happy accident that he does; the point seems to be that it is his nature to love us. In a broadly logical (or metaphysical) sense, it could not have been otherwise.[1] That this is, at the very least, a natural interpretation seems indisputable. Commenting upon 1 John 4:8, the conservative New Testament scholar, Leon Morris, thus wrote: "*God is love.* This means more than 'God is loving.' It means that God's essential nature is love. He loves, so to speak, not because he finds objects worthy of His love, but because it is His nature to love. His love for us depends not on what we are, but on what He is. He loves us because He is that kind of God."[2]

But this interpretation, which seems to me exactly right, is in fact more controversial than some might expect. Many theologians, most notably some of the Augustinians, reject the idea that lovingkindness is an essential property of God; John Calvin, for example, explicitly considered this idea and explicitly rejected it, as we shall see. And the reason for his rejection is clear: If God freely chooses to make

1. That is, it is logically impossible that God should *both* create someone *and* fail to act in loving ways toward that person.
2. D. Guthrie and J. A. Motyer (eds.), *The New Bible Commentary,* rev. ed. (Grand Rapids: Eerdmans, 1970), 1267.

some persons, but not *all,* the object of his love and mercy—if, that is, he freely bestows his love and mercy upon a limited elect, as Calvin insisted—then it must be possible for God not to love someone; and if that is so much as possible, then loving-kindness is not one of his essential properties.

Unfortunately, not all theologians in the Augustinian tradition are as clear on this point as Calvin himself was (and in the end even Calvin contradicted himself). According to Daniel Strange, for example, "God does not have to love all of humanity . . . for Him to be love."[3] But you might as well say: "God does not have to believe all true propositions in order to be omniscient." If it is so much as possible that God should not believe a true proposition, then omniscience is not one of his essential properties; and similarly, if it is so much as possible that God should not love someone, then love is not one of his essential properties either. So clearly the question of whether loving-kindness is an essential property of God is not merely academic but goes to the heart of Augustinian theology. Let us therefore pose a twofold question: how *do* the Augustinians interpret the Johannine declaration that God is love?—and what, if any, are the exegetical and theological merits of their interpretation?

In Search of an Augustinian Interpretation

When I first began to wonder how the proponents of limited election might interpret 1 John 4:8 and 16, I immediately encountered three difficulties as I began to search for an answer.

First, not all the proponents of limited election seem to regard these texts as particularly important. Louis Berkhof, for example, wrote an entire systematic theology without citing either of the texts in question;[4] and though Calvin did comment upon them briefly in his commentary on 1 John, he evidently did not regard them as important enough even to mention in his *Institutes of the Christian Religion.* When one thinks about it, this is truly astonishing. Calvin's *Institutes* is a monumental work of over 1,500 pages; in it he sought to provide an exhaustive summary of Christian doctrine, as he understood it, along with the biblical support for it. In the Westminster Press edition, the index of Bible references alone is 39 pages of small print with three columns per page. And yet, in this entire work, as

---

3. Daniel Strange, "A Calvinist Response to Talbott's Universalism" in Robin A. Parry and Christopher H. Partridge, *Universal Salvation? The Current Debate* (Grand Rapids: Eerdmans, 2004), 157.

4. See Louis Berkhof, *Systematic Theology* (Grand Rapids: Eerdmans, 1931).

massive and thorough as it is, Calvin never once found the Johannine declaration that God is love important enough to discuss. How, one wonders, could this have happened? Here is a statement that, to all appearances at least, provides a glimpse into the nature of the Christian God, and in his *Institutes* Calvin ignored it altogether; he did not even try to explain it away.

A second difficulty I encountered as I began my search was that the proponents of limited election are sometimes inconsistent in the various claims they make. When he contemplated God's relationship with the redeemed in heaven, for example, Jonathan Edwards wrote: "The Apostle tells us that God is love, 1 John 4:8. And therefore seeing he is an infinite Being, it follows that he is an infinite fountain of love. Seeing he is an all-sufficient Being, it follows that he is a full and overflowing and an inexhaustible fountain of love. Seeing he is an unchangeable and eternal Being, he is an unchangeable and eternal source of love."[5]

Here Edwards said that God is an "infinite," "overflowing," "inexhaustible," "unchangeable," and "eternal source of love." But when he contemplated God's relationship to the damned, Edwards also wrote: "In hell God manifests his being and perfections only in hatred and wrath, and hatred without love."[6] By "hatred without love," he evidently had in mind an attitude quite incompatible with love. So how, I ask, are we to reconcile the second quotation with the first? Suppose Edwards had said, in one place, that God's *righteousness* is "infinite," "inexhaustible," "unchangeable," and "eternal," and then had said, in another, that God acts toward some people—say, the nonelect—in some expedient way *without righteousness*. That would have posed a similar problem of interpretation. How could God's righteousness be both infinite and eternal if it is also limited in the sense that he sometimes acts without righteousness? And similarly, one wonders, how could God be an infinite, inexhaustible, overflowing, and eternal source of love if his love is also limited in the sense that he sometimes acts without love? Like Strange, Edwards appears to have embraced a logical inconsistency.

Perhaps the most serious difficulty I encountered, however, was a seemingly intentional kind of subterfuge. Consider how the Reformed theologian, J. I. Packer, interprets 1 John 4:8 and 16 in his

---

5. Jonathan Edwards, *Charity and Its Fruits,* reprinted in Paul Ramsey (ed.), *Works of Jonathan Edwards, Volume 8: Ethical Writings* (New Haven and London: Yale University Press, 1989), 369.

6. Ibid., 390.

book *Knowing God*.[7] A strong proponent of limited election, Packer in effect asks whether the proposition, *God is love,* expresses "the complete truth about God." By way of an answer, he juxtaposes two assertions. He begins one section with this italicized sentence as a caption: *"'God is love' is not the complete truth about God so far as the Bible is concerned";*[8] then, three pages later, he begins his next section with this italicized sentence as a caption: *"'God is love' is the complete truth about God so far as the Christian is concerned."*[9] From the perspective of a Christian who looks to the Bible as an authority, however, these captions are even more perplexing than Edwards's apparent inconsistency. If the proposition, *God is love,* does not express the complete truth about God so far as the Bible is concerned but does express the complete truth about God so far as the Christian is concerned, it would seem to follow that either the Bible or the Christian is mistaken.

And what, one wonders, does Packer mean by "the complete truth about God" anyway? In a perfectly obvious sense, the proposition, *God is love,* does *not* express the complete truth about God, not if God is also omnipotent and omniscient; but that would be true, I should think, both so far as the Bible is concerned (at least on Packer's account) and so far as the Christian is concerned. Does Packer really want to say that the Christian's perspective is different from that of the Bible?

Clearly not. Like Edwards, Packer has simply stumbled over a text that he finds difficult to incorporate into his overall theological perspective. As a close reading of his discussion will reveal, a recognizably consistent pair of theses lie behind the confused forms of expression in the two captions quoted above. The thesis of his second caption is really this: "According to the Bible, God loves the Christian with a perfect form of love"; and the thesis of his first caption is really this: "According to the Bible, God does *not* love *all* human beings with a perfect form of love." We can show that these are indeed Packer's theses in the following way. Packer makes two excellent and profound points. The first concerns the nature of God's actions: "This is what God does for those he loves—*the best He can*; and the measure of the best that God can do is omnipotence!"[10] The second concerns a condition of God's own happiness, which "will not be complete," says

---

7. J. I. Packer, *Knowing God* (Downers Grove: InterVarsity, 1973), 106–15.
8. Ibid., 108.
9. Ibid., 111.
10. Ibid, 115.

Packer, "till all His beloved ones are finally out of trouble."[11] Accordingly, Packer leaves us with exactly three possibilities: either (1) all persons will eventually be reconciled to God, or (2) God's own happiness will never be complete, or (3) God does not love all created persons. Now Packer clearly rejects both (1) and (2), and that leaves only (3), namely, that God does not love all created persons.

So far as I can tell, moreover, Packer sees all of this clearly, though he fails to make it explicit. His confusing caption—"'God is love' is not the complete truth about God so far as the Bible is concerned"—is merely his way of opting for (3) without calling too much attention to it. But in the end his readers are bound to ask the obvious question: "Does the Johannine declaration imply that God loves all persons, or does it not?" To this question Packer can give one of three possible answers: "Yes," "No," and "I don't know." As we have just seen, the answer he in fact gives is, "No," but it almost seems as if he recoils from the answer he gives. He probably felt a burden to express himself with sensitivity and caution on a difficult matter, lest he put off his readers with a clear statement of his own position. So he ends up trying to conceal his position, even as he articulates it, behind a curtain of ambiguous and confusing language.

The Loving Nature of God

It is hard to avoid the conclusion that the Augustinians, who restrict God's love and mercy to a limited elect, really have no clear idea how to handle 1 John 4:8 and 16. As a further illustration, consider how Calvin flatly contradicted himself when he was forced to say something about these texts, however briefly, in his commentary on 1 John. He began by observing, correctly, that the author of 1 John "takes as granted a general principle or truth, that God is love, that is, that his *nature* [or essence] is to love men" (my emphasis). He then went on to write: "But the meaning of the Apostle is simply this—that as God is the fountain of love, this effect flows from him, and is diffused wherever the knowledge of him comes, as he had at the beginning called him light, because there is nothing dark in him, but on the contrary he illuminates all things by his brightness. Here then he does not speak of the essence [or the nature] of God, but only shows what he is found to be by us [i.e., by the elect]."[12]

---

11. Ibid., 113.
12. John Calvin, *Commentaries on the Catholic Epistles* (Grand Rapids: Eerdmans, 1948), 239.

Having just told us that the Johannine declaration *is* a statement about the nature of God, Calvin went on to provide some additional reasons for taking it so: just as God is light in the twofold sense that "there is nothing dark in him" and "he illuminates all things by his brightness," so God is love in the sense that he is the source or "fountain of love." But then, by way of a conclusion that seems to come from nowhere, Calvin flatly contradicted himself and took it all back: in declaring that "God is love," he concluded, "the Apostle . . . does not speak of the essence [or the nature] of God, but only shows what he is found to be by us" [i.e., by the elect]. Nor did Calvin explain himself any further; he simply moved on to other matters.

Though such an explicit contradiction is no doubt bewildering, Calvin's conclusion that "the Apostle . . . does not speak of the essence [or the nature] of God" remains just what his overall theological perspective requires. It also indicates that he saw more clearly than Packer does exactly where the issue must be joined. The issue is not, as Packer has caricatured it, whether the proposition, *God is love,* expresses the complete truth about God. The issue is whether it expresses a truth about the nature or essence of God—whether, in other words, it ascribes an essential property to God. If it does, then God could not possibly fail to love someone or fail to seek anything other than the best for those whom he does love.

Consider now how Packer defends his Calvinistic interpretation of the Johannine declaration. Even as Calvin compared the divine attribute of love with that of light, so Packer points to two other Johannine statements "of exactly similar grammatical form": "God is light" and "God is spirit"; he then informs us that the "assertion that God is love has to be interpreted in the light of what these other two statements teach."[13] But these other two Johannine statements unquestionably *are* statements about the essence (or the nature) of God. In 1 John 1:5 (NKJV), we read that "God is light and in him is no darkness at all." This is not a declaration to the effect that, by a happy accident, God *happens* to be free from all darkness, all impurity, all unrighteousness; nor is it a declaration that God has *chosen* to remain free from all darkness in his relationship to some fortunate people only. It is instead a declaration about the essence (or nature) of God. And similarly for the assertion in John 4:24 that God is spirit.

As Calvin acknowledged in a comment upon this passage, "Christ himself calls God in his entirety 'Spirit'"; and this implies "that the

---

13. Packer, *Knowing God,* 109.

whole essence of God is spiritual, in which are comprehended Father, Son, and Spirit."[14] But then, if *God is spirit* implies "that the whole essence of God is spiritual," why should not *God is love* likewise imply that it is God's essence (or nature) to love? Packer insists that the latter proposition is a mere "summing up, *from the believer's standpoint* [my emphasis], of what the whole revelation set forth in Scripture tells us about its author."[15] But just what is that supposed to mean? Would Packer (or Calvin, for that matter) interpret the statement that God is spirit in the same way? Would he describe this as a mere "summing up, from the believer's standpoint," of the revelation about God? Certainly Calvin never described God's spiritual nature in this way, and I doubt that Packer would either. He would surely recognize that, given the spiritual nature of God, the expression "from the believer's standpoint" adds little but confusion.

Given Packer's own principle of interpretation, therefore, we are entitled to conclude that, in Johannine theology at least, God is love in exactly the same sense that he is spirit and is light; that is, it is as impossible for God not to love someone as it is for him to exhibit darkness rather than light.

In at least one place, moreover, Packer seems to acknowledge all of this. For he writes: "To say 'God *is* light' is to imply that God's holiness finds expression in everything that He says and does. Similarly, the statement 'God *is* love' means that His love finds expression in everything that He says and does."[16] But if God's holiness "finds expression in everything that He says and does," and his love likewise "finds expression in everything that He says and does," then in God there is no such thing as a holy act devoid of love or a loving act devoid of holiness. Accordingly, God's holiness and his love must be, at least, logically compatible; and if that is true, then the presence of divine judgment and divine wrath—which are but particular expressions of God's holiness—would no more imply the absence of God's purifying love than the presence of his love would imply the absence of his holiness.

The Paradox of Exclusivism

Our discussion so far has underscored two points: first, that the Johannine declaration that God is love is without question an as-

---

14. John Calvin, *Institutes of the Christian Religion*, ed. Ford Lewis Battles (Philadelphia: Westminster, 1960), 1.13.20.

15. Packer, *Knowing God*, 108.

16. Ibid., 111.

sertion about the essence (or nature) of God, and second, that, so interpreted, this single declaration is utterly inconsistent with any doctrine of limited election. But let us now set these two points aside for a moment, and let us grant, at least for the sake of argument, the possibility that God might not truly love all people. If we grant that assumption, then it may appear as if God is utterly free, as Calvin insisted, to will the good for some, namely the elect, and not to will it for all others.

But the appearance is misleading. If loving-kindness were merely an accidental property of God and not part of his essence, then it would indeed be possible that, for some sinner s, God does not truly love s. It would not follow, however, that God could *both* love some person s^* who also loves s *and,* at the same time, fail to love s. It would not follow, for example, that God could *both* love Isaac, who loved his son Esau so dearly, *and,* at the same time, hate Esau in the sense of willing that Esau should come to a bad end. Nor would it follow that God could *both* love Jacob, who eventually came to love Esau as a brother (see Gen. 33:10), *and* literally hate Esau. To the contrary, even if loving-kindness were not part of God's essence, God still could not love some persons (the elect) without loving all other persons as well.

Consider first a mere awkwardness in the doctrine of limited election. If God has commanded us to love our families, our neighbors, and even our enemies, as the New Testament consistently affirms, then a doctrine of limited election carries the awkward implication that God hates (or simply fails to love) some of the ones whom he has commanded us to love. Jesus declared that we are to love our enemies as well as our friends, so that (a) we might be children of our Father in heaven and (b) we might be perfect even as our Father in heaven is perfect (see Matt. 5:43–48); that is, we are to love our enemies because God loves them, and we should be like God in just this respect. So why should God command us to love some of the ones whom he himself fails to love? The reply that we can never know in this life who are not the objects of God's love may seem to provide a practical reason for loving all, lest we fail to love a true object of God's love. But such an answer hardly accords well with the words of 1 John 4:8, "Whoever does not love does not know God, for God is love."

Though the above paragraph registers a mere awkwardness in the doctrine of limited election, a more substantial puzzle emerges as soon as we ask ourselves how God could possibly love Isaac without loving Esau as well. According to Packer's excellent statement, quoted above: "This is what God does for those he loves—*the best He can*; and the measure of the best that God can do is omnipotence!" So just what is the best that omnipotence could do for Isaac? Or, to put it another way, what is the nature of the good that God wills for those whom he does love? He no doubt wills that they should achieve happiness of some kind. But just what is the relevant *kind* of happiness? Let us call it true *blessedness* or, to borrow Richard Swinburne's expression, *supremely worthwhile happiness.*[17]

Among the various conditions of such happiness, two are especially relevant for our present purposes. If I should be so unloving as to take pleasure from the misery of others, then whatever pleasure I take from it would be far removed from true blessedness; and if I should remain blissfully ignorant of some tragedy that, if known, would undermine my happiness altogether, then my blissful ignorance would not be worth much in the end. Accordingly, my happiness will qualify as supremely worthwhile, a form of true blessedness, only when (a) I am (finally) filled with love for all others and (b) no false beliefs or ignorance of any kind are essential to it. If God truly loves (or wills the best for) Isaac, therefore, then he wills that Isaac should achieve true blessedness in the end; he wills, in other words, that Isaac should become the kind of person who loves (or wills the best for) all others, including Esau.

Consider next the way in which love, or willing the good for another, binds people's interests together even as it renders them more vulnerable to misery and sorrow. Whenever two people are bound together in love, their purposes and interests, even the conditions of their happiness, are so logically intertwined as to be inseparable. Paul acknowledged this point when he commented concerning his fellow worker Epaphroditus: "He was indeed so ill that he nearly died. But God had mercy on him, and not only on him but on me also, so that I would not have one sorrow after another" (Phil. 2:27). Given Paul's love for his friend, then, any good that befell his friend would also be a good that befell Paul; and any evil that befell his friend would likewise be an evil that befell Paul. It is a point about the logic of love that the New Testament endorses again and again. First John 4:20 thus declares: "Those who say, 'I love God,' and hate their brothers

---

17. See Richard Swinburne, "A Theodicy of Heaven and Hell," in Alfred J. Freddoso, *The Existence of God* (South Bend, Ind.: University of Notre Dame Press, 1983).

and sisters, are liars"; they are liars because it is simply not possible to hate those whom God loves and, at the same time, to love God. Or, as Jesus put it in his much misunderstood account of the judgment of nations: "As you did it to one of the least of these my brethren [or loved ones], you did it to me" (Matt. 25:40 RSV).

But the reverse is true as well. Just as we cannot love God and hate those whom he loves, neither can God love us and, at the same time, hate (or even fail to love) those whom we love. If I truly love my own daughter, for example, and love her *even as I love myself,* then God cannot love (or will the best for) me unless he also loves (or wills the best for) her. For I am not an isolated monad whose interests are distinct from those of my loved ones, and neither is anyone else. If God should do less than his best for my daughter, therefore, he would also do less than his best for me; and if he should act contrary to her best interest, he would also act contrary to my own.

Calvin seemed to believe, however, that I might at least *experience* God as loving and kind, provided that I am one of the elect, even if God should choose not to love some of my own loved ones. But except in a case of blissful ignorance, which is not true blessedness, how could that be true? Could Isaac, consistent with his love for Esau, both *know* that God refused to love (indeed hated) his beloved son and, at the same time, experience God as loving and kind? Not unless he were somehow mentally deranged.

Suppose that in the aftermath of a boating accident my daughter and I should both start floundering in the water, too far apart to be of help to each other; suppose further that a man in another boat could easily rescue both of us, if he should choose to do so; and suppose, finally, that he should choose to rescue me (by throwing me one of several life rings in his possession) even as he permits my daughter to drown. We might imagine him to reason as follows: "If I permit the girl to drown, the man will be even more thankful for his own rescue and will therefore be even more inclined to reward me handsomely."

As twisted as such "reasoning" surely is, it seems comparable to the following: "If God passes over some sinners and refuses to extend his mercy to them, then the fortunate elect, despite their love for some of the lost, will be even more thankful for the (gratuitous) mercy extended to them and will therefore have even more grounds to praise God for their own undeserved salvation." Is the latter "reasoning" any better than the former? Clearly not. Unless he were in some way ignorant of God's attitude, Isaac could no more experience as loving and kind a God who literally hated Esau than I could experience as loving and kind a man who refused to throw a needed life ring to my daughter.

So herein lies a paradox, it seems, at the heart of Augustinian theology. The idea that God loves some people but not all, that he loves Isaac but not Esau, or that he divides the human race into the elect and the nonelect, is necessarily false. For even if, as Calvin insisted, the proposition, *God is love,* does not express a truth about the essence of God—even if God could have chosen not to love us—he could not choose to love some of us without also choosing to love all of us. That is why Paul, at least, so often spoke in terms of corporate wholes, the most important of which was the human race as a whole; even if it were possible that God should withhold his mercy from the human race as a whole, he must either extend it to the human race as a whole or extend it to no sinful humans at all. The reason, as we have seen, has to do with the inclusive nature of love.

For any two people, *s* and *s**, you choose, either a bond of love will exist between them where *s* wills the best for *s**, or it will not. If such a bond does exist, then God cannot will the best for *s* without willing the best for *s** as well. But even if such a bond does *not* exist, God still cannot will the best for *s* unless he wills that *s* should become the kind of person who is filled with love for, and therefore wills the best for, all others. And God cannot will that *s* should become the kind of person who wills the best for all others, I contend, unless God himself wills the best for them as well. Hence, God cannot love one person unless he loves all others as well.[18]

The Sin of Exclusivism

The argument of the previous section establishes, I believe, that Augustinian exclusivism or the doctrine of limited election entails a logical absurdity. But there is another side to the argument, which I have not yet emphasized, and in expressing this other side I run the risk of offending some who are far more virtuous and far more loving than I. For it does seem to me that a belief in limited election is, in one important sense, an expression of sin or human rebellion. Does this mean that, as I see it, those who accept such a doctrine or think they find it in the Bible are worse sinners than those of us who do not accept it? Of course not. Many deeply engrained and culturally condi-

18. For a more rigorous statement of the argument, see my article, "The Doctrine of Everlasting Punishment," *Faith and Philosophy* (January 1990): 30–34 and endnote 30.

tioned patterns of thought, like the "us versus them" mentality, may reflect sinful tendencies common to the human race as a whole, and perhaps all of us, at various times in our lives, unknowingly express such sinful tendencies in a variety of different ways.

But in what sense, one may ask, does Augustinian exclusivism express a sinful pattern of thought? It expresses, first of all, a temptation as old as religion itself: the temptation to distinguish between the favored few—to which, of course, we belong—and everyone else. We see the crudest manifestation of this temptation, perhaps, in some of the primitive religions, where people seek the favor of God (or the gods) in an effort to achieve an advantage over their enemies. Here the aim seems to be to possess the tribal god, or at least to pacify him with sacrifices, so that one can control him and even use him as a weapon against one's enemies. The last thing one may want, at this stage in one's religious development, is a God whose love and mercy extends to all persons including the members of enemy tribes, and the last commandment one may want to hear is that we must love our enemies as well as our friends.

In no way, however, are such attitudes of exclusivism limited to primitive religion; to the contrary, they are widespread and persistent, and they lie behind some of the most important religious struggles in many different ages. In the Old Testament, no less than in the New, we encounter a prophetic tradition that not only condemns such attitudes but testifies to their persistence and destructive power. A good early example is the story of Jonah and his refusal to preach to the Ninevites. For according to the story, Jonah's disobedience arose from his hatred of the Ninevites: the fact that he simply did not want them to repent and be saved. When they did repent and the Lord therefore spared their city, Jonah became so angry and distraught that he literally wanted to die.

Now a doctrine of limited election ultimately reflects attitudes similar to those of Jonah. For those who accept such a doctrine either sincerely desire that God's mercy should extend to all people, or they do not. If they do, then they are, given their own theology, more merciful than God; and if they do not desire this, then their attitudes are little different from Jonah's in this regard. We thus approach another logical impossibility built right into the heart of Augustinian theology. So long as I love my daughter as myself, I can neither love God nor worship him unless I at least *believe* that he loves her as well. For my love for God, if genuine, entails, first, that I respect God and approve of his actions; second, that I am grateful to him for what he has done for me; and third, that my will is, on the important issues at least, in conformity with his will.

But if I truly love, or desire the best for, my daughter and God does not, then (a) my will is *not* in conformity with God's will in this matter, (b) I could not consistently approve of God's attitude toward my daughter, and (c) neither could I be grateful to him for the harm he is doing to me. Nor is this merely to register a point about my own psychological makeup; the whole thing, I want to suggest, is *logically* impossible. As a matter of logic, either I do not love my daughter *as myself*, or I do not love God with all my heart, or I do not believe that God himself fails to love my own daughter.

Of course people are not always consistent and do not always see all the implications of their own beliefs; neither do they always believe what they *think* they believe. I have known several people who, after some tragedy or the death of a loved one, discovered that they did not really believe everything they had previously thought they believed. Still, certain beliefs—a racist ideology would be an example—unquestionably do interfere with a person's capacity to love. If a racist is also a Southern gentleman, then he may be gracious, loving toward his family and friends, and a person of many good qualities; his demeanor may be utterly different from that of skinheads or members of the American Nazi Party. But for as long as he *truly* believes that he belongs to a superior race or that his black neighbors are less than fully human, his racist ideology will interfere with his capacity for love and will inevitably separate him from some of his neighbors; he cannot, in other words, *both* hold his racist beliefs *and* love his black neighbor as himself.

Neither could the first-century Jews *both* believe that God restricts his love and mercy to the physical descendants of Abraham *and* love their Gentile neighbors as themselves. And for similar reasons neither can those Christians who believe that God has divided the world into the elect, whom he loves, and the nonelect, whom he despises, *both* love their neighbors even as they love themselves *and*, at the same time, love with all their heart a God who refuses to love some of their own loved ones.

Lest I be misunderstood here, I should perhaps repeat a point made at the beginning of this section. My point is not that exclusivists in theology or even racists are, on balance, worse than anyone else. I presume that, when God finally perfects our love for others, we shall all find that we have had to shed some deeply ingrained beliefs. But the fact is that some beliefs, particularly faulty beliefs about God, do undermine our capacity for love and do separate one person from another. When we finally learn to love our neighbor even as we love ourselves, therefore, we shall find that such beliefs have fallen away from us like the shackles they are.

Part 2: God's Unrestricted and Unconditional Mercy

For God has imprisoned all in disobedience so that he may be merciful to all (Rom. 11:32).

We have seen so far that the Augustinian understanding of limited election is utterly inconsistent with the loving nature of the Christian God and, in particular, utterly inconsistent with the Johannine declaration that God *is* love. We have also seen that this doctrine is riddled with logical impossibilities in any case. But we have not yet addressed St. Paul's view of the matter or the view of the New Testament in general. So in this part of my essay, I shall argue that the Augustinian understanding of limited election is not only inconsistent, but obviously inconsistent, with the whole thrust of Pauline theology.

Not only did Paul nowhere *embrace* a doctrine of limited election; he was, so I shall argue, a vigorous opponent of this doctrine, which he clearly regarded as heretical. The clarity and power of his explicit and sustained argument against it, moreover, explains why it virtually disappeared from the early church for several centuries until St. Augustine finally revived it in the early fifth century. Of course Paul combated the specific form that the doctrine had taken in his own day: the idea that God restricts his mercy to a single nation, namely the nation of Israel. He did not address—or try to anticipate—every conceivable form that the heresy might take in the future; he did not specifically discuss, for example, the Augustinian view that restricts God's mercy to a limited elect drawn from all nations and all classes of people. He did not discuss this view because he had never heard of it. For his purposes it was enough to point out that God will save everyone "who calls on the name of the Lord" (Rom. 10:13) and "everyone who has faith" (Rom. 1:16), whether the person be a Jew or a Greek. But though Paul never discussed Augustine's particular version of limited election, he did address and explicitly reject the understanding of justice and mercy that underlies it; so in that respect, his doctrine, set forth in Romans 11, that God is merciful to all and merciful even in his severity clearly did rule out the Augustinian view, as we shall see.

Are Justice and Mercy Separate and Distinct Attributes of God?

As the first Christian thinker to endorse a doctrine of limited election, Augustine's influence over subsequent generations of Christian thinkers was enormous, in part because he set forth a simple and captivating theological picture. But his simple picture also rests upon a faulty philosophical idea, one that perverts, I believe, the biblical understanding of both God's loving nature and his sovereignty in the matter of salvation. What the Augustinian picture finally illustrates, therefore, is the power of a faulty philosophical idea, particularly when articulated with skill and conviction, to influence how subsequent generations read the Bible and even what they are able, and not able, to see in it.

So just what was Augustine's faulty philosophical idea? It was the idea, to which he clung tenaciously in his later life, that justice and mercy are distinct and different attributes of God. In the *Enchiridion,* he thus argued that all human beings, by reason of their relationship to Adam, are part of "a corrupt mass"; all of them, the children no less than the adults, therefore, *deserve* everlasting punishment. He argued further that God selects from this corrupt mass a limited elect, drawn from all classes and all nations, to which he extends his mercy; having made *them* a special object of his love, he saves them from their sin. The rest God simply leaves in their sin and guilt, and they have, Augustine insisted, no grounds for complaint thereupon. For God merely gives them the punishment they deserve.[19] So the rest are objects of God's justice, but not his mercy, and that is possible only if justice and mercy are distinct and different attributes of God.

Such a faulty understanding of justice and mercy is by no means restricted to the Augustinians, however. For in his great epic poem *Paradise Lost,* John Milton, who clearly rejected any doctrine of limited election, nonetheless described Christ's willingness to die for our sins this way:

> No sooner did thy dear and only Son
> Perceive thee purpos'd not to doom frail Man
> So strictly, but much more to pity inclin'd,
> Hee to appease thy wrath, and end the strife

---

19. See Augustine, *Enchiridion,* 20.

> Of Mercy and Justice in thy face discern'd
> Regardless of the Bliss wherein hee sat
> Second to thee, offer'd himself to die
> For man's offense.[20]

According to Milton, then, the fall of the human race produced a conflict within the heart of God, a "strife" between his justice and his mercy, and Christ's atonement somehow managed to resolve the conflict. Presumably the source of the conflict was this: As a righteous judge, God willed something for the fallen human race that he could not possibly will in his role as a loving father; and as a loving father, he willed something that he could not possibly will in his role as a righteous judge. As a righteous judge, he willed that justice should prevail; and since justice requires retribution for sin, he was quite prepared to punish sin—in hell, for example—without any regard for the sinner's own good. But as a loving father, he also wanted to forgive sin and to permit his loved ones to escape the terrible punishment they deserved on account of their sin.

Hence the strife within the heart of God, and hence the need for an atonement that would appease the wrath of God—that is, satisfy his justice—and put an end to the strife. It is almost as if, according to Milton, Christ died not to effect a cure in us but to put an end to a bad case of schizophrenia in the Father. That may be a bit of a caricature, but it illustrates the point that, according to Milton and a host of Augustinian theologians, Christ died in order that God might be merciful to sinners without doing violence to his own sense of justice.

It is noteworthy, however, that Augustine's understanding of justice and mercy flatly contradicts his own commitment to the philosophical doctrine of divine simplicity: the difficult (and, I suspect, finally incoherent) idea that each attribute of God is identical with God himself and with every other attribute of God.[21] But however incoherent the *full* doctrine of divine simplicity may be—and we can

---

20. Bk. III, 403–10.

21. In *De Trinitate* Augustine wrote: "God is truly called in manifold ways, great, good, wise, blessed, true, and whatsoever other thing seems to be said of Him not unworthily: but his greatness is the same as His wisdom; for He is not great by bulk, but by power; and His goodness is the same as His wisdom and greatness, and His truth the same as all those things; and in Him it is not one thing to be blessed, and another to be great, or wise, or true, or good, or in a word to be Himself" (6.7). Note, however, that Augustine here identified God's greatness not with his love but with his *power*, and Augustine also identified God's goodness with his greatness; Augustine thus seems to have reduced everything to mere power. It seems to me, however, that one can defend a doctrine of absolute simplicity *and* be faithful to the biblical witness only if one identifies God's power as the creative and transforming power of love.

simply let the proverbial chips fall where they may on that issue—the idea that God's *moral nature* is simple seems to me both coherent and profound. According to this idea, God's love is identical with his mercy, which is identical with his justice, which is identical with his holiness, which is identical with his righteousness, etc. So how, one wonders, could Augustine accept *both* this kind of identity, which his own doctrine of divine simplicity also implies, *and* a doctrine of limited election?

In the case of Augustine, it is possible that, after embracing a doctrine of limited election, he simply changed his mind on the matter of divine simplicity. But a more recent Augustinian, Daniel Strange, embraces both limited election and divine simplicity in the context of the same essay![22]—an incoherent combination, if ever there was one. Consider again Strange's curious assertion, quoted above, that "God does not have to love all of humanity . . . for Him to *be* love." Would Strange make a similar claim about God's justice? Would he say that God does not have to treat all people justly in order to be just? I doubt it. But given the doctrine of divine simplicity, God is perfectly just in his treatment of all people only if he is perfectly loving, perfectly compassionate, and perfectly merciful in his treatment of them all as well. So if God is not perfectly loving, perfectly compassionate, and perfectly merciful in his treatment of the nonelect, then he is not perfectly just in his treatment of them either.

Clearly, then, no proponent of limited election can consistently accept a doctrine of divine simplicity or consistently agree with George MacDonald, who once wrote: "I believe that justice and mercy are simply one and the same thing: without justice to the full there can be no mercy, and without mercy to the full there can be no justice."[23] Neither, therefore, can a proponent of limited election accept Paul's clear and explicit argument in Romans 11 that all of God's actions—even his severity toward the disobedient—are, in the end, an expression of his boundless mercy.

Romans 11: An Explicit Argument against Limited Election

The argument of Romans 11 is exquisitely simple. God is merciful to all; therefore, the doctrine of limited election is false. What we encounter here is a glorious vision of mercy without limit of any

---

22. See Strange, "Calvinist Response," 155.
23. George MacDonald, "Justice" in Rolland Hein, ed., *Creation in Christ* (Wheaton: Harold Shaw, 1976), 77.

kind—a severe mercy, perhaps, but mercy nonetheless. For even in the case of the disobedient, those who have refused to call upon the name of the Lord, Paul insisted that God permits their disobedience and permits them to stumble only for the purpose of being merciful to them. In verse 7 Paul thus wrote: "What then? Israel failed to obtain what it was seeking. The elect obtained it, but the rest were hardened" (or blinded). He then explicitly asked whether God's severity toward these unbelievers—the hardening of their hearts, for example—implied an ultimate rejection of them: "Have they [the nonremnant who were cut off and hardened] stumbled so as to fall?" (v. 11). "Is this a doctrine of limited election?" he in effect asked. And his reply was most emphatic: "By no means!" Are there limits of any kind to God's mercy? By no means!

It seems as if the proponents of limited election inevitably stumble and fall themselves whenever they confront Paul's devastatingly simple answer to his own simple question. According to John Piper, for example, the hardening of which Paul spoke in verse 7 "is a condition that leaves part of Israel unresponsive to the gospel and so excludes them from salvation."[24] Excludes them from salvation? Would that be forever or just temporarily? If Piper means only that the nonremnant Jews were excluded from salvation temporarily, then they were no different, in that respect, from Paul himself. For Paul was also unresponsive to the gospel and was even a religious terrorist before he finally repented and became reconciled to God on the road to Damascus.

If Piper means, however, that the non-remnant Jews were excluded from salvation forever—and the whole thrust of his argument suggests that this is indeed his meaning—then he has flatly contradicted Paul's own words in verse 11. For as John Murray has pointed out, the construction at the beginning of verse 11 (translated "So I ask") "is Paul's way of introducing a question intended to obviate a conclusion which might seem to follow from what precedes."[25] It is almost as if Paul had said, in other words, "Don't make the mistake of interpreting my previous remark in the way that John Piper does, that is, in a way that implies ultimate rejection." So how does Piper square his interpretation of verse 7 with Paul's own clarification in verse 11? Well, he never mentions verse 11, at least not in the work where he

---

24. John Piper, *The Justification of God: An Exegetical and Theological Study of Romans 9:1–23* (Grand Rapids: Baker, 1983), 158.

25. John Murray, *Epistle of Paul to the Romans,* vol. II (Grand Rapids: Eerdmans, 1960), 75, n. 18.

gives the above interpretation of verse 7. And when challenged in another context with Paul's explicit claim that those who had stumbled, according to verse 7, did not stumble so as to fall (with ultimate consequences), Piper replied as follows: "Notice that this [i.e., the "they" in verse 11] is not a reference to all Jews, but to Israel as a corporate whole conceived of as an entity that endures from generation to generation made up of different individuals from time to time."[26]

But that could not possibly be right because in verse 7 Paul had already distinguished between three groups of people: Israel or the nation as a corporate whole, "the elect" or the faithful remnant, and "the rest," that is, the nonremnant Jews who were hardened. Now the antecedent of "they" in verse 11 could not possibly be the faithful remnant; they are not the ones who stumbled and were hardened. Nor could it be the nation as a corporate whole, for Paul had just distinguished between two groups within that corporate whole: the faithful remnant who did not stumble and were not hardened and "the rest" who did stumble and were hardened. Accordingly, the antecedent of "they" in verse 11 must be "the rest," the nonremnant Jews or the ones whom God had hardened. Even the Reformed New Testament scholar John Murray admitted this when he asked: "Is not the denotation of those in view [in verse 11] the same as those mentioned in verse 7: 'the rest were hardened'? And is not Paul thinking here of those in verse 22: 'toward them that fell, severity'?"[27] The answers are, "Yes" and "Yes."

But somehow Murray failed to draw the obvious conclusion that "they" (i.e., the nonremnant Jews) did not fall with ultimate consequences and therefore were not excluded from salvation. Perhaps, like many others, Murray was simply unable to fathom the idea that in Paul's scheme of things God's severity, even the hardening of a heart, is itself an expression of mercy; Murray therefore insisted, even as Piper does, that "those who stumbled did fall with ultimate consequences." But that could not possibly be right either. For the "denotation of those" mentioned in verse 11 is not only "the same as those mentioned in verse 7"; it is also the same as those mentioned in verse 12, that is, those whose "full inclusion" will mean so much more than the stumble that made their full inclusion possible.

In Paul's own words: "Now if their stumbling means riches for the world, and if their defeat means riches for the Gentiles, how much more will their full inclusion mean!" And again: "For if their rejec-

---

26. John Piper, "Universalism in Romans 9–11? Testing the Exegesis of Thomas Talbott," *The Reformed Journal,* 33:7, 12.

27. Murray, *Romans,* 75.

tion is the reconciliation of the world, what will their acceptance be but life from the dead!" (v. 15). Throughout the entire chapter Paul was talking about the unbelieving Jews ("the rest"), and throughout the entire chapter his third-person plural pronouns consistently refer back to the unbelieving Jews and not to Israel as a corporate whole.

Now Paul fully appreciated, it seems, the radical nature of his thesis that God's severity, no less than his kindness, is an expression of mercy; he fully appreciated that his readers would find such a teaching, which is so foreign to our ordinary ways of thinking about justice and mercy, hard to understand and therefore hard to accept. To forestall the anticipated objections, therefore, he in effect warned his readers to be wary of their normal ways of thinking and told them not to regard themselves as wiser than they are (v. 25) in the face of a fundamental mystery, which is this: "A hardening has come upon part of Israel," he said, "until the full number of the Gentiles has come in. And so all Israel will be saved" (vv. 25–26). God may have hardened part of Israel, but he did so, Paul insisted, as a means of saving all of Israel and all of Israel *including those who were hardened.* And lest a reader still miss the point, Paul repeated it one more time with an absolutely explicit statement: Though the unbelieving Jews were in some sense "enemies of God" (v. 28), they nonetheless became "disobedient in order that they too may now receive mercy" (11:31 NIV). You simply cannot get any more explicit than that. But though Paul's *specific* point about his disobedient kin was glorious enough, the general principle (of which the specific point is but an instance) was even more glorious yet: "For God has imprisoned *all* in disobedience so that he may be merciful to *all*" (11:32, my emphasis).

The message of Romans 11, then, is that God is always and everywhere merciful, even as he is always and everywhere righteous. His rejection of a sinner, if we can call it that, is always temporary and always serves an overriding redemptive purpose; even when he shuts people up to their disobedience—blinding their eyes, hardening their hearts, or cutting them off for a season—he does so as an expression of his mercy or compassion for them. Nor can one counter this glorious message by insisting, as so many have, that Paul's "all Israel" in 11:26 does not include, for example, Israelites who have already died. For though I think that this is quite mistaken,[28] I am not here

---

28. As Jan Bonda has put it: "The only argument adduced against this view [that Paul literally had in mind all Israel] is that the dead are excluded from this number. But this exclusion wreaks havoc with the interpretation of Romans 11:26a. . . . It denies that God's redemption in Christ includes all generations since Adam, while this is precisely the

presenting Romans 11 as a complete argument for universalism. I am instead presenting it as Paul's argument against limited election, against the idea that God sometimes acts righteously but without mercy or compassion, as if that were even a logical possibility.

For whether sinners are free to reject God forever, God himself never rejects anyone. In that respect, the central claim of Romans 11 is in perfect agreement with Lamentations 3:22, 31–32: "The steadfast love of the LORD never ceases, his mercies never come to an end. . . . For the Lord will not reject forever. Although he causes grief, he will have compassion according to the abundance of his steadfast love; for he does not willingly afflict or grieve anyone." The God described here is not one who restricts his mercy and compassion to a chosen few.

Consider, finally, two important features of Romans 11:32. First, Paul's use of *for* shows that verse 32 is not, as some have supposed, a mere summary of verses 30 and 31; nor is it a mere summary of anything else in the chapter. As the grand finale of Paul's theological essay, verse 32 makes a general claim that grounds or explains several specific points made in the chapter. As an illustration, suppose that I should say something like the following: "You know that Hollywood stars, however highly they may think of themselves, are mere mortals in the end, and the same is true of sports heroes and famous politicians. For, however highly they may think of themselves, all humans are mere mortals." Here it is obvious that my claim about all humans is not a mere summary of my several claims about Hollywood stars, sports heroes, and famous politicians; nor do these specific instances of my generalization provide an excuse for denying that it also applies, for example, to schizophrenics with delusions of immortality. And similarly for Paul's general claim in 11:32: why is it, according to Paul, that the nonremnant Jews who stumbled did not stumble so as to fall with ultimate consequences? Because God is merciful to all. Why was the hardening that came upon part of Israel destined to be but one contributing factor in the salvation of all Israel? Because God is merciful to all. Why did Paul's unbelieving kin become "disobedient in order that they too may now receive mercy"? Because God is merciful to all. "O the depth of the riches and wisdom and knowledge of God!" (11:33).

---

point Paul wants to make. If we grasp that, then we know that if all Israel will be saved, this will include all Israelites who have died." Jan Bonda, *The One Purpose of God* (Grand Rapids: Eerdmans, 1998), 184. See also footnote 28 on p. 184.

Second, the parallel structure of 11:32, so typical of Paul, should eliminate any possibility of ambiguity. For the whole point of such a parallel structure is for the first "all" to determine the reference of the second. And it is simply inconceivable, to my mind at least, that Paul had here forgotten, or simply did not have clearly in view, the whole thrust of his teaching throughout his letter that each and every human being, with the one exception of Jesus Christ, has been shut up to disobedience.[29] It is likewise inconceivable, therefore, that Paul did not mean to say what his sentence in fact does say, which is that God is merciful to each and every human being. As I have expressed the point elsewhere:

> According to Paul, the *very ones* whom God "shuts up" to disobedience—whom he "blinds," or "hardens," or "cuts off" for a season—are those to whom he is merciful; his former act is but the first expression of the latter, and the latter is the goal and the *purpose* of the former. God hardens a heart in order to produce, in the end, a contrite spirit, blinds those who are unready for the truth in order to bring them ultimately to the truth, "imprisons all in disobedience so that he may be merciful to all."[30]

When "All" Really Means All

A remarkable feature of the standard Augustinian exegesis of the Bible is how often "all" arbitrarily becomes *some,* and Augustine's own explanation of 1 Timothy 2:4, where we read that God wills or "desires everyone to be saved and to come to the knowledge of the truth," illustrates the point nicely. Though the meaning of this text seems clear and straightforward, here is how Augustine tried to explain it away: "The word concerning God, 'who will have all men to be saved,' does not mean that there is no one whose salvation he doth not will . . . but by 'all men' we are to understand the whole of mankind, in every single group into which it can be divided. . . . For from which of these groups doth not God will that *some* men from every nation should be saved through his only-begotten Son our Lord?"[31]

So it is not God's will, said Augustine, to save every individual from every group and every nation; it is merely God's will to save all

---

29. But see Murray, *Romans,* 103, for an example of someone who claims that, even if Paul did not literally forget the whole thrust of his previous teaching on this matter, neither did he here have it in view.

30. Robin A. Parry and Christopher H. Partridge, eds., *Universal Salvation? The Current Debate* (Grand Rapids: Eerdmans, 2004), 34.

31. *Enchiridion,* 27.

kinds of people, that is, *some* individuals from every group and every nation.

But why should anyone accept such an interpretation as that? In support of it, Augustine pointed to the context, which singles out a specific group of people—not several groups, mind you, but a single group—for special mention. Though we should pray for all people (1 Tim. 2:1), the text specifically mentions "kings and all who are in high positions" (1 Tim. 2:2). Seizing upon this reference, Augustine argued that God wills salvation only for the elect, only for some persons from all groups: "kings and subjects; nobility and plebeians; the high and the low; the learned and the unlearned; the healthy and the sick; the bright, the dull, and the stupid," etc.[32] But that will never do. For the text explains exactly why "kings and all who are in high places" are singled out for special mention. We should pray for those in positions of authority, it says, so that "we may lead a quiet and peaceable life" (1 Tim. 2:2). The mere fact that the text provides a special (and quite understandable) reason we should pray specifically for those whose job it is to keep the peace—the kind of prayer, incidentally, that one can hear almost any Sunday in some churches—hardly justifies Augustine's contention that "all humans" really means "some humans from all classes and all nations."

The text goes on to specify a second reason we should pray for all; we should do so because "Christ Jesus, himself human . . . gave himself a ransom for all" (1 Tim. 2:5). The full passage (1 Tim. 2:1–2:7) thus includes three references in sequence to all humans. We are to pray for all humans (1 Tim. 2:1), first, because God wills or desires the salvation of them all (1 Tim. 2:4), and second, because Jesus Christ gave himself as a ransom for them all (1 Tim. 2:5). Now the "all humans" in 1 Timothy 2:1 could not possibly be limited to some from all classes and all nations. For even if one should accept a doctrine of limited election and should hold that the reason we are to pray for all people is that we have no way of knowing who is elect and who is not, it would still be true that, according to our text, we are to pray for all people, not just some of them. So unless one supposes, in the absence of any grammatical or textual evidence at all, a shift of reference in the text, the "all" whose salvation God sincerely desires includes everyone for whom we are to pray, and the "all" for whom Jesus gave himself as a ransom includes everyone whose salvation God sincerely desires.

---

32. Ibid.

In the words of the New Testament scholar Luke Johnson, "As the one God wills the salvation of all, the one mediator gives himself for all."[33] No other interpretation is even remotely plausible. The Arminians can rightly deny that, taken by itself, 1 Timothy 2:1–7 entails universalism, because the text leaves open the question of whether God's desire for the salvation of all will ever be satisfied. But the Augustinian interpretation requires that we simply ignore what is right there before our eyes.

When we turn, furthermore, to a theological context such as Romans 5:12–21, where Paul identified his reference class with great clarity, we discover just how carefully he sometimes used the expression "all humans" (or more literally "all men"). For here Paul made abundantly clear that, when he spoke of all humans, he had in mind the whole mass of humanity with only two possible exceptions: the first and the second Adam. And he excluded the second Adam, or Jesus Christ, from his "all humans" for several obvious reasons: First, he did not think of Jesus as merely human—*fully* human, perhaps, but not *merely* human; second, he did not think of Jesus as a sinner, and in 5:12 he identified his reference class as all humans *who have sinned*; and third, for the very reason that he did think of Jesus as the savior of all, he did not include Jesus among the "all" who are being saved.

But in Romans 5, at least, Paul also seems to have excluded the first Adam from his "all humans." For in 5:14 he distinguished Adam, who first sinned and brought doom upon the entire human race, from those whose sins had a less profound effect upon the human race as a whole; he also called Adam a "type" of Jesus Christ or of "the one who was to come," and he did so to indicate that Adam and Jesus Christ stand in an analogous relationship to the whole of humanity. So in that sense he distinguished both Adams from his "all humans" or the whole of humanity.[34] And in 5:15 he continued to contrast "the one" and "the many" in two instances: In the first, Adam is "the one" who stands in a special relationship to "the many" or the whole of humanity; in the second, Jesus Christ is "the one" who stands in a special relationship to "the many" or the whole of humanity. As Paul

---

33. L. T. Johnson, *The First and Second Letters to Timothy*, Anchor Bible (New York: Doubleday, 2001), 197.

34. This in no way implies, of course, that Adam was excluded from salvation. He was excluded from Paul's "all humans" only by reason of the analogy between the first and the second Adam. But Jesus and Jesus alone was excluded from both the class of sinners and the class of redeemed sinners.

himself put it in Romans 5:15, "If the many died by the trespass of the one man, how much more did God's grace and the gift that came by the grace of the one man, Jesus Christ, overflow to the many!" (NIV). So insofar as Adam brought doom upon the human race as a whole and Jesus Christ undid the doom and restored the human race to life, neither of them was strictly in view when Paul spoke of "all humans," which included all the merely human and sinful descendants of Adam.

It is absolutely clear, then, that in Romans 5 Paul employed the two expressions "all humans" and "the many" to pick out exactly the same group of individuals. As John Murray has pointed out: "When Paul uses the expression 'the many,' he is not intending to delimit the denotation. The scope of 'the many' must be the same as the 'all men' of verses 12 and 18. He uses 'the many' here, as in verse 19, for the purpose of contrasting more effectively 'the one' and 'the many,' singularity and plurality—it was the trespass of 'the one,' . . . but 'the many' died as a result."[35]

Similarly, it was the righteous act of "the one," but "the many" are granted justification and life as a result. In order to eliminate any possibility of ambiguity, moreover, Paul then employed one of his favorite devices in verses 18 and 19: a parallel structure and a "just as, . . . so also" construction. Given such a parallel structure, it is simply inconceivable, to my mind at least, that Paul intended to shift reference within the context of a single sentence. He could easily have written: "Therefore just as one man's trespass led to condemnation for all humans, so also one man's act of righteousness brings justification and life to some of them, or to all of the specially favored, or to some people from all nations and classes." But Paul used every grammatical device he could think of to avoid this kind of misinterpretation. The whole point of his parallel structure and the "just as, . . . so also" construction was to make two parallel statements about exactly the same group of individuals; the whole point was that *all of those* who are subject to condemnation, as a result of Adam's sin, are also the beneficiaries of Christ's act of righteousness.

Mind you, I am not, at this point, presenting Romans 5:18 as an explicit statement of universalism; I am claiming only that you cannot escape a universalistic interpretation by insisting that the second "all" is restricted in a way that the first is not. For Paul intentionally

---

35. John Murray, *Romans*, 192–93.

constructed his sentence in a way that would make it obvious that both instances of "all" pick out exactly the same group of individuals. But the specter of universalism no doubt explains why so many strive so mightily to explain away the clear sense of the text. According to Douglas J. Moo, for example, "Paul's point [in verses 18–19] is not so much that the groups affected by Christ and Adam, respectively, are coextensive, but that Christ affects those who are his just as certainly as Adam does those who are his."[36] In support of this widespread contention, Moo appeals to Paul's use of "all" in other contexts.[37] "That 'all' does not always mean 'every single human being,'" he writes, "is clear from many passages, it often being clearly limited in context (c.f., e.g., Rom. 8:32; 12:17–18; 14:2; 16:19)"; hence, there is "no linguistic barrier," he concludes, to supposing that the second "all humans" is more restrictive than the first.[38]

But in fact there are serious "linguistic barriers" to Moo's interpretation, most notably the parallel structure of Paul's sentence and the care with which he distinguished between "the one" and "the many" with respect to his "all humans." Nor do any of Moo's references have the slightest relevance to these "linguistic barriers." We can certainly agree with him that in neither Paul nor any other author does "all" always mean "every single human being"; in the statement, "All rocks have weight," for example, "all" obviously does not mean "every single human being." And if this seems like a rather cutesy remark, I would point out that in two of Moo's cited examples, Romans 14:2 and 8:32, the relevant reference class is not even that of human beings! Consider Romans 14:2, where the unstated reference class is that of *edible foods:*[39] Whereas some, Paul in effect said, believe in eating all edible foods, both meat and vegetables, others believe in eating vegetables only. More often than not, the reason that an implicit reference class, such as edible foods, is left unstated is as familiar as it is simple: When the context already makes a reference class clear, it is simply not necessary to state it explicitly. Not even Romans

36. Douglas J. Moo, *The Epistle to the Romans* (Grand Rapids: Eerdmans, 1996), 343.

37. In support of his claim that the second "all humans" in 5:18 is more restrictive than the first, Moo also appeals to Paul's consistent emphasis on the necessity of faith and belief and to his reference in 5:17 to "those receiving the abundance of grace." But this is more relevant to the question of whether 5:18 teaches universalism than it is to the question of whether Jesus did something on behalf of all humans or the human race as a whole. In any event, see Part 4 for a further discussion of this matter.

38. Moo, *Romans*, 343–44.

39. Because Paul was no doubt opposed to cannibalism, a more accurate statement of his reference class would be that it includes all edible nonhuman flesh and vegetables.

3:23, where Paul declared that all have sinned, explicitly identifies the relevant reference class of human beings.

Following Moo's strategy, therefore, one could always contend that even in Romans 3:23 "all" is "limited in context," because neither dogs nor birds nor unfallen angels have in fact sinned. It is a neat trick: First misidentify a reference class; then, argue that "all" is "limited in context" because it does not refer to each and every member of your misidentified reference class.

As an illustration of just how faulty the Moo strategy is, suppose that a future racist society should come to regard our country's Declaration of Independence as a sacred document, and suppose further that some scholars in this society, being determined to explain away the statement, "All men are created equal," should scour other letters and documents of the time in order to find instances where "all" is used rather loosely. We might suppose that they find "some fifty places," perhaps in some narratives of the Revolutionary War, where "the words 'all' and 'every' are used in a limited sense" (whatever, exactly, that unclear expression might mean). Would this have any bearing on the meaning of "all men" in the statement, "All men are created equal," as it appears in the Declaration of Independence? It is hard to see why it should. And it is no less hard to see how the Moo/Boettner strategy is even relevant to the correct interpretation of Romans 5:18 or any other universalistic text in Paul.

When examining the use of "all" in any text, it is always critical to distinguish between two different sorts of contexts: those where "all" is combined with a relevant noun, which either explicitly fixes or helps to fix the reference class, and those where it is not combined with a relevant noun. In the latter contexts, it is up to the reader to identify the reference class accurately—which, in the case of Paul's letters, is rarely a difficult task. For whenever Paul used "all" in the context of some theological discourse, he seems always to have had in mind a clear reference class, stated or unstated, and he referred distributively to every member of that class. When he said that God "accomplishes *all* things according to his counsel and will" (Eph. 1:11), he did not, it is true, literally have in mind everything, including numbers and propositions and sets of properties; he had in mind every *event*. Everything that happens in the world, he was claiming, falls under God's providential control. And similarly for his remark that "*all* things work together for good to them that love God" (Rom. 8:28 KJV); here he meant not just *some* events, but *all* events. Or again, when Paul asserted that "God has put *all* things in subjection" to Christ (1 Cor. 15:27), he clearly had in mind all *created* things; and so, as he pointed out himself, this does not include the Father (15:28). But it does include every member of the class he had in mind.

Beyond that, Paul never spoke of the human race as a whole, at least not in a context of doctrinal exposition, in a way that omitted anyone—except, perhaps, the first and the second Adam. And even if he had spoken rather loosely in some contexts, that would have had no relevance to those contexts, such as Romans 5:18; 11:32; and 1 Corinthians 15:22, where he employed special grammatical devices for the purpose of eliminating all ambiguity. Nor is there a single shred of evidence that by "all" Paul ever meant "some" or that by "all humans" he ever meant "some humans from all classes." And because he explicitly stated that God is merciful to all and merciful even in his severity, he also explicitly rejected any view that would restrict God's mercy to a limited elect.

Part 3: Understanding Romans 9

I will have mercy on whom I have mercy, and I will have compassion on whom I have compassion (Rom. 9:15).

Romans 9–11 is a sustained theological discourse in which Paul took up the problem of Jewish unbelief and systematically defended his thesis that God has every right to extend his mercy to all the descendants of Adam, including Gentiles. The body of discussion is sandwiched between Paul's expression of "great sorrow and unceasing anguish" in Romans 9:2 and his expression of great joy and wonder at the end of chapter 11. So just what transformed Paul's "unceasing anguish" over the condition of his unbelieving kin into ecstatic praise at the end of chapter 11? Was it not precisely the message of chapter 11?

As something of an aside, I would point out that in Romans 9–11 we encounter a literary structure much like that of a fairy tale. Essential to any good fairy tale, according to J. R. R. Tolkien, is the "sudden joyous 'turn'" and the consolation it brings. A good fairy tale thus "denies (in the face of much evidence, if you will) universal final defeat . . . [thereby] giving a fleeting glimpse of Joy, Joy beyond the walls of the world, poignant as grief."[40] In a similar vein, Paul's discourse

---

40. J. R. R. Tolkien, "On Fairy-Stories," in *The Tolkien Reader* (New York: Ballantine, 1966), 68.

in Romans 9–11 begins with "unceasing anguish" and the *apparent* "dark side of any doctrine of election," as the New Testament scholar, James Dunn, has called it.[41] The apparent darkness may seem to include God's supposed hatred and rejection of Esau, the hardening of Pharaoh's heart, and a lot of "orc-talk" about how Paul's beloved kin are little more than "vessels of wrath fit for destruction." No wonder the discourse begins with "unceasing anguish!"

But then comes the sudden joyous turn at the end of chapter 11. We learn that we have misconstrued the whole story, and we finally begin to penetrate the glorious eschatological mystery behind it all: how rejection is always temporary and always serves a merciful purpose, how even the hardening of a heart is an expression of mercy, and how the election of one, such as Jacob, is always on behalf of all others, including Esau. As James Dunn has correctly summarized the point, "God hardens some in order to save all; he confines all to disobedience in order to show mercy to all."[42] So all is grace and mercy in the end, and no lesser vision could have transformed Paul's "unceasing anguish" into his ecstatic praise of God at the end of chapter 11.

My point is that we must allow the glorious eschatological vision at the end of our "fairy tale" to reshape our understanding of the whole story, and that is only a sound exegetical procedure anyway: It would be exegetically irresponsible not to interpret the early stages of Paul's argument, as developed in chapter 9, in light of Paul's own conclusion in chapter 11. But it sometimes seems as if the Augustinians stop reading, either literally or metaphorically, around 9:24 or so. In the *Enchiridion,* for example, Augustine set forth a summary of Christian doctrine, as he understood it; and though his summary is saturated with quotations from Romans 9, it contains not a single reference to Romans 11, which he evidently regarded as less essential than Romans 9 to Paul's understanding of divine mercy.

I find this truly astonishing, sort of like Calvin's failure in the *Institutes* even to mention the Johannine declaration that God is love. No less astonishing to me is that John Piper could write an entire book on Romans 9:1–23 without ever citing either Romans 11:11 or 11:32. The implication of such omissions is that these texts have no relevance to a correct interpretation of Romans 9. But the issue of their *relevance* should be utterly noncontroversial, because it is sim-

41. James D. G. Dunn, *The Theology of Paul the Apostle* (Grand Rapids: Eerdmans, 1998), 511.

42. James D. G. Dunn, *Romans 9–16,* vol. 38b, Word Biblical Commentary (Dallas: Word, 1988), 696.

ply not possible that God should *both* refuse to extend his mercy to Esau *and,* at the same time, extend it to all, as 11:32 at least *appears* to say he does. So how can Piper give a responsible interpretation of Romans 9 without even mentioning a text that functions as the conclusion of Paul's argument and at least *appears* to contradict Piper's own interpretation?

Be all of that as it may, I shall now argue that the real message of Romans 9 is just the opposite of what the Augustinians have claimed it to be.

St. Paul's Inclusive Understanding of Election

In Romans 9:6 Paul insisted that the widespread unbelief among his Jewish kin carried no implication that "the word of God had failed"; and when he spoke of God's "purpose in election" (v. 11 NIV) and how it continued through the choice of Jacob "not by works but by his call" (v. 12), his implication was again that this "purpose in election" had not failed. But just what did he mean by "God's purpose in election?"

Based upon Ephesians 1:9–10, we can say that God's purpose in election expresses his eternal "good pleasure"; it is simply his decretive will, as the Augustinians often call it, "a plan for the fullness of time, to gather up all things in him [Christ], things in heaven and things on earth." Given the close association and similarity of structure between Ephesians 1:10 and Colossians 1:20, we can also infer that "this plan to gather up all things" in Christ is a plan to reconcile all people to God through Christ. For as Colossians 1:19–20 explicitly states, "God was pleased [i.e., it was God's good pleasure[43]] . . . to reconcile to himself [through Christ] all things, whether things on earth or things in heaven, by making peace through his blood, shed on the cross" (NIV).

In view of the stress that the Augustinians typically place on God's "good pleasure" or decretive will, they would do well, I believe, to place an equal stress on texts, such as Ephesians 1:20 and Colossians 1:20, that tell us exactly what God's good pleasure or decretive will or purpose in election is. In the latter text Paul applied the concept of reconciliation, which is explicitly a redemptive concept, to the entire creation; he also specifically associated this reconciliation with

---

43. The difference between saying, "God was pleased to reconcile," and saying, "It was God's good pleasure to reconcile," is like the difference between saying, "I desire to do such and such," and saying, "I have a desire to do such and such."

238 — PERSPECTIVES ON ELECTION: FIVE VIEWS

the peace that the blood of the cross brings and specifically cited his own readers (v. 21) as examples of the kind of reconciliation he had in mind. Without question, therefore, he had in mind the reconciliation of all people in the full redemptive and restorative sense.[44] God's "good pleasure" or decretive will, in other words, is precisely his loving will to be merciful to all (Rom. 11:32), to reconcile the entire world (or all of humanity) to himself (2 Cor. 5:19), and to achieve this end through the death and resurrection of Jesus Christ.

But if that is true, if it is God's "good pleasure" or "purpose in election" to reconcile all of humanity to himself, why the initial *appearance* of exclusion in Romans 9? Why the division between Isaac and Ishmael, between Jacob and Esau, and between "the children of the flesh" and "the children of the promise"? There is, I believe, a relatively simple explanation. Paul normally spoke of an all-encompassing election *in Christ*; in Ephesians 1, for example, he asserted merely that God chose "us"—not one person rather than another (e.g., Isaac rather than Ishmael), but simply *us*—"in Christ before the foundation of the world" (1:4). And this predestined "us" in no way *requires* a rejected "them."

But at the beginning of Romans 9, Paul's interest was more historical, as he wrestled with the meaning of Jewish unbelief. Among the many advantages that belong to the Israelites, he listed these two: "Theirs are the patriarchs, and from them is traced the human ancestry of Christ, who is God over all" (9:5 NIV). He then went on to review[45] some early (and utterly familiar) Jewish history: how Israel had come into being as a nation in the two generations following Abraham, and how the line of descent from Abraham to Jesus had begun with the election of Isaac and Jacob. One could hardly overemphasize, moreover, the importance that Paul placed on this idea that Jesus Christ was the promised offspring (or seed) of Abraham. In his letter to the Galatians, he had earlier written, "Now the promises were made to Abraham and to his offspring; it does not say 'And to offsprings,' as of many; but it says, 'And to your offspring,' that is, to one person, who is Christ" (Gal. 3:16). In Romans 9, however, the emergence of Israel as a nation and the line of descent between

---

44. For why the reconciliation of which Paul speaks in Colossians 1:20 is not a mere subjugation of hostile powers, see my remarks in Parry and Partridge, op. cit., 22–25.

45. Romans 9:5 is, of course, the conclusion of the opening section in this theological discourse. But a point that James Dunn makes concerning the transition from 9:13 to 9:14 is also relevant here: "As so often with Paul the conclusion to a section . . . serves also as introduction to the next section." Dunn, *Romans 9–16,* 538.

Abraham and his seed, namely Jesus Christ, was the focal point of his attention. That line of descent could not possibly have passed through both Isaac and Ishmael, and neither could it have passed through both Jacob and Esau.

In the relevant historical context being reviewed in Romans 9, therefore, election has both a particular and a universal aspect; and both are reflected in the original promise to Abraham. The particular aspect emerges clearly in the promise, to which Paul alluded in Romans 9:9, that Sarah would give birth to a child and would thus provide Abraham with a line of physical descent, so that he could become the father of a great nation and a blessing to all nations. Neither Ishmael nor any child not born of Sarah, however righteous that child might turn out to be as an adult, could have fulfilled this part of God's promise to Abraham. But the promise also had an obvious universal aspect which already included, so Paul stated in Galatians 3:8, the central message of the Christian gospel. For the essence of that promise was that through Abraham's offspring, identified in Paul's mind as Jesus Christ, God would bless all nations, not just the nation of Israel. Observe also that neither Ishmael nor Esau were Israelites or descendants of Jacob; they were passed over, therefore, in exactly the same sense in which all other Gentiles living at the time were likewise passed over.

It seems to me a pointless exercise, then, to deny, as some commentators do, that in Romans 9 Paul had in mind the election of the specific individuals named "Abraham," "Isaac," and "Jacob." When Paul spoke of Jacob's election (9:11) and cited the Old Testament prophecy that the "elder shall serve the younger" (9:12), it is true that he lifted his quotation from a context in which nations, not individuals, were definitely in view. In Genesis 25:23, we thus read that the Lord declared to Rebecca: "Two nations are in your womb, and two peoples born of you shall be divided; the one shall be stronger than the other, the elder shall serve the younger." Similarly, when Paul quoted the words, "I have loved Jacob, but I have hated Esau" (9:13), which he lifted from an oracle that the prophet Malachi had delivered to Israel, he again quoted from a context in which nations, not individuals, were in view. But the issue here is Paul's context, not these Old Testament contexts; and given the use to which the New Testament writers typically put the Old Testament, we cannot suppose uncritically that the Old Testament context from which Paul lifted his quotations determined his own use of them.

According to F. F. Bruce, among others, Paul did indeed have in view the peoples of Israel and Edom, rather than the Old Testament characters who bore the names "Jacob" and "Esau";[46] and according to Johannes Munck, "Romans 9:6–13 is speaking neither of individuals and their selection for salvation, nor of the spiritual Israel, the Christian church. It speaks rather of the patriarchs, who without exception became the founders of peoples."[47] It is doubtful, however, that even Malachi would have disassociated the individuals, Jacob and Esau, from their progeny, the latter being seen as but an extension of the former. And furthermore, when Paul indicated that the election of Jacob took place before the twins were "born or had done anything good or bad" (9:11), he surely did have the individuals, Jacob and Esau, principally in view. Was not the whole point to illustrate "God's purpose in election": how it continues "not by works but by his call" (9:11–12)? And was not the familiar struggle between Jacob and Esau for the birthright—the fact that it went to the younger brother rather than to the older one—just what illustrated his point in a forceful way? Ernst Käsemann thus seems at least half right when he comments: "The quotations [from Genesis and Malachi] are taken out of their context. . . . For Paul is no longer concerned with two peoples and their destiny, . . . but timelessly . . . with the election and rejection of two persons who are elevated as types."[48]

But on what textual grounds does Käsemann suppose, along with so many others, that the election of one person implies the rejection of another? For many, the idea that rejection is the inevitable "dark side" of election functions almost like an *a priori* assumption. James Dunn thus writes: "The election of one implies as an unavoidable corollary the nonelection, that is, rejection, of another."[49] But why should that follow? Why should the election of Isaac and Jacob in particular imply the rejection of Ishmael and Esau? For that matter, why should the election of Abraham imply the rejection of all others, living at the time, whom God could have called out but did not? In fact, since election is an expression of love, as even the Augustinians agree, the *logic* of election is just the opposite of what Dunn has said. For as we have already seen, God could not love Jacob without also

---

46. See F. F. Bruce, *The Epistle of Paul to the Romans* (Grand Rapids: Eerdmans, 1963), 193.

47. Johannes Munck, *Christ & Israel: An Interpretation of Romans 9–11* (Philadelphia: Fortress, 1967), 42.

48. Ernst Käsemann, *Commentary on Romans* (Grand Rapids: Eerdmans, 1980), 264.

49. Dunn, *Theology of Paul,* 511.

loving Esau (assuming that both exist), and neither could he make Jacob the object of his electing love without making Esau its object as well.

The critical exegetical issue, however, concerns not the logic of election, but Paul's own view of the matter, and not one word in Romans 9–11 implies a final and irrevocable rejection of Ishmael, Esau, Pharaoh, the nonremnant Jews, or anyone else. To the contrary, Abraham was chosen as a blessing to all nations, including Esau and his progeny; and for exactly the same reason, Jacob was chosen on behalf of Esau as well. So yes, God does, according to Paul, elect or choose individuals for himself. But God never treats anyone as an isolated monad, and the election of one person is always on behalf of others; it reaches beyond the chosen person to incorporate, in a variety of complex ways, the community in which the person lives and, in the end, the entire human race.

That is why the idea of a "remnant, chosen by grace" (Rom. 11:5) played such an important role in Paul's argument that God has not rejected his people as a whole (11:1). For contrary to what the Augustinians would have us believe, it was not a mere tautology that Paul here defended, something like: "A remnant, chosen by grace, proves that God has not rejected the remnant, chosen by grace." Instead, the "remnant, chosen by grace," proves that God has not rejected the whole of which the remnant is a part. The faithful remnant is always a pledge, in other words, on behalf of the whole and also the proof that "the word of God" or his "purpose in election" has not failed (9:6). Or, as Paul himself put it in 11:16, "If the part of the dough offered as first fruits [or the faithful remnant] is holy, then the whole batch [that the faithful remnant represents] is holy" in God's eyes as well.

God's Severe Mercy: Three Examples

If you fail to interpret Romans 9 in light of Paul's own conclusion in Romans 11, or fail to appreciate Paul's inclusive understanding of election (how the salvation of a single individual is a pledge on behalf of the human race as a whole), then Romans 9 is apt to appear dark and unforgiving. For Paul's understanding of God's love and mercy was anything but sentimental. But once we begin to glimpse the merciful purpose behind God's severity, as Paul explains it in Romans 11, Romans 9 turns out to be no problem at all.

Consider first the quotation in 9:13 from the prophet Malachi: "I have loved Jacob, but I have hated Esau." It is important to set aside, right at the outset, a distracting irrelevancy. In an effort to ameliorate things a bit, Charles Hodge suggested, as have many others, that in Romans 9:13 "hatred" does not imply *"positive disfavour,"* but instead means only *"to love less, to regard and treat with less favour."*[50] And even Dunn, despite his accurate understanding of chapter 11, likewise writes: "To 'love' Jacob (that is, to lavish love on Jacob) means to 'hate' Esau (that is, to withhold such affection from Esau)."[51] But why should that be true? Why should my love for my son (even lavishing love on my son) imply a withholding of love from my daughter? If I were so much as to love my daughter *less* than I do my son, then that would surely imply a defect in my moral character; and similarly, if God were even to have loved Esau *less* than he did Jacob, then that too would have diminished his holy character and have contradicted Paul's repeated declaration that God shows no partiality to anyone.

What we have in 9:13, therefore, is an obvious case of hyperbole, where hyperbole is *by intention* literally false. We encounter an almost identical hyperbole in the words of Jesus: "Whoever comes to me and does not hate father and mother, wife and children, brothers and sisters . . . cannot be my disciple" (Luke 14:26). Though no Christian would likely misinterpret these words to mean that we should *literally* hate the members of our family, some do misinterpret them to mean that we should love the members of our family *less* than we do Jesus. But Jesus' hyperbole, no less than Paul's use of the quotation from Malachi, is *by intention* literally false. Was it not Jesus, after all, who commanded us to love others, including the members of our family, even as we love ourselves? And was it not Jesus who pointed out (in the parable of the sheep and the goats) that anything less than a perfect love for those whom Jesus loves is also less than a perfect love for Jesus himself? If that is true, then it is simply not possible to love our family *less* and, at the same time, to love Jesus *more*. Accordingly, we hate the members of our family in the relevant metaphorical sense only when we love them more, not less; and similarly, God hated Esau in the relevant metaphorical sense only because he loved him to the fullest extent possible, not less.

So just what is the relevant metaphorical sense in which, according to Paul's hyperbole, God supposedly hated Esau? The answer is implicit in what we have already said. The election of Jacob unto salvation carried no implication of Esau being rejected. But in addi-

---

50. Charles Hodge, *Commentary on the Epistle to the Romans* (New York: A. C. Armstrong and Son, 1896), 490.

51. Dunn, *Theology of Paul,* 511.

tion to being chosen as children of God, such patriarchs as Abraham, Isaac, and Jacob were *also* chosen to play a unique role in redemptive history—one that also involved their earthly concerns and perceived interests in important ways. We are all familiar, as Paul's Jewish readers certainly were as well, with the bitter struggle between Jacob and Esau for the birthright and for their father's blessing: how (through Jacob's trickery) Esau lost the very thing that, given all the conventions governing ancient Semitic society, was rightfully his. Because Jacob and Esau both wanted, or thought they wanted, the same thing, their perceived interests had come into conflict; and so not even God could have settled this particular conflict without appearing to favor one of the twins over the other.

It is often that way. The events that transpire in our earthly lives often do favor the perceived interests of some over those of others; and with respect to many earthly struggles, a winner does indeed imply a loser. In the case of Jacob and Esau, God had already decided, even before they were "born or had done anything good or bad," who would win and therefore who would lose in their struggle for the birthright (Rom. 9:11). Esau was destined to lose not because he deserved to lose but in order that God's "purpose in election"—that is, the means by which he extends his mercy to all people including Esau—might continue. The prophecy to Rebecca, "The elder [Esau] shall serve the younger" [Jacob], thus captures the full and complete meaning of God's so-called hatred of Esau.[52]

Consider next the hardening of Pharaoh's heart to which Paul alluded in 9:17–18. Those who view such hardening as an instance of God causing someone to sin have simply failed to acquaint themselves, I believe, with the intricacies of causal-sounding language. But though God's hardening of Pharaoh's heart was in no way a *sufficient* cause of any sin, it was nonetheless an instance of what, according to Romans 11:32a, he does to every descendant of Adam (except Christ): He simply shut Pharaoh up to, or imprisoned him in, his own disobedience. Here two points in the Exodus account are perhaps relevant: First, God consistently hardened Pharaoh's heart in connection with the single command, "Let my people go," and second, Pharaoh was essentially a coward who had exalted himself above the Hebrews for many years (see Exod. 9:17).

---

52. For additional reasons God's love for Jacob and his hatred of Esau express exactly the same attitude, see my remarks in Parry and Partridge, *Universal Salvation,* 38–39.

So perhaps the first question to ask is this: How would Pharaoh likely have responded if God had *not* hardened his heart and therefore had *not* given him the strength to stand in the presence of the "signs and wonders" performed in Egypt? The obvious answer is that Pharaoh would most certainly have caved in much sooner than he did. Does this mean that he would also have repented? Clearly not. Being easily cowed in the presence of superior power, which is just what the plagues in Egypt represented, is no real virtue. So God simply gave Pharaoh the strength to stand, or at least renewed his strength between various plagues, so that he would not be cowed too easily.

But that is only half the story. According to Romans 11:32b, the other half is that God's actions toward Pharaoh, like his actions toward anyone else, were also an expression of mercy. Here we might speculate that, had God permitted Pharaoh to be cowed too easily—after the first plague, let us suppose—then Pharaoh's haughty arrogance would have remained largely hidden, at least from his own view. It is a familiar fact of experience: Cowardice sometimes "protects" us from the sin we secretly wish to commit. When sheer cowardice prevents a man from committing adultery, for example, it may also "protect" him from a terrible web of lies and deceit, a true prison of sorts. So if the transformation of a heart is far more important than outward conformity to moral rules and even more important than cowardly obedience to the command of God, then having the strength to act upon one's innermost desires might easily serve a redemptive purpose.

In the case of Pharaoh, his God-given strength to disobey God's command no doubt revealed to him, in a way that perhaps nothing else could have revealed, the self-destructive and self-defeating character of his own self-exaltation. And however one interprets the hardening of Pharaoh's heart, we can be confident that God gave him exactly what he needed at the time and exactly what would do him the most good over the long run. When the walls of water were crashing over his head and all of his evil plans and ambitions were clearly coming to ruin, Pharaoh may then have been, for all we know, in a far more hopeful condition than he ever had been at any previous time during his earthly life.

Consider, finally, Paul's distinction in Romans 9:22 between the vessels of mercy and the vessels of wrath and why, in the context of Paul's overall argument, every vessel of mercy must represent the destruction of a vessel of wrath. Just who were, first of all, the vessels of wrath that occupied Paul's attention here? Were they not precisely Paul's unbelieving kin about whom he expressed such "unceasing anguish" at the beginning of Romans 9? And were they not also the non-remnant Jews whose hearts, according to 11:7, were hardened? If so, then the vessels of wrath to which Paul referred in Romans 9:22 were the ones concerning whom he later made two claims: first, that "as regards election they are beloved, for the sake of their ancestors" (Rom. 11:28), and second, that "they have now become disobedient in order that they too might receive mercy." So clearly, Paul's distinction between vessels of mercy and vessels of wrath, like his distinction between the new creation in Christ and the old person that the new creation replaces, could not possibly be a distinction between those *individuals* who are, and those who are not, objects of God's mercy.

To the contrary, a vessel of wrath just *is* the old person, even as a vessel of mercy just *is* the new creation in Christ. For as Paul himself explicitly stated in his letter to the Ephesians,[53] using a slightly different metaphor, even Christians (or the new creations in Christ) first came into this earthly life as "children of wrath" (Eph. 2:3); they were at one time, in other words, "vessels of wrath fit for destruction." And just as a new creation in Christ requires the absolute destruction of the old person, so every vessel of mercy represents the absolute destruction of some vessel of wrath. In no way, therefore, do such expressions as "children of wrath" or "vessels of wrath" represent a determinate and eternally fixed category of individuals; and if Paul himself, like everyone else, first came into this earthly life as a vessel of wrath (call him Saul), then a paraphrase that captures part of the meaning of 9:22–23 is this: "What if God, desiring to show his wrath and to make known his power, has endured with much patience Saul, a vessel of wrath fit for destruction, in order to make known the riches of his glory for Paul, a vessel of mercy that he has prepared beforehand for glory?"

Because the paraphrase is intended to startle, I should perhaps clarify one point: I make no claim here that at the time of writing 9:22 Paul was consciously contrasting his former life as an unbeliever (or as a vessel of wrath) with his then present life as an apostle of Christ; nor do I have any doubt that in 9:22 Paul had Pharaoh and the unbelieving Jews principally in view. But if Paul himself, like all other Christians, first came into this earthly life as a vessel

---

53. Here I adopt the traditional assumption that Paul was indeed the author of Ephesians, as I believe he was.

of wrath, as he surely did, then God endured with much patience this particular vessel of wrath, along with all the others, in order to make known the riches of his mercy to the believing Paul. What the above paraphrase illustrates, therefore, is only what Paul himself explicitly stated in 11:32. In Romans 1 Paul also spoke of God giving people over "to impurity" (1:24), "to degrading passions" (1:26), "to a debased mind and to things that should not be done" (1:28); God forces people to experience, in other words, the consequences of their sinful actions and to confront the life they have chosen to live. He does this to all people, including Pharaoh, because in no other way could he be merciful to each and every one of them, as 11:32 explicitly states that he is.

Is There Injustice on God's Part?

After reviewing briefly the election of Isaac and Jacob, Paul went on to raise a question about injustice (Rom. 9:14–16). But why should a question concerning injustice even arise at this point? Was it because Paul really did accept a seemingly unjust doctrine of limited election? Clearly not. It was Paul's opponents, not Paul, who believed in limited election; his opponents would have seen no injustice, for example, in the election of Isaac and Jacob, or even in a literal interpretation of "I have hated Esau." It was not this reminder of history, in other words, that motivated the question about injustice; it was rather the implication in Paul's teaching that election depends not upon physical descent from Abraham (9:6–8) and not upon works (9:12), but upon God's sovereign mercy alone (9:16). What seemed unjust to Paul's contemporaries was his teaching that the Gentiles could attain "righteousness through faith" (Rom. 9:30) without converting to Judaism, without keeping the Jewish ceremonial law, and without having their males circumcised. For as they saw it, such teaching implied that God, having broken his promise to Abraham, was unjustly extending his mercy to the Gentiles.

Paul's question, then, is essentially this: "Has God acted unjustly in extending his mercy to Gentiles as well as to Jews?" Paul's remarks about Jacob and Esau, which occur just prior to the question, are not what generate the question but part of his *answer* to the question. Like a good debater, he meets his opponents on their own ground and prepares them for his answer even before raising the question. For none of Paul's opponents would have denied God's right to violate human tradition and convention in the matter of Jacob and Esau. According to tradition—that is, according to the conventions governing ancient Semitic society—the birthright, the blessing, and the headship of the tribal family should have passed from Isaac to Esau rather than from Isaac to Jacob. But if none of Paul's opponents would have denied God's right to violate that tradition, then neither, Paul in effect argued, should they deny God's right to violate the tradition that would restrict God's mercy to the physical descendants of Abraham, or at least to the circumcised and to those who keep the Jewish law.

Having disarmed his opponents even before raising his question, Paul then sets forth his unassailable answer, a quotation from Exodus 33:19 in which the Lord declares: "I will have mercy on whom I have mercy, and I will have compassion on whom I have compassion." This is an idiomatic expression that stresses not the *indeterminacy* of God's mercy, as some Augustinians have supposed, but rather its *intensity* and *assuredness*. As one Old Testament scholar, Frederick Bush, has pointed out,[54] "The meaning that the expression is normally given in English, i.e. an arbitrary expression of God's free, sovereign will, makes almost no sense in the context" of Exodus 33:19, where it is a revelation of the very name, or essence, or goodness of God. It is, says Bush, "equivalent to 'I am indeed the one who is gracious and merciful.'"

And similarly for Paul's own context. To all of those, such as many of Paul's own kin, who would insist that God has no right to extend his mercy to a given class of persons—whether it be the Ninevites in Jonah's day, the Gentiles in Paul's day, or the non-Christians in our own day—Paul in effect quoted the Lord as saying: "I will have mercy upon whomever I please." There is absolutely nothing in view here except God's unlimited and inexhaustible mercy—a mercy that, although no doubt severe at times (as Esau and Pharaoh might well have attested), is nonetheless utterly reliable and therefore secures our hope for the future. For as Paul had already pointed out in the first part of Romans 3, no human disobedience or unfaithfulness can nullify the faithfulness of God. God will continue to meet our true spiritual needs and to consume all that is false within us, regardless of what choices we make, good or bad. So however important these choices may be for the here and now, or even for the immediate future, our *destiny* "depends not upon human will or exertion, but upon God who shows mercy."

---

54. Frederick Wm. Bush, "'I Am Who I Am': Moses and the Name of God," *Theology, News and Notes* (Pasadena: Fuller Theological Seminary, Dec. 1976), 11.

Part 4: The Triumph of God's Salvific Will

*For I am persuaded, that neither death, nor life, nor angels, nor
principalities, nor powers, nor things present, nor things to come, nor
height, nor depth, nor any other creature, shall be able to separate us
from the love of God, which is in Christ Jesus our Lord
(Rom. 8:38–39 KJV).*

According to Christian universalists, the death and resurrection
of Jesus Christ achieved a complete victory over sin and death—an
eschatological victory, if you will, but one that already guarantees the
eventual destruction of both. God will not, therefore, merely quar-
antine evil in a specific region of his creation, a dark region known
as hell; he will instead destroy it altogether, as the annihilationists
also insist. But whereas the annihilationists believe that God will in
the end annihilate some of his own loved ones, some of the very ones
created in his own image, the universalists believe that God will eventually destroy evil in the only way possible short of annihilating the
objects of his love: by saving them from their sins.

Christ Victorious

So how should a Christian understand Christ's victory over sin
and death? According to Romans 5:12–21, Jesus Christ rescued the
entire human race from the doom and condemnation that Adam
originally brought upon it and, in the process, unleashed the power
that will eventually bring justification and life to all human beings. As
we have already seen, both instances of "all humans" in verse 18 pick
out exactly the same group of individuals; there is simply no question
about that. Nor is there any doubt that, according to this text, Jesus
Christ did something *on behalf of* all human beings or the human
race as a whole. But if, as some Arminians might contend, he brought
to all people something less than full justification and life—an *offer* of
salvation, perhaps, or a possibility of some kind that each individual
remains free to reject—then the possibility of an ultimate defeat remains. For the possibility yet remains that Christ might be less successful in saving the human race as a whole than Adam was in cor-
rupting it. So did Paul contemplate such a possibility in Romans 5?

In support of an affirmative answer, some commentators, such as
Douglas Moo and John Blanchard, appeal to 5:17, where the expres-
sion "those who receive the abundance of grace" appears. According to
Moo, "The deliberately worded v. 17, along with the persistent stress

on faith as the means of achieving righteousness in 1:16–4:25, makes it clear that only certain people derive the benefits from Christ's act of righteousness."[55] And similarly for Blanchard: "The only ones [according to 5:17] who 'reign in life' are 'those who receive God's abundant provision of grace and of the gift of righteousness'; those who do not receive these things remain under the devastating reign of death."[56]

Note Blanchard's words "those who do not receive these things." Where in the context of 5:17 did Paul say anything about a group of people *not* receiving "God's abundant provision of grace"? Where did he even leave this open as a possibility? Suppose that I should comment upon those who receive the precious gift of life from their biological parents. Would my comment carry any implication that some people do not receive this precious gift? Of course not. So why struggle so hard, even to the point of drawing an obviously fallacious inference, just to overpower a text, such as 5:18–19, that is as glorious as it is clear? Let us concede, at least for the sake of argument, that 5:17 endorses this idea: (1) only those sinners receiving the abundance of grace will be saved. From (1) it simply does not follow that (2) some sinners will never receive the abundance of grace, and neither does it follow that (3) not all sinners will be saved. Even worse for Blanchard's interpretation is the following: If you simply conjoin (1) above with the assertion in 5:18 that Christ brings justification and life to all human sinners, it follows, as a deductive consequence, that all human sinners will indeed receive the abundance of grace. So unless Blanchard is prepared to foist upon Paul his own fallacious inference,[57] verse 17 provides no grounds whatsoever for supposing that some people will never receive the abundance of grace.

To the contrary, the expression "much more surely," which appears in both verses 15 and 17, provides an additional reason for supposing that the effects of Christ's one act of righteousness, as Paul understood them, are far greater, and therefore far more extensive, than the effects of Adam's disobedience. As M. C. de Boer has argued: "Unless the universalism of vv. 18–19 is taken seriously . . . 'how much

---

55. *Romans*, 344.

56. John Blanchard, *Whatever Happened to Hell?* (Durham: Evangelical, 1993), 198.

57. It is truly astonishing how many commentators draw virtually the same fallacious inference at this point. Douglas Moo clearly draws such a fallacious inference in the passage quoted above, and so did H. C. G. Moule when he contended that "the whole Epistle, and the whole message of St. Paul about our acceptance" of Christ counts against a universalistic interpretation of Romans 5:18." Moule, *Romans* (Washington: Christian Literature Crusade, 1975), 151.

more' is turned into 'how much less,' for death is then given the last word over the vast majority of human beings and God's regrasping of the world for his sovereignty becomes a limited affair."[58] And that surely *is* the issue. Which is greater and therefore more extensive: the effects of Adam's sin, or the effects of Christ's act of righteousness? Which will triumph in the end: sin and death (at least in the lives of millions), or Jesus Christ?

Unlike Blanchard and Moo, Howard Marshall at least recognizes that we cannot read into 5:17 any implication that some will *not* receive the abundance of grace. But Marshall nonetheless contends, incorrectly, that Paul left such an eventuality open as a possibility. For according to Marshall, "Paul's statement [in 5:17] means that all individuals will be saved provided that they believe, and it is left open whether they will do so."[59] Marshall thus assumes, as do Blanchard and Moo, that in 5:17 Paul used the verb *lambano* ("to receive") in a sense that would mean something like "to take hold" or "to accept believingly." But it is nearly certain that Paul was *not* using *lambano* in this way; indeed, he almost never used it this way in any context, such as Romans 5, where the thing received is divine judgment, divine grace, or a divine gift of some kind. In any such context as that, Paul always thought of God as the active agent and human beings as the *recipients* of some divine action.

In Romans 13:2, for example, those who receive (or incur) judgment do so in the same passive way that a citizen might receive a summons to court, a criminal might receive a prescribed punishment, or a boxer might receive severe blows to the head; and in Romans 1:5, those who "have received grace and apostleship" do so in the same passive way that a newborn baby might receive life. Similarly, as John Murray has argued, the "word 'receiving' [in 5:17] . . . does not refer to our believing acceptance of the free gift but to our being made the

---

58. M. C. de Boer, *The Defeat of Death: Apocalyptic Eschatology in I Corinthians 15 and Romans 5* (Sheffield: Sheffield Academic Press, 1988), 175. Arland J. Hultgren has also expressed the point powerfully: "As Adam was the head of humanity in the old eon, leading all to destruction, so Christ is the head of humanity in the new age which has dawned, leading all to justification and life. The grace of God in Christ amounts to 'much more' than the trespass of Adam and its effects (5:17). All of humanity is in view here without exception." *Christ and His Benefits: Christology and Redemption in the New Testament* (Philadelphia: Fortress, 1987), 54–55.

59. I. Howard Marshall, "The New Testament Does *Not* Teach Universal Salvation," in Parry and Partridge, *Universal Salvation,* 65.

recipients, and we are regarded as the passive beneficiaries of both the grace and the free gift in their overflowing fullness."[60]

Does this mean that, according to Paul, salvation is possible apart from faith or belief? Not at all. It could mean, consistent with the rest of what Paul wrote, that even our faith and belief are a work of God within. But even that seems a stretch in the present context, where the focus of Paul's attention was the objective work of Christ, not our personal faith or belief in response to it. If the latter had been his concern here, as it was in chapter 4, he would have used the same verb here, namely *pisteuo* ("to believe" or "to trust"), that he used in chapter 4; he would not have chosen a verb that is just as applicable to the recipients of judgment as it is to the recipients of grace. That he chose the verb *lambano* shows that his intention in Romans 5 was to compare the *effects* Christ's act of righteousness with those of Adam's sin. He insisted that Christ more than undid the harm that Adam had inflicted on the human race as a whole; Christ defeated death on behalf of all people and unleashed into the cosmos the power that will bring eternal life to them all (see v. 21).[61]

If any doubt should remain concerning how Paul understood Christ's ultimate triumph over sin and death, 1 Corinthians 15:20–28 should, I believe, finally put it to rest. For here we read that Christ

---

60. Murray, *Romans*, vol. 1, 198. Richard Bell, following M. E. Boring, makes a similar point in "Rom. 5:18–19 and Universal Salvation," *New Testament Studies* 48 (2002): 429.

61. Having argued, correctly, that in 5:17 *lambano* is being used in a passive sense and that in 5:18 the expression "justification and life" implies eternal salvation, John Murray's own arguments seem to render universalism an inescapable consequence of 5:18. Murray therefore appealed to the wider context of Pauline thought in order to argue that Paul could not have meant to say what his words in fact do say. He thus wrote: "When we ask the question: Is it Pauline to posit universal salvation? the answer must be decisively negative (*cf.* 2 Thess. 1:8, 9). Hence we cannot interpret the apodosis in verse 18 in the sense of inclusive universalism." Murray therefore concluded that the second "all humans" in 5:18 must be more restrictive than the first. But that is, very simply, a fallacious inference, similar to the following, which we might imagine to appear in a commentary on 2 Thessalonians: "When we ask the question: Is it Pauline to posit eternal damnation? the answer must be decisively negative (*cf.* Rom. 5:12–21). Hence we cannot interpret 2 Thessalonians 1:8–9 in any sense that implies an eternal separation from God." Murray gives no reason whatsoever, either good or bad, for why we should adjust our understanding of Romans 5:18 in light of our understanding of 1 Thessalonians 1:8–9 rather than adjust our understanding of 1 Thessalonians 1:8–9 in light of our understanding of Romans 5; 11; 1 Corinthians 15, and other universalistic texts in Paul. In fact, there are good exegetical reasons for supposing that *destruction* is a redemptive concept in 1 Thessalonians 1:8–9, as it clearly is in 1 Corinthians 5:5 where the pronounced judgment is equally as harsh; there are also decisive grammatical reasons for denying that 1 Thessalonians 1:8–9 carries any implication of separation from God. On these points see Thomas Talbott, "A Pauline Interpretation of Divine Judgment," in Parry and Partridge, *Universal Salvation*, 40–43 and 49, n. 10.

will turn his kingdom over to the Father only after he has destroyed *every* competing rule and *every* competing "authority and power" (v. 24). The victory pictured here is thus absolute and total, with death being the last enemy to be destroyed (v. 26). A literal translation, however, would be, "The last enemy, death, is being destroyed" (present passive), which could imply, as Anthony Thiselton suggests, that "the *process* of annihilation" has been "*already set in motion* by Christ's (past) death and resurrection." In any event, Christ must continue to reign "until he has put all his enemies under his feet" (v. 25); and when all things are finally brought into subjection to Christ, "then the Son himself will also be subjected to the one who put all things in subjection under him, so that God may be all in all" (v. 28). All separation from God will then be a thing of the past. "Death will be no more; mourning and crying and pain will be no more, for the first things [will then] have passed away" (Rev. 21:4).

Now just what did Paul mean when he suggested that Christ would "put all his enemies under his feet"? Verse 27 implies an equivalency between someone's being put under the feet of Christ and someone's being brought into subjection to him, and Paul's clear implication here is that some people, who are not in subjection to Christ at one time, are then brought into subjection to Christ at some later time. So how should we understand this idea of someone *not yet* being in subjection to Christ? If the powers and authorities that Christ is bound to destroy involve *competing wills,* then the answer is clear: a competing will (or a will not yet in conformity with Christ's own will) is, for that very reason, not yet in subjection to Christ; that is, it has not yet been reconciled to God through Christ. For there is but one way in which a competing will can be brought into subjection to Christ: it must be won over so that it voluntarily places itself in subjection to Christ. No willing agent, after all, could ever be *entirely* in subjection to Christ involuntarily; the very idea is self-contradictory. If one should be subdued against one's will, or defeated in battle like John Milton's Satan, then one's *will* would precisely not be in subjection to Christ. Indeed, even after being defeated in battle, Milton's Satan found that "the mind and spirit remains / Invincible":

What though the field be lost?
All is not lost; the unconquerable Will,
And study of revenge, immortal hate,
And courage never to submit or yield:
And what else is not to be overcome?

> That Glory never shall his wrath or might
> Extort from me.[62]

The author of such a speech could hardly be in subjection to Christ, and so, as Milton's Satan illustrates (perhaps contrary to Milton's own intention), there is but one way for God to defeat a rebellious will and to bring it into subjection to Christ. He must so transform the will that it voluntarily places itself in subjection to Christ. God could easily annihilate, no doubt, anyone with a rebellious will, but that would neither bring the rebellious will into subjection to Christ nor satisfy God's loving nature. As a paradigm of subjection, therefore, we need look no further than Christ's own subjection to the Father, as depicted in 1 Corinthians 15:28. No one would deny, I presume, that Christ's subjection to the Father is voluntary and implies voluntary obedience; it finds perfect expression in the prayer that Jesus uttered shortly before his arrest and crucifixion: "Yet, not my will but yours be done" (Luke 22:42). That is the only coherent form that absolute subjection could take. If, as is not even possible, Christ's will should be in conflict with the Father's on some important point, if he should not want to comply with his Father's will but should nonetheless be forced to do so *against* his will, then he would be no different from Milton's Satan in this regard. But according to our text, *all* things and therefore *all* wills will eventually be brought into subjection to Christ in the same sense in which Christ places himself in subjection to the Father, a sense that clearly implies voluntary obedience and reconciliation in the full redemptive sense.

The destruction of the last enemy, which is death, carries the same implication of universal reconciliation. For death is a spiritual condition that involves far more than the corruption and disintegration of the body, and it is closely associated in Pauline thought with the power of sin itself (see Rom. 8:2). If "the flesh" in Pauline theology involves "the whole personality of man as organized in the wrong direction,"[63] and if to "set the mind on the flesh is death" (Rom. 8:6), as Paul explicitly declared, then death, like sin, includes anything that separates us from God. And not even God, therefore, can destroy death altogether while keeping sin alive throughout an eternity of hell. For as I have elsewhere stated: "Death is destroyed (and all of its bad effects nullified) only to the extent that those subject to death are made alive. Indeed, if death should achieve a final victory in the life

---

62. *Paradise Lost,* Bk. I, 105–11.

63. See Leon Morris's entry on "flesh" in *The New Bible Dictionary* (London: Inter-Varsity, 1962), 426.

of a single person, then that would provide a clear answer to Paul's rhetorical question: 'Where, O death, is your victory?' (1 Cor. 15:55). But the question is not supposed to have an answer."

So even if Paul had never written the words: "as in Adam all die, even so in Christ shall all be made alive" (1 Cor. 15:22 KJV), we could still be confident that, according to Paul, all of those who die in Adam will in fact be made alive in Jesus Christ. For the bringing of all things into subjection to Christ already entails that all persons will eventually belong to Christ,[64] and the final destruction of death already entails that all who are subject to death will be made alive. The parallel structure of 1 Corinthians 15:22, so similar to Romans 5:18 and 11:32, merely makes explicit, then, what is already implicit in the context. When the power of the cross, which is the transforming power of love, successfully brings every rebellious will into conformity with Christ's own loving will and Christ then turns his kingdom over to the Father, then and only then will God truly be all in all.

Victory or Defeat?

Paul's grand vision of a total victory over sin and death thus stands in luminous contrast to the Arminian picture of a defeated God. For though the Arminians insist, even as the universalists do, that God at least wills or desires the salvation of all sinners, they also hold that some sinners will defeat God's will in this matter and defeat it forever. As C. S. Lewis once put it, "I willingly believe that the damned are, in one sense, successful, rebels to the end; that the doors of hell are locked on the *inside*."[65] So even though God himself never rejects anyone, at least not forever, he will nonetheless permit some of his loved ones to reject him forever, if that is what they should irrationally choose to do. In the case of the damned, at least, God grants ultimate sovereignty not to his own loving will but to an utterly irrational human decision.

---

64. Even as many argue that the second "all" in Romans 5:18 is more restrictive than the first, so many argue that the second "all" in 1 Corinthians 15:22 is more restrictive than the first. According to Gordon D. Fee, for example, Paul's intention in 1 Corinthians 15:22 was to assert that "in Christ all *who are in Christ* will be made alive." Fee, *The Epistle to the Corinthians* (Grand Rapids: Eerdmans, 1973), 750. But even if we should accept that dubious claim, it does nothing to restrict the second "all" in 1 Corinthians 15:22. For Paul's whole point in the subsequent verses was that everything that might have had the power, were it not destroyed, to prevent some from belonging to Christ and thereby to restrict the second "all" in 1 Corinthians 15:22 will be destroyed.

65. C. S. Lewis, *The Problem of Pain* (New York: Macmillan, 1944), 115.

Now Jerry Walls, for one, objects to my putting the matter this way. For all such talk of God suffering a defeat, he argues, "is cleverly misleading at best": "God's love can be declined but it cannot be defeated. The only meaningful sense in which God's love could be defeated would be if he ceased to love those who rejected him and his love turned into hate. But in my view he never stops loving those who reject him. Rather, his love shines all the brighter by remaining steadfast in the face of such rejection."[66]

And I certainly agree with Walls concerning this: a loving God, who values human freedom, will no doubt *permit* his loved ones to do many things that he would prefer them not to do. So as Walls goes on to write: "Even Talbott must agree that things happen in this world that God does not prefer unless he wants to say that all atrocities down the ages have been willed and determined by God."[67] That is correct. In no way do I believe, for example, that God directly caused the atrocities at Auschwitz; nor do I believe that he wills or desires such moral evils as the rape and murder of innocent children. At the very most, he willingly permits such atrocities as Auschwitz, not for their own sake but for the sake of some greater good or some larger redemptive purpose—a greater good not only for people in general, but especially for the victims of such atrocities themselves.

I nonetheless find Walls's complaint perplexing, to say the least. How can he deny that the damnation, or even the loss, of millions whose salvation God sincerely desires would represent a tragic defeat of God's loving purposes for them? Contrary to what Walls implies, you do not in general defeat a loving purpose by bringing about that the loving purpose no longer exists or by turning someone's love into hatred; you defeat a loving purpose by preventing it from being realized. So if Walls truly believes, as I know he does, that God sincerely wills or desires the salvation of all, he surely must concede that the eternal loss of a loved one would represent a horrendous defeat of God's loving purpose for the human race as a whole. Indeed, if someone's rejecting God forever does not count as a defeat, why should someone's repentance and faith count as a victory? Or suppose, as is logically possible on Walls's view, that all human sinners should freely and irrevocably reject Christ, despite God's best efforts to save them. Would that not count as a defeat? If not, then the concept of *defeat*

---

66. Jerry Walls, "A Philosophical Critique of Talbott's Universalism," in Parry and Partridge, *Universal Salvation,* 122.
67. Ibid.

seems empty of meaning; if so, then the loss of a single loved one should count as a defeat as well.

A distinction that I have drawn repeatedly (and Walls ignores in the passage quoted above) is between *irreparable* harm, on the one hand, and harm that can be repaired or canceled out at some future time, on the other. When we humans confront the possibility of serious and irreparable harm—that is, harm that no mere human can repair or cancel out at some future time—we feel justified in interfering with someone's freedom to inflict such harm. We feel justified, first of all, in preventing one person from harming another irreparably; a loving father may thus report his own son to the police in an effort to prevent the son from committing murder. And we may feel justified, secondly, in preventing our loved ones from harming themselves irreparably as well; a loving father may thus physically overpower his teenage daughter in an effort to prevent her from committing suicide.

This does not mean, of course, that a loving God, whose goal is the reconciliation of the world, would prevent every suicide, every murder, or every atrocity in human history, however horrendous such evils may seem to us; it follows only that he would prevent every harm that not even omnipotence could repair at some future time, and neither suicide nor murder is necessarily an instance of that *kind* of harm. Just as loving parents are prepared to restrict the freedom of the children they love, so a loving God would restrict the freedom of the children he loves, at least in cases of truly irreparable harm. The only difference is that God deals with a much larger picture and a much longer time frame than that with which human parents are immediately concerned.

So the idea of *irreparable* harm—that is, of harm that not even omnipotence can repair—is critical, and Paul's doctrine of unconditional election (along with the closely associated doctrine of predestination) is his doctrine that, despite the many atrocities in human history, God never permits truly irreparable harm to befall any of his loved ones.[68] From the beginning—that is, even "before the founda-

---

68. If God draws the line at *irreparable* harm and therefore never permits such harm to befall his loved ones, then neither the unpardonable sin of which Jesus spoke, nor the sin of apostasy, as described in Hebrews 10, nor punishment in the age to come is an instance of irreparable harm. I set forth my reasons for believing that the unpardonable sin and the sin of apostasy are both correctable, however unforgivable they may be, in *The Inescapable Love of God* (Parkland, Fla.: Universal, 1999), 103–6. And I set forth my reasons for denying that the punishment associated with the age to come is unending in Parry and Partridge, *Universal Salvation*, 43–47, 51 n. 20–n. 30, 269–70 n. 33.

tion of the world"—God built into his creation, so Paul insisted, a guarantee that his salvific will would triumph in the end. Accordingly, all of those whom God "foreknew he also predestined to be conformed to the image of his Son. . . . And those whom he predestined he also called; and those whom he called he also justified; and those whom he justified he also glorified" (Rom. 8:29–30). Arminians typically argue that the predestination (or foreordination) of which Paul here spoke rests upon foreknowledge, where foreknowledge, as they interpret it, is a mere precognition or prevision of someone's faith, or of someone's decision to accept Christ, or of someone's free choice of one kind or another.

But a twofold objection to any such interpretation seems to me utterly decisive: first, the object of God's foreknowledge in 8:29 is simply people, not their faith or their free choices, and second, Paul used the same word "foreknow" (*proegno*) when he wrote: "God has not rejected his people whom he foreknew" (Rom. 11:2). And here Paul had in view not the faithful remnant whose proper choices, one might claim, God had already foreknown; instead, he had in view those unbelieving Israelites of his own day who had rejected Christ and whose hearts were still hard and impenitent. They were foreknown, in other words, despite their disobedience, and they remained objects of God's electing love ("as regards election they are beloved, for the sake of their ancestors"), not because they had made the right choices, but because "the gifts and the calling of God are irrevocable" (Rom. 11:28–29).

To be foreknown in the relevant Pauline sense, then, is simply to be loved beforehand. All of those whom God has loved from the beginning—that is, all the descendants of Adam—are predestined to be conformed to the image of Christ. So not only did Paul hold that Jesus Christ achieved a complete victory over sin and death; he also held that there was never the slightest possibility that God would lose any of those loved ones whose salvation he had already foreordained even before the foundation of the world.

Predestination without Determinism

That Paul believed in predestination now seems to me undeniable. The Augustinian mistake lies in the doctrine of limited election, which so clearly contradicts the central teaching of the New Testament; it does not lie in the doctrine of unconditional election, which confronts us on almost every page of the New Testament. When the latter doctrine is divorced from the idea of limited election, it no longer inspires fear and anxiety but inspires instead the greatest conceivable hope and sense of consolation. Still some may wonder about the role of free choice and moral effort in Paul's predestinarian scheme. Just what role do free choice and moral effort play in our lives if our eventual salvation is secure from the beginning? Fortunately, Paul not only addressed this question directly but also provided a clear answer to it.

Because our eternal destiny, as Paul understood it, lies in God's hands and not in our own, it is indeed secure. But Paul also provided a clear picture of how our choices, even if causally undetermined, could nonetheless play an essential role in a redemptive process whose end is foreordained and therefore secure. "Note then," he wrote in Romans 11:22, "the kindness and the severity of God: severity toward those who have fallen, but God's kindness toward you, provided you continue in his kindness; otherwise, you also will be cut off." As this text illustrates, Paul clearly believed that our own actions—even our free choices, if you will—determine how God will respond to us in the immediate future; they determine, in particular, the form that God's perfecting love will take. If we continue in disobedience, then God will continue to shut us up to our disobedience, thereby forcing us to experience the consequences of our choices and the life we have chosen to live; in that way, we will experience God's perfecting love as severity. But if we repent and enter into communion with God, then we will experience his perfecting love as kindness.

Our free choices, then, have real consequences in our lives and they determine how we will encounter God's grace in the future; but whichever way we choose, God's perfecting love will meet our true spiritual needs perfectly. For Paul's whole point in Romans 11 was that God's severity, no less than his kindness, is a means of his saving grace; his severity toward part of Israel, for example, is only one of the means whereby he saves all of Israel in the end, as we have seen.

Essential to the whole process, then, is that we exercise our moral freedom—not that we choose rightly rather than wrongly but that we choose freely one way or the other. We can choose today to live selfishly or unselfishly, faithfully or unfaithfully, obediently or disobediently. But our choices, especially the bad ones, will also have unintended and unforeseen consequences in our lives; as the proverb says, "The human mind plans the way, but the LORD directs the steps" (Prov. 16:9). A man who commits robbery may set off a chain of events that, contrary to his own intentions, lands him in jail; and a woman who enters into an adulterous affair may discover that, even though her husband remains oblivious to it, the affair has a host of unforeseen and destructive consequences in her life. In fact, our bad choices almost never get us what we really want; that is part of what makes them bad and also one reason God is able to bring redemptive goods out of them. When we make a mess of our lives and our misery becomes more and more unbearable, the hell we thereby create for ourselves will in the end resolve the ambiguity and shatter the illusions that made the bad choices possible in the first place.

That is how God works with us as created rational agents. He permits us to choose in the ambiguous contexts in which we first emerge as self-aware beings, and he then requires us to learn from experience the hard lessons we sometimes need to learn. So in that way the consequences of our free choices, both the good choices and the bad ones, are a source of revelation; they sooner or later reveal—in the next life if not in this one—both the horror of separation from God and the bliss of union with him. And that is why the end is foreordained: all paths finally lead to the same destination, the end of reconciliation, though some are longer and a lot more painful than others.

But if our salvation is guaranteed from the beginning and guaranteed no matter what choices we make in the present, then where is the incentive, many would ask, to repent and to enter into communion with God? Why not just keep on sinning if we are going to be saved anyway? That question, however, betrays a terrible confusion. Paul himself, I would point out, raised a similar question: "Should we continue in sin in order that grace may abound?" (Rom. 6:1). And he never rejected, furthermore, the assumption behind the question, namely, that the more we sin, the more grace will indeed abound. To the contrary, he endorsed this assumption when he wrote, "Where sin increased, grace abounded all the more" (Rom. 5:20). Not in a million, or a billion, or even a trillion years could our sins ever outduel the grace of God. So why did Paul answer his own question, correctly, with his characteristic, "By no means"?

He did so because of his firm conviction that sin is utterly irrational. For how, he in effect asked, could those who have "died to sin," and therefore understand its true nature, continue to sin (6:2)? Is not sin (or anything that separates us from God) precisely the problem, the very thing making our lives miserable? And similarly, that the misery and discontent that sin brings into a life can serve a redemptive purpose—because it can provide in the end a compelling motive to repent—hardly implies that one has a good reason to keep on sinning and to continue making oneself more and more miserable in the process.

Accordingly, the well-worn analogy of the grand master in chess remains as apt as ever. When a grand master plays a novice, it is foreordained, so to speak, that the grand master will win but not because he or she causally determines the novice's every move or even predicts each one; the end is foreordained because the grand master is resourceful enough to counter *any* combination of moves that the novice might freely decide to make. And similarly for the infinitely wise and resourceful God: he has no need to exercise direct causal control over our individual choices in order to "checkmate" us in the end; he can allow us to choose freely, perhaps even protect us from some ill-advised choices for a while, and still undermine over time every conceivable motive we might have for rejecting his grace. For once we learn for ourselves—after many trials and tribulations, in some cases—why separation from God can bring only greater and greater misery into our lives and why union with him is the only thing that can satisfy our deepest yearnings and desires, all resistance to his grace will melt away like wax before a flame.

Conclusion

Christian universalists believe that, apart from a corporate salvation of the human race as a whole, there can be no real grace and no worthwhile salvation for any individual. For where is the grace in a doctrine of limited election? Is God being gracious to an elect mother, for example, when he makes the baby she loves an object of his "sovereign hatred,"[69] and does so, as some believe he did in the case of Esau, even before the child has done anything good or bad? In the end, it seems, a doctrine of limited election replaces grace with a *horrible decree,* one that separates the redeemed forever from some of their own loved ones; and perhaps no other doctrine, not even the doctrine of everlasting punishment itself, has *as a matter of historical fact* produced so much anxiety in the lives of those who actually believe it. It also flatly contradicts Paul's explicit and repeated teach-

---

69. According to G. C. Berkouwer, the Dutch theologian Hermann Hoeksema described God's attitude toward the nonelect as the "sovereign hatred of his good pleasure." For the quotation from *Het Evangelie,* see Berkouwer, *Divine Election* (Grand Rapids: Eerdmans, 1960), 224.

ing that God, being merciful to all (Rom. 11:32), shows no partiality to anyone, and it is riddled, in any case, with logical impossibilities, as we have seen. So if a Christian were forced to choose between the doctrine of limited election and that of conditional election, the latter would be by far the preferable choice.

But the doctrine of conditional election, which requires that grace be supplemented by our human free choices, also carries some unfortunate implications. For it too carries the threat, at least, that some of our loved ones will eventually be lost forever; it also undermines the Christian's solidarity with the human race as a whole and seems to provide the redeemed with grounds for boasting. If our own free choices determine our ultimate destiny in heaven or hell and the redeemed are those whose free choices are of a superior moral quality (because, unlike the damned, they did not reject Christ), then that difference, at any rate, is not a matter of grace at all. But beyond all of that, the consistent testimony of the New Testament is that, like a good shepherd who pursues the one lost sheep "until he finds it" (Luke 15:4), the Hound of Heaven pursues all of his loved ones until he finally reconciles them all to himself.

The gospel is truly good news, therefore, and truly glorious in its utter simplicity. Its message is that the death and resurrection of Jesus Christ has already achieved a complete victory over sin and death in this sense: though these defeated enemies of true blessedness remain a terrible part of our present reality, their eventual destruction is already guaranteed and so also, therefore, is the reconciliation of the world and every person in it. For no power in the universe, not the power of death itself and not even the power of our own recalcitrant wills, can finally "separate us from the love of God in Christ Jesus our Lord" (Rom. 8:39).

CHAPTER 8

Responses to Thomas B. Talbott

Response by Clark H. Pinnock

I welcome this lively exposition of the doctrine of universal reconciliation. I have often wondered how many evangelicals take this view. I have come across one or two of them, but they were still "in the closet" on the topic and didn't want it mentioned. (They might lose their teaching jobs.) I have the impression that, once an evangelical takes this position, he ceases to be considered as evangelical. So the case would have to be made by some bold fellow like Talbott who doesn't worry much about what the evangelical "powers that be" think of him. I welcome his able defense of universalism and expect that it will help others get into the discussion. As to the substance, I hope that Talbott is right and that hell will lack for inhabitants. It is something that I hope for but not something that I know as dogmatic truth.

Like Karl Barth, Talbott holds that God has elected the entire human race for salvation in Jesus Christ. He goes further and claims that God not only elects the whole race but will succeed in saving it, thanks to his powerful grace and determination. Were Talbott an Arminian, he would put the emphasis on divine persistence and argue that God will keep trying to save them all until he succeeds. Our author, however, being a Calvinist, puts the accent on divine sovereignty. Thus he believes that God's election is unconditional and his grace irresistible. He believes God never fails to get what he wants. The puny human may try to defeat God's purposes for it, but he cannot succeed. No one can finally reject God if God has decided otherwise.

Talbott needs to understand that salvation is conditional upon faith. God has made himself vulnerable by making creatures who are free to accept or reject him. He is not a deity of raw power but a Creator and Savior who suffers with and because of us. We can disappoint him and nullify his plan for us. The Bible is clear in teaching that there will be a final judgment which will issue in the justification of some and the condemnation of others. This is contrary to Talbott's view that there are really no bad consequences for one's rejecting of Christ in this life. He interprets a few texts as pointing to universal salvation, though they only teach universal opportunity, and offers unconvincing interpretations of judgment texts.

The problem with Talbott lies in his doctrine of God. He does not take seriously enough the reciprocal nature of God's dealings. God desires us to reciprocate his love and gives us freedom to make this possible. But with free will comes the possibility that humans may fail to receive God's grace but instead reject it. Because love cannot be forced, it is possible that some will reject it—even ultimately and finally. Talbott accepts the general idea that love cannot be forced (he is not a compatibilist) but not in the final situation.

Is God defeated then? I think not, because God's love is demonstrated whether it is accepted or rejected. God's love can be declined, but God is not defeated. His plan would only be defeated if God ceased to love those who reject him and/or if his love were to turn into hate. But God never stops loving them. His light shines even brighter by remaining steadfast even in the face of rejection. God's will was to make free creatures to whom he could offer his love while knowing that the possibility existed that some of them might reject it. His choice to create such a world means ultimately that his will is done even though things happen in the world that God does not approve such as any sinner being lost.

Response by Robert L. Reymond

Thomas Talbott's four-part essay on universal reconciliation argues (1) that the doctrine of limited election is inconsistent with the Johannine declaration that God is love, (2) that the doctrine of limited election contradicts Paul's teaching in Romans 11, (3) that the advocates of limited election have misunderstood Romans 9, and

264 — PERSPECTIVES ON ELECTION: FIVE VIEWS

(4) that, unlike the doctrine of limited election, the doctrines of unconditional election and irresistible grace do reflect Paul's teaching. In sum, Talbott argues for a universal reconciliation between God and all mankind, viewed both distributively and individually, and for the doctrine of "inclusive election." Because of the limited space we are allotted for our responses, I will leave the analysis of his syllogistic arguments to others who have more of a proclivity to evaluate them than I,[1] saying only this much about them, that one must agree with his premises (which I for the most part do not) before one can agree with his conclusions.

Talbott's Understanding of God's Love

With respect to Talbott's argument—contending as he does that not a single passage in the Bible would require a person to accept the doctrine of an eternal hell—for the ultimate eschatological reconciliation of every human being to God, in opposition I would first insist, as J. A. Motyer observes, that the Old Testament contains the "suggestion of diversity of destiny for the godly and the ungodly."[2] What are these Old Testament "suggestions of diversity of destiny" to which Motyer refers? Obviously, I cannot offer an exhaustive response to this question, but I will mention several such intimations.

First, one should recall the distinction God drew between the antediluvian world as a whole on the one hand and Noah and his family on the other: "The Lord saw how great man's wickedness on the earth had become, and that every inclination of the thoughts of his heart was only evil all the time. . . . So the Lord said, 'I will wipe mankind, whom I have created, from the face of the earth.' But Noah found grace in the eyes of the Lord" (Gen. 6:5–8 NIV; see 1 Pet. 3:19–20; 2 Pet. 2:5). To say the least, such a division among men would seem to disallow the doctrine of universalism.

Although our sin infuriates God and deserves his immediate judgment, he is, as Moses says, a God of love who is "slow to anger" (Num. 14:18 NIV). Nahum says the same thing (Nah. 1:3). And God himself (Exod. 34:6), David (Pss. 86:15; 103:8), Joel (Joel 2:13), Jonah (Jon. 4:2), and Nehemiah (Neh. 9:17) tell us that Yahweh is "slow to anger and *abounding in steadfast lovingkindness.*"

---

1. See, for example, William Lane Craig, "Talbott's Universalism," *Religious Studies* 27 (1991), 297–308.
2. J. A. Motyer, "Destruction," *Baker Dictionary of Theology,* edited by Everett F. Harrison (Grand Rapids: Baker, 1960), 260.

God is indeed "slow of anger and abounding and rich in his stead-fast love," and he keeps the sword of his wrath sheathed. That sword, I can imagine, struggles to get free, but God's patient long-suffering puts its hand on the sheath and says, "Stay! Not yet!" And so he continues to give sinners time to learn of him and to repent in order that he may bring all of his chosen ones to himself. And this is all *because* he is "long-suffering" and *because* he takes no pleasure in punishing the sinner but rather in showing him mercy (Mic. 7:18). Even the absence in God of a will to spare a particular sinner does not imply the absence in him of profound pity toward him even as he consigns him to perdition. *Even as God with moral indignation consigns impenitent sinners to hell, he pities them.*

Nothing I have said about God's long-suffering, however, should be construed to mean that I believe that God will not finally punish the impenitent sinner for his sin because the Scriptures are clear that his wrath against sin is also a perfection of his divine nature (see Deut. 32:39–41; Rom. 1:18; 1 Thess. 1:10). Not only does God swear by his holiness (Ps. 89:35), but he also swears by his wrath (Ps. 95:11). One day in the future, so say the prophets Nahum (1:2, 5, 8) and Malachi (4:1), in concert with the other prophets' teaching about the Day of the Lord, God will take vengeance on his adversaries and pour out his wrath upon his enemies. Paul says of the impenitent in Romans 2:5, "Because of your stubbornness and your unrepentant heart, you are storing up wrath against yourself for the day of God's wrath, when his righteous judgment will be revealed" (NIV). Consequently, we must not look to Talbott's unbiblical index of universal reconciliation to comprehend the greatness of God's love; we must look to other measuring indices for this.

Let the readers consider how much they love their sons. Could they give them to die for their enemies? Consider, you fathers who have only one son, does it not seem that God loved us even better than he loved his one and only Son? For many a father has given a son to the service of his country and many a mother's son has become a casualty of war. We regard theirs as honorable deaths. But to what did God give his Son? To some profession in the pursuit of which he might still enjoy his company? To some service that all mankind would respect? To an honorable death? No! He gave his Son to exile among men; he sent him down to hunger and thirst amid poverty so dire that he had no place to lay his head; he sent him down to the scourging and the crowning with thorns, to the giving of his back to wicked smiters and his cheeks to those who plucked out his beard. And finally, the Father gave his Son up to death on the cross—a type of execution so ignoble and reprehensible that it was reserved for the meanest and lowest criminal types. And on the cross he gave him up, still further, to the awful forsakenness expressed in "the strangest utterance that ever ascended from earth to heaven" (Murray)—that cry of dereliction: "My God, my God, why have you forsaken me?" We hesitate to say it, but say it we must: in those hours at Calvary, God the Father became a sonless Father, and God the Son a fatherless Son—for us men and for our salvation.

The point I have attempted to make by this short discourse on God's love is that, while the Bible speaks of God's essential nature as love, it also *concretizes that love in a special way.* The Bible would say that we must not measure the nature and depth of God's love, as Talbott does, by the universal reach or expansiveness of its extension, thereby overthrowing the biblical teaching on election.

I would insist that Talbott's index for the measurement of the essence of God's love, namely, a universal expansiveness that must encompass every single human being, is unscriptural, ineffectual, and inappropriate. Rather, the indices by which we should attempt to measure adequately God's love (and we are bound to fail) are the *extraordinary object* of its affection—this *sinful* world—and the *indescribably expensive costliness* of God's bounteous gift to us—the sacrifice of his Son in the person and work of Jesus Christ. Talbott has missed both of these measuring indices in his effort to universalize reconciliation with God.

Talbott's Understanding of Romans 9 and 11

Paul writes in Romans 11:32, "God has bound all men over to disobedience so that he may have mercy on them all" (NIV). Talbott declares, "The argument of Romans 11 is exquisitely simple. God is merciful to all; therefore, the doctrine of limited election is false." But is Talbott's representation of Paul's argument exegetically defensible? I do not think so. Talbott (with Arminians in general) alleges that the second half of the verse should be understood to teach that God's reach of mercy is as expansive and all encompassing as the disobedience of men is said to be in the first half of the verse, which is just to say that God wills his salvific mercies for all men without exception which means in turn that limited election is false.

Two things must be said in response: First, it is incredible that Arminians would use this verse at all to teach their inclusive election; for in doing so, in the interest of making room for human freedom as the decisive factor in men's salvation, they must completely ignore the verse's primary lesson that God is the sovereign subject of both verbs. He is the one who is first credited with shutting "all" up to disobedience in order that he may show mercy to all. Where then is any room for free agency as the decisive factor in salvation in this Pauline declaration (see Rom. 9:11:15)? Second, as everywhere else, the double "all" must be interpreted within its universe of discourse.

In my opinion Talbott, finding as he does his doctrine of an all-inclusive universalism in Romans 11, does precisely what must not be done, namely, reading Romans 11 in isolation from the plain, explicit limited election and particularism of Romans 9, thereby again overthrowing the biblical teaching on predestination and particular election.

I hope these criticisms—that he fails to have a biblical understanding of sin, that he fails to measure God's love by the appropriate indices, and that he has misunderstood Romans 9 and 11—will move Talbott to rethink his entire theology and to come to a more biblical understanding of God's love and election. Perhaps we can talk *mano a mano* sometime about this matter; I would like that very much.

Before I close I want to make a personal appeal to Talbott, something that I would not normally do in an academic work such as this one: in your article, "On Predestination, Reprobation, and the Love of God," *Reformed Journal* (Feb. 1983), you reject the God of the Reformed faith, declaring the Reformed doctrine of predestination to be a "complete absurdity" (14). You then write: "I will not worship such a God, and if such a God can send me to hell for not so worshipping him, then to hell I will go" (14). But the God of the Reformed faith, I am bold to declare, Dr. Talbott, is the one living and true God whether you like it or not. So I respectfully say to you: "If you do not worship him, he *will* send you to hell and send you there *forever*. Therefore, centrally concerned as you are with the doctrine of the reconciliation of others to God, I implore *you* on Christ's behalf: *Be reconciled to God* by repenting of your reliance on your inappropriate method of measuring God's love and placing your heartfelt trust in God's great sacrifice at Calvary." To aid you I would recommend that you read Geerhardus Vos's article, "The Spiritual Doctrine of the Love of God," in *Redemptive History and*

Biblical Interpretation: The Shorter Writings of Geerhardus Vos, edited by Richard B. Gaffin (Grand Rapids: Baker, 1981).

Response by Bruce A. Ware

On the one hand, I found this essay to be extremely well-written and carefully-argued, and for this I give to Dr. Talbott my heartfelt commendation. I appreciate not only the force of the logic he employed but also the endeavor to account for numerous texts of Scripture. For these reasons I consider this a formidable essay. On the other hand, I can hardly believe that someone who knows the whole of the Bible, including the numerous teachings about the final judgment and the certainty of hell, could make this proposal with a straight face. I don't believe, though, that Talbott presented his essay as an exercise in artistic sarcasm. I take it that he means what he says here. But how can he? Is it possible that he is oblivious to the fact that interpreted the way he has, the texts he cites and discusses stand in a mutually-exclusive relation to the meanings (at least *prima facie*) of numerous other texts? Does the Bible present contradictory teachings? Does the God of the Bible speak out of two sides of his mouth? This, it seems to me, is the chief weakness of Talbott's essay. He simply does not acknowledge the abundant evidence to the contrary and attempt some measure of explanation.

Consider just a few texts which provide explicit and clear teaching about the reality and horror of a hell to come, which teaching stands directly contrary to Talbott's thesis.

And if your hand causes your downfall, cut it off. It is better for you to enter life maimed than to have two hands and go to hell—the unquenchable fire, where their worm does not die, and the fire is not quenched. And if your foot causes your downfall, cut it off. It is better for you to enter life lame than to have two feet and be thrown into hell—the unquenchable fire, where their worm does not die, and the fire is not quenched. And if your eye causes your downfall, gouge it out. It is better for you to enter the kingdom of God with one eye that to have two eyes and be thrown into hell, where their worm does not die, and the fire is not quenched (Mark 9:48-48;[3] cf., Matt 5:29-30; 18:8-9 for similar statements by Jesus).

---

3. The phrase, "where their worm does not die, and the fire is not quenched" appears in these verses three times. The first two occasions (Mark 9:44, 46) do not appear in the earliest manuscripts. But the last statement in 9:48 is original.

Then He will also say to those on the left [i.e., the goats], "Depart from Me, you who are cursed, into the eternal fire prepared for the Devil and his angels! . . . And they will go away into eternal punishment, but the righteous into eternal life" (Matt 25:41, 46; cf., Matt 25:31-46 for larger context; and John 5:28-29).

This will take place at the revelation of the Lord Jesus from heaven with His powerful angels, taking vengeance with flaming fire on those who don't know God and on those who don't obey the gospel of our Lord Jesus. These will pay the penalty of everlasting destruction, away from the Lord's presence and from His glorious strength (2 Thess 1:7b-9).

And He has kept, with eternal chains in darkness for the judgment of the great day, angels who did not keep their own position but deserted their proper dwelling. In the same way, Sodom and Gomorrah and the cities around them committed sexual immorality and practiced perversions, just as they did, and serve as an example by undergoing the punishment of eternal fire (Jude 6-7).

And a third angel followed them and spoke with a loud voice: "If anyone worships the beast and his image and receives a mark on his forehead or on his hand, he will also drink the wine of God's wrath, which is mixed full strength in the cup of His anger. He will be tormented with fire and sulfur in the sight of the holy angels and in the sight of the Lamb, and the smoke of their torment will go up forever and ever. There is no rest day or night for those who worship the beast and his image, or anyone who receives the mark of his name" (Rev 14:9-11).

The Devil who deceived them was thrown into the lake of fire and sulfur where the beast and the false prophet are, and they will be tormented day and night forever and ever. Then I saw a great white throne and One seated on it. Earth and heaven fled from His presence, and no place was found for them. I also saw the dead, the great and the small, standing before the throne, and books were opened. Another book was opened, which is the book of life, and the dead were judged according to their works by what was written in the books. Then the sea gave up its dead, and Death and Hades gave up their dead; all were judged according to their works. Death and Hades were thrown into the lake of fire. This is the second death, the lake of fire. And anyone not found written in the book of life was thrown into the lake of fire (Rev 20:10-15).

Clearly, there are many pertinent and forceful texts which present teachings that are exactly contrary to the position Talbott argues. But what about the interpretation he gives of the texts he does deal with? And what about the force of his logical argumentation? Does he have it right here? On the contrary, there are numerous problems in the case makes. Consider first the main argument he develops from 1 John 4:8, that "God is love" and hence, God could not (i.e., as a logically impossibility) love all people in the world and not also do everything in his power to bring about what is best for them. By this reasoning, God must save all people, argues Talbott. Just two comments can be given here. First, if God is logically bound to love as much as he possibly can love, it would be impossible for him to create a world that he could love, for he could always create yet one more person to love. Something is wrong with the reasoning Talbott employs when the very notion of 'God's loving as fully as can be done' is itself a logical impossibility. So, God cannot create a rock bigger than he can lift, and he cannot create a world in which maximal love is manifest. Second, and much more important, the Bible presents the love of God very differently than does Talbott. Yes, God is love, no question. That is, no one gives to God the love that he possesses; rather, it is intrinsic to his very being as the eternal and self-sufficient God that he is. But, to say that 'God is love' does not require that we also hold that God must love all people in the same way, or to the same degree. God's love, as is his mercy and grace, is freely given, which means (among other things) that his love may be extended or withheld, as he chooses. How else can we understand a statement like this about God's disposition toward Jacob and Esau respectively: "And not only that, but also when Rebekah became pregnant by Isaac our forefather (for though they had not been born yet or done anything good or bad, so that God's purpose according to election might stand, not from works but from the One who calls) she was told: The older will serve the younger. As it is written: Jacob I have loved, but Esau I have hated" (Rom 9:10-13). Lest one wonder about the force of the Pauline quotation, "Jacob I have loved, but Esau I have hated," one need only look at Malachi chapter 1 from which this quotation is taken, and the context makes clear that God defines his love for Jacob precisely by his hatred toward Esau. In the opening verses of Malachi 1, Israel is said to have asked God the question, "How have You love us?" And God's reply, giving evidence of the truthfulness and genuineness of his love for Israel (Jacob), says,

> "Wasn't Esau Jacob's brother?" This is the LORD's declaration. "Even so, I loved Jacob, but I hated Esau. I turned his mountains into a wasteland, and gave his inheritance to the desert jackals." Though Edom [i.e., the land where the descendents of Esau settled] says: "We have been devastated, but we will rebuild the ruins," the LORD of Hosts says this: "They may build, but I will demolish. They will be called a wicked country and the people the Lord has cursed forever" (Malachi 1:2b-4).

The love of God is a complex notion biblically, not a simple one. It has numerous senses, as Don Carson has helpfully shown.[4] And one of those senses, which turns out to be the most prominent sense of God's love in the Bible, is this: God has a special, deep, selective, particular, covenantal, and saving love for his own people. Recall, husbands are to love their wives as Christ loved the Church (Eph 5:25). But doesn't this analogy indicate that I should have for my own wife—which surely is a particular and very special love—that is like Christ's love for his own bride, the church? I love my wife in ways I love no other woman, and Christ loves his bride the church in a way he manifests only to those who are members of his church. The particularity of God's love is all through the Bible, and Talbott simply does not acknowledge this. If he did, the force of his major logical argument that sets the tone of his paper would be shown to fail.

Second, I can only comment generally on the force of Talbott's textual argument for universalism. There is no question that a number of passages of Scripture speak of a future day of cosmic or universal reconciliation. What a glorious biblical truth this is! Yet, these passages that speak of universal reconciliation in no way cancel out so many other texts that make clear that heaven and hell are both realities, that only some are saved, not all. To see that Scripture speaks of both universal reconciliation and particular, saving reconciliation, consider this text:

> For God was pleased to have all His fullness dwell in Him, and through Him to reconcile everything to Himself by making peace through the blood of His cross—whether things on earth or things in heaven. And you were once alienated and hostile in mind because of your evil actions. But now He has recon-

---

4. D. A. Carson, *The Difficult Doctrine of the Love of God* (Wheaton, IL: Crossway, 2000).

ciled you by His physical body through His death, to present you holy, faultless, and blameless before Him—if indeed you remain grounded and steadfast in the faith, and are not shifted away from the hope of the gospel that you heard (Co. 1:19-23a).

Clearly Paul celebrates a sense in which the atoning death of Christ won a cosmic or universal reconciliation, making peace through his cross for all things in heaven and earth. But this cannot be interpreted rightly in context to indicate universal salvation. If Paul meant that this cosmic reconciliation was universally salvific, why would he continue to say what he does to these believers? He proceeds by saying that they have been reconciled by Christ's death and will be holy and blameless in the end *if* they continue in the faith. The conditional 'if' indicates that only those who truly persevere to the end will be saved. But of course, if this is the case, then the opposite is also true, i.e., those who profess faith in Christ but fail to persevere and by this demonstrate that their faith was false, will be lost. Therefore, it simply cannot be the case that Paul has taught in the previous verses that all would be saved.

It is difficult to know exactly what this universal reconciliation spoken of in Scripture will be like. Passages like Col 1:20, Rom 8:19-25, and 1 Cor 15:22-28 all speak of this glorious future reality. I think most likely that these texts mean that in the end, sin and its deceptive power will be vanquished altogether. The rebellion will be over, the lies and deception of sin will be exposed for the falsehoods that they are, and every knee will bow and every tongue will confess that Jesus Christ is Lord, to the glory of God the Father (Phil 2:9-11). Does this mean that all will be saved? Certainly not! But it means that every person in heaven and hell will be disabused of the lie that they are central in the universe, not God. Every person will know that Christ is Lord, that God is God, and as a result, there will no longer be any resistance to God—yes, including in hell! I depart from C. S. Lewis at this point who insisted that in hell the rebellion continues. "I willingly believe," says Lewis, that the damned are, in one sense, successful, rebels to the end; that the doors of hell are locked on the *inside*."[35] Lewis' view here makes a mockery of the universal reconciliation and universal acknowledgement that Christ is Lord that Scripture celebrates. It also vastly underestimates the horror of hell, to imagine that those living there would choose to stay if granted the opportu-

---

5. C. S. Lewis, *The Problem of Pain* (New York: Macmillan, 1962), 127 (author's emphasis).

nity to leave. No, heaven and hell are real, and they are opposite in the qualities of life each offers its respective inhabitants. But what they have in common is that knowledge of the truth, finally and fully, of who the real God really is, of salvation being only through faith in Christ, and of Christ's exclusive and rightful lordship over all, will be universally understood and embraced. All in hell as well as in heaven will acknowledge that God's ways are perfect and just. Yes, there is universal reconciliation, but not universal salvation, and his failure to make this distinction is responsible for the main flaw in Talbott's textual argumentation.

Response by Jack W. Cottrell

Talbott's present essay is the only writing of his that I have read; thus my comments are based on it alone. I will address three main problems found therein.

The first is a problem of *methodology*. Most would agree that it is wrong to predefine a key theological term and then interpret the biblical data according to the predefinition. This is what Calvinism does, for example, with the term *sovereignty*. Talbott seems to do the same with the word *love*. Many of his conclusions related thereto are philosophical speculations based on "the logic of love."

In exposing certain errors in Augustinianism, Talbott makes two points about love with which I agree; i.e., "love is part of God's nature or essence," and, therefore, his love necessarily embraces every human being and not just a "limited elect." These good points, however, are negated by three major "faulty philosophical ideas" of the same kind that Talbott attributes to Augustinians.

The first faulty idea has to do with the *content* of love; that is, the nature of God's love is presented in such a way that *by definition* it leads to universal salvation. For example, divine love is described as completely unconditional; but this is not true in a crucial sense explained below. Also, according to Talbott, "God's love no doubt does preclude a literal *hatred* of someone and therefore does preclude a final rejection of his loved ones." This also is not true; see below. Again, God's "purifying love . . . is bound to destroy all that is false within us"; i.e., it must necessarily, unconditionally do so. Finally, by nature a loving God cannot allow his creatures to bring "irreparable harm" upon themselves. Simply to assert that such is the nature of love, however, begs the question of universal salvation.

The second faulty idea related to love is the application of the philosophical concept of divine simplicity to the moral nature of God. Talbott says this concept is incoherent when applied to the full nature of God but is coherently and properly applied to his moral nature. This means that all of God's moral attributes (love, mercy, justice, holiness, righteousness, wrath, etc.) are identical to one another; they are all one and the same. Thus everything God does must be an expression of his love and equally an expression of his justice and wrath.

Three serious problems are involved here. It seems arbitrary and inconsistent (incoherent?) to apply simplicity to part of God's nature and not to all of it.[6] Also, in Talbott's system the simple moral nature of God in the end reduces to love and love alone. Every other moral attribute loses its identity and integrity and becomes just one of the ways love expresses itself. This applies especially to what we call God's wrath, justice, or severity (see Rom. 11:22) and even to the description of God as a "consuming fire" (Heb. 12:29). Finally, such love-reductionism is difficult to justify in view of the extensive biblical teaching on God's holy wrath,[7] which is described in terms of terror (Heb. 10:31), hatred (Pss. 5:5–6; 11:5), curses (Matt. 25:41), retribution (Deut. 32:35), and vengeance (Ps. 94:1–3). Looking at Scripture as a whole, it seems utterly indefensible to say that "God's severity, no less than his kindness, is an expression of mercy."

The third faulty idea about love is Talbott's failure to distinguish between (on the one hand) love as an attitude (attribute) that resides within the nature of God, and (on the other hand) love in the form of objective gifts and benefits offered to and received by individuals. Only the former aspect of God's love is unconditional and universal; Talbott's error is to say that these characteristics apply also to the latter aspect.

The second main problem in Talbott's essay relates to his *exegesis* of specific key texts. This applies especially to his treatment of Romans 9–11, which is interpreted in such a way that it functions as

---

6. In reality, it should not be applied to God at all in its philosophical sense. See Jack Cottrell, *What the Bible Says about God the Creator* (Joplin, Mo.: College Press, 1983), 37–40.

7. See Jack Cottrell, *What the Bible Says About God the Redeemer* (Joplin, Mo.: College Press, 1987), 275–319; see especially pp. 286–88.

a central proof text for his view. In my judgment he misses the whole point of the passage.

The misunderstanding begins with what Talbott identifies as the problem Paul is dealing with in these chapters, i.e., a complaint from the Jews that God is being unjust toward them by allowing the Gentiles to be saved without requiring them to convert to Judaism. The issue is stated thus: "Has God acted unjustly in extending his mercy to Gentiles as well as to Jews?" This, I believe, is a wrong reading of these chapters.[8] What Paul is dealing with here has nothing to do with the Gentiles directly (as if he were addressing the Judaizing controversy again). Here the Jews' complaint was not that God is unjust for saving the Gentiles but that he is unjust for *not* saving all the Jews. Having wrongly understood God's promises to the patriarchs as including guaranteed salvation for all Jews, they saw God's present rejection of most of them as a violation of these promises (Rom. 9:6, 14).

Talbott's misunderstanding of the main issue being dealt with leads to a second crucial error, namely, his interpretation of all references to predestination (election) in these chapters as primarily *election to salvation*. He sees "God's purpose in election" in Romans 9:11 as equivalent to Ephesians 1:9–10 and as expressing God's universal salvific plan, "the means by which he extends his mercy to all people including Esau." He sees verse 15 (and Exod. 33:19) as God's assertion that he has the sovereign right to save whomever he pleases—even Gentiles!

Another text misinterpreted as teaching universal salvation is Romans 5:12–21. Talbott is absolutely correct to insist, contra Augustinianism, that the salvation language in these verses must be as universally applied as the references to sin and condemnation. I agree: "According to Romans 5:12–21, Jesus Christ rescued the entire human race from the doom and condemnation that Adam originally brought upon it." But Talbott misses the main point of his own statement, i.e., that this text is referring *only* to the condemnation that *Adam* brought upon the race. Any potential "original sin" was *completely* nullified for all of Adam's progeny by Christ's one saving act; all babies are born instead in the "original grace" of Jesus Christ.[9] Christ's death does "much more" than this (Rom. 5:15, 17); i.e., it also

---

8. See Jack Cottrell, *The College Press NIV Commentary: Romans* (Joplin, Mo.: College Press, 1998), 2:23–303, for the explanation and defense of my understanding of these chapters.

9. See Jack Cottrell, *The Faith Once for All* (Joplin, Mo.: College Press, 2002), chapter 9. See also Cottrell, *The College Press NIV Commentary: Romans,* 1:330–68.

saves us from our *personal* sins. This, however, is conditioned upon one's freewill acceptance of Jesus. Only the cancellation of *Adam's* sin is universal and unconditional.

I must comment also on Talbott's misuse of 1 Corinthians 15:20–28 as supporting universal salvation. First, he contends that being under the feet of Christ and being brought into subjection to him imply a willing, voluntary surrender resulting in reconciliation and redemption. This is not consistent, however, with Ephesians 1:19–22, which uses this same language to refer to what Jesus has already accomplished (aorist tense) in reference to demonic powers. This was certainly not a willing surrender on their part.

Second, Talbott goes to great lengths to insist that "all" in 1 Corinthians 15:22 really means *all* human beings. But we cannot suspend the most basic rules of hermeneutics here, i.e., consideration of context and comparison with other biblical teaching. We know that context sometimes limits the "all" to which a text refers, e.g., Matthew 10:22 (Mark 13:13; Luke 21:17); Mark 1:37; John 17:21; 1 Corinthians 6:12 (1 Cor. 10:23; Titus 1:15); 1 Corinthians 14:24; 2 Timothy 1:15; 4:16; Revelation 22:21. In 1 Corinthians 15 Paul is obviously speaking to and about Christians (see vv. 1–2, 18–20). The "all" in verse 22b means all "who are Christ's" (v. 23). Likewise passages such as Romans 8:38–39 and Revelation 21:4 must be understood in context as referring only to believers.

My last problem with Talbott's universalism has to do with the *means* by which the ultimate goal will be accomplished. This problem has several facets, not the least of which is the role of Jesus in the salvation process. Talbott clearly asserts that the "complete victory over sin and death" is accomplished by "the death and resurrection of Jesus Christ." But how? Consistent with his view of a love-only God, Talbott clearly rejects any view of Christ's death that resolves a tension within God's nature between his love and his wrath. This all but eliminates any concept of substitutionary atonement involving true propitiation and sets the stage for a moral-influence view of the cross. Talbott criticizes John Milton for espousing the former view, a view that says "Christ died not to effect a cure in us"—implying that, as Talbott sees it, this is exactly what the death of Jesus accomplishes. This is explicitly affirmed when Talbott refers to "the power of the cross, which is the transforming power of love" that will ultimately bring "every rebellious will into conformity with Christ's own loving will." Salvation thus is a process of *purification* accomplished by the "consuming fire" of God's "purifying love," "when God finally perfects our love for others." This view falls far short of the biblical teaching of the cross as a work of redemption and propitiation (Rom. 3:24–26).

In the final analysis, though, Talbott's version of universal, unconditional election leaves no room for a truly free will. He realizes that his view will cause some to "wonder about the role of free choice and moral effort," and he himself declares that it is "essential to the whole process . . . that we exercise our moral freedom." The bottom line, though, is that whatever Talbott means by "moral freedom," in the end it is superfluous for the salvation process. He speaks as if it is a real part of the process, e.g., the will "must be won over" so that it *voluntarily* subjects itself to Christ; "our free choices . . . determine which path we are now traveling" on our way to heaven. But he also declares that God's purpose in election will be accomplished "regardless of what choices we make, good or bad." Our *destiny* depends not on our choices but only "upon God who shows mercy," as in Romans 9:16. "If our own free choices determine our ultimate destiny," there is no such thing as grace, and God is not sovereign.

Talbott declares that the salvation of every human being is absolutely guaranteed. Freewill choices affect the *way* we get to heaven, but "all paths finally lead to the same destination . . . though some are longer and a lot more painful than others." But if this is the case, we may legitimately question the nature of the "love" that Talbott says determines everything God does. If we are all destined for the same end, why does God give us just enough "freedom" to make the journey miserable? Talbott admits that his view is the same as Augustinianism in that he believes in unconditional election and irresistible grace, though he believes these apply to all human beings and not just to a limited elect. But at least in the Augustinian scheme, God does not subject some of his elect to an undefined, indeterminate post-mortem gauntlet before the end is finally achieved.

CHAPTER 9

Divine Election as Corporate, Open, and Vocational

CLARK H. PINNOCK

What a joy it is and what a privilege to be asked to reflect upon the important subject of divine election in a book where others, worthy scholars all, set forth their insights alongside my own and interact. What an opportunity too for readers to see the range of interpretive options and consider where they themselves stand. I am particularly glad to be able to deal with this particular subject because, although it is a glorious truth, it is also for many a dark tenet and a heavy burden. Alongside issues of interpretation then lie issues of pastoral concern. I find myself wanting to offer believers relief by presenting the doctrine to them as the really good news it is. I would be delighted if many readers would experience surprise and delight at what I have to say. Theology sometimes creates distress, but it can also open the doors of understanding. It can restore the joy of our salvation by removing barriers to insight. Without accepting his views in their entirety, I resonate with Karl Barth's bold declaration: "The doctrine of election is the sum of the gospel because, of all the words that can be said or heard, it is the best: that God elects man and that God is for man as the One who loves in freedom."[1]

---

1. Karl Barth, *Church Dogmatics* II/2 (Edinburgh: T. & T. Clark, 1957), 3.

Divine election (I will be contending) is not about a few sinners being selected arbitrarily for salvation and the rest being consigned to hellfire. Rather it is about God's willing the salvation of all nations and calling an elect people in order to realize it. God's love does not fall short—it is a perfect, not a partial, loving. How we handle election speaks volumes about our understanding of the character of God and the universality of the gospel. How we handle divine election will say a lot about our vision of Christianity as a whole. Does God love the world, or does he pick and choose who will live and who will die by what criteria God only knows and decides? Is God good? Is God fair? Is God loving? There is a lot at stake in this discussion. The key thing to remember in my view is that divine election does not exclude but aims at the salvation of the nations. It upholds and does not negate the truth that God is light, and in him there is no darkness at all (1 John 1:5).

Weighing heavily on my mind as I write is the realization that many people inside and outside the churches have been devastated by the teaching, both narrow and exclusive, stemming from Augustine. Though purporting to inspire in us awe before a sovereign God, what it does is lead us to doubt God's loving character. I want to overcome if I can election's unhappy returns and give my readers relief from the effects of this awful interpretation so that they might learn once again to rejoice in the overflowing grace of God. Everyone (I think) knows that election is not much preached about these days, and understandably so, because the traditional version contains little gospel. What I will contend is that, when rightly understood, it invites being proclaimed and proclaimed boldly.[2]

This is my thesis: *divine election is best understood when we take it to be corporate and vocational.* Election is about a people and their God-given task. It is about ecclesiology and missiology. This (I maintain) is the preponderant witness of the Bible on this subject. We see it in what Peter writes: "You are a *chosen race* (corporate), a royal priesthood, a holy nation, God's own people, *in order that* (vocational) you may proclaim the mighty acts of him who called you out of darkness into his marvellous light" (1 Pet. 2:9).[3] Election is not about the destiny of individual persons for salvation or damnation but about God's calling a people who in the New Testament setting live

---

2. James Daane, *The Freedom of God: A Study of Election and Pulpit* (Grand Rapids: Eerdmans, 1973), 6.

3. For the scriptural witness, see especially William W. Klein, *The New Chosen People: A Corporate View of Election* (Grand Rapids: Zondervan, 1992).

according to the faithfulness of Jesus Christ and proclaim good news to the world. The goal of the electing will of God is not the salvation of a few but the gathering of the nations into an eschatological fellowship. Calling an elect people is a means to that noble end as the community discharges its task of cooperating with God in bringing it about.[4] The focus is not on the salvation of the elect body itself (though this is assumed) but on the hoped-for consummated new humanity.

Through the prophet Amos, God refers to the working of his elective will even among the Philistines and the Arameans, in a way parallel to his choice of Israel, as if to say that the election of Israel is not something entirely unique and without parallel (Amos 9:7). We are given more than a hint here of a philosophy of history based on the election of many nations in all their variety. If one covenant is good, two or more covenants are surely better. The work of God is not restricted to a covenant with Jews and another one with Christians. Might not the story of another people contain traces of God's loving care making them too a people of God also? Does it not say in the Apocalypse, "They will be my peoples (plural)," and, "The kings of the earth will bring their glory into it" (Rev. 21:3, 26 AT)[5]

Much distress has been caused by the way in which the doctrine of election has been interpreted in individualistic (not corporate) and abstract (not historical and vocational) terms. It has missed the central point of election and been responsible for troubling God's people, raising doubt into their minds as to whether they are elect—as if this could possibly be a question for believers. Thinking instead of election as corporate and vocational spells relief. In this view election is about God's calling a people in the midst of history (initially Israel and subsequently the church of Jews and Gentiles), not to a salvation which is exclusively theirs but to a salvation which is open to everybody. In tender love God has chosen a people for himself and given them a universal salvific vocation. Election is not an end in itself but foreshadows the reconcili-

---

4. If my favorite exegetical source is William Klein, my favorite systematic authority is Wolfhart Pannenberg, *Systematic Theology,* vol. III (Grand Rapids: Eerdmans, 1993), 457. One finds a similar orientation in Catholic authors, too, like Walter Kasper, *The God of Jesus* (New York: Crossroad, 1986), 139, 165.

5. Pannenberg, "The thought of election as a religious category for the historical constitution of the cultural order," *Systematic Theology,* vol. III, 484–88. This line is also pursued in Clark H. Pinnock, *A Wideness in God's Mercy: The Finality of Jesus Christ in a World of Religions* (Grand Rapids: Zondervan, 1992), ch. 1 and in Jacques Dupuis, "God and Peoples in History," *Toward a Christian Theology of Religious Pluralism* (Maryknoll, N.Y.: Orbis, 1997), ch. 8.

ation of the world; and, as such, it is a broad and not a narrow concept. Thus it presents a joyful and not a fearful prospect.

The elect body is the vehicle of the love of God for all nations. Election has a communal character; and, as far as individuals are concerned, it focuses on the functions that they will perform on humanity's behalf. I cannot say it often enough: election is an inclusive, not an exclusive, category. It does not spell exclusiveness relative to others who are passed over but signals a movement toward the inclusion of all the rest.[6]

As for the place of the doctrine in systematic theology, I am inclined to position it under ecclesiology, not in theology proper as Barth does and not in soteriology as Calvin does.[7] I put it under the doctrine of the church since in election God chooses a people for his name's sake and for the sake of world missions. It was eccentric (I think) of Barth to place it under the doctrine of God, to make the point in support of the precious truth of God's universal salvific will. Of course I grant the point and agree that election does express it. But why detract from the corporate and vocational nature of election which is primary? What Barth uses election for (to establish God's universal salvific will) is better done directly by an appeal to the texts which plainly teach it, like Titus 2:11 and 1 Timothy 2:4. As for Calvin's putting election under soteriology and in a double predestinarian manner, one can only wish that he had let that piece of Augustine's legacy languish and fade as all the Eastern and most of the Western churches have wisely done.

This is what I will be arguing: that believers are chosen in Christ and caught up in God's offer of salvation as a people who have the whole of humanity in view. The election of the community is part of God's comprehensive will to save humankind. It is not aimed at a few souls and them alone but at humankind as a whole. Election is also not a mark of pride, a self-distinction from others who are presumed to be rejected. It begins modestly, in the call of Abraham, but has in view the blessing of the nations (Gen. 12:3). It begins with a few but aims at summing up all things in Christ (Eph. 1:9). Being "elect" signifies that one is taking part in the future of God's salvation and ultimately the consummation of creation. It is (at this point) an open

---

6. For Pannenberg's overall treatment of the subject, see "Election and History," *Systematic Theology,* vol. III, ch. 14 and idem, *Human Nature, Election, and History* (Philadelphia: Westminster, 1977).

7. See Barth, "The Place of the Doctrine in Dogmatics," *Church Dogmatics* II/2. 76–93.

question exactly which individuals will finally belong to the eschatological fellowship and which will not. While there is no guarantee of
universal reconciliation, the door is open to the salvation of all who
repent (2 Pet. 3:9). And every Christian can and should hope for a
large salvific result. Meanwhile, the church serves as a provisional
representation of the eschatological fellowship of humanity to be renewed in the kingdom of God and works toward the ingathering of
an ever-larger fellowship. The church is an open catholic community
symbolizing the destiny of all mankind.

Historical Developments

Theology is an unfinished business and a human construction
even when it is based upon divine revelation. As Paul put it, what we
now know is partial and preliminary to the fuller understanding that
will be ours at the Lord's return (1 Cor. 13:12). Theology is always a
venture and may require that we grow and mature as hearers of the
Word of God. Traditions can be precious, but the developments in this
case had an unhappy beginning.[8] There has always been, as Barth put
it, "a problem of a correct doctrine of the election of grace." That's
putting it mildly. Few doctrines have been so misunderstood, and
few have caused so much controversy and suffering. Folks without
number have been vexed by the thought that God aims to bring only
a handful of souls to heaven and to consign the rest to the rubbish
heap, making it sound as if God only cares for a select number and
not for humanity at large. It sounds as if God has a double plan, one
for elect people and the other for reprobate people even before history
began! Who has not felt at some time or other that this is a travesty,
including (and perhaps especially) its defenders, who have the misfortune of having to live with it?[9]

The central problem of election is easy to grasp. Historically, the
doctrine has been taken to mean the election of individuals. Surpris-
ingly, this has been true of both the predestinarians and the nonpre-

---

8. On the history of the development of the doctrine of election, see Wolfhart Pannen-
berg, *Systematic Theology*, vol. III, 435–62; Karl Barth, *Church Dogmatics* II/2, 3–93;
G. C. Berkouwer, "The Doctrine of Election in Historical Perspective," *Divine Election*
(Grand Rapids: Eerdmans, 1960), ch. 2; and Paul K. Jewett, "A Historical Overview" in
Election and Predestination (Grand Rapids: Eerdmans, 1985), 5–23.

9. No issue so disturbed John Wesley more than this perverse reading of the divine
sovereignty. See Randy L. Maddox, *Responsible Grace: John Wesley's Practical Theology*
(Nashville: Kingswood, 1994), 54–58. Reformed believers too (I have gathered) experience painful uncertainty about how to deal with this piece of tradition.

destinarians. On the one hand the church fathers before Augustine, such as Origen, wishing to avoid determinism, stressed the freedom of human subjects as the basis of election and the origin of the distinction between the elect and the nonelect. At least this takes into account the historical nature of election and does not place the blame of reprobation on God. It simply grounds election in the divine foreknowledge. Seeing in advance our future conduct, God sets us on the way to salvation or perdition on the basis of our own free and foreseen decisions. Divine election rests on God's knowledge of the future free choices of human beings. In effect then, God endorses our self-election. We choose God and God returns the compliment. But this is not altogether satisfactory because it reduces the meaning of election as an unconditional act of God's grace and makes it more than a little redundant. It turns God's election into a human act of self-election.[10] Nevertheless, it is better than the other early view of election—Augustine's.

The first true predestinarian was Augustine. The church fathers before him would certainly have rejected his views, holding as they did to libertarian freedom. The bishop of Hippo corrected Origen's mistake only to make things much worse. Somehow he got the idea that election was an act of God for saving individuals prior to any prevision of the future conduct of the creature. For him election was an expression of divine sovereignty, unconditionally and not based on anything the creature has done. Now it has to do only with God's good pleasure and, as such, is said to be comforting and a reason to thank God. That is as may be, but at the same time it created a set of problems which are legendary. Calvin did not exaggerate when he admitted that his doctrine of election, whereby God predestines some to salvation and others to destruction, is "dreadful indeed" (*Institutes* 3.23.7). What could be more inconsistent, he muses, than that, out of the common multitude of needy persons, some should be predestined to salvation and others to destruction. Such a doctrine would surely undermine a theologian's ability to hold and defend the goodness of God, who because of this now appears to be the author of a great evil. As Dave Hunt cryptically and rightly asks, "What love is this?"[11]

How surprising it is that John Henry Cardinal Newman, when he celebrated Augustine's theological legacy, did not include among his contributions to theology the doctrine of sovereign saving grace.

10. Origen discusses it in his commentary on Romans 8.
11. Dave Hunt, *What Love Is This? Calvinism's Misrepresentation of God* (Sisters, Oreg.: Loyal, 2002).

It had become for him a branch on the tree of doctrinal development to be pruned. As Jaroslav Pelikan observes: "His doctrine of double predestination was repudiated in later generations but even the repudiation was formulated in Augustinian terms."[12]

Some who adopt the Augustine framework interpret it more rigorously than others. Supralapsarians among the Calvinists emphasize the absolute sovereignty of God even in respect of sin and the fall. After all, the divine Potter can do exactly as he likes with the clay. In this view, God does not just permit the fall; it is an integral part of the divine decree even though it makes God appear to be the author of evil and equally the cause of both salvation and damnation. Infralapsarians (on the other hand) are a little squeamish. Even while holding to double predestination, they wish to introduce an element of conditionality into it, as Arminians do. But it doesn't really help them since even for them the fall is part of the divine decree and everything that happens is part of the greater good. But the infralapsarians feel better if they can say that the damned actually deserve to be damned and God is not to be blamed. Neither view, however, can really avoid blaming God for this gloomy situation.[13]

With regard to both these traditions of divine election in the early church (Origen and Augustine), one is on the horns of a dilemma. On the one hand, if the distinction between the elect and nonelect rests on human conduct which God foreknew, election has little gracious character. It is little more than self-election. Furthermore, it assumes exhaustive definite foreknowledge, whose ontological grounding is uncertain and which I cannot accept on either scriptural or philosophical ground. On the other hand, if election is solely a result of a decision on God's part whereby the nonelect are passed over for no reason, where is the justice in that? And why would God be calling the nations to come to him if no one who has been excluded beforehand can respond, being denied the grace of the Holy Spirit?

What a bad start this notion of election had in the history of doctrine! Both models diminish the truth of it, Origen by making it trivial and Augustine by making it revolting. One view makes God nominally sovereign, waiting to rubber-stamp human decisions; the other makes God a tyrant who hides behind mystery. It is little wonder why the church at the Synod of Orange (A.D. 529) took a more moderate position. It rejected double predestination and attributed

---

12. Jaroslav Pelikan, *The Emergence of the Catholic Tradition 100–600* (Chicago: University of Chicago Press, 1971), 293.

13. Louis Berkhof, *Systematic Theology* (Grand Rapids: Eerdmans, 1938), 118–25.

the condemnation of anyone to his or her own resistance to grace. And in the case of the elect, though their faith is a gift, grace is not thought to be irresistible, which would do violence to human freedom. The council was seeking a better way, as we all should be. Surely the Scriptures do not warrant either of the two original paths taken by the tradition.[14]

Karl Barth, the greatest theologian in the Calvinistic tradition, writes: "I would have preferred to follow Calvin's doctrine of predestination much more closely, instead of departing from it so radically. I would have preferred, too, to keep to the beaten tracks when considering the basis of ethics. But I could not and cannot do so. As I let the Bible speak to me on these matters, as I meditated on what I seemed to hear, I was driven irresistibly to reconstruction" (*Church Dogmatics* II/2, x). What concerned Barth most (and what concerns me, too) was the way in which Calvin's doctrine placed a shadow over the goodness and saving purposes of God. It made it sound as if God were saying to humanity, not "yes," but "yes" and "no." Barth was concerned that the doctrine in this form denied God's universal salvific will, and he spoke of "the pathetic inhumanity" of the traditional view. He even quoted John Milton as saying: "I may go to hell but such a God will never command my respect."[15]

Election as Corporate and Vocational

The election traditions of the Bible point us in a different direction.[16] Election in the Bible has to do with God's strategy for the salvation of the nations. The calling of a new people with its new way of being together in the world, this is God's plan to turn the world right-side up. It has to do with what Yoder calls "the original revolution."[17] Our election texts do not focus on God's eternal choice of individuals for salvation or damnation but emphasize the election of a people with a history-making vocation. Even Jewett admits that "in the Bible the elect are generally spoken of as a class, not as individuals per se." (Not that this prevented him from devoting most of his

---

14. The Thomistic sleight of hand does not avoid the alternatives in holding both that God sovereignly selects and those elected freely assent, though it is (admittedly) a "mystery" of which one cannot comprehend the truth. See Norman L. Geisler, *Chosen but Free* (Minneapolis: Bethany, 1999), ch. 3.

15. *Church Dogmatics* II/2, 13.

16. "Eklegomai," *Theological Dictionary of the New Testament,* ed. Gerhard Kittel, vol. IV (Grand Rapids: Eerdmans, 1967), 144–92.

17. John H. Yoder, *The Original Revolution* (Scottdale, Pa.: Herald, 1971).

book to individual election anyhow.)[18] The Bible speaks in corporate terms about election, and plural language dominates these texts. We do not find the individualistic emphasis which is so commonly held. Where individuals are seen as chosen, it is always for a task and for some supportive role in salvation history. William Klein concludes his study: "The [biblical] data present an impressive case that election is not God's choice of a restricted number of individuals whom he wills to save but the description of that corporate body which, in Christ, he is saving."[19]

The solution to the problem of divine election is (I think) to view it as corporate and historical, not as individualistic and abstract. The late Colin E. Gunton captures the point when he observes that theologians have treated the notion "as more concerned with the other-worldly destiny of a limited number of human beings than with the destiny, in and through time, of the whole world."[20]

While it is true that the election of Israel could be understood, as Jonah may have understood it, in negative terms vis-à-vis other nations, it actually has a more benign meaning. Israel is called to be a witness to everyone. Election begins with the call of Abram. After the cataclysm of Babel, he was chosen to be the one in whom all the nations of earth will be blessed (Gen. 12:3). In the calling of this man to leave home and go somewhere else, a step was taken in the story of salvation. Obviously, the patriarchs were not chosen for their goodness—what a rogue Jacob was!—but to be the means, nevertheless, for the redemption of the world. This is a strange sovereignty true enough, but it is the way in which God decided to work. God established a special relationship with Abram with world-transforming potential. The covenant, unilateral in origin, was bilateral in its outworking. God committed himself to this covenant with Israel, a lowly tribe, and established a relationship which will eventually include all peoples. Israel was and is God's experimental garden, a place where things are tried out for the benefit of all mankind.[21]

Divine election has mission in view. It carries with it responsibilities whether they are mentioned or not. God declares: "You shall be my treasured possession out of all the peoples. Indeed, the whole

18. Jewett, *Election and Predestination*, 47.
19. Klein, *The New Chosen People*, 266.
20. Colin E. Gunton, *The Christian Faith: An Introduction to Christian Doctrine* (Oxford: Blackwell, 2002), 31.
21. Hendrikus Berkhof, *Christian Faith: An Introduction to the Study of the Faith* (Grand Rapids: Eerdmans, 1979), 230–49.

earth is mine, but you shall be for me a priestly kingdom and a holy nation" (Exod. 19:5). The election is of a people (it is corporate); Israel is God's holy people and treasured possession. God says: "You are a people holy to the LORD your God. The LORD your God has chosen you out of all the peoples on earth to be his people, his treasured possession" (Deut. 7:6). God gave Israel a most-favored-nation status and for a reason. God said: "If you obey me fully and keep my covenant, then out of all nations you will be my treasured possession" (Exod. 19:5 NIV). Israel was not called to an exclusive salvation but to a priestly vocation intended to bring the whole world to God. She was bound to God by a special love which is meant to spread to the whole world.

Similarly, the church is not the realm of exclusive salvation. Its calling is to reconcile the nations to God through its praise and ministry. The church is the means by which the world will return home to God. This understanding mitigates the exclusivity while pointing to the divine calling and central role we have been given in God's purposes for the world.

Election then is not for privilege but for service.[22] God chooses a people to serve him. The corporate side is unconditional. As for individuals, there was no guarantee that each and every one would always enjoy the privileges. Indeed, they could be cut off from the people (Exod. 12:19). God remains faithful to his people but has expectations—the vocational aspect. God expects things from his people. He expects them to keep God's covenant and live holy lives. God warns, "You only have I known of all the families of the earth; therefore I will punish you for all your iniquities" (Amos 3:2). They have been blessed, but with favor come expectations. God loves the people in Israel but has a ministry in mind for her, namely, a mediating role in the salvation of the world. Isaiah expresses the heart of it. Most succinctly God says, "I will give you as a light to the nations, that my salvation may reach to the end of the earth" (Isa. 49:6). The idea of a priestly kingdom suggests that Israel is going to serve as a representative people and will have a mediating role within the wider world. This is made plain in the New Testament, too. The church is not an

---

22. H. H. Rowley, *The Biblical Doctrine of Election* (London: Lutterworth, 1950), 43; Jack Cottrell, "Predestined to Service," *The Faith Once for All: Bible Doctrine for Today* (Joplin, Mo.: College Press, 2002), 389–90.

end in itself; it has been given the power of the Spirit in order to take the gospel to the world and to make disciples of every nation.[23]

What is the thinking behind a corporate and vocational election? The election of a people creates a community which has the potential to be and to become an exemplary anticipation and advance representation of the eschatological fellowship for which humanity itself is destined in the kingdom of God. God calls a people in order to change history. Because of his love for the whole race, God reached out to Abram and set in motion a plan to reconcile sinners. He called into being a people bearing God's name among the nations, a vehicle through which history could be brought to its intended consummation. Election was the historically essential presupposition without which the subsequent history of salvation could not have unfolded the way it did. The community, graciously chosen, would be God's covenant partner with the salvation of the whole race in view.

Let me say it again: the goal of election is the creation of a people and not, in the first instance, the salvation of solitary individuals. It establishes the firstfruits of a new humanity whose praise and whose distinctive way of being in the world is God oriented. Under the law of Christ, the church has a way of being in the world (a polity, if you like) which corresponds to Israel's way but which also allows for changes consequent upon the movement from being a particular ethnic group (Israel) to being a community which incorporates every nation (church). The church is like Israel in being called out and distinguished from the rest of humankind but unlike Israel in that representatives from every nation are openly included, not needing to be circumcised and not having to cease to be the particular people they are as Gentiles.

Under this interpretation election does not narrow things down but opens things up. The community as a chosen race does not spell exclusivity relative to others who are passed over but carries with it the promise of the inclusion of humanity. The aim of God's electing purposes is the fellowship of a renewed humanity in the kingdom of God. It does not have to do with elect individuals in abstraction from history but with God's having a people to bear him witness. Notice, the number of the redeemed remains open to anyone and everyone who is brought into the fellowship by the preaching of the gospel. Whereas individuals are the focus of the conventional views of elec-

23. Karl Barth, "The Holy Spirit and the Sending of the Christian Community," *Church Dogmatics* IV/3 (Edinburgh: T. & T. Clark, 1962), 681–901.

tion, the election of a people is the issue in the Bible's traditions. Amid the strife of world history, God's elect people are called upon to offer a model of his kingdom. The elect are pressed into the service of a greater fellowship; election is not for their benefit alone.

The church is the elect community, and individual believers are caught up into it by faith and baptism. As God's people in the service of the kingdom, they are an anticipation of the unity of humanity under God. The community points beyond itself to the final purposes of God. The church is not an end in itself but a sign of the coming kingdom. God calls a people so that they can be involved in the restoration of the world. Election is a movement toward a goal, not an end in itself. In electing, God puts us to work and makes us partners in the mending of creation. It is often overlooked that election is not a call to privilege but to service. One's "vocation" as a believer is not the job by which to earn a living. Our calling is to be partners in God's work of salvation. Mission and outreach, not salvation as our private possession, is the goal of election. Too often we have taken our own salvation to be the goal and assigned mission to paid emissaries. Too often we can be so busy edifying ourselves that we have little time for our neighbor. Barth notes that the Bible contains stories of calling, not stories of conversion as such, and the goal of them is to bear witness. Like Paul's "conversion," it was an event in the history of mission as this "instrument" which God has chosen comes on line (Acts 9:15).

To reiterate: the elect community is a provisional representation of the future of humanity. Having experienced salvation, it proclaims the mighty acts of God to everyone. It is not that faith is first exercised in the human heart and the church is added as an afterthought. God is aiming to establish a new human community, and the church is the firstfruits of it and imperfectly embodies what is coming. Pannenberg writes: "The human society at which God's eternal election aims will find its definitive form only in the eschatological fellowship of the kingdom of God. God's work of election in history is oriented to those that are still on the way to this goal."[24] One could say that the church has an eschatological horizon and is the proleptic manifestation of the kingdom of God in history. It is the beachhead of the new creation and the sign of the new order in a world that is coming to an end (1 Cor. 7:29).

What about individuals then? Election is corporate and comprehends individuals in association with the elect body. Whereas in the

---

24. Pannenberg, *Systematic Theology,* vol. III, 463.

Augustinian tradition, election to salvation is unconditional for individuals and contingent when it comes to the elect body, in the Bible election to salvation is unconditional for the elect body and contingent when it comes to individuals. This is how I see it: God's mercy is freely available and the elect body open to any and all who hear God's call.[25] When we preach the gospel, we give to people outside the community an opportunity to become members of the elect people of God. Before the foundation of the world, God chose to have a people and destined them to be holy and blameless in love. When a person believes in Jesus, he or she is incorporated in the body of Christ, and all that had been predestined for the group now applies to that person as well. God is sharing his life with the world and does so through the instrumentality of Jesus Christ and his church.

God knows that some will respond but not (I submit) exactly who. He has predestined the church to be conformed to the image of his Son and uses it to bear witness to the rest of humankind. The election of Israel, too, did not have in view only salvation; it also had in mind a priestly vocation, intended to bring the whole world to God. The love by which God loves the church is meant to spread into the whole world. The church is not a community intended for a salvation exclusively its own. It comes with a calling to reconcile the world to God through its praise and ministry.

God foreknew his bride. It says that "those whom he foreknew he also predestined to be conformed to the image of his Son" (Rom. 8:29). What he foreknows is a group of people (believers) in contrast to another group (unbelievers) whom he did not foreknow. Obviously Paul is not talking about prior information here! This is not foreknowledge in the cognitive sense. It has to do with loving people ahead of time. As his people we are preloved by God. It is not that God foreloved select individuals as opposed to others whom he did not love. What God loved from the foundation of the world was the bride of Christ considered as a corporate whole. There is no reason to suppose that God knew precisely who would constitute and make up the elect body.[26]

---

25. Robert Shank, *Elect in the Son: A Study in the Doctrine of Election* (Springfield, Mo.: Westcott, 1970), ch. 2.

26. Gregory A. Boyd, *Satan and the Problem of Evil: Constructing a Trinitarian Warfare Theodicy* (Downers Grove: InterVarsity, 2001), 117–19. Boyd casts light on these realities by supplying this experience. "Suppose I decide at the last minute to attend a theology conference in which, to my surprise, a person delivers a paper on Milton's *Paradise Lost*. At the end of the presentation I ask, 'When was it decided that we would listen to that paper?' To which the conference organiser responds, 'It was decided six months

God's calling is a genuine calling, and it takes place in time. It is not all decided from eternity. It calls for a decision here and now. Peoples' fate is not sealed one way or the other. The early attempts to understand election were not successful. Whether the distinction between the elect and the nonelect rests on observing their conduct through foreknowledge, thereby undermining the gracious character of election, or whether it rests solely on the decision of God whereby he simply passes over the nonelect irrespective of their conduct runs up against the category of God's calling. In either case there is no room left for a free decision to the call of God on the part of the creatures in their historical situations. It results in a monstrosity—an outer calling for everybody and an inner calling only for some.[27]

God's election of the people is the basis of God's election of individuals who associate with it by saying "yes" to God's call. The obedience of faith is what makes our "calling and election sure" (2 Pet. 1:10 NIV). Remember the widow who is God's elect and who calls out for justice (Luke 18:7). She is one of the suffering elect people of God who will experience God's protection and salvation. Faithful Jews and faithful Christians are "the elect" then, not because God pretemporally and arbitrarily chose them and not others but because they belong by faith to his chosen people and are members of the elect body. "Elect" is a status enjoyed by all believers including all in the future who will believe in Jesus.

To reiterate: whereas for Calvin election applies to individuals unconditionally and who comprise the corporate body incidentally, for the Bible election is corporate and comprehends individuals in association with the elect body. That Christ will present the elect people, the bride, to himself is unconditional. But, as for individuals, he will present them only if they continue in the faith which is contingent (Col. 1:23). In my reading of the Bible, election is God's choice of a people; and, when individuals are said to be chosen, it is in connection with the people and for the people.[28]

---

ago.' It was not decided six months ago that I *individually* would hear this paper. Rather it was decided that whoever chooses to attend this conference would hear this paper. Now that I and the others have decided to attend this conference, we can all say, 'It was decided (predestined) six months ago that *we* would hear this paper.' What was decided for the group as a whole gets individually applied as individuals decide to align themselves with the group."

27. Pannenberg, "Election and Calling," *Systematic Theology*, vol. III, 447–55.

28. Jack Cottrell believes that individuals too are elect from the beginning: *The Faith Once Delivered: Bible Doctrine for Today* (Joplin, Mo.: College Press, 2002), ch. 22.

What might be meant then by the New Testament sometimes saying that God "foreknows" his people (Rom. 8:29; 1 Pet. 1:2)? Light is shed on this in Romans 11:2, where Paul says that God has not rejected his people whom he "foreknew." In Christ, before the foundation of the world, God foreknew and foreloved all believing creatures. They have a special place in God's heart and a glorious future whoever they are. In creating the universe, God decided that (at least) some of his creatures would share in the divine life. He decided that some would become conformed to the image of the perfect humanity manifested in Jesus and would constitute a new community. God decided that there would be such creatures and that he would call them into communion with himself through the church. He committed himself to justify them if they responded. God foreknew them, in that he had decided that there would be some such creatures, that some of them would respond and be glorified. It is not necessary to believe that God knew in particular exactly who they would be. God is simply envisaging and intending that there will be some and determining (predestinating) that some will be conformed to the image of his Son. By means of repeated and patient preparation and assistance, some will respond affirmatively without God knowing exactly who.

In speaking of an elect people, God is not talking about specific individuals but a group or a class, the membership of which is still undetermined. God does not have to know from eternity past exactly which persons would actually be conceived and born and which would respond to his call. Who they all are is something that will manifest itself. One should not equate foreknowing with foreseeing. It is a relational and not merely a cognitive term. Only one individual is said to have been elect by name—Jesus Christ; everyone else who is elect is elect in him. When we believe, we step into the realm of God's everlasting love.[29]

Israel in the Old Testament and the church in the New Testament are considered the chosen people of God. What should we think about how things stand with unbelieving Israel now? Has Israel been superseded by the church, or is she still God's people? Many Christians have thought of Israel as discarded, as a negligible people now passed over and deserving of no appreciation. But this does not seem to be Paul's view: "God has not rejected his people whom he foreknew" (Rom. 11:2 NRSV). He adds: "The gifts and the calling of God are irrevocable"

---

29. S. M. Baugh takes exception to this approach: "The Meaning of Foreknowledge" in *The Grace of God, the Bondage of the Will,* ed. Thomas R. Schreiner and Bruce A. Ware (Grand Rapids: Baker, 1995), ch. 7.

(Rom. 11:29). God is faithful to his promises in spite of intransigence. "If we are faithless, God remains faithful—he cannot deny himself" (2 Tim. 2:13). He says, "They are enemies and yet they are still loved" (Rom. 11:28). Indeed, Paul adds, God has even found a way to redeem the situation. In the wake of Israel's unbelief, the salvation of both Jews and Greeks has become a possibility, a net gain. Therefore, our calling regarding Israel is not to ignore them or merely tolerate them or even make them a special target of mission, but (as Paul says) we are "to make them jealous" (11:11, 14). That is, we are so to live out the gospel of Jesus Christ and so to witness to messianic fulfillment that Israel will reconsider and experience a change of heart.

The church is to confront Israel, not in a battle of words but in committed competition—something which so far has not been very convincing. So far, looking at the unredeemed state of the world and, alas, of the church too, the Jews have not yet found it possible to accept Jesus as the Messiah. But we can sympathize; we too regret the unredeemed nature of the world and the church. And we too pray, "Thy kingdom come, thy will be done on earth as in heaven." We too await fulfilment and consummation.[30]

Election as Christocentric and Representational

The foundations of the doctrine of election as corporate and vocational are laid in the Old Testament. The New Testament supports this pattern and enriches it. What I see is the corporate-vocational doctrine with a Christological-representational twist. In brief, we are faced with the election of Jesus Christ and a double representation in him of Israel and humanity at large. Owing to the failure of Israel to heed God's call in the old covenant and to recognize Jesus' proclamation, Peter says, "The stone that the builders rejected has become the very head of the corner" (1 Pet. 2:7). And, he adds, Jesus the Christ is now what is chosen and precious in God's sight (1 Pet. 2:4). Through the wisdom of God, the faithful Son of the Father is carrying the mission of Israel forward and is creating a new form of the elect people alongside her. Now we hear about a bridegroom and an elect bride, chosen in Christ. Now we hear about a last Adam, who embodies the

---

30. Hans Küng, "The Church and the Jews" in *The Church* (New York: Sheed and Ward, 1967), 132–50; R. Kendall Soulen, *The God of Israel and Christian Theology* (Minneapolis: Fortress, 1996); David Novak, *The Election of Israel: The Idea of the Chosen People* (Cambridge: Cambridge University Press, 1995); Scott Bader-Saye, *Church and Israel after Christendom* (Boulder, Colo.: Westview, 1999).

new humanity. We hear how it is that, in him, through faith and baptism, we as individuals become part of the elect servant and of the new creation itself.

The Election of Jesus Christ

We noticed in the Old Testament how, although election is fundamentally corporate, individuals are "chosen" to play important roles in the life of the community. In the Hebrew Bible, God chooses the heroes of the nation: Abraham (Neh. 9:7), Jacob (Ps. 135:4), Moses (Num. 16:5,7), David (1 Sam. 13:13–14), Amos (Amos 7:14–15), Jeremiah (Jer. 1:4–8), etc. God also chooses the priesthood and various kings and prophets. Similarly in the New Testament, Jesus chooses apostles to follow him. Individuals are elected to tasks in God's mission.

Most striking in this context is the choice of one individual—Jesus Christ—whose vocation it is to be the Savior of the world. We hear God's voice at the baptism of Jesus: "You are my Son, the beloved; with you I am well pleased" (Mark 1:11). God says at the transfiguration: "This is my Son, my Chosen; listen to him" (Luke 9:35). This was no election to salvation (Jesus did not need to be saved) but to service. In particular, he is the one through whom God brings salvation. Dying on the cross, he was taunted in these terms: "He saved others; let him save himself if he is the Messiah of God, his chosen one!" (Luke 23:35). God has chosen this individual to be the Savior of the world. This was to be his calling and election.[31] No other specific person is pretemporally chosen in this way.

Much about the future is as yet undecided. It awaits for agents to have their "say so." Much belongs to the category of "what might be." But not everything is merely possible. God has decided on certain things. The defining event of history, the death and resurrection of Jesus, is one of those things. They did not just happen. They were part of God's plan for the redemption of the race from long ago. It was certain that Jesus would suffer crucifixion and triumph over death, but that does not imply that everything about these events was fixed. Figures like Pilate and Herod played their roles, but of their own free will. There was a combination of the divine purpose and human machinations. It was a vile murder but also something much more (Acts 2:23). It was the plan of God to provide a redeemer. The Son would be delivered up into the hands of evil men, but God would

---

31. Compare Richard A. Muller, *Christ and the Decree: Christology and Predestination in Reformed Theology from Calvin to Perkins* (Durham, N.C.: Labyrinth, 1986).

override their plans. God decreed the salvation of the world through Jesus but did not approve of all the means by which it was brought about. For example, God did not approve or ordain that men should curse him and spit on him. It was a vile murder but one which God used for the world's salvation. Here we have a predestined event with nonpredestined players.[32]

The Representation of Israel

Before Jesus came, Israel had been God's experimental garden, a place where God could try things out and see what kind of a response he would get. Israel was God's vineyard from which he expected a good yield but which often proved unproductive. It was an experiment that could become decisive for the world, which is why God "chose" them. He wanted a people to receive his love and walk in his ways. Sadly, it did not always work out that way. God is faithful, but how unfaithful we humans are! Relentlessly the prophets exposed the sins of Israel. How near to failure God's experiment with this people would seem to be. But the prophets did not give up hoping. They kept on believing that "in that coming day" God will restore his people (Ezek. 36:32). On the boundaries of the New Testament, we meet up with John the Baptist who like an Old Testament prophet announces the strong One who is to come and who will bring the kingdom of God near. Languishing in prison, John experienced doubts, but Jesus reassured him and carried it through. Like John, we believe that Jesus Christ was God's next and decisive step in a continuation of the way he had gone and the path he had trodden with Israel long before. At last the kingdom of God was among us.

The point and meaning of the election of Israel is now to be found in Jesus of Nazareth. Her vocation is seen in the presence of this one person. Jesus is the concrete realization of God's dealings with his people and reveals the shape of the preparatory history. In the New Testament the election is narrowed down to Jesus Christ himself. The need for his role arose from the failure of Israel and from the fact that something else had to be done if the goal is to be reached, namely, reaching of the nations. Someone had to act in Israel's name and on Israel's behalf. This is what Jesus Christ did as "minister to the circumcision" (Rom. 15:8).

Something new then was being built on the history of Israel in which God's call became particular in a decisive way. The offices of

---

32. Gregory A. Boyd, *God of the Possible* (Grand Rapids: Baker, 2002), 44–45.

the prophets, priests, and kings of Israel, through whom God dealt with Israel, are now seen to be concentrated in Christ who is the concrete realization in person of God's dealings with his people and revealing of the shape of the preparatory history. In him God's universal reconciling design is exposed and achieved. The role of Jesus was not isolated from the foregoing history of Israel. This is not an isolated epiphany but a decisive phase in the path that had been followed for centuries. Jesus was a decisive step and a continuation of the way God had gone with Israel before. John the baptizer may have seen the covenant event between God and the people ending in a great judgment, but Jesus saw this as a great opportunity to play a unique and definitive role to act on God's behalf. The way has opened up for him to serve as Israel's representative, as the obedient servant in whom the covenant could be made firm. He knew that he was the elect of God and chosen with purpose. He was sent by the faithful God to an unfaithful people to realize the covenant on behalf of Israel.

Israel responded to this divine initiative, with rejection but it issued in a breakthrough, nevertheless. The age of salvation had arrived, even though Israel still did not enter in. Even with the Gentiles flooding in, God's dispute with Israel remains undecided. Had the age of salvation moved toward completion in accordance with the prophetic vision, the way would have been open for a new world community with Israel at the core plus all those from the nations who would turn to Israel's God. But because the majority in Israel withdrew from it, the appearance of Jesus, contrary seemingly to the intent, led to two forms of the people of God: with Israel continuing the old covenant as if Jesus had not come and the Gentiles with a remnant of Jews operating out of a new covenant through Jesus and the Spirit. In line with the way in which God achieves his goals with open routes, the process toward the renewal of the human race has gotten under way.

A new facet in the doctrine of divine election is now visible. Election is now seen as relative to the Son, to his mission, death, and resurrection. Jesus is "the elect" par excellence and God has chosen to elect us "in him." We become part of the corporate "us" in the body of Christ. Election does not create a scheme which divides humankind into two camps. God's election of Jesus extends to all who are "in him" and who will be "in him." Election is God's "yes" to the human race. Believers participate in his election by faith and baptism. God's choice of him extends to all those who are in him. Election is God's choice of a bride for his Son. He has ordained that those in Christ by faith would belong to it.[33]

Often we view salvation in juridical terms. But it needs also to be understood as participation in Jesus Christ. By faith we share in his death and resurrection. In a mysterious and mystical way, believers enter into a new realm and constitute a new humanity. They belong to a new corporateness which signifies the age to come. In Christ, with Christ, into Christ, and through Christ—all such expressions speak of a new corporate reality. It is the presence of the risen Lord with us in the community which is his body and the realm of the Holy Spirit. Christ is conceived of as a kind of location into which the convert is inserted. It makes us all part of the process of world transformation. Participatory union with Christ is the heart of Paul's theology. In him we are elect, called, justified, sanctified, redeemed, and made alive.[34]

The Representation of Humanity Itself

In a broader way, Jesus represents not only Israel but humanity itself. In Paul's writings, Christ and Adam are representative figures which are compared and contrasted. Paul writes: "Just as one man's trespass (Adam's) led to condemnation for all, so one man's act of righteousness leads to justification and life for all (Christ's)" in Romans 5:18. Or again: "For as all die in Adam, so all will be made alive in Christ" (1 Cor. 15:22). In such expressions, Adam is humanity itself, an individual who represents the whole human race. Jesus Christ is also a representative figure, the eschatological counterpart of primeval Adam. Each begins an epoch which is established by their action. In this way human beings are viewed as being either "in Adam" or "in Christ." Adam represents a fallen humankind, while Jesus is the type and prototype of the new humanity which is to come. He is the author of a new humanity and the embodiment of human destiny. The way God found in his wisdom to deal with the problem of human

---

33. Markus Barth, *Ephesians* (New York: Doubleday, 1975), 105–9; Robert Shank, *Elect in the Son: A Study of the Doctrine of Election* (Springfield, Mo.: Westcott, 1970), ch. 2.

34. Richard N. Longenecker, *Paul: Apostle of Liberty* (New York: Harper & Row, 1964), 156–80; James D. G. Dunn, "Participation in Christ," *The Theology of Paul the Apostle* (Grand Rapids: Eerdmans, 1998), 390–412; Paul S. Fiddes, *Participating in God* (Louisville, Ky.: Westminster/John Knox, 2000). Other scholars warn against exaggerating the category of the corporate: Stanley E. Porter, "An Assessment of Some New Testament-related Assumptions for Open Theism in the Writings of Clark H. Pinnock" in *Semper Reformanda: Studies in Honour of Clark H. Pinnock*, ed. Stanley E. Porter and Anthony R. Cross (Carlisle, UK: Paternoster, 2003), 167–75.

sin was to send his Son in solidarity with humankind in its existence under the powers of sin and death.

Paul's logic would be summed up later in the classic formulations of Gregory of Nazianzus: "What has not been assumed cannot be healed" (*Epistle* 101.7). And in the formulation of Irenaeus: "Christ became what we are in order that we may become what he is" (*Adversus Haereses* 5). Or, in Athanasius: "He became man that we might become divine" (*De Incarnatione* 54).[35]

What does this mean? I think that it means that, in the coming of Jesus, the future of God's reign that he proclaimed was present by anticipation. He was himself a sign of the coming kingdom of God. In an antithesis to the old humanity, Jesus spells the origin of a new human being, a reality that has overcome sin and death. Thus Jesus is the eschatological new human being, and we who are elect in him look to the summing up of all things in him. Election is oriented toward the goal of consummation. Pannenberg writes: "In the coming of Jesus the future of God and his reign that Jesus proclaimed were present by anticipation. In person, Jesus was a sign of the coming divine rule, so that by him and in fellowship with him people may be assured even now of their participation in the future salvation of God."[36]

The gospel is about our becoming truly human. It is about the humanization of men and women. Being a Christian is about being human in a new way. It is about having a new orientation in thought and life. It is about being oriented to God and not to idols. Salvation is aimed at man's well-being. It involves having a new orientation, a new approach to life, a new standard, and living model for our relations to God and the neighbor. The goal is that we may live differently—more genuinely, more humanly, more like Jesus. It's about the new creation which is coming to be. It is about Jesus Christ.[37]

Barth is right to focus on the election of Jesus Christ who represents the whole race. Not just Israel and church but all of humankind is elect in him. Jesus is God's elect; and, if we are elect, it is in and with his election. In contrast with the Reformed tradition, according to which God has elected some for salvation and others for perdition, Barth maintains that God's election is centered on Christ only.

---

35. Russell P. Shedd, *Man in Community: A Study of St Paul's Application of Old Testament and Early Jewish Conceptions of Human Solidarity* (London: Epworth, 1958); James D. G. Dunn, "Adam," *The Theology of Paul the Apostle*, 199–204, 241–2.

36. Pannenberg, *Systematic Theology*, vol. III, 435. See also his "Anthropology and Christology," *Systematic Theology*, vol. II (Grand Rapids: Eerdmans, 1994), 297–323.

37. Hans Küng, *On Being a Christian* (London: Collins, 1976), 249–77, 552, 602.

It refers to this one individual and not to individuals at large. He has a Christological doctrine of election which reveals his will to save and not reject Adam's race. In election, God is for us, not against us. In him, the entire race has been chosen for salvation. He repudiates double predestination. God's decision to be gracious leaves no doubt. All humanity swims in a sea of grace whether they know it or not. Barth reads the Bible through the lens of Jesus. His cross reveals God's grace for all people, not just a few lucky ones.[38]

But Barth takes this too far. He takes this to imply the actual justification of humankind and (therefore) moves in the direction of universal salvation. It is as if grace cannot ultimately be defeated in anybody's life. It's a kind of Reformed universalism. If God can save anyone and everyone, he will surely do so, given the combination of unconditional election and irresistible grace for Barth. How could it be otherwise? But Barth does not hold the objective and the subjective in proper tension. Faith is the condition for the concrete realization of salvation which does not take effect apart from it. It has nothing to do with merit (Rom. 4:16). But we need to leave room for a human response. It is right to be optimistic about every one since Christ has died for them. There is no necessity that any be lost. But God's love must woo them and win them. Universal opportunity, yes; universal salvation, not likely. God's love appeals to human freedom; it does not swallow it up. To those who say no to God finally, he gives them what they want most—the opportunity to be themselves, enslaved forever by the autonomy they have demanded.[39]

God's desire to save all sinners is clear, and election does not contest it. Indeed, election is an instrument and means to make salvation happen. It is a corporate category and comprehends individuals in association with the elect body. The goal is to have creatures who participate in the trinitarian fellowship which will be actualized at the final consummation. The community of faith now is an expression but not the final expression of God's will to love. At this time election means selection, but the number of the elect remains open to all who may later on be added. Election comprehends all men and women potentially and no one unconditionally. It is open to all. Faith is the

---

38. I. Howard Marshall, "For All, for All My Saviour Died," in *Semper Reformanda: Studies in Honour of Clark H. Pinnock,* ed. Stanley E. Porter and Anthony R. Cross (Carlisle, UK: Paternoster, 2003), 322–46.

39. Donald G. Bloesch, *Jesus Is Victor: Karl Barth's Doctrine of Salvation* (Nashville: Abingdon, 1976), ch. 7; Jerry L. Walls, *Hell: The Logic of Damnation* (Notre Dame: University of Notre Dame Press, 1992), ch. 5.

subjective means and baptism and eucharist are the outward means of identification with Christ in his election.

No Horrible Decree, No Self-selection

A person could be in considerable agreement with what has been said so far and still maintain that there is, in the Bible, in addition to these truths, a divine election alongside them which does involve the selection of certain individuals to be saved and not others. What if there were, in addition to corporate election with a vocational focus, what John Frame calls "a stronger kind of election"?[40] Might there also be what has been called a soteriological double predestination? Is there a selection/election of individuals underneath the corporate/vocational dimension? Although I do not find the Bible to be teaching such a belief—the election of certain individuals to salvation and the predestination of the rest to damnation—it must be taken seriously because it has been widely accepted since Augustine, especially in Calvinistic circles. Although this notion in my view derives from bad habits of interpretation, built up over the generations, nevertheless, it is important to remove this obstacle to a good understanding which has dogged our path for centuries and placed a dark shadow over a basic tenet of the Christian message that "God desires everyone to be saved and come to a knowledge of the truth" (1 Tim. 2:4).[41]

One reason election as a selection of individuals to be saved has seemed a plausible interpretation despite its doubtful morality is that modern readers find it hard to grasp the biblical notion of corporate solidarity. The Bible may be familiar with the idea whereby community is prior to the individual, but we are not used to thinking in these terms. It is not that individuality is foreign to the Bible or that individuals are swallowed up into the group; it is just that biblical writers find thinking about an elect "body" easier than we do. We tend more naturally to think of the individuals who make it up. It is not as easy for us to think of people receiving election as part of an elect body. We are more used to thinking of God electing "me" rather than God electing "us." We have to recognize that our election as believers

---

40. John Frame, *No Other God: A Response to Open Theism* (Phillipsburg, N.J.: Presbyterian & Reformed, 2001), 98.

41. Consider "the salvation debate" in *Across the Spectrum: Understanding Issues in Evangelical Theology,* ed. Gregory A. Boyd and Paul R. Eddy (Grand Rapids: Baker, 2002), ch. 9. Some like Paul Helm are content to say that God does not love men and women equally. See Kevin J. Vanhoozer, ed., *Nothing Greater, Nothing Better* (Grand Rapids: Eerdmans, 2001), 185.

is the result of our participation and incorporation by faith and baptism in the body of Christ. What gives us hope is not a speculation as to whether we are chosen. It is membership in the community that gives us hope since God has chosen the bride in Christ and for Christ before the foundation of the world. Everyone who believes is part of this elect group, and the others are free to believe and enter into it.

God chose a people without determining the specific individuals who would belong to it. Every believer who is in Christ is chosen and predestined to be holy and blameless. This is God's purpose for them and the grace that they were given "in Christ Jesus before the ages began" (2 Tim. 1:9). As R. P. Shedd writes: "Election does not have an individual emphasis in Paul, any more than it did for Israel in the Old Testament. Rather, it implies a covenant relationship through which God chooses for himself a people. This collectivism is of supreme importance for understanding the implications of election in Christ."[42]

It is natural for us Westerners to ask how there can be an elect body without the selection of individuals to populate it. The fact is though that this is not a biblical problem. Strong individualism, however, is foreign to the Bible's way of thinking where the perspective is corporate. Our individual chosenness rests on our being partakers in the body of Christ and in our affiliation in his church. Election is not God's choice of a restricted number of individuals whom God is willing to save—it is a description of the corporate body which God is in fact saving through Jesus. Election is not a limit on the mercy of God but its very expression. Individuals become part of the elect body simply by responding to the call of God.[43]

Having appealed to texts in support of divine election as corporate and vocational, as Christocentric and representational, I must now say something about important texts to which others (especially Calvinists) refer and determine whether they can be reasonably interpreted in the way I am suggesting.

In a most important text, Paul writes: "Just as he chose us in Christ before the foundation of the world to be holy and blameless before him in love" and then he adds, "as a plan for the fullness of time to gather up all things in him" (Eph. 1:4, 10). Notice the grand sweep there is in Paul's vision. He looks back to the pretemporal election in Christ of a people and then forward to the fulfilment of God's plan for human history. He is not talking about the otherworldly destiny

42. R. P. Shedd, *Man in Community,* 133.
43. Klein, *The New Chosen People,* 36–42, 257–68.

of a limited number of people but about the destiny of creation itself. What we have here is the election of a people for the sake of the rest. It is an expression of God's will to save humanity through the agency of this community. The elect are the people whose role it is to bring salvation to the world. The focus is not on individuals; God would save everyone if he could (1 Tim. 2:4). Individuals will be called to salvation through the mission of the church and will become elect when incorporated into the elect body by faith in Jesus.

What is happening is that God's choice of Jesus now extends to all who are "in him." As members of the community, they share in the benefits of God's gracious choice. As Klein writes, "Christ is the principally elected one and God has chosen a corporate body to be included in him."[44] As Markus Barth writes, "Election in Christ must be understood as the election of God's people. Only as members of that community do individuals share in the benefits of God's gracious choice."[45]

Paul again writes: "For those whom he foreknew he also predestined to be conformed to the image of his Son, in order that he might be the firstborn within a large family. And those whom he predestined he also called; and those whom he called he also justified; and those whom he justified he also glorified" (Rom. 8:29–30). In Romans 11:2 Paul speaks of Israel as the people "whom God foreknew." In this text too, he is not thinking of individuals but of the people as a whole who had turned away from God. In both texts he is envisaging a people, and God's "foreknowledge" of them in each case is not a precognition of them as individuals but a loving of them in advance as a group. He is thinking of the elect body which is predestined to be conformed to the image of God's Son. In these texts Paul is not saying that God previsioned all the actual individuals who would be saved. He is saying that the church (and Israel) as a corporate reality has always been in God's heart. He is viewing them as a body, not as individuals.[46]

Had Paul meant to speak of individuals, he would have fallen into a self-contradiction. If foreknowledge here means precognition, why would God be said only to preknow believers? Does he not foreknow

---

44. Ibid., 180.
45. Marcus Barth, *Ephesians* I (Garden City, N.Y.: Doubleday, 1974), 108.
46. Despite Jack Cottrell, *The Faith Once for All,* 390–98. I confess, too, to having difficulty believing that God possesses complete foreknowledge of what humans will do with their (libertarian) freedom. What would the ontological grounding be for that? How can libertarianly free human decisions be known infallibly ahead of time?

unbelievers too? And is every believer "called, justified, and glorified?" Surely not. Did he not say that persons can fall from grace (Gal. 1:4)? Can one not be justified and not glorified? Paul is not speaking to the issue that interests us most, as to whether God knew in advance which specific individuals would belong to the elect body. That question (thank God) is open. All who confess Christ are subsumed under God's plan and are part of that body. Paul is not talking about individuals elected in eternity but about the historical saving plan of God. God has in mind a chosen race that will take the salvation of God to the nations. Paul is contemplating the purpose of God for his elect people. Pannenberg writes: "Only in detaching the statements in Romans 8:29–30 and 9:13, 16 from the context of salvation history in which Paul set them makes it possible to link them to the abstract notions of election that since the days of Origen and Augustine have been determinative in the history of the doctrine of predestination."[47]

Romans 9–11 represents a tremendously important block of teaching. In it Paul is speaking about God's purpose in the election of Israel. It grieves him so deeply that the Jews have turned away from the gospel that he writes, "I have great sorrow and unceasing anguish in my heart" (Rom. 9:2). Later on, he confesses, "My heart's desire and prayer to God for them is that they may be saved" (Rom. 10:1 NRSV). Paul faced a tremendous conundrum. How is it that God can be said to remain faithful to his people which he had chosen and at the same time could be calling Paul to preach a gospel for Jew and Greek?

What makes it tolerable for him is the insight that even Israel's unbelief plays a role in God's plan. Specifically, it opened the door for Gentiles to be saved. Paul writes, "Through their stumbling, salvation has come to the Gentiles" (11:11). This is what he had said to the church at Antioch about the success of his mission: "God . . . opened the door of faith for the Gentiles" (Acts 14:27). What a tribute to God's competence and resourcefulness (Rom. 11:33). As for Israel, God will deal with them in his own way and time; but in the meantime our task as Jews and Gentiles in the body of Christ is to live in such a way that the Jews can infer from our lives that we are worshiping the God of Israel in truth.

Paul's remarks in Romans 9–11 are about God working in world history to show mercy to both Jew and Gentile (11:32). It's not about the salvation of individuals per se. The emphasis on sovereignty is to emphasize the freedom of God to do things in his way without in any

---

47. Pannenberg, *Systematic Theology*, vol. III, 444.

way casting doubt about the broad goal of salvation. If in fact (perish the thought) the unbelief of the Jews were due to God's decision and, therefore, was something God sovereignly wanted, why would Paul experience sorrow, and why would he want the people to be saved whom God does not want saved? He makes clear that Jews missed salvation because they do not strive for it on the basis of faith but works (Rom. 9:32).

Paul's subject in Romans 9–11 is salvation history with the goal of global outreach. There is no hidden decree here but only good news through and through. God has not annulled his covenant with the Jews. There is still a remnant of the faithful, as there was in the days of Elijah. At the moment (granted), and for the time being, the relationship is going through a rough patch. Nevertheless, the people of God are expanding with the flowing in of the Gentiles. And our hope is that, at least by his return, the Jews too will be saved (Rom. 11:26). People who struggle with Romans 9–11 would be greatly helped if they would stop reading it as if it were about divine pan-causality and start reading it as being about God's covenant faithfulness.[48] God is not addressing the issue of the salvation of individuals in Romans 9. He is pondering the issue of God's covenant with Israel. "Has God's word failed?" Has the covenant been rescinded? At stake here is God's fidelity to Israel as his covenant partner, not double predestination. It has to do with God's sovereignty to use Gentiles, if he chooses to. If they believe and the Jews refuse, that will not stop God from carrying on with his plan to reach all the nations. God is a flexible potter who knows how to work with willing clay. Did anyone before Augustine read Romans 9 in a deterministic way?

Romans 9–11 is about the sovereignty of God to do things his way and the orientation is corporate. There is no arbitrariness as regards individuals. God's goal is to have mercy on both Jews and Gentiles (Rom. 11:32). To achieve it, God even uses something as horrific as Israel's unbelief. Paul writes: "Even before they had been born or had done anything good or bad (so that God's purpose of election might continue, not by works but by his call) she was told, 'the elder shall serve the younger.' As it is written, 'I have loved Jacob, but I have

---

48. John Sanders, *The God Who Risks: A Theology of Providence* (Downers Grove: InterVarsity, 1998), 120–24; Klein, *The New Chosen People,* 166–67, 173–76; Shank, *Elect in the Son,* 117–25. John Frame writes: "These are hard sayings (Rom 9–11) and I myself could wish that the passage presented fewer challenges to those who would expound it in today's theological environment" (102). I hope I have indicated that there is a better and less painful a way of being faithful to these Scriptures.

hated Esau'" (Rom. 9:11, 13). The point is that God decided that the line should go through Jacob, not through Esau. This was God's sovereign choice and had nothing whatever to do with individual salvation. God simply chose Jacob and his offspring rather than Esau and his offspring. Paul quotes Malachi to make his point where the issue is clearly two nations and not individuals.[49] It is all about God as the flexible potter who can work the clay into ever new forms (Jer. 18:4; Rom. 9:21).

Some read Romans 9 as if God loves some and hates others, but this is wrong.[50] Geisler refutes this notion effectively. He argues that the passage is not speaking about individuals but about nations. The "Esau" Paul refers to is the nation of Edom and the "Jacob" is the nation of Israel, as the Malachi reference makes clear (Mal. 1:2–3). As for Pharaoh, he hardened his own heart before God hardened it. God sent the plagues to get him to repent; but, since he refused, the result was well deserved hardening. The vessels of wrath were not destined to destruction against their will. They deserved to be put aside, God having endured their disobedience long enough.[51] One simply cannot read Romans 9 this way. The idea that God has decided unilaterally to leave some untouched by grace is a scandalous note and in flagrant opposition to the gospel. It conceals the outrageous love of God revealed to all humanity in the cross and puts it under the shadow of God's supposed equally outrageous hatred. To this reading we must say no.

Not every text which is relevant to election mentions the word. There are also indirect "proofs" which are appealed to. For example, there are texts that seem to assert that everything is foreordained, in which case the salvation of individuals must be foreordained along with everything else. In Psalm 139, for example, we read, "In your book were written all the days that were formed for me, when none of them as yet existed" (v. 16 NRSV). A text like this seems to support a predestinarian outlook which could undergird the election and/or rejection of individuals. However, in this poem (and it is a poem), the psalmist gives expression to the intimacy of God's acquaintance with him. He reflects on how God cared for him from conception and wrote down in a book all that what was possible for this human life. The language is not perfectly clear as to what is exactly implied. It

---

49. Klein, *The New Chosen People*, 173–75.

50. Donald J. Westblade, "Divine Election in the Pauline Literature," in *The Grace of God, the Bondage of the Will*, ch. 3; Thomas R. Schreiner, "Does Romans 9 Teach Individual Election to Salvation," in *The Grace of God, the Bondage of the Will*, ch. 4.

51. Norman L. Geisler, *Systematic Theology*, vol. II (Minneapolis: Bethany, 2003), 380.

does not say, for example, that everything that will ever happen in this lifetime is written down. And elsewhere in the Bible we are told that what is written down in such a book can be changed (Exod. 32:33; Rev. 3:5). What is "predestined" then may not actually occur! It may be conditional and dependant on other factors. God's plan for us all is a flexible one and takes account of every possibility. We should not read too much into a text like this. Of course God knows an incredible amount about our future since he is infinitely wise, but this does not prove that his knowledge is strictly limitless with respect to the future.[52]

In the book of Acts, Luke writes, "When the Gentiles heard this, they were glad and praised the word of the Lord; and, as many as had been destined for eternal life became believers" (Acts 13:48). Apart from the verb "destined," the context makes the meaning plain. The action of the Jews, having decided not to accept the message, leads Paul to turn to the Gentiles. Thus the door is now open to them to enter into salvation (Acts 14:27). What does this "being destined" or "disposed (Greek *tasso*) for eternal life" mean then? The context decides it. It means that the Gentiles believed because of the fact that God's plan of salvation, given Israel's negative decision, now includes them. The Jews had rejected the gospel, but the Gentiles were eager to receive it. Those who reject the message are unworthy of eternal life while others who accept it reveal by their response to God's Word that they are numbered with the saints. The word *disposed* has to be understood in the context where the meaning is after all very clear.[53]

Admittedly, Acts 13:48 comes close to suggesting that God might determine who will believe. But there is no mention of any pretemporal election, and the narrative is clear. The Jews have disqualified themselves by their rejection while the Gentiles have an open door and are opting in. William Neil remarks: "It is not in any sense narrowly predestinarian, as if some are scheduled for salvation and others for damnation. In this case, the Jews of Antioch as a whole rejected the offer of eternal life, while some—by no means all—of the Gentiles accept it. Those who accepted the gospel fulfil the purpose of God that all men shall be saved and by their response show that they are worthy to be numbered with the saints of heaven."[54]

52. Terrance E. Fretheim, *The Suffering God: An Old Testament Perspective* (Philadelphia: Fortress, 1984), 57.
53. Klein, *The New Chosen People*, 108–10, 121.
54. William Neil, *Acts of the Apostles* (London: Oliphants, 1973), 161.

Again Luke writes, "The Lord opened [Lydia's] heart to listen eagerly to what was said by Paul" (Acts 16:14). Though not strictly an election text, this verse is cited because it seems to support the notion that sinners are totally depraved and (therefore) cannot respond to God unless coerced. Given their sinful condition, only efficacious and not merely prevenient and assisting grace can help. In this way, the Calvinist view of election may be thought to rest on and be inferred from its dark view of sinful man's plight. What really motivates its view of election then is its anthropology. Were grace merely assisting, it would never be sufficient. Were grace not irresistible, it would involve a human factor and not be by grace alone.[55]

But we should not read too much into this text. In conversion, there is always a divine side and a human side (salvation is, after all, by grace through faith). While this text truly mentions only the divine side, it does not deny that there is a human side. The opening of her heart was God's work; the response of faith was hers. Given the type of personal relationship that we enjoy with God as significant creatures, we know that God does not go in for manipulative measures. The Bible issues innumerable and sincere invitations for people like Lydia to respond to God's message. They by no means assume that people cannot believe. Quite the contrary. These invitations reveal that God wants freely chosen and truly personal relations with us. God makes the initial move by saying yes to us. Then it is our turn to respond with a yes or a no. Such a response cannot be coerced.[56]

In another text Paul writes, "For we know, brothers and sisters beloved by God, that he has chosen you [literally "knowing your election"], because our message of the gospel came to you not in word only, but also in power and in the Holy Spirit and with full conviction" (1 Thess. 1:4–5). Paul knew that these disciples were associated with the elect body because of their ready reception of the gospel which confirmed to him their elect status. He means that, when people hear the gospel and respond to it, they establish their inclusion in the elect body. As Peter puts it, they make their calling and election sure (2 Pet. 1:10). This is how Paul knows where they stand *vis a*

---

55. Paul Helm spells the logic out in *Divine Foreknowledge: Four Views,* 63–64, 169–70.

56. Vincent Brummer, "Can We Resist the Grace of God," *Speaking of a Personal God* (Cambridge: Cambridge University Press, 1992), 68–89; Harry R. Boer, "The Responding Imago," in *An Ember Still Glowing: Humankind as the Image of God* (Grand Rapids: Eerdmans, 1990), ch. 5.

vis Christ's elect body. There is no hint here that God chose specific people to respond and not others. Perish the thought.

In another text, Paul is thankful, he says, "because God chose you as the firstfruits for salvation through sanctification by the Spirit and through belief in the truth" (2 Thess. 2:13). Paul could say that of this or any congregation that God chose them as a community to be the firstfruits of salvation through the work of the Spirit in their lives and through faith in Jesus Christ. Notice here again the double agency: the Spirit's work in us and our response to the call of God. The Thessalonians really were the firstfruits of a new humanity. For this purpose God called them through the proclamation of Christ Jesus. God's action in us is necessary but not causally sufficient. One is saved by responding to the work of God in one's life.

If we prefer the reading in verse 13 which says, not "firstfruits," but God chose you "from the beginning" to be saved (the manuscript evidence is evenly divided), the meaning would not change because it has always been God's purpose to save sinners in this way. God did choose a community in Christ pretemporally which gets actualized in history by the work of the Spirit and through people's faith. Both facets must be present. In some of its forms synergism must be resisted but not in every form. Augustine's extreme rejection of it has been a terrible burden for the churches. Fortunately his radical monergism of salvation was rejected by the Eastern church and was never completely accepted by the Western churches. And although important to the conservative reformers, it was powerfully critiqued by Wesley and replaced by an evangelical synergism which is by now, I think, nearly universally accepted.[57]

In 2 Timothy, Paul remarks that God "saved us and called us with a holy calling, not according to our works but according to his own purpose and grace. This grace was given to us in Christ Jesus before the ages began" (2 Tim. 1:9). Here Paul is affirming that God's call to salvation does not result from the works that we do but from God's own loving heart according to a plan which was put into effect before history started. Before creation, God elected Jesus Christ and all of us in him to be his elect people.

In a mysterious text the Lord Jesus says to the apostles, "To you it has been given to know the secrets of the kingdom of heaven, but to them it has not been given" (Matt. 13:11 and parallels, Mark 4:11

---

57. Roger E. Olson, *The Story of Christian Theology: Twenty Centuries of Tradition and Reform* (Downers Grove: InterVarsity, 1999), 271–76, 469–72, 612.

and Luke 8:10). In context, Jesus is giving his disciples insight into the in-breaking of the kingdom of God. They are wondering how it is that some are given to know and some not. (This is a question which still puzzles.) The truth is that in God's purpose those who reject the truth in Jesus, who turn a blind eye and a deaf ear to it, do not find salvation. His parables reveal the truth to those who have eyes to see and ears to hear but does not do so for those with calloused hearts. Those with hardened hearts bring judgment on themselves. Jesus did not make them blind; he speaks in this way because they are blind. We should not interpret the phrase "it is given" to refer to a divine choice to save or to damn. Those who respond to the message are blessed and stand to gain more insight; while those who reject the truth doom themselves and never grow insight. God's rejection of anyone is always and only a response to man's prior rejection of him.[58]

In John's Gospel, Jesus says, "Everything that the Father gives me will come to me and anyone who comes to me I will never drive away" (John 6:37). It sounds like a done deal, doesn't it? But notice that it's everything (neuter) not everybody which is the Father's gift, calling attention to the collective aspect of the gift. God gives Jesus, among other things, a company of believers, and Jesus will not reject any of them who look to him and come to him.

Again Jesus says, "No one can come to me unless he is drawn by the Father who sent me" (John 6:44). This is certainly true. Apart from prevenient grace, no one can come to Jesus. This is a central truth shared by us all. But there is no reason to suppose that this is a selective or irresistible drawing or pulling. If it were saying that, it would lead to universal salvation, since (later on) Jesus says he will "draw" everyone (John 12:32). Jesus is not saying that God only draws some and them in a coercive manner while abandoning the rest. He is simply saying that there is no salvation apart from the divine initiative. As he says later on, "No one can come to me unless it is granted by the Father" (John 6:65). No one can obtain salvation without divine enablement. But that assistance is neither coercive nor irresistible. Anyone at all is eligible to be drawn by the Father.

Concerning unbelievers, Peter writes, "They stumble because they disobey the word, as they were destined to do" (1 Pet. 2:8). Is it that they are meant to stumble and disbelieve, or is it their disobedience which dooms them? Surely it is not that they were destined to disobey the word and thus stumble. Peter is saying that those who disobey the

---

58. On these texts, see Klein, *The New Chosen People,* 72–79.

word of God are going to stumble—that's inevitable. If people will not accept the gospel, they are doomed. There is no thought about God's appointing some people to disobey. They stumble because of their disobedience, not because they are unpredestined. How could one seriously believe that the God and Father of our Lord Jesus would appoint people not to believe for his glory? What kind of glory is that?

Jesus said, "For many are called, but few are chosen" (Matt. 22:14). What does he mean by that? In the context of the parable, there is a larger group who are invited but prove unworthy and a smaller group who respond to the invitation. The chosen ones are marked out as God's elect because they respond in the proper way. They came to the supper and wore the prescribed wedding garment. The parable makes plain that any who were not among the "chosen" were unchosen because they refused the call. It was in their power to be among the chosen, but they preferred to remain aloof. God calls us, but whether to associate with the elect body or not is ours to decide. God issues the call, but it is up to us to be among the elect. The challenge is not to remain aloof or hang around outside the banquet hall.

Luke reports that in Antioch Paul and Silas "related all that God had done with them, and how he had opened a door of faith for the Gentiles" (Acts 14:27). In saying that God "opened the door of faith," were they making a predestinarian statement? I don't think so. They were simply reporting how God had now opened up possibilities of missionary work among the Gentiles. Now that most of the Jews had declined the gospel, the way was open to the Gentiles. In this case, God brought good out of evil. Now the doors of the kingdom are thrown open to any and all who believe.

Jesus said to the disciples, "You did not choose me but I chose you. And I appointed you to go and bear fruit" (John 15:16). Jesus chose these men to be disciples and to be his friends, not servants. Therefore, he was telling them everything he was doing and everything he had heard from the Father. He has chosen and appointed them to join him in his mission. Being chosen for salvation does not come into the picture. This is a vocational election to go and bear lasting fruit as his disciples.

Jesus says, "The Son gives life to whomever he wishes" (John 5:21). Of course Jesus gives life to whomsoever he chooses, but who are they? They are those who honor him by hearing his word and believing. There is no secret election here. There is a conditional element; honoring Christ is the important issue, and this was precisely what his opponents were not doing. The way to life is faith in Jesus. He does not give it to a select few who have been arbitrarily favored. No, Jesus gives life to all who believe. These are the terms of the deal.[59]

John records, "They could not believe, because Isaiah also said, He has blinded their eyes and hardened their hearts" (John 12:39). Does this mean that God prevented the Jews from responding? How could anyone suppose that? Their nonresponse was due to their hardheartedness. If and when God hardens people, it comes as a response to prior unbelief and disobedience, and there was a precedent in Isaiah's day of it. How can anyone come to faith when they spurn God's word? It would be a contradiction in terms. Continual rejection can only incur God's hardening, such that faith becomes virtually impossible. It can consign a person to a state of intractable unbelief. God's hardening of them was a response to the adamant self-will of these people. The person who rejects God's word incurs a divine response where faith becomes an impossibility.

I know many other verses are quoted in this connection, but I have referred to enough of them to make my point. Scripture does not require believers to hold to the seemingly pernicious doctrine of soteriological double predestination, and what a relief! To get a sense of how problematic such a doctrine is, one only has to listen to what its defenders say. The best of them know well how heavily burdened it is with extraordinarily difficult problems. Calvin himself was candid when he admitted that it is "a dreadful decree" (*Institutes* 3.23.7). Millard Erickson concurs: "Of all the doctrines of the Christian faith, certainly one of the most puzzling and least understood is the doctrine of predestination. It seems to many to be obscure and bizarre."[60] With regard to these matters, John S. Feinberg writes, "Sometimes it would be easier not to be a Calvinist. An intellectual price tag comes with any conceptual scheme but the one that comes with Calvinism seems beyond the resources of human intelligence to pay."[61] It makes one long for them to be set free from this burden and for the world at large to be told how unnecessary all this is.

You can feel the pain when Calvin struggles with what he calls five "false accusations" which to the non-Calvinist seem to be very much on target (*Institutes* 3.23). Though he considers the doctrine

---

59. Despite Robert W. Yarborough, "Divine Election in the Gospel of John," in *The Grace of God, the Bondage of the Will*, ch. 2.

60. Millard J. Erickson, *Christian Theology*, 2nd ed. (Grand Rapids: Baker, 1998), 921.

61. Feinberg in *The Grace of God, the Bondage of the Will*, 459.

"unjustly burdened" by them, the fact is that these criticisms seem well-founded to me. They are so insoluble that one can only admire Calvin for his honesty in not just sweeping the problems under the table. To his credit he doesn't.[62] First, he wonders if his doctrine of election does not make God a tyrant. This is a reasonable suspicion in light of the arbitrary way God is said to assign some to salvation and others to damnation. To be honest, it does sound "more like the caprice of a tyrant than the lawful sentence of a judge," as he puts it. Even the sin which makes men so hateful to God was, he says, ordained by God, and toward them God acts with neither mercy nor justice. In the end, given this doctrine, one can only give up and admit that God can do whatever he wants and that we have no right to question it. Suppose a man had two sons, both of them equally guilty of a misdemeanor, and he punished one but not the other. There's no getting around it—such a father is unfair. And if he gets glory from it, he ought to be ashamed.

Second, Calvin wonders whether his doctrine of election does not take all guilt and responsibility away from man. Indeed, it would seem to. After all, Adam's fall and all our unrighteousness are decreed by God and not merely permitted. (Calvin rejects the category of permission.)[63] How then can we be said to have any role in our own calamity? This is a great mystery. Calvin's doctrine means that we have no choice in whether we are saved. We are treated as puppets and not as real persons. Our freedom is, as Helm delicately put it, "a deterministic freedom."[64] For most of us, this is no freedom at all. We have no meaningful responsibility in any of this.

Third, Calvin worries whether his doctrine might not suggest that God shows partiality. Yes, it would appear so. Though everyone needs mercy equally, divine mercy is dispensed only to some. Clearly this is unfair with respect to distributive justice. In this view, it means that many people will never have an opportunity to be saved. This makes God a respecter of persons and partial. God does play favorites and loves men and women unequally. This would involve God in unjust judgments contrary to Scripture (Lev. 19:15; Acts 10:34–35). Calvin has the burden of retributive justice, which lacks a basis in hu-

---

62. A more recent example in this vein: Loraine Boettner, "Objections Commonly Urged against the Reformed Doctrine of Predestination," in *The Reformed Doctrine of Predestination* (Grand Rapids: Eerdmans, 1941), 205–96.

63. John Calvin, *Institutes of the Christian Religion,* Library of Christian Classics, 2 vols., ed. John T. McNeill, trans. Ford Lewis Battles (Philadelphia: Westminster, 1960), 1.18.1.

64. Paul Helm, *The Providence of God* (Downers Grove: InterVarsity, 1995), 66–68.

man responsibility, and also the burden of distributive justice, which is dispensed arbitrarily.[65]

Fourth, Calvin worries that his doctrine of election might destroy zeal for an upright life. Indeed, if God has decided either death or life for everyone unconditionally, it makes no difference how we conduct ourselves, since the predestination cannot be helped or hindered. It would seem to put any sense of responsibility into jeopardy. It would seem to discourage any and all motives to exertion. What would be the basis for preaching the gospel to the nonelect?

Fifth, in a similar vein, he asks whether it would not make admonitions meaningless and whether it might not be unfavorable to good morality? It would seem to do so if the means as well as the ends are predetermined. (Thankfully, we humans do not always follow the logic of our presuppositions and are saved from their dire consequences.)

The most troubling aspect of Calvin's position is not mentioned. His doctrine of double predestination contradicts the universal salvific will of God which lies at the heart of the gospel. Paul writes that God "desires everyone to be saved and to come to the knowledge of the truth" (1 Tim. 2:4). He also states, "We have our hope set on the living God, who is the Savior of all people, especially of those who believe" (1 Tim. 4:10). He writes, "The grace of God has appeared, bringing salvation to all" (Titus 2:11). And Peter writes that God does not want "any to perish" (2 Pet. 3:9). Although Calvin's view claims to be based on the Bible, it is not. In teaching that grace is given only to a limited group and that God passes over the rest of mankind, it is at odds with Scripture. It fails to do justice to the teachings of the Bible, in which God's will for the salvation of mankind is expressed. I. Howard Marshall writes, "We must be content simply to register our feeling of certainty that this is a false interpretation of the New Testament."[66]

At stake is the loving character of God. Though God's love is central in worship and piety, there can be a disparity when it comes to

65. Bruce R. Reichenbach, "Freedom, Justice, and Moral Responsibility" in *The Grace of God, the Will of Man: A Case for Arminianism,* ed. Clark H. Pinnock, ch. 15.

66. I. Howard Marshall, *Kept by the Power of God: A Study of Perseverance and Falling Away* (London: Epworth, 1969), 195. More recently, see Marshall, "For All, for All My Saviour Died," 322–46. Despite John Piper, "Are There Two Wills in God? Divine Election and God's Desire for All to Be Saved," in *The Grace of God, the Bondage of the Will,* ch. 5; J. I. Packer, "The Love of God: Universal and Particular," in *The Grace of God, the Bondage of the Will,* ch. 18.

theology. The tradition has had great difficulty handling this theme.[67] Preferring abstract categories like immutability and/or apathy and/or sovereignty, it has driven love away from the center of the Christian message. It has not been able to think of God along the lines of a personal, loving, and relational God. If we highlight the abstract categories, we will not be able to make the love of God primary and will find ourselves able to imagine a doctrine as awful as Augustine's. If you start with philosophy and allow natural theology to operate, you will have great difficulty in speaking of God's love as anything more than mere beneficence in which God cares for us but not about us. You will miss the deepest truth of all, that God is essentially relational and loving. Even theologies as good as Erickson's do not make the love of God primary but promote formal doctrines undergirded by philosophical assumptions which undermine the centrality of love. For John Frame, God's power, not God's love, is primary, and this is typical.[68]

God is a triune communion of love who does not love merely occasionally or arbitrarily but essentially. We have a triune and relational God who creates out of love and for love. We have a God who brings into being significant others who can experience divine love and reciprocate it. Love is not just an attribute among many which may or not kick in. It is the nature of God and central to God's project. It's not just one of the *loci* but belongs to the structure, the point of integration and thematic unity. If you accept the biblical picture of divine love, you will find yourself needing to reconsider the abstract categories that have been used for God, and you will have nothing whatever to do with the horror of double predestination. Let us not start with the metaphysical being of God and then insert love somewhere down the line as an add-on. This is the heart of the matter: the triune God loves in freedom and longs for relationships with his significant creatures. God is for us; his "yes" is greater than our "no."[69]

The grace and love of God are at stake. What I want to say with Jerry Walls is that "God will do everything he can, short of overriding

---

67. Kevin J. Vanhoozer, ed., *Nothing Greater, Nothing Better: Theological Essays on the Love of God* (Grand Rapids: Eerdmans, 2001), ch. 1.

68. John M. Frame, *A Theology of Lordship: The Doctrine of God* (Phillipsburg, N.J.: Presbyterian & Reformed, 2002).

69. Thus Karl Barth, having established the reality of God as the One who loves in freedom (*CD* II/1), is compelled to turn the tradition of Augustinian election on its head (*CD* II/2). Lewis Smedes, too, turns his back on paleo-Calvinism in his memoirs: *My God and I: A Spiritual Memoir* (Grand Rapids: Eerdmans, 2003), ch. 19.

freedom, to save all persons. Indeed, God will compensate for a lack of opportunity to receive salvation in this life and will make sure that all persons have a fair and full opportunity to receive the eternal life for which all persons were created. If this is so, then all persons will have the opportunity to experience full satisfaction and happiness. The only ones who will not do so will be those who freely and decisively refused the offer of grace."[70]

Conclusion

In this essay, I have lifted up God's sovereign and unconditional election, which is corporate and vocational in nature, ecclesiological and missiological. It involves no horrible decree, no double predestination, and no God of doubtful character. My aim has been to formulate a doctrine which is truly God's election (that is, it is not our own self-election) and one which can be celebrated (that is, it is not an arbitrary selection). This subject constitutes a huge pastoral concern. I share Dave Hunt's lament when he writes, "My heart has been broken by Calvinism's misrepresentation of the God of the Bible and the excuse this has given atheists not to believe in him."[71]

Exclusivity, in the sense of a restrictiveness of salvation, is a hard habit to break. Once people get it into their head that they are specially privileged, it is hard for them to remember that these privileges belong to others also. The Jews of the Old Testament believed that they were God's favorites and sometimes entertained the idea that he had no use for other nations. But God is not the special property of one group. Those who know God are meant to make him known. Divine election is a wonderful gospel doctrine. God has unconditionally elected a people to serve as the vehicle of salvation for the whole of humanity. He has not limited his efforts to save a few individuals as an end in itself. His is an election without a shadow. God has chosen a people for the sake of all the nations. This interpretation of it upholds the perfect love and goodness of God. God's ways are fair; he saves all he possibly can. He does not leave anyone out arbitrarily.

Once you see divine election as the election of a people for the sake of everybody else, it becomes possible to say to all and sundry: you are all loved, you are all chosen to be God's children. Do not

---

70. Jerry L. Walls, *Heaven: The Logic of Eternal Joy* (Oxford: Oxford University Press, 2002), 130.

71. Hunt, *What Love Is This?*, 414.

believe the lies that the world is telling you. Don't believe either the theological mistakes that create anxiety. Truth is, you are God's beloved. And your being chosen does not mean that others are not chosen, too. They, too, enjoy God's embrace. Therefore, I say to every reader: make your calling and election sure (2 Pet. 1:10). Accept your vocation as a member of the elect body in Christ. Let us join in the original revolution and be a distinctive people and salt of the earth. Let us be a people who march to the beat of a different drummer.

CHAPTER 10

Responses to Clark H. Pinnock

Response by Bruce A. Ware

Clark Pinnock states up front the heart of the position that he argues for in his essay. "This is my thesis," he writes, "divine election is best understood when we take it to be corporate and vocational. Election is about a people and their God-given task. It is about ecclesiology and missiology. This (I maintain) is the preponderant witness of the Bible on this subject." So here is what I understand Pinnock to be claiming: divine election in Scripture is not about God's choice of those specific individuals whom he will save. Rather, divine election is about God's choice to have a people through whom his message of salvation may be proclaimed and by which people may be saved. In that sense, then, divine election is both corporate and vocational. It is corporate in that it does not discriminate among persons, picking those who are in or out. Instead, God chooses to accept all who will come to him. And this election is vocational in that when they come, he then chooses them for the missiological vocation of declaring God's saving grace in Christ.

I heartily agree with part of Pinnock's thesis. There are in fact many instances in Scripture where divine election is to service or vocation. Having acknowledged where I agree with Pinnock, I'll develop briefly two areas where I disagree with him. First, I simply do not believe it to be true that the "preponderant witness of the Bible" on the subject of divine election is both corporate and vocational. Pinnock seems to miss the most obvious other biblical theme in which divine election is employed, and that is for God's choice of those whom he will save. At times this choosing for salvation is corporate so that the new covenant, for example, is made with "the house of Israel and the house of Judah" (Jer. 31:31). Amazingly, what this text says is that God will do a work among the ethnic, national people of Israel in which he will "place [his] law within them and write it on their hearts" (Jer. 31:33). The result will be that they will know the Lord, obviously indicating their true devotion to and love for God, and so surely they are saved. This is confirmed when we read that God "will forgive their iniquity" and "remember their sin no more" (Jer. 31:34).

Notice here, though, that this corporate salvation of Israel is not the same sort of corporate election to which Pinnock refers. Pinnock's notion of corporate election envisions God's choosing an empty set of people, i.e., a hypothetical group whose specific composition is made up not by God's choosing but by each individual's choosing who wishes to enter the group. But this notion of corporate election does not reflect the new covenant promise of God to Israel. Rather, in the new covenant, God says to the already formed "set" or "group" of people whose constituent members are all those who are ethnically Jewish; he says to these Jews that he *will* save them. So here we have corporate election (exactly the same kind as we find in Romans 11, by the way), but it is the promised election to salvation of *all* the members of this group who make up "the house of Israel and the house of Judah" (Jer. 31:31; cf., Rom. 11:26).

But another prominent theme in Scripture relating to divine election has to do with God's choice of those specific individuals whom he will save. In Romans 8:29–30, Paul clearly indicates specific individuals whom he has predestined to save. Perhaps the element within the whole sequence stated in these verses that shows this most clearly is when we read, "And those whom he called he also justified" (Rom. 8:30). Now, as one contemplates what divine calling is here, it should be clear that it cannot refer to what is often labeled the "general call." That is, this is not the general evangelistic presentation of the gospel calling all who hear to come and be saved—as would happen, for example, in a Billy Graham crusade. This simply cannot be the case because in this text all of those who are called are also justified. We might wish it were the case that all of those to whom Billy Graham preached the gospel would be justified (i.e., saved), but we know better. So instead, here we have a call that effects the justification of those called.

Shall we not think of this, then, as the "effectual call" made to specific individuals to distinguish it from the "general call" of gospel proclamation made indiscriminately to all people. Understanding the particularity and individuality contained in this phrase, we now can see that Paul must have had in mind the same particularity and individuality previously when he said, "Those whom he foreknew he also predestined . . . and those he predestined he also called" (Rom. 8:29–30). Notice it is "those" whom he predestined, and "those" whom he called, and "those" whom he justified, and "those" whom he glorified—all in one glorious and unbroken chain of God's gracious saving work. Indeed, election is to salvation; and while this election to salvation is sometimes corporate (in a different sense than Pinnock means, however), it is also, gloriously, individual.

Second, the distinctiveness of Pinnock's openness model presents particular problems that nonopenness Arminians do not face. Because Pinnock denies that God knows or can know the future free choices of human beings, it follows that God cannot know from eternity past precisely who will be saved. No doubt this is one of the reasons that his notion of corporate election being of the empty set filled with those who, in time, choose to come, appeals to him so strongly. But can this view stand up under biblical scrutiny? Consider, for example, Ephesians 1:4 (NIV) where Paul writes, "For he chose us in him before the creation of the world to be holy and blameless in His sight." As has often been observed to counter the Arminian position that this text is about God's choosing Christ as the one who saves us, the direct object of "he chose" is not Christ but it is "us." Paul does not say merely that God chose to provide salvation for those who would come. Rather, he says that God chose particular persons to be saved.[1] And when did this choosing take place?

Paul's answer here shows one of the ways the openness view fails biblically, for this choice of those whom he would save took place before God created the world. Then it must be the case that God had foreknowledge of those individual persons. But if so, the entire structure of the openness model collapses. Imagine for a moment all of the contingencies and previous choices in history leading up to "you"

---

1. The reader should compare Paul's exact wording in Ephesians 1:4 with Pinnock's paraphrastic interpretation. Pinnock writes, "Before the foundation of the world, God chose to have a people and destined them to be holy and blameless in love." I propose that Paul's statement and Pinnock's are saying two different things.

existing. If God knew before the foundation of the world that "you" would exist, he also foreknew a multitude of future free choices and actions of his human creatures. Therefore, Pinnock's proposal not only removes from divine election the central place of salvation, both corporate and individual, that many texts present, but it also removes the deeply personal and cherished biblical notion that God knew "me" and "you" before he created the world, and that in his grace, he has chosen some among the totality of fallen humanity to save, by his grace.

Response by Jack W. Cottrell

Pinnock and I agree on some of the most fundamental aspects of the doctrine of predestination. Regarding the nature of man, we both accept the general Arminian view of libertarian free will, contra Augustinianism. We both accept the universality of God's love, of God's salvific will, and of the call of the gospel (John 6:44). We share the same basic critique of the Augustinian view, i.e., that it makes God ultimately responsible for the lostness of the lost, renders meaningless the biblical affirmations of God's salvific will (e.g., 1 Tim. 2:4; Titus 2:11; 2 Pet. 3:9), and distorts the nature of God's love.

I believe that Pinnock is correct when he interprets much of the biblical teaching on predestination in terms of corporate and vocational election. This theme is definitely present, e.g., in Romans 9. But I reject Pinnock's central thesis that biblical election is *corporate* and *vocational* to the practical exclusion of individual predestination to salvation and damnation. The Bible's teaching on this subject is not a matter of either/or, but both/and.

When Pinnock says that election is vocational, he means that the group is primarily chosen to fulfill a particular mission or task upon the stage of world history. God is working out his redemptive purpose within history, and he chooses first Israel and then the church as his instruments for accomplishing this purpose. Sometimes particular individuals are chosen for specific roles in this drama (e.g., Abraham, Jacob, the apostles), but this affects only their earthly service, not their eternal destinies. Regarding individual election either to salvation or to damnation, Pinnock clearly says, "I do not find the Bible to be teaching such a belief." Indeed, he notes, "Election is not about the destiny of individual persons for salvation or damnation but about God's calling a people who . . . proclaim good news to the world."

I have two main observations regarding Pinnock's approach. First, his rejection of the predestination of individuals to salvation (and damnation) is a necessary implication of his denial of God's foreknowledge of human freewill choices. Anyone who accepts the reality of truly free will, and at the same time denies God's precognition of choices made thereby, must also reject individual predestination. Without foreknowledge, God cannot know in advance what individuals will even exist, much less have any basis for predestining them either to heaven or to hell. On the other hand, if divine foreknowledge of human freewill choices is a fact, then individual election is inescapable.

Pinnock's denial of exhaustive divine foreknowledge has been clearly stated in other places.[2] In his present essay Pinnock restates his view: "I confess, too, to having difficulty believing that God possesses complete foreknowledge of what humans will do with their (libertarian) freedom." Affirming openness, he says, "Much about the future is as yet undecided. It awaits for agents to have their 'say so.'" Especially, it is "an open question exactly which individuals will finally [be saved] and which will not." "God knows some will respond but not (I submit) exactly who."[3]

I agree with Pinnock about the reality of libertarian free will, but I strongly disagree with his view of divine foreknowledge. The reality of divine foreknowledge is clearly taught in the Bible,[4] as is its connection with predestination.[5] Contra Pinnock, Romans 8:29 cannot be reinterpreted in terms of corporate predestination. The result of the predestination in this verse is conformity to the likeness of Christ, which in this context (vv. 11, 23) refers to the bestowal of a glorified body in heaven, as indicated by the reference to Christ as the "firstborn," i.e., "from the dead" (Col. 1:18).[6] This is best understood in terms of individuals.

Pinnock rejects individual election based on foreknowledge because he says it is contrary to salvation by grace. If "divine election rests on God's knowledge of the future free choices of human beings," this means simply that "God endorses our self-election"; and "it turns God's election into a human act of self-election." This trivi-

---

2. E.g., Clark Pinnock, *Most Moved Mover* (Grand Rapids: Baker, 2001), 48–49.
3. Without foreknowledge, how can he really know that even *some* will respond?
4. Jack Cottrell, *The Faith Once for All* (Joplin, Mo.: College Press, 2002), 85–87.
5. Ibid., 394–98.
6. See Jack Cottrell, *The College Press NIV Commentary: Romans* (Joplin, Mo.: College Press, 1996), I:503.

alizes election, picturing God as "waiting to rubber-stamp human decisions." This results in "foreknowledge thereby undermining the gracious character of election."

My second main observation concerning Pinnock's approach is that he attempts to justify his view of election as corporate and vocational by making God's election of *Israel* a paradigm for all other forms of election, including that of Christ and that of the church. This, however, is in my judgment a serious error. God's predestination of Israel is *not* such a paradigm.

Pinnock's understanding of election becomes in my opinion increasingly bizarre and seriously unbiblical. He describes God's call and use of Israel as an *experiment* which, unfortunately, did not work out.[7] This explains why Jesus came, namely, to continue to pursue the same purpose for which Israel was chosen but at which she failed. "The faithful Son of the Father is carrying the mission of Israel forward." "The point and meaning of the election of Israel is now to be found in Jesus of Nazareth." Jesus is the next and "decisive phase in the path that had been followed for centuries," a "continuation of the way God had gone with Israel before." Christ's goal, like that of Abraham and Israel, is to bring all the nations of the earth into a world community wherein all will share God's covenant blessings together.

In this brief space I can only begin to point out how extremely erroneous I believe this concept of election to be. First, I believe it misrepresents the covenant God made with Abraham as something that could be extended beyond the actual coming of Jesus and applied to the church under the new covenant. By what means were Abraham and his descendants to be a blessing to all families of the earth? By one means alone, namely, that through them the Savior of all mankind was to be brought into the world. The coming of Jesus was *the fulfillment* of the covenant with Abraham (Acts 13:33). The Abrahamic covenant and vocation have been fulfilled; they do not apply to the church.

Second, the same applies to Israel as a nation. What is true of Abraham is true of Israel as such. Israel had one purpose only, i.e., to prepare for the first coming of the Messiah. Neither Abraham nor the nation of Israel was chosen to personally preach God to the other nations of the world. When Jesus came, Israel's national vocation was fulfilled (Rom. 9:5; Gal. 3:28; Col. 3:11).

---

7. God's lack of foreknowledge would be a major factor here.

Third, and perhaps most seriously, Pinnock's view of Christ's election seriously threatens the uniqueness and effectiveness of Christ's saving work. To say that Jesus simply took over the mission at which Israel failed (as Pinnock understands it) is to say that his main work was epistemological, i.e., to reveal and to proclaim. Surely this diminishes the role of his death and resurrection. The most serious question, of course, is this: if the experiment with Israel had not failed, would Christ's coming, death, and resurrection have been necessary at all? This seems to be implied by Pinnock's discussion, especially in statements such as this: "The need for [Christ's] role arose from the failure of Israel and from the fact that something else had to be done if the goal is to be reached, namely, reaching of the nations."

Fourth and finally, the whole idea that predestination as it applies to Christians in the new covenant age is simply a continuation of the corporate, vocational election of the nation of Israel under the old covenant is based upon a false understanding of the relation between Israel and the church. God purposed to use national Israel to prepare for the first coming of Christ. That purpose has been accomplished, and that covenant has been terminated.[8] The church has some continuity with Israel (Rom. 11:17–24), but it does not simply take Israel's place and continue Israel's vocation. The church's continuity with Israel is not with the nation as such, but with the "Israel within Israel," as in Romans 9:6.

A right understanding of Romans 9 would go a long way toward resolving this whole issue. I believe Augustinians are wrong to say this chapter refers to unconditional election to *salvation* and then to use it as a paradigm for the doctrine of predestination as such. But I believe Pinnock is equally wrong to (rightly) say that it is about the election of the *nation* of Israel (along with some individuals within it) unto vocation or service, and then likewise to use it as a paradigm for the doctrine of predestination as such.

Response by Thomas B. Talbott

How should Christians respond to a teaching, even one with seemingly impressive biblical credentials and a long history of acceptance within the (Western) church, if that teaching appears morally

---

8. Pinnock is seriously wrong to say that the Old Covenant with Israel still continues "as if Jesus had not come," and that "God has not annulled his covenant with the Jews." Whatever happened to the book of Hebrews? and Galatians 3:28? and Colossians 3:11?

repugnant to them and utterly inconsistent with a God in whom there is no darkness at all? I was reminded of this question, which I have reflected upon many times throughout the course of my life, when I read the first few pages of Clark Pinnock's chapter. For as Pinnock points out in his chapter, correctly, "Many people inside and outside the churches have been devastated by the teaching, both narrow and exclusive, stemming from Augustine [that God restricts his mercy to a chosen few]. Though purporting to inspire in us awe before a sovereign God, what it does is lead us to doubt God's loving character."

And what, I would also ask, does a church that preaches such a doctrine have to offer those most desperate for a word of consolation? What can it offer the wife whose husband dies in unbelief, or the mother whose son leaves the faith, or the teenager whose best friend commits suicide? The teaching that, for all we know, God himself hated some of our own loved ones from the beginning and hated them in the same literal sense that he supposedly hated Esau is merely a prescription for more pain, more misery, and more fear.

But Pinnock has an advantage that many Christians have not had. As a scholar with scholarly resources at his fingertips, he is in a position to counter, at least to his own satisfaction, the exegetical arguments of those who would, in the opinion of many, slander the name of God. My question, however, concerns those Christians who have no such advantage; it concerns, for example, a simple peasant woman who may have lived in the vicinity of Geneva during Calvin's own lifetime. Having no knowledge of Greek or Hebrew, no real understanding of the Bible's historical background, and no reasonable way to counter Calvin's superior scholarship, her only grounds for opposing a doctrine of limited election might have been her *moral conviction* that a worthy object of worship could not possibly be an unloving and unjust tyrant. So how, then, should she respond when told to suppress her own moral conviction and to bow humbly before the Scriptures (as someone else interprets them, of course)?

I know of no better answer to this question than the one that George MacDonald gave: "Do not try to believe anything that affects you as darkness. Even if you mistake and refuse something true thereby, you will do less wrong to Christ by such a refusal than you would by accepting as His what you can see only as darkness."[9] So it matters not, according to MacDonald, what "affects you as darkness," whether

---

9. George MacDonald, "Light," reprinted in Rolland Hein, *Creation in Christ* (Wheaton: Harold Shaw Publishers, 1976), 42.

a racist interpretation of the curse of Ham, an appeal to Paul in support of institutional slavery, or an appeal to Romans 9 in an effort to persuade you that the Christian God is something less than all loving and all merciful: If the teaching strikes you as morally repugnant, you should say "either the thing is not what it seems, or God never said or did it."[10] For given the complexities in *any* interpretation of the Bible as a whole (see my comments on Robert Reymond), the façade of bowing humbly before the Scriptures is no excuse for accepting, in opposition to your own deep-rooted moral convictions, a seemingly blasphemous picture of God.

Can There Be Inclusive Election without Universalism?

To his credit, Pinnock underscores the inclusive nature of election as we encounter it in the Bible. The election of anyone, he observes, "foreshadows the reconciliation of the world and, as such, it is a broad and not a narrow concept." The election of Abraham, Isaac, and Jacob, for example, was on behalf of the entire human race, including Ishmael and Esau. So, he writes, "Election is an inclusive, not an exclusive category. It does not spell exclusiveness relative to others who are passed over but signals a movement toward the inclusion of all the rest." Pinnock even goes so far as to endorse Karl Barth's understanding of election, at least in this respect: "Barth is right to focus on the election of Jesus Christ who represents the whole race. Not just Israel and church but all of humankind is elect in him."

Now so far, this accords nicely with the emphasis of my own chapter. But Pinnock also claims that Barth goes "too far" because his inclusive understanding of election seems "to imply the actual justification of humankind and (therefore) moves in the direction of universal salvation." Is this not precisely what Romans 5:18 says, however? Or consider Romans 11:26. Contrary to what Pinnock seems to suggest, this text expresses far more than a vague hope that Jews as well as Gentiles will be saved; it instead makes a confident prediction that *all* Israel will be saved.

Does God Interfere with Human Freedom?

Consider more closely now the Pinnock/Walls claim that "God will do everything he can, short of overriding freedom, to save all persons." Though I tend to agree with the sentiments behind such a claim, we cannot finally assess it until we achieve some degree of

---

10. Ibid.

clarity concerning what would, and would not, count as an interference with human freedom. Suppose that I am standing atop the
Empire State Building with the intention of committing suicide by
jumping off and plunging to my death below, and consider two different ways in which God might interfere with my freedom in this
matter. He might, in the first place, simply cause me to change my
mind; that would effectively prevent the suicide from occurring. Or
he might, alternatively, permit me to leap from the building and then
cause me to float gently to the ground like a feather; that too would
effectively prevent the suicide from occurring.

I am not free to accomplish some action or to achieve some end,
in other words, unless God permits me to have the thing I have chosen, however confusedly I may have chosen it; and neither am I free
to separate myself from God, or from the ultimate source of human
happiness, unless God permits me to experience the life I have chosen
and the full measure of misery that it entails.

As I see it, then, damnation is a process whereby the damned
gradually learn from experience the true meaning of separation from
God. At the beginning of our lives, we might never have guessed that
we cannot reject the Creator and Father of our souls without rejecting ourselves, or oppose God's will for our lives without opposing,
schizophrenically perhaps, our own will for our lives. Neither might
we have guessed that submission to God is not really submission to
an external will or external power at all; it is merely a way of acknowledging and honoring our own deepest desires and yearnings, the very
desires and yearnings that God in his love also yearns to satisfy. So
in our confusion we make wrong choices, and at this point God can
either permit us to follow our chosen path, thereby respecting our
freedom, or to interfere with our freedom to follow it.

So does a guarantee of universal salvation require that God interfere with human freedom in inappropriate ways? Not at all. As surprising as it may at first appear, it is freewill theism, not universalism,
that postulates an inappropriate interference with human freedom.

To illustrate the point, let us suppose, as we do in our discussion
of Jack Cottrell, that I should hold, for whatever reason, the false belief that fire does not burn but instead produces highly pleasant sen-
sations. This time, however, let us compare two different scenarios:
(1) However absurd it may seem, here we imagine that God wants to
preserve my freedom to shove my hand into fire; so whenever I freely
choose to do so, he protects me from the fire and from its power to

burn and to cause pain. He does this because he knows that a severe burn would shatter my illusion about fire and thereby remove my libertarian freedom to repeatedly shove my hand into the fire. (2) Here we imagine that God does nothing either to prevent me from freely acting upon my illusion or to prevent the fire from burning my hand; so when I do shove my hand into the fire, the resulting burn shatters my illusion about fire, removes the only motive I had for shoving my hand into the fire, and effectively removes my libertarian freedom to repeatedly shove my hand into the fire.

Consider, finally, how similar freewill theodicies of hell are to our first scenario above. According to Jerry Walls, whose view Pinnock seems to endorse, "Hell may afford its inhabitants a kind of gratification which motivates the choice to go there"[11]; and more than that, says Walls, the damned may even experience a kind of illusory happiness: "Those in hell may be almost happy, and this may explain why they insist on staying there. They do not, of course, experience even a shred of genuine happiness. But perhaps they experience a certain perverse sense of satisfaction, a distorted sort of pleasure."[12] Though Walls denies that the damned are *genuinely* happy, he does not deny that they *believe* themselves to be happy; to the contrary, he insists that, for some lost souls, the illusion of happiness may endure forever and with sufficient conviction to explain why they never leave their preferred abode in hell.

And though Walls later characterizes the above comments as something of an overstatement,[13] he never does justice, so far as I can tell, to the New Testament picture of "weeping and gnashing of teeth" in both the fiery furnace and the outer darkness. But if separation from God finally includes separation from every possible good in life and even from all human relationships, including such improper ones as master and slave, then not even God can *both* respect a person's choice to live apart from him *and* protect that person from the consequences of such a choice.

Accordingly, only by *interfering* with our freedom to continue separating ourselves from him could God protect us from the sheer horror of doing so; and for that reason alone, no genuinely free agent

---

11. See Jerry L. Walls, *Hell: The Logic of Damnation* (Notre Dame: University of Notre Dame Press, 1993), 128.

12. Ibid., 126.

13. See Jerry Walls, "A Philosophical Critique of Talbott's Universalism," in Robin A Parry and Christopher H. Partridge, *Universal Salvation? The Current Debate* (Grand Rapids: Eerdmans, 2003), 121.

could possibly cling forever to the illusion that a life apart from God is more desirable than the bliss of union with God. It is hardly surprising, of course, that in a context of ambiguity, ignorance, and deception most of us, if not all of us, should initially find the broad road that leads to further separation (and finally to destruction) more attractive than the narrow road that leads to more abundant life. For at the beginning of our earthly lives, we are all programmed to pursue our own interests as we perceive (or in many cases misperceive) them; and furthermore, our natural fears often tempt us to seek refuge in power relationships of various kinds.

So as the consequences of our sinful choices continue to reveal— first in this life, then in hell, and even in the outer darkness, when necessary—the sheer horror of a life apart from God, the illusions that make such choices possible in the first place will eventually fall away from us like the shackles they are.

Whereas we can indeed freely choose, therefore, to live apart from God, at least for a while, we cannot *both* experience the full measure of such a life *and* escape the horror that it entails. Neither can we both experience such a life and cling forever to the illusion that it includes some possible good or another for us. And neither, therefore, can we both experience such a life and freely embrace it forever. Since in the nature of the case, then, there can be no freedom to reject God forever, our salvation finally rests upon God's faithfulness to us and not upon our own human will or exertion. And that, I should think, is a conclusion that Pinnock would also welcome, particularly in light of his own rejection of both self-selection and a horrible decree.

Response by Robert L. Reymond

I have struggled more with writing this response to Clark Pinnock's essay than with my other three responses in this volume, often searching for just the right word over against the almost-right word, since he claims to be an evangelical and is thus my brother in the faith. I would have preferred to write a more favorable response but found myself unable to do so.

Pinnock's essay is a sustained appeal to the church and especially to Calvinists to rethink their traditional views of predestination (infralapsarianism and supralapsarianism) and to interpret divine election as inclusivistically corporate and vocational. While he states that Romans 8:29 speaks of God corporately "foreloving" the bride of

Christ, he wrongly concludes that this means that God "foreknew and foreloved all *believing* creatures" (emphasis supplied) and that "there is no reason to suppose that God knew precisely who would constitute and make up" his Son's bride, that in fact "it is not necessary to believe that God knew in particular exactly who [these believing creatures] would be," since, indeed, "much about the future is as yet undecided. It awaits for agents to have their 'say so.'"[14]

He injects into his appeal along the way what he apparently believes are superiorly accurate and insightful expositions of "Calvinist texts"[15] that allegedly show Calvinism to be pernicious error and his own view to be correct. He concludes from what can only be described as a string of very casual exegetical encounters with these texts of Scripture: "Scripture does not require believers to hold to the (seemingly) pernicious doctrine of soteriological double predestination, and what a relief!" He is fooling himself here, of course, and is, in my opinion, placing his teaching in jeopardy before God as "wood, hay, and stubble."

Pinnock also exhibits a patronizing spirit when he expresses sadness over the burden that we Calvinists, "who have the misfortune," he says, "of having to live with [our views of predestination]," have to bear because of our "awful interpretation" of election, an interpretation that the "bad habits" of our "gloomy" misreading of Scripture through the lenses Augustine and Calvin have forced upon us. In fact, he "longs for [us] to be set free from this burden." But could it be that it is the Spirit of God, working by and with the Scripture itself in our hearts—not Augustine, not Calvin—who humbles us before our sovereign God and draws us to love and worship him? We Calvinists believe so and therefore find it all pleasure and a great honor, not a burden, to live with our views of predestination.

If my contribution to this volume grieves Pinnock, as I am rather sure it will, he should know that I am equally grieved, if not more

---

14. In his chapter in *The Openness of God* (Downers Grove, Ill.: InterVarsity, 1994), Pinnock argues that God's knowledge does not include a complete knowledge of the future for if it did "the future would be fixed and determined" and human freedom would be an illusion (121). Pinnock also argues that the God of Scripture has also freely limited his power for the sake of unabridged human freedom (112–13). He views God's sovereignty as open and flexible, a sovereignty of "infinite resourcefulness in the subtle use of power" rather than a sovereignty that "dominates, manipulates, coerces, and tyrannizes" people. What a mean-spirited, inflammatory, not to mention fallacious, list of pejorative verbs to describe the system of his Calvinistic opponents!

15. Ephesians 1:4, 10; Romans 8:29–30; 9–11; Psalms 139:16; Acts 13:48; 16:14; 2 Thessalonians 2:13; 2 Timothy 1:9; Matthew 13:11 with its parallels in Mark 4:11 and Luke 8:10; John 6:37, 44; 1 Peter 2:8; Matthew 22:14; Acts 14:27; John 15:16; 5:21; 12:39 in this haphazard order.

so, by his. I am grieved by his temerity in actually suggesting that the Bible is more supportive, over against the classical Augustinian/Calvinist doctrine of double predestination, of his inclusivistically corporate and vocational view of election. I am grieved by his willingness to rely for his ever-emerging understanding of election on men such as Karl Barth, who, in his opinion, is the "greatest theologian in the Reformed tradition," Markus Barth, Wolfhart Pannenberg who is his "favorite systematic authority," Hendrikus Berkhof, H. H. Rowley, and Hans Küng, none of whom are evangelicals and who are, at best, neoorthodox.

I am grieved by his essay's explicit advocacy of the "open theism" that he himself helped to spawn in the last few years in order to make room for and to legitimatize libertarian freedom. This is a view that states that God restricted himself at creation with respect to his omniscience and therefore is as ignorant of future so-called "free" actions of moral agents as mankind itself is. This is a view, in light of the many predictions that God makes about future events, that places God within the ranks of the idols of this world[16] and makes him no better than a soothsayer or a fortune-teller when he predicts things that often necessarily entail the so-called "free" actions of moral agents, which predictions also necessarily include messianic prophecies. This is a view that also renders such prophecies, at the time that he makes them, at best, wishful thinking on God's part.

This is a view that fails adequately to answer the following four basic questions. How can such a risk-taking, self-limiting God who rarely if ever intervenes in the free choices and actions of moral agents really know, *without ever "robbing" creatures of their freedom,* that

---

16. God himself declared that a major distinction between himself and all the false gods of this world is his infallible ability to predict the future and to bring that future to pass precisely as he declared it would be over against the inability of all the false gods either to predict the future or to bring it to pass. Isaiah teaches this in the following verses: Isaiah 41:22, 27 (NIV): "Bring in your idols to tell . . . what is going to happen . . . I was the first to tell Zion, 'Look, here they are.'" Isaiah 42:8–9 (NIV): "I am the LORD . . . new things I declare; before they spring into being, I announce them to you." Isaiah 43:12 (NIV): "I have proclaimed . . . I, and not some foreign god among you." Isaiah 44:7–8 (NIV): "Let [your idol] declare . . . what is yet to come—yes, let him foretell what will come." Isaiah 45:18, 21 (NIV): "For this is what the LORD says . . . 'Who foretold this long ago, who declared it from the distant past? Was it not I, the LORD?'" Isaiah 46:10–11 (NIV): "I make known the end from the beginning, from ancient times, what is still to come . . . What I have said, that will I bring about; what I have planned, that will I do." Isaiah 48:3–5 (NIV): "I foretold the former things long ago, my mouth announced them and I made them known; then suddenly I acted, and they came to pass . . . I told you these things long ago; before they happened I announced them to you so that you could not say, 'My idols did them, my wooden image and metal god ordained them.'"

history will end the way he envisions and predicts? Can this God who does not know the future in its entirety hold false views about the future? If not, why not? How can God make his salvation available to all, as Dr. Pinnock believes he must,

> given his ignorance about the innumerable people and events and relationships involved? We all know how human beings are conceived. Presumably most of those conceptions occur as the result of voluntary human behavior, that is, the kind of future human actions Pinnock's God cannot know. It would seem to allow that Pinnock's God cannot then know what human beings will exist in the future. Much of the access that these humans will have to salvation would, it seems, depend upon the voluntary actions of themselves and others. But Pinnock's God must be largely ignorant about this as well.[17]

Also note his essay's vision of election that is based more on Barthian Christomonism ("Christ is the *only* elect man; *all* men are elect in him.")[18] than it is on solid exegesis of the biblical text, and finally, what he writes about classical Calvinism. It is a well-known fact that Dr. Pinnock over the years has become a vehement foe of Calvinism. He despises the predestinarian theology of John Calvin's *Institutes of the Christian Religion,* the most influential systematic theology ever written,[19] for that is exactly what one is holding when he holds in his hands Calvin's *Institutes* — the work more fiercely and persistently opposed than any other work of the sixteenth century and twice ordered by the Sorbonne (the theological faculty of the University of Paris) to be burned, which burnings occurred in 1542 and 1544 in front of Notre Dame Cathedral in Paris; the work that one Roman Catholic authority of the day vilified as "the Koran or rather the Talmud of heresy";[20] the work whose author became Rome's most hated enemy; the work described by Will Durant, the twentieth-century American humanist historian, as "the most eloquent, fervent, lucid, logical, influential, and terrible . . . in all the literature of the religious revolution . . . developing the thought of [its author's] predecessors to ruinously logical conclusions," whose author, because of his doctrine of predestination, "darkened the human soul with the most absurd and

---

17. Ronald H. Nash, *Is Jesus the Only Savior?* (Grand Rapids: Zondervan, 1994), 131.

18. See my monograph, *Barth's Soteriology* (Philadelphia: Presbyterian and Reformed, 1967).

19. See my *John Calvin: His Life and Influence* (Ross-shire: Christian Focus, 2004) for an overview of his life's accomplishments.

20. Florimond de Raemond, counsellor of the Parlement of Bordeaux, *Historie de la naissance, progrez ed decadence le' hérésie de ce sèicle* (Paris, 1605).

blasphemous conception of God in all the long and honored history of nonsense";[21] but also a work, because of the world's recognition of its great worth, that has been translated into Spanish (1540), Italian (1557), Dutch (1560), French, partially by Calvin himself but the whole overseen by him (1560), English (1561), German (1572), Czech (1617), Hungarian (1624), Arabic (perhaps), Japanese (1934), Russian (1999), Korean (date unknown), and portions in Chinese.

I am shocked at Pinnock's slanderous misrepresentation of John Calvin when he says of Calvin: "You can feel the pain when he struggles with what he calls five 'false accusations'" concerning his doctrine of election; "He wonders if his doctrine of election does not make God a tyrant"; "he wonders whether his doctrine of election does not take all guilt and responsibility away from man"; "He worries whether his doctrine might not suggest that God shows partiality"; "He worries that his doctrine of election might destroy zeal for an upright life"; and, "In a similar vein, he asks, whether [his doctrine] would not make admonitions meaningless and whether it might not be unfavorable to good morality."

None of Pinnock's six assertions about Calvin is true; they are all scandalous misrepresentations of the Swiss Reformer's attitude toward the biblical doctrine of double predestination.[22] The truth of the matter is that Calvin does not exude "pain" or "struggle with" these accusations; he does not "wonder if" these accusations have merit to them; he does not "worry whether" these accusations have merit to them; and he does not ask whether his doctrine could have deleterious effects on good morality.

Rather, Calvin writes as one convinced by Holy Scripture that none of these accusations carries any water.[23] He regards them as

---

21. Will Durant, *The Reformation,* in *The Story of Civilization* (New York: MJF Books, n.d.), 6:460, 465, 490.

22. Arminians, including Cottrell and Pinnock in the present volume, have often observed that Calvin described reprobation as he understood the Bible's teaching about it as a "horrible decree": "The decree indeed is horrible, I confess," he writes (*Decretum quidem horribile, fateor.*) (*Institutes,* 3.23.7). (His French version of the *Institutes* reads here: *Je confesse que ce décret nous doit épouvanter.*) Arminians apparently think or at least want to convey the notion that his word *horribile* carries the negative connotation that it does today of "vile" or "repulsive" and that Calvin was describing reprobation as a "vile decree." But both the Latin *horribile* and the French *épouvanter* mean "dreadful" here in the sense of "awesome" as is evident from his phrase, *horribilis Dei maiestas* ("God's dread [or "awesome"] majesty") in *Institutes,* 3.20.17. Therefore, John T. McNeill writes in the Battles translation of the *Institutes,* 1, 955, fn 17: "Calvin is awestruck but unrelenting in his declaration that God is the author of reprobation."

23. William J. Bouwsma states in *John Calvin: A Sixteenth Century Portrait* (Oxford: Oxford University Press, 1988), 172: "(Calvin] stated [the doctrine of predestination]

"unjust," as "foolish," as "impious," as "absurd," as "blasphemous," as "malicious," as "shameless."[24] Pinnock has fabricated a caricature of Calvin out of whole cloth, to say the least, by his representation of Calvin here, presumably in the interest of leading his readers into thinking that, if even Calvin himself had problems with his theology, then they too may feel that they should question whether Calvinism is biblical. Just to the contrary, the lay Christian has every right to question, in light of Pinnock's fabricated caricature of Calvin here, whether *his* representations of the teaching of Scripture are not also fabrications created to serve his theological ends. Certainly his cavalier handling of Scripture stands in sharp contrast to Calvin's exegetical and theological prowess and is ground for not a little skepticism of his credibility.

While it greatly pains me to say so, I must for the sake of truth and the health and well-being of Christ's church express my long-held conviction[25] that Pinnock's teaching[26] simply cannot be trusted and that the evangelical church should stop providing him its lecture platforms and publishing houses to propagate his errors unless, as

---

firmly. . . . 'No one who wishes to be thought religious,' he wrote [in *Institutes*, 3.21.5], 'dares simply to deny predestination, by which God adopts some to hope of life and sentences other to eternal death.' He did not shrink from its harshest implications."

24. I urge my readers to check this out for themselves by consulting Calvin's *Institutes*, 3.23.

25. See my *A New Systematic Theology of the Christian Faith*, 2nd ed. (Nashville: Thomas Nelson, 2001), 346–80.

26. In recent times Pinnock has advocated both the doctrine of inclusivism that contends that people from other religions will be saved by Christ without knowing Christ (see his "Acts 4:12—No Other Name Under Heaven" in *Through No Fault of Their Own*, ed. William V. Crockett and James G. Sigountos [Grand Rapids: Baker, 1991], 113, and his *A Wideness in God's Mercy* [Grand Rapids: Zondervan, 1992] and the doctrine of the impenitent sinner's final annihilation, body and soul. In "The Destruction of the Finally Impenitent," *Criswell Theological Review* 4, no. 2 (1990): 246–47, he is unrestrained in his outright rejection of the doctrine of hell as eternal conscious torment: "I consider the concept of hell as endless torment in body and mind an outrageous doctrine, a theological and moral enormity, a bad doctrine of the tradition which needs to be changed. How can Christians possibly project a deity of such cruelty and vindictiveness whose ways include inflicting everlasting torture upon his creatures, however sinful they may have been? Surely a God who would do such a thing is more nearly like Satan than like God, at least by any moral standards, and by the gospel itself. . . . Surely the God and Father of our Lord Jesus Christ is no fiend; torturing people without end is not what our God does." Millard J. Erickson in his *The Evangelical Mind and Heart* (Grand Rapids: Baker, 1993), 152, cautions Pinnock to be more temperate: "If [Pinnock] is going to describe sending persons to endless punishment as 'cruelty and vindictiveness,' and a God who would do so as 'more nearly like Satan than God,' and 'a bloodthirsty monster who maintains an everlasting Auschwitz,' he had better be very certain he is correct. For if he is wrong, he is guilty of blasphemy. A wiser course of action would be restraint in one's statements, just in case he might be wrong."

with this volume, other scholars are given the opportunity to monitor his assertions and to caution his audiences about his teaching.

I am glad a tradition exists in the church that affords scholars the right before they die to write retractations. I sincerely hope that Pinnock will avail himself one day of this privilege and publicly retract his misrepresentation not only of Calvin but also of Calvinism; I call upon him to do so. I also sincerely and eagerly hope that Pinnock and I will have the opportunity to talk together sometime, either publicly or privately, about the issues I have raised in this response.

Author Index

Subject Index

Prepared by Travis S. Kerns